OPERATION UNDERWORLD

OPERATION UNDERWORLD

How the Mafia and US Government Teamed Up to Win World War II

MATTHEW BLACK

CITADEL PRESS
Kensington Publishing Corp.
www.kensingtonbooks.com

CITADEL PRESS BOOKS are published by

Kensington Publishing Corp.
119 West 40th Street
New York, NY 10018

All Kensington titles, imprints, and distributed lines are available at special quantity discounts for bulk purchases for sales promotions, premiums, fundraising, educational, or institutional use. Special book excerpts or customized printings can also be created to fit specific needs. For details, write or phone the office of the Kensington sales manager: Kensington Publishing Corp., 119 West 40th Street, New York, NY 10018, attn: Sales Department; phone 1-800-221-2647.

CITADEL PRESS and the Citadel logo are Reg. U.S. Pat. & TM Off.

ISBN: 978-0-8065-4215-7

First Citadel hardcover printing: January 2023

10 9 8 7 6 5 4 3 2

Printed in the United States of America

Library of Congress Control Number: 2022943476

ISBN: 978-0-8065-4217-1 (e-book)

for Brooklyn

Contents

What follows is a true story . . .

PROLOGUE

The fire started with a spark in the grand salon on the Promenade deck of SS *Normandie*. At 2:30 p.m. on Monday, February 9, 1942, barely two months after the disaster at Pearl Harbor that plunged the United States into war, New Yorkers on the West Side of Manhattan looked to the sky in horror as a giant plume of black smoke turned day into night. Thousands of people were inside their offices that occupied New York City's pristine skyscrapers when a sight from the harbor drew their attention away from their work. Even miles away, people on the ground could see the smoke: The second largest ship in the world— SS *Normandie*—was ablaze while in port at Pier 88 on the Hudson River. The sight was familiar to what people had seen in recent newsreels—looking like the blazing ships recently destroyed in Pearl Harbor.

Was New York under attack?

The call to the fire department didn't come until fourteen minutes after the blaze was first reported. In that time, the fire had made advances in every direction. What had started as a small blaze mid-deck had risen to the top deck, as a fifteen-mile-an-hour northwesterly wind pushed the conflagration hundreds of feet toward the bow. As the ship's ventilators worked into overdrive to pump out the smoke, their thirst for oxygen drove the fire downward—breathing toward the bowels of the boat. In a short amount of time, *Normandie* was an inferno.

The luxurious French-made ocean liner arrived in the Port of New York at the outset of WWII two and a half years earlier seeking refuge from German attack. *Normandie* remained idle at Pier 88 after the French government fell to the German war machine and was replaced with a puppet regime. Then, just days after the Pearl Harbor attack, the US government seized the boat from France by right of angary. In early February 1942 it was only two weeks away from being fully converted to a troop transport ship. It was to be renamed *Lafayette* and would be able to ferry fifteen thousand soldiers across the Atlantic Ocean in one run. It was also so fast that it could outrun any U-boat that tried to chase it. Now it was on fire, and the strategic value to the enemy was obvious to many who watched it burn.

Had *Normandie* been sabotaged?

Lieutenant Commander Charles Radcliffe Haffenden—who was in command of B-3 section (the investigative arm) of the Third Naval District, Office of Naval Intelligence (ONI)—was one of the principal men who had been tasked with preventing such an attack from happening. Though his command stretched across the Eastern Sea Frontier—comprising Connecticut, New Jersey, and greater New York—the Port of New York was the crown jewel of his command. Now a ship was burning in port.

The late call to the fire department had alerted the navy. Men from the Third Naval District Intelligence Office at 90 Church Street in Lower Manhattan—where Haffenden kept his official office—were summoned to the scene. They jumped into yellow taxis and their own cars and headed north, but upon approach, they were quickly stalled.

Everyone from air wardens to sailors and auxiliary firemen was called to help with the fire and the hundreds of injuries being sustained at Pier 88. Busy Manhattan streets were quickly clogged with taxis and automobiles filled with first responders who arrived piecemeal. Vendors walked away from their stands, and though the temperature was just above freezing, a massive crowd of onlookers gathered at the end of West 48th Street. Fifteen hundred firefighters who had received the late call filtered in and arrived at a scene of chaos—no one on Pier 88 had begun to fight the fire. New York fire hoses could not attach to the boat's original French fittings, and the ship's own firefighting systems were mostly out of service. The only help to contain the blaze came from the Hudson River, as firefighting ships nuzzled up against the port side and blasted water in high arcs onto *Normandie*'s deck.[1]

New York City Mayor Fiorello La Guardia arrived, and so did Admiral Adolphus Andrews, who was the commander of the Third Naval District. La Guardia and Andrews looked on helplessly as a ship nearly one thousand feet long (a full one hundred feet longer than HMS *Titanic*), with three smokestacks so large that each could have swallowed the Holland Tunnel twice over, lit up the cold, rainy day. They watched as hundreds of men scrambled around on the pier that ran the length of the boat. They also saw sailors escaping from the ship on skinny ladders that swayed in the wind, and a few who fell helplessly into a sea that was so cold large chunks of ice had formed on the surface.

The New York Fire Department was tenacious, and after hours of fighting and nearly three hundred casualties (and fortunately only one death), they successfully extinguished the blaze. In their zeal, however, they hurled so much water on board (about six thousand tons) that it collected belowdecks and was causing the ship to become unstable. By nightfall the ship was illuminated with spotlights, and it was clear that it was listing dangerously to port. Counter-flooding efforts were tried and failed, as divers tried to open compartments underneath the ship. In the early hours of February 10, 1942, clattering sounds were heard in the massive ship. The lights were turned off and the press was taken away, under orders from Admiral Andrews. Then suddenly, *Normandie* capsized to port—away from the pier—and slowly slid into a murky pool of mud, ice, and water. Listing eighty degrees and stuck, the ship was lost.

It was a disaster for the navy—one of the most important ships the United States had in the Atlantic Ocean was destroyed in a very public fashion. Overnight, a dense fog of soot settled as far away as Times Square, as low clouds trapped the smoke. The next day, the smoke was there to greet the tens of thousands of New Yorkers who went to Pier 88 to see the wrecked, giant ship for themselves.

Commander Haffenden, meanwhile, assigned some of his best men to investigate what happened. Prior to the fire, spy rings had already been identified in New York City by the navy and the FBI, with most of them seeking information about ship movements. Without a doubt, there were more out there that had yet to be exposed. They may not have known what had caused the fire, but the men in B-3 section of ONI in the Third Naval District carried on as if the ship had been sabotaged by enemy spies. Whether it was sabotage or not, Haffenden simply didn't have any of his men in place on the piers to give his superiors assurances that such a catastrophe wouldn't happen again.

If the fire had been an act of sabotage—by German or Italian spies—Haffenden and his command were going to have to think of something fast to combat the threat. Months of investigating the waterfront had yielded limited results at best. Gaining access to the piers of the Port of New York was going to require unconventional solutions, which was a challenge that Haffenden welcomed.

As *Normandie* settled into the muddy bottom of the Hudson River for all to see, Haffenden and his section started working on a plan that was so audacious and dangerous that some of the lieutenant commander's own men would question if they should even go along with it.

PART I

CHAPTER 1

Cerberus at the Gates

Lieutenant Commander Charles Radcliffe Haffenden's blood pressure was rising. After the eighty-three-thousand-ton *Normandie* was lost, the commander of the B-3 investigative section of Naval Intelligence, with his team, was tasked with figuring out what happened, and what measures could be put in place to prevent it from happening again. The problem was, he didn't have many answers, but that didn't stop the questions from his superiors at ONI in Washington, DC. Haffenden's preliminary reports indicated that the fire was an accident—sparked by a welder who ignited a pile of kapok life preservers—but that wasn't good enough for his superiors, or himself for that matter. If it happened again, or if he couldn't guarantee that it wouldn't happen again, his mission would be considered a failure. In February of 1942—just two months into World War II—this meant combating threats of all kinds.

The Duquesne Spy Ring was an example of the type of threat the navy faced. The ring had been exposed and busted by the FBI not even two months ago. The FBI rounded up over thirty conspirators across the country, all loyal to the German Reich. Most of them were charged with "conspiracy to transmit to a foreign government information vital to the national defense of the United States," and almost half had been arrested in New York City, caught collecting and transmitting Allied ship movements in and out of the Port of New York. The spies had just been sentenced to prison last month, amassing over three hundred years of incarceration between them. But there were more enemy spies out there.

There had been a curious incident last year in Manhattan where a man was struck and killed by a taxicab as he crossed the street. He had no labels on his clothes, and despite the fact that his ID said he was Señor Don Julio Lopez Lido of Spain, he had a notebook containing German writing. This writing had the names and assignments of US soldiers, a list presumably made to pass on to the enemy. Furthermore, another man grabbed Lido's briefcase and ran away as Lido lay dying in the street. This other man was still at large.

The United States military and law enforcement weren't even close to becoming aware of all the enemy spy rings that had been operational for some time. Some were only picking up steam and others were firmly entrenched in American society, as the enemy had been preparing for war for a decade, leaving the US desperately behind in its ability to combat threats from enemy legions in Europe, armadas in the Pacific Ocean, and spies and saboteurs at home.

President Franklin Delano Roosevelt had previously authorized the secretary of the navy to place the Port of New York under the protection of the navy. The Port of New York was the second largest natural port in the world, and busier than any other port worldwide. It comprised 240 miles of waterway that was formed by New Jersey to the west, Long Island to the east, and Manhattan Island in the middle, isolated by two main waterways—the Hudson and East Rivers. All along the Manhattan waterfront there were over one hundred football field-length piers, spaced out about the size of a city block and typically with giant warehouses attached for housing outgoing and incoming cargo.

This cargo was vulnerable, as it was moved to and from the warehouses by civilian longshoremen, many of whom weren't Americans. The cargo itself increasingly became war materials and supplies destined for England, and protecting it was of vital importance. England was relying on this cargo to survive, and if it did not make it to its destination, the English could be forced to capitulate, leaving the US in a terrible strategic position.

The navy high command gave responsibility for defending the port to the Third Naval District, which was commanded by Admiral Adolphus Andrews. The Third Naval District Intelligence Office was run by a man named Captain Roscoe MacFall, who was an experienced leader, having previously captained the battleships *California* and *West Virginia*. Those two battleships now rested on the bottom of Pearl Harbor, after sustaining at least six torpedo and three bomb hits between them. MacFall's resolve to combat the enemy could not be questioned. He had previously planned on retiring after forty years in the navy, but that had been pushed back because of the war.

MacFall's executive officer was a dear friend of his named Captain William Howe, who had been in the navy for thirty-four years. The two officers oversaw seven sections within ONI, including B-3 section, which was led by Commander Haffenden. Haffenden had an extremely large amount of autonomy, but he operated at the direction of MacFall, Howe, and another more secretive man, who was the spymaster at Naval Intelligence Headquarters in Washington, DC.

Since MacFall, Howe, Haffenden, and other sections of the Third Naval District were mandated to protect the Port of New York, they were responsible for making sure that there was no interference in the movement of troop supplies and ammunition onto transport ships. Nothing could stop the flow of supplies in the war effort, they were told—nothing.[1]

In early December 1941, in the aftermath of the Pearl Harbor attack, MacFall, Howe, and Haffenden sent sailors from B-3 section to scout the Hudson River piers on the West Side of Manhattan and farther south. They also talked to longshoremen in Brooklyn and tried to speak with supply shop owners and ship captains at Fulton Fish Market.

No one was saying anything, as the longshoremen and stevedores were mostly Italians, and they practiced their strict code of acting "D 'n' D," or "Deaf and Dumb," when confronted by nosey authorities. "Mum" was the word, as the ancient Padrone System, brought over from the old world, ruled their behavior. It mandated that they didn't cause any trouble for their bosses, and that certainly meant never talking to any authority figure about anything, ever, or it could mean their life. And the people who might kill them were the very people who employed them.[2]

Another reason the longshoremen in Brooklyn were not talking to the navy was because President Roosevelt had declared that the country's six hundred thousand nonnaturalized Italians be classified as "enemy aliens." It was insulting, and it was an unwise move to offend the very people who were handling the materials that were being transported for war.[3] By late February 1942, Haffenden and his section had failed to produce a single informant on the waterfront. Every officer at ONI had been trained to know that developing informants was essential for counter-intelligence work, and on the waterfront, B-3 was coming up short.[4]

Haffenden had several men in his command who had worked in the New York District Attorney's Office prior to the war, and they, at least, were able to tell him who was in charge on the docks—criminal elements, mainly of Italian and Irish ethnicities. The Italians who controlled the docks—primarily in Manhattan and Brooklyn—were part of a very large criminal syndicate that ran the unions, transportation in and out, and loading—basically every job that handled weapons and supplies. It was this syndicate that Haffenden was trying, in vain, to infiltrate.

"Sabotage" was a word that ran rampant in both New York City and ONI after *Normandie* met its very public end. Those fears were amplified by the sight of anti-aircraft batteries set up at some very visible places in the city, including by the Brooklyn Bridge and in front of the New York Public Library. Air raid drills had already been conducted, and President Roosevelt himself even said during a fireside chat that "Today's threat to our national security is not a matter of military weapons alone. We know of new methods of attack—the Trojan Horse, the Fifth Column that betrays a nation unprepared for treachery. Spies, saboteurs and traitors are the actors in this new energy."

These threats were exactly what Haffenden was up against on the waterfront. If the enemy infiltrated the harbor, and posed as a longshoreman, the missions he could carry out were terrifying. As unthinkable as they were, it was Haffenden's job to be one step ahead. That meant getting information about sabotage activity, however he could get it.

In B-3 section, Haffenden may have commanded over one hundred investigators from the New York District Attorney's Office, FBI agents, and cops who had joined the war effort, but Haffenden himself was never a member of law enforcement of any kind.

He had been a good-looking man in his youth, with a poise and cunning in his eyes, but now he wasn't sleeping, and he wasn't placing much emphasis on keeping himself in shape and healthy. He was now completely devoted to his job. His dark hair was mostly gone. His waistline was expanding, he had a double chin, and his only exercise was a weekly golf game. His face still lit up, as he always found energy in leadership. He gave off an infectious enthusiasm, and exuded confidence well beyond his abilities. He was also creative, and equipped with an imagination that was so extravagant that at times it had to be reined in by his superiors. At other times, it manifested into strokes of pure genius.

He had been born to Myles Radcliffe and Clarabel Haffenden on November 2, 1892, in Manhattan. Myles was an Englishman, and Clarabel was an American-born Pennsylvanian of German extraction. The two met shortly after Myles immigrated, when he was working as a wine importer and merchant. After Charles was born, the family left the city and relocated to Staten Island. At the turn of the twentieth century, Staten Island barely had a building over two stories, and was dominated by the brewing industry. Charles grew up in what felt like a small town, and was drawn to the fast pace and adventure in the big city, which was close by.

As a young man, Haffenden was swept up in the national furor

over the United States' entry into World War I. He joined the
navy in 1917 and was commissioned as an ensign after training at
the Pelham Bay Park Naval Training Station. During the war
years Haffenden served aboard the SS *President Grant*. It was an
eighteen-thousand-ton troop transport ship that had six large
masts from bow to stern, with one giant smokestack in the middle. It was given a camouflage paint job, as it ran the gauntlet of
the Atlantic Ocean while evading a new and terrifying enemy—
German U-boats. Eight runs to and from Europe in 1918 saw
President Grant transport forty thousand troops to the war zone
in Western Europe. Haffenden served well and was promoted to
lieutenant j.g. just six months after completing training. His service aboard the *Grant* gave him special knowledge of the nightmare that would occur if a loaded troop transport were lost to the
enemy, which was one of the reasons he took the loss of *Normandie* so personally. He knew all about the fear that sailors felt
when confronted by the U-boat menace on the high seas, and the
anxiety that they could be killed at any moment by a silent
enemy.[5]

After the Allies won the war and his service was over, he remained part of the navy reserve, which was a post that he held
proudly and was happy to boast about to anyone who would listen. He was a talker and liked to brag, a man whose charisma
grabbed people's interest and made it hard for them to let go.

When he returned from WWI, he was beaming with confidence and tried his luck as an entrepreneur. First, he tried to start
his own business—manufacturing decorated boxes—but he
failed after only eighteen months. He also tried to become a diamond wholesaler, which didn't last long either. Becoming an entrepreneur was not in the cards for Haffenden, so he decided to go
the corporate route. He worked as a salesman for a brick concern,
then in the marketing department of the National Biscuit Company.

During this time, he sweet-talked the love of his life, Mary
Coates Estes, into marrying him. Mary was from Macon, Georgia, and the daughter of a traveling salesman. Her family was

well-off; she had grown up with a brother and three live-in servants—a coachman, a cook, and a maid. Haffenden had grown up with a servant too, and he promised Mary that he would be able to provide the luxuries that she was accustomed to.

Not only was keeping this promise difficult, but the Haffendens also had a rough time starting a family. In early 1925, Mary got pregnant, and since Haffenden had yet to establish himself and save enough money to buy a place where they could start a family, the expectant couple decided to move in with Haffenden's mother. It was an odd situation, as she had recently divorced Haffenden's father and moved in with Haffenden's new stepfather in Queens.

At the end of the year, close to Christmas, the Haffendens were crushed when Mary gave birth to a stillborn child—it was a girl whom they named Mary. The Haffendens decided that they needed a change of scenery, so they moved to Georgia, where Mary was from, and were determined to try again to start a family. Two years after suffering the loss of their daughter, Mary gave birth to another girl. They named her Mary Adelaide, and two years later, Mary gave birth to another child—a boy this, whom they named Charles.

With a growing family, Haffenden wasn't done with trying to become successful, and being from Manhattan, he dreamed of being a big shot in the city. He brought his family back to New York and worked hard to become vice president and general manager of the Fry Gasoline Pump Company in Rochester, and finally president of the Wiley-Moore Corporation in Queens from 1937 to 1939.

The Wiley-Moore Corporation built exhibits for the New York World's Fair, held in Flushing in 1939. The Haffenden family moved into a six-bedroom house at 35-25 167th Street in Flushing, Queens. It was on a beautiful lot with trees and plenty of space, and their home was a beautiful farm-style house with a sloping roof and two white pillars at the doorway that gave it a Southern feel.[6] Times were good, as the Haffenden family had a live-in Irish maid and their daughter, Mary Adelaide, lived in

Massachusetts, where she attended the Northfield School for Girls. But it proved to be both a prosperous and weird time in Haffenden's life.

The New York World's Fair opened on April 30, 1939, on an unseasonably hot Sunday that turned into rain in the night, and soured Albert Einstein's lighting of new fluorescent lights as part of the opening ceremony. It was a sign of things to come.

Flushing Meadows—Corona Park in north Queens—was transformed. At the center of all the exhibitions and new structures were a 610-foot-tall obelisk (over fifty feet taller than the Washington Monument) named the Trylon and a nearly two-hundred-foot-diameter and eighteen-story-tall globe called the Perisphere.[7] The two structures embodied the fair's theme—"The World of Tomorrow"—as inside the Perisphere was a miniature model of the city of the future—"Democracity." The theme of democracy was being celebrated in honor of George Washington's first inauguration one hundred fifty years earlier in Lower Manhattan—and how far democracy had come.

In witnessing and helping create the exhibitions that dazzled people's minds and transported them to places at the far reaches of the world, grand ideas began to populate Haffenden's mind, as his imagination was awakened. The fair displayed a future built on business and commerce where fancy gizmos were going to be made available to the public, as exhibits were dominated by some of America's biggest corporations—Westinghouse, AT&T, RCA, and Chrysler.

Eventually, Haffenden made it over to the RCA pavilion, and witnessed an exhibit that enabled people to see themselves on a television set. At the time, the television was such an unknown that RCA had to build a TV with a transparent case so viewers could see that what appeared on the tube was not magic. When President Franklin Roosevelt spoke on opening day, he was filmed, and it was the first time a US president had been seen on live TV.

Haffenden had hoped that his job at the Wiley-Moore Corporation would springboard him into the next executive position. But even as the fair got going, world events spiraled out of control.

On opening day, a fleet that was supposed to show up at the fair was suddenly called into action in the Pacific. The Czech Pavilion went unfinished for the first month because that country had been consumed by Germany. More bad news came over the summer, and it was capped off on September 1, 1939, when Germany invaded Poland, officially starting World War II, and interrupting so many lives worldwide. For a while, the fair was a welcome distraction from events in Europe, but as "the World of Tomorrow" held events celebrating a utopian future of democracy, the present looked as though it was unfolding into an ominous alternate reality.

On July 8, 1940, just a couple weeks after "the miracle at Dunkirk," and nearly three months before the New York World's Fair even ended, Haffenden was pulled away from a fantasy world and called up for active duty in the navy. Every New Yorker who visited the fair felt it—there was a dark cloud of evil hovering over the promise of the World of Tomorrow. Whatever energy they had that was meant for dreaming about the future had to be shifted to confronting a monumental struggle, the price of which was the soul of the world.

When Haffenden was called up for active duty, he reported for counterintelligence training. He was certainly smart, but none of what he had accomplished during his prior civilian career made him a good fit for Naval Intelligence, or work as an investigator. Now he was in charge of an entire section of investigators. In fact, many of them resented the fact that they had to answer to someone they viewed as an unqualified superior.[8] This disdain for Haffenden wasn't limited to his subordinates either, as the head of the Domestic Branch of ONI also had it in for Haffenden. His name was Captain Wallace Phillips, and had Phillips not been reassigned prior to the outbreak of war, Haffenden would likely not have been promoted to his current position. He had to hope that Phillips wouldn't be coming back to the Third Naval District.[9]

But Haffenden did have his fans too, and a big reason for Haffenden's positive reputation among investigators was because of shoulders he rubbed up against in certain social circles of New

York City. First and foremost, he was a registered Democrat and supporter of Tammany Hall—the political powerhouse of New York City for nearly a century. And since the mid-1930s, Haffenden had also been the president of the New York Adventurers Club and served as the coordinator of the Executives Association of Greater New York.

Both of these clubs had a common thread beyond Haffenden, as one of the most famous private investigators in the country had served as president of each—Raymond Schindler. Schindler had been running his own investigation business since 1912, and he attracted not only executives to these clubs, but also fellow investigators (and at least one wannabe). Associations with Schindler and the investigators who naturally flocked to him gave Haffenden an extremely large pool of qualified men to recruit for counterintelligence. It made him the perfect candidate to run a section of investigators for the navy in New York City.

Haffenden did indeed learn a lot from Schindler over the years, as he picked up several of his habits, such as dictating notes into a Dictaphone. In the early twentieth century, a Dictaphone was revolutionary technology, but was outdated when Haffenden took over Schindler's office in room 196 at the Hotel Astor on Broadway. As coordinator of the Executives Association, Haffenden was given access to three rooms previously used for association activities. Now one of them was Haffenden's "off the record office,"[10] which he could use as a secret headquarters and keep his most confidential informants protected. It was also a place where he could operate outside the view of watchful eyes at his official office at 90 Church Street in Lower Manhattan.

In mid-February 1942, while Haffenden was alone in room 196, he sat in the chair of one the greatest investigators in the world, dictating notes into Schindler's Dictaphone, as he read the inbound intelligence reports through his horn-rimmed glasses. Puffing on a pipe as he read, he certainly looked the part, but if Haffenden couldn't find out what he needed, then he'd be demoted, or possibly discharged. Then not only would

American lives be lost, but those who resented him, and his lack of experience, would be proven right, and he would always be a "wannabe."[11]

On February 19, 1942, President Franklin D. Roosevelt signed Executive Order 9066. It mandated that all people of Japanese descent who lived in the western United States be interned at several designated camps. The American government was deathly afraid of "enemy aliens" attacking the country. One of the reasons the government took such a drastic step was because of shortcomings during the First World War.

The Black Tom explosion of 1916 was on Roosevelt's mind when he signed the order; he even said, "We don't want any more Black Toms." The Black Tom explosion had been set off back in 1916 by German agents in conjunction with Communist activists who were also foreigners. The agents targeted a series of munitions warehouses on Black Tom Island in New York Harbor and ignited an explosion so big that it was heard in Maryland, hit 5.0 on the Richter scale, and created a crater that was over sixty-five thousand square feet.[12] It took nearly a decade to figure it out, but it was Naval Intelligence that finally concluded that the United States had been attacked.

While people of Japanese descent were deplorably being rounded up for detention, the war had failed to impact the daily lives of people in New York City. Feelings of dread abounded, but Major League Baseball had plans to start on time in April (though many of its stars were leaving the league to join the military). Baseball fans were excited because all three of New York's teams were supposed to be good in the season of '42, as the New York Yankees had just beaten the Brooklyn Dodgers in the previous World Series. Joe DiMaggio had been the American League's Most Valuable Player.

The city's population mostly stayed the same, as the largest manufacturing city in the country failed to secure early war production contracts. Small factories, which New York City was full of, had nothing to produce, and more jobs were actually lost than gained.

Air raid drills happened periodically, but by February 1942, New York City hadn't changed any of its routines. Night baseball games were still held at the Polo Grounds and Ebbets Field, despite emitting an extraordinary amount of light. Floodlights still lit up Manhattan's tallest buildings—the Empire State Building, the Chrysler Building, and Rockefeller Center. Times Square still had a dizzying array of lights from advertisers. Wrigley's fish blew neon bubbles, and at 44th and Broadway—just blocks from the Hotel Astor—the Camel cigarette man blew five-foot-wide steam rings (to look like smoke) every four seconds. The Depression had caused most of the theaters to shut down on Broadway, and in Times Square they were replaced by dime-a-dance halls and movie grind houses, while prostitutes (male and female) and drug peddlers roamed the streets. Now with talks of spy rings in the press, coupled with the *Normandie* fire, everyone became suspect.

Saboteurs in the city were the biggest threat to ships in port, but for the entire US Atlantic Fleet, there loomed a much more dangerous, and lethal, unseen enemy—German U-boats. Forty Allied ships had been destroyed by U-boats at sea during the ongoing Battle of the Atlantic by the time one ship—*Normandie*—went down in port. The rest of the month of February saw thirty-one more US ships sent to the bottom of the Atlantic, some of them torpedoed within eyesight of the East Coast.[13] The US Navy simply did not have enough warships to protect their merchant fleet, which was responsible for ferrying all the valuable cargo on the piers to England in February 1942. U-boat attacks were so effective on the US merchant fleet that England was being choked off from US supplies, which was threatening to create a total collapse of their forces. The threat to US coastal waters off what was called the "Eastern Sea Frontier" was considered a "grave national emergency" by navy commanders.

Haffenden and MacFall were told there was no way the Germans were achieving such success on the high seas alone—

impossible. Their submarines were not equipped to run the gauntlet of the Atlantic, slip quietly into the dark waters off the American coast, destroy US shipping, and then resupply in ports all the way back in occupied France. They didn't have the fuel, food, or supplies to operate independently so far away from their sub pens. Haffenden's latest intelligence spoke to this fact, and it was startling.

Thousands from the navy, Coast Guard, and Merchant Marines had been killed, but there were more than a fair share of survivors. Some of them had even been pulled aboard German U-boats and interrogated, before being sent adrift in the open ocean. The ones who were rescued by US forces had strange things to share, and what they reported made its way through the channels of Naval Intelligence to Haffenden and MacFall. American supplies—packaged with their name branding—were seen belowdecks inside German U-boats.

This meant that the Germans might be rendezvousing out at sea with people from mainland North America. And if these people could supply food, then they could also supply other things, such as fuel and distilled water, which were liquid gold to a U-boat at sea.

Still, it was plausible that the U-boats had simply scavenged the supplies from the ships they sank. But then another report came in that turned that theory on its head—sliced bread, unmistakably baked in America, was seen inside a U-boat. The Germans had bread, of course, and could even bake it in their U-boats. But even though sliced bread makers had been invented almost fifteen years earlier, nobody outside of the United States sold loaves of pre-sliced bread.[14]

Food and supplies cost money, and that meant there were profits to be made. But who would do such a thing—sell out their country, presumably for the right price? German spies were one threat, but there was another avenue that had to be explored—Haffenden and MacFall believed the answer lay in the Italians in New York, especially members of the underworld, who perhaps still held their native Italy closer to their hearts than the America they had adopted (and exploited). Haffenden's creative mind, along with those at ONI, was extremely concerned that the Germans could persuade these Italians to aid their cause.[15]

After all, criminal elements had run this sort of mission before—for over a decade actually—during the time of Prohibition. In those days, fast rumrunner-piloted boats from the mainland rendezvoused just beyond the three-mile boundary of US coastal waters with British ships carrying whisky and Scotch. If the rumrunners accomplished their mission with such success then, they could do it again. Haffenden thought about this because under his command was a seasoned lieutenant named Joe Treglia, who in a previous life had been a rumrunner.

The lieutenant was secretive and kept a low profile—given his past, it was for a good reason. But he confided in Haffenden, whom he trusted, and respected. Treglia was short, with an athletic build full of muscle.[16] Treglia was a first-class officer, and Haffenden was happy to have him not only because he was an Italian-American, had expertise in the underworld, and was smart, but also because he was one of the only actual seamen in his command.

As they began to see that criminal gangs of New York were connected to their two problems—being unable to infiltrate the docks and stopping anyone from completing a resupply mission with the enemy, Haffenden and MacFall needed to answer some questions: Could underworld figures be recruited as informants? How reliable of an informant would a career criminal be? And if criminals could be trusted, could they be used for counterespionage?

The place to find the answer to these questions, Haffenden and MacFall concluded—or at least the next place to ask them—was the New York County District Attorney's Office.

That office had just recently been occupied by a newbie named Frank S. Hogan. Hogan had worked for the previous DA— Thomas Dewey. Dewey had just vacated his post on January 1, 1942, leaving Hogan at the helm of one of the most rat-infested ships in all of America—New York County (i.e., Manhattan). Hogan already had cases in progress against various criminals who controlled the waterfront. If there was an honest man who could give Haffenden and MacFall answers, this was him.

The two officers resolved that the easiest way to set up a meeting with Hogan was through one of their men who had previously worked in the DA's office. This was a junior lieutenant named James O'Malley. O'Malley phoned Hogan, and let him know that the navy had interest in contacting underworld figures for the purposes of obtaining information. The two set up a meeting at Hogan's office at 155 Leonard Street in Lower Manhattan, and not far from 90 Church Street. For the initial meeting, it was decided that MacFall—not Haffenden—would make overtures, and O'Malley would come along as well.

At 11 a.m. on March 7, 1942, a cold and partially rainy Saturday, MacFall and O'Malley arrived at a tall building that had a concrete base and was topped with more concrete that rose to the clouds. Inside, Hogan had a big office with high ceilings and white walls, and a window that took up most of the back wall. The district attorney sat behind his desk, which was situated diagonally in a corner. Never afraid to address the elephant in the room, Hogan had a small elephant cigarette lighter in the middle of his desk. He was forty years old and tall, with a high forehead and light, thinning hair. He was also an athlete, and easy to talk to, mainly because his smile had a way of calming people. People felt comfortable opening up to him, which had helped him gain many convictions. Hogan was behind his desk when he received the two officers. O'Malley was present at the meeting for the sole purpose of introducing MacFall to Hogan, and once that had been accomplished, Hogan immediately opened a side door that led to another office, and asked a man to join the meeting—Assistant District Attorney Murray Gurfein, who was head of the rackets bureau.[17]

Gurfein was a crusader who was fearless in his unrelenting attacks on New York waterfront criminals. He was as smart as he was uncompromising, and certainly the expert on the people whom the navy feared were aiding the enemy. He had dark hair, pudgy baby cheeks, and a fat nose that looked like it had been broken a couple times. He was family man with a wife and two daughters. Gurfein was only in his mid-thirties, but he had already put some of New York's biggest criminals behind bars while working under Hogan and Dewey.

MacFall had gray hair, a prominent gray mustache, and cunning eyes that revealed, despite his old age, he was as sharp as a tack. He opened up the discussion, and, being a former sea captain, got straight to the point.

"It's possible," he started, "that the disclosure of information as to the convoy movements and assistance in refueling of enemy submarines might be traced to criminal elements of Italian or German origin on the waterfront in the metropolitan area."[18]

MacFall went on to explain that the navy felt that the motivation of these "criminal elements" to betray their country could stem from trying to profit, or perhaps because many of them were Italian and therefore could be enemy sympathizers. Furthermore, they had opportunity to act on these motives, as they possessed the capability to conduct resupply missions to the enemy.

The navy needed to know if there was any basis for these theories. Would Hogan be willing to turn over the information he'd obtained from various waterfront criminal prosecutions to the navy for review?

"There is nothing in the office the navy cannot have," Hogan replied.[19]

With that settled, Hogan then brought the group's attention to Gurfein, who stood at his side. Hogan told MacFall that Gurfein was the expert, and not only would he tell the navy what he knew, but he would also arrange for his underworld contacts to supply them with whatever other information they needed.

"These underworld contacts," Gurfein started, "often have information about many illegal activities long before the regular police authorities."

This was great news to MacFall, but it raised an obvious question: Could they be trusted?

Gurfein assured him the answer was yes, and added that these men loved America.

MacFall was blown away. Not so much by the answer, as by the confidence the young assistant district attorney showed when he said it. How could they love America when they seemed to be actively working against and exploiting it? Smart as he was, it was difficult for an old sailor to understand.

Gurfein assured MacFall that if any of these racketeers did anything to hurt the navy, there were sanctions the DA's office could impose on them.

This was truly compelling. MacFall told the two prosecutors that one of his direct subordinates, Lieutenant Commander Charles Haffenden, would be the navy's representative for the operation. Hogan made a similar move and designated Gurfein as his office's representative. As for O'Malley—who didn't say a word beyond introductions—he was designated as a liaison between the two offices, for now.[20]

Over the next two-and-a-half weeks, Haffenden had two of his young officers pore through case files provided by the DA's office. For this task, Haffenden used James O'Malley and another lieutenant j.g., named Anthony Marzulo. Marzulo had also previously worked in the DA's office, as an investigator under Thomas Dewey. He was in his early thirties, was of Italian descent, and had thick black hair and big black eyebrows. He was a linguist who not only spoke Italian, but also various Sicilian dialects. He had mixed feelings about his Italian heritage, and wanted to be thought of as an American. He despised the Italian criminal gangs of New York, as he felt they gave his ethnicity a bad name. To combat them, he had gone to law school, before becoming an investigator in the DA's office.[21]

Haffenden used Marzulo's and O'Malley's expertise to pick out a few connected underworld figures to use as contacts. But both young officers were having a hard time with Haffenden's orders, as the idea of working with these underworld figures ran counter to everything they had learned and practiced up until then—they only worked with criminals to have them rat out other criminals. Marzulo thought so little of them that he was wondering if it was even ethical to develop informants of this nature. As he read about their horrible crimes in case file after case file, he began to feel that using the very people he was trying to put behind bars to help the navy seemed absurd. They were terrible citizens, after all, and they probably wouldn't, and couldn't help anyway.

So Marzulo prayed on it, and then decided to have a chat with his mentor. In confidence, he provided classified information to a man named John O'Connell, who was a former investigator for the DA and the FBI. O'Connell listened to Marzulo's concerns and put it this way: "Since survival of the United States and successful carrying out of our war effort is involved, every means available to the armed forces and agencies of our Government should be utilized."[22]

With that, Marzulo made his peace with the nature of the mission, having learned a valuable lesson in the difference between peacetime law enforcement and wartime counterespionage.

After flagging a few cases with Marzulo and showing them to Haffenden, O'Malley made arrangements for another meeting with Hogan. On a cold Wednesday, March 25, 1942, Haffenden, Marzulo, and O'Malley met Hogan in his office. Just like before, after introductions, Gurfein was brought into the meeting.

Haffenden repeated some of the information that was already known, and used it as a segue into his main question: Could underworld informants on the waterfront be developed? The case files provided by the DA's office didn't give the three officers any confidence about the men they were trying to contact.

Was there a member of the underworld Hogan knew of who could help the navy?

Just like at the last meeting, Hogan assured the eager lieutenant commander that Gurfein knew the answer to that question much better than he did. Then Hogan gracefully bowed out of the conversation, as Haffenden, Marzulo, and O'Malley moved with Gurfein to his office.

What kind of person was the navy looking for?

Haffenden had something very specific in mind: He was looking for an Italian American who was a leader in the underworld, and he preferred someone who was connected with waterfront activities.

Gurfein was ahead of the three officers—and he already knew the perfect person to contact: a business agent with the United Seafood Workers Union, Local 359, and a mid-ranking member in the Luciano crime family,[23] which dominated most of Manhattan. He was also reportedly a member of what was known as the "mob" (or much less commonly known as the "mafia"), an Italian criminal organization that was centrally located in New York City, but controlled many rackets across the country.

The name Gurfein came up with was Joseph "Socks" Lanza, who was a bulldozer of a man at five-foot-eight and over 250 pounds. He had short, thick, dark hair, brown eyes, big lips, and despite being forty-one years old, he had about a gallon of baby fat still in his face.

Aside from his nickname, "Socks," Lanza was also known as the "Czar of Fulton Fish Market." Fulton Fish Market in Lower Manhattan—next to the Brooklyn Bridge—was his fiefdom. It was also the largest fish market in the world, selling somewhere in the neighborhood of 400 million pounds of fish a year, which was good enough to constitute 25 percent of all the fish sold in the country. Lanza controlled every racket in the market. It was his territory within the Luciano family, which was one of five "families" of the mafia that controlled just about every racket in the city.

One of those rackets was in transports, where Lanza was charging a fee for unloading fishing boats. These boats ranged from clippers with high masts to small trawlers that were powered by steam.[24] His dominance over the transport racket made Lanza an even better contact, as it was one of Haffenden's theories that fishing boats could very well be the vessels that were resupplying U-boats at sea. If anyone knew anything about that kind of operation, it would be Joe "Socks" Lanza.

Lanza also just happened to be under indictment for extortion and conspiracy, stemming from an arrest in early 1941. That meant that while Gurfein was actively working hard to slap Lanza with a stiff prison sentence, he was also recommending him to the navy for a highly sensitive, supremely important counterespionage mission.[25]

With the four men agreeing on contacting Lanza, Gurfein then made a suggestion: If they were going to contact these underworld figures, they should first approach their attorneys. After all, Gurfein didn't know many of them personally, and the ones he did know wouldn't like seeing or talking to him. Haffenden thought this was a good idea, and it was agreed that Gurfein would set up a meeting with Lanza's lawyer, and then try to establish contact with Lanza himself. If everything went according to plan, then perhaps Lanza would cooperate with Haffenden directly.

If they were successful in recruiting Lanza, Haffenden felt that he had the perfect man to work with Lanza and keep a close eye on him—Marzulo. But Marzulo told Haffenden this was not a good idea. Marzulo explained that one of the last cases he worked on before joining the navy involved Socks Lanza. Lanza had been arrested for a crime that involved four co-conspirators. When some of them went on the run, it was Marzulo who tracked them down. He was confident that Lanza knew who he was, and the site of Marzulo might make him uncooperative and jeopardize the mission.

"It might be more fruitful," Marzulo said reluctantly to Haffenden, "if another experienced officer were assigned to this mission rather than myself." Marzulo hated refusing a mission, but Haffenden agreed.[26]

As for O'Malley, he was increasingly finding himself at odds with Haffenden. He was often sighted coming out of Haffenden's office shaking his head, or placing his hands on his head while making a facial expression that reflected his inner conflict. Having already accomplished his mission of introducing MacFall and Haffenden to the DA, O'Malley's role would dwindle going forward. Unlike Marzulo, he was unable to make himself comfortable with the mission of working with underworld informants.[27]

Gurfein didn't waste any time, and when the three sailors left his office, he went right back to Hogan. After everything was explained to him, Hogan gave Gurfein the green light to contact Lanza's lawyer. Gurfein walked back into his office and dug up the lawyer's telephone number. He called a man named Joseph Guerin at his office at 60 Wall Street.

Gurfein told him there was something they needed to discuss, and Guerin—excited that the DA was reaching out to him—promptly agreed to meet the following morning.

At 10:15 a.m. on March 26, 1942,[28] Guerin arrived at the assistant district attorney's office hoping for good news about his client's case. Instead, Gurfein told him about an elaborate plan devised by the navy to recruit powerful underworld figures to aid in the Battle of the Atlantic. He also told Guerin that fishing boats from Fulton Fish Market could possibly be resupplying German U-boats. In typical Gurfein fashion, he spared no detail.

Guerin was speechless.

The assistant DA went on to explain that helping the navy was Lanza's patriotic duty. He was not offering anything in return for his cooperation.

"This is a war effort," Gurfein said pointedly, "and has nothing to do with the indictment or anything else. It is a separate and distinct matter, and inasmuch as it is a war effort, Mr. Lanza may be willing to cooperate."

Guerin was still absorbing what he had just been told when he agreed to ask his client if he'd like to help. He went back to 60 Wall Street and telephoned Lanza, who held his offices at Meyer's Hotel on Peck Slip, right across the street from Fulton Fish Market. Guerin told him it was important for him to come to his office immediately. Lanza dropped everything and went to his lawyer's office.

That afternoon when Lanza arrived, Guerin explained what the assistant DA had told him earlier in the day. He said that the navy thought that Lanza could help stop all the ships being sunk. Lanza was excited about the opportunity. He loved his country.[29]

"I'd love to help put an end to those sinkings," he said.[30]

Guerin telephoned the assistant DA and told him that Lanza was ready to cooperate. Gurfein then gave them instructions to meet him at 11:30 p.m. that night. They were to stand on the corner of West 103rd Street and Broadway and wait for his signal. All parties involved had reason to take precautions and make sure that no one saw them together. Anyone who knew Gurfein would want to know what he was doing. Anyone who knew Lanza would tag him as a snitch, and that undoubtedly would result in his death.

Meeting northeast of Central Park was far enough away from Lanza and Gurfein's downtown offices that no one would recognize them.

Lanza and Guerin met up at 9 p.m. and had dinner. At 11:30 p.m. they arrived at the designated spot as the temperature began to plummet. They were both startled when they heard a car horn honking repeatedly. They looked to see a yellow Sunshine taxi-cab with the back door open. An arm was sticking out and it was waving them toward the car. Lanza and Guerin walked to the sedan and found Gurfein in the backseat. The two men piled in, and Gurfein told the driver to take them a few blocks west to Riverside Park.

It was cold that night, and especially so right on the Hudson River. It was dark, but the sky was relatively clear, with a waxing moon whose light illuminated their facial features as their eyes adjusted to the dark. As the temperature continued to drop into the mid-thirties, they huddled together on a park bench to shield each other from the biting wind, like Emperor penguins. Gurfein and Guerin took up half the bench, while Lanza took up the other half.

"You could be of help," Gurfein told Lanza. "You know all the business representatives, seamen and captains, and riggers, and all ship deck hand men."[31]

Gurfein told Lanza it was his patriotic duty as a citizen, and this was his chance at redemption for all the crimes that he had committed. Gurfein had chosen the spot carefully, as the bench they were sitting on was right next to the final resting place of President Ulysses S. Grant. The massive mausoleum had big white Greek columns and a classical dome, and held the Civil War general who rose from obscurity to become the savior of the union. In that vein, Gurfein added that any efforts by Lanza to help the navy would not be taken into consideration when prosecuting his case—Lanza owed this to his country.

No deal in Lanza's case?

Gurfein assured Lanza once again: There would be no deal.

Lanza thought about it and was also not dissuaded by his attorney.

"I go along 100 percent," Lanza assured Gurfein.[32]

Satisfied, Gurfein told the other two men that he was going to set up a meeting between them and a man from Naval Intelligence named Commander Haffenden. Lanza had trouble saying his name. Then Gurfein got up and each man went his separate way into the night, with a lot to ponder.

After Gurfein shared the good news with Haffenden, the lieutenant commander invited Lanza and his lawyer to meet him in his office at the Hotel Astor. The two men were to knock on the door of room 200, and Haffenden would see them shortly after. Haffenden then began preparing for what he hoped would be his newest informant, who also happened to be a vicious killer and hardened criminal. Haffenden had no law enforcement experience and had never dealt with a person like Lanza. Thus, he had no idea about the intoxicating effect his journey into the underworld's domain would have on his life. To accomplish his mission, Haffenden needed someone to get him inside this realm, and Lanza was the chosen beast to meet him at the gates of the underworld.

CHAPTER 2

An Unholy Alliance

At 2:15 p.m. on March 30, 1942, Lieutenant Commander Charles Radcliffe Haffenden was an excited man. As he sat in his secret office in room 196 on the mezzanine floor of the Hotel Astor in midtown Manhattan, he waited to meet what he hoped was his newest informant.

The Hotel Astor was located in Times Square between 44th and 45th Streets on Broadway, which was one of the busiest main arteries in Manhattan. Four lanes of New York City traffic bustled on the thoroughfare, with sedans of very similar design. Sunshine and taxicabs dominated the streets. They had big grills that rose to a high point in the middle and bug-eye lights on each side—painted yellow to distinguish them from so many cars of the same concept and design. If it were nighttime, the Camel cigarette man and lights that spelled "Hotel Astor" would be illuminated above.

The Hotel Astor was a massive twelve-floor rectangular building with a limestone base, a dark red-brick body, and a sloped top made of slate and copper. The roof was ornate, with sculptures and design elements such as big stone dormers, and a rooftop garden that was considered the most beautiful of its kind in the city.

The Hotel Astor was also known for its enormous and plush ballroom, as it catered to an upscale clientele and delighted in hosting events. Upon arrival at the main entrance on Broadway, guests walked into a gigantic, open lobby and two marble-and-bronze staircases on either side lead to the mezzanine level. Once on the mezzanine gallery, visitors looked over the lobby, a billiard room, a palm garden, and restaurants, including the German Hunter's Room, which was "bristling with trophies of the rod and gun."[1]

The halls were decorated with Greek columns, ornate wood carvings and finishes, baroque carpeting, marble floors, and European decor. From the left staircase, it was a short walk to room 200, which was the entrance to the Executives Association's offices. The floor was mostly devoted to servant's quarters, with the exception of the three adjacent rooms rented to the association.

Haffenden needed this informant—badly—so he had gone to a few extra lengths to ensure he had Lanza's attention. One of those lengths involved meeting him at the Hotel Astor instead of 90 Church Street. That environment might have been a bit intimidating for Lanza, with naval officers and armed Marines busying themselves like bees. Haffenden also didn't want to bring Lanza around his Church Street office because he didn't want anyone to know that he was developing an underworld informant.

Of course, Haffenden told MacFall about Lanza, and Captain Howe had been involved in the planning, but there were only a handful of people who knew about the meeting between Haffenden and Lanza.

Haffenden had chosen a weekday, when room 200 would've normally been staffed by a receptionist, but he placed one of his yeomen there instead. The room had had the beds taken out and was a rectangle shape with a bathroom, a floor-to-ceiling window in the back, and an adjoining door on the side that led to room 198. Room 198 was often used as a waiting room, but it also served as Haffenden's executive secretary's office—Mrs. Elizabeth Schwerin.

Schwerin wasn't actually in the navy, and only served Haffenden because she was secretary to the coordinator of the Executives Association. She had been serving in that capacity since 1933, and when Haffenden became coordinator he got the office, and Schwerin. Upon Haffenden's insistence on using the association's offices, Schwerin was questioned, vetted, trained, and granted security clearance by the navy.

Her office also had a bathroom, a door that led to the corridor, and as much as the Executives Association tried to cancel out the busy décor by painting the walls white, they could do nothing to hide the dizzying carpet that looked like it was moving. Schwerin's office also had a floor-to-ceiling window in the back, and a fireplace in the corner. Another adjoining door led to Haffenden's inner sanctum in room 196.

Suites in the Hotel Astor had design-heavy European styles, but the Executives Association had redecorated, and just as in Schwerin's office, room 196's busy walls were painted white. There was a floor-to-ceiling window that looked out onto 44th Street, a fireplace in the corner, and a bathroom on the opposite side.

The room was very much an office, as it had a desk and seats for visitors. Haffenden sat at a glass-topped desk, with Ray Schindler's Dictaphone to his left, and while he was reading the same report for the fifth time, he kept reaching for his pipe and stopping himself, as he didn't want the office filling with smoke.

Behind him, there was a table up against the wall. It had trays for incoming and outgoing correspondence, a pile of files, and a photograph of his family and another one of his mother. It was all meant to look innocuous, as there was a safe hidden in the wall, and also a revolver in a locked case.

Room 196 is where the interconnecting doors stopped. There was a door to the corridor if Haffenden wanted to greet visitors himself, but today, making Socks jump through some carefully placed hoops just might impress him. Normally, room 196 was where Haffenden came to take off his navy attire and replace it with regular civilian clothes that he kept in the closet. But today, Haffenden had gotten spruced up for the occasion, wearing his dress uniform, complete with ribbons of merit he'd received from the last war. He hoped it would make an impression on Lanza.

Socks Lanza arrived at the Hotel Astor with his attorney, Joe

Guerin, just before 2:30 p.m. in room 200, where the two men found Haffenden's yeoman.[2]

"This is Mr. Guerin calling to see Lieutenant Commander Haffenden," Guerin said.[3]

The yeoman nodded, stood up, walked to the door that led to room 198, and knocked before opening the door.

"Commander Haffenden's visitors are here," said the yeoman to Schwerin.

"Send them in," she said.

Schwerin had been briefed about Haffenden's guests, and it was a good thing she had, because no one like Lanza had been in those offices before. She did a double take when seeing the man, who was as wide as the door he entered through but still managed to be wearing a bespoke suit. Lanza also wanted to make an impression; he was just as excited as Haffenden to be in this meeting.

Schwerin invited the men to have a seat on a sofa, and soon after they were joined by another guest—Assistant DA Gurfein. Schwerin then used their electronic interoffice communication to alert Haffenden that his visitors had arrived.

Haffenden stopped reading, removed his horn-rimmed glasses, and told Schwerin to send them in. Schwerin opened the door and invited the three men into Haffenden's office. Haffenden greeted them, made introductions, and invited the men to sit down. Lanza and Guerin sat down, then an awkward moment ensued. Gurfein, still standing, started speaking.

"Mr. Lanza understands that if he helps the navy in any matters, he is doing so voluntarily," Gurfein started. "The District Attorney's Office has made no promise to him in exchange for his cooperation."

Guerin and Lanza looked at each other as Gurfein stated his disclaimer like he had practiced it the night before.

"We hope that Mr. Lanza will be useful to the navy. Thank you," Gurfein concluded.[4] Haffenden then suggested that maybe, perhaps, the assistant DA would be more comfortable leaving. Gurfein agreed. Not only for security reasons did his exit make sense, but deep down, Gurfein didn't want to know what was about to ensue. It might involve illegal activity, and Gurfein wanted no part in that.[5] After excusing himself, he opened the door he had come through, leaving the officer, the lawyer, and the gangster to discuss the details of what Haffenden had in mind.

Haffenden opened the conversation by asking Lanza if he was a patriot.

Lanza answered that he was, and that Haffenden could call him Joe. In fact, Lanza was a registered Democrat and a member of Tammany Hall. He took pride in his involvement in politics, and thought it would impress Haffenden.

He was right, as Haffenden was also a Tammany man.

Haffenden then told Lanza that the war was not going well for the United States as far as the movement of supplies across the Atlantic was concerned. He told Lanza about the U-boat threat, which had been covered in the newspapers for Lanza to read, but not at length, as the US government was actively censoring the worst aspects of the war. Haffenden then told Lanza he was worried that fishing boats might be aiding the enemy. He then asked if Lanza was willing to help find out if this was true.

"I will do anything to stop the sinkings if the fishing smacks are involved," Lanza stated.

Haffenden then told Lanza about his fear of rumrunners supplying U-boats, and wondered what kind of fishing boats were operating in deep waters off the Atlantic Coast.

"The mackerel season is going on," said Lanza. "These are little boats, this mackerel fleet, and they're run by nothing but Italians and Portuguese."

Italians—that was interesting. Where did they operate?

"Around North Carolina and South Carolina, Virginia, and Atlantic City, and all up Delaware, and all up through there," Lanza answered. "I will ferret out whatever I can."

Haffenden thanked him, but that's not what he was looking for. He wanted to use Lanza as an informant, not an active agent. He needed Lanza for information, and for another extremely important reason—his access to union records.

Did Lanza have access to any union records?

Yes, he did.

Could Lanza use this access to get Haffenden's spies proper identification? Could Lanza get them this proper identification so they could pass themselves off as regular workers on the docks? Could Lanza provide access without anyone knowing about it?

Lanza said he could to all three questions. "All right," he started, "you let me know where you want the contacts made, or what you want, and I'll carry on."

After a little over a half an hour of discussion, Haffenden felt confident that he had a new informant who could help. He kept the meeting going until five past three. This was on purpose, as Haffenden's carefully laid plan to lure Lanza in required one final touch. He instructed his most trusted civilian agent—who was a civilian investigator on the navy payroll—to arrive at precisely 3 p.m. Five minutes later, Haffenden took Lanza's address, home telephone number, and the number to his office at Meyer's Hotel, and then walked him to the door leading back to room 198.

"I'll call you up again, Joe," said Haffenden. "And you come up to see me."

When Haffenden opened the door, Schwerin was at her desk, and on a sofa waiting for them was a man named Dominick Sacco. Sacco had thinning hair and was a little old for the intelligence work he was doing. He had a prominent chin, ears that stood out, and droopy eyes that only opened halfway. He was also tall, well over six feet, and had an athletic build. Since he was trusted by Haffenden and an Italian American, Haffenden thought Sacco was a good fit to be Lanza's liaison.

Haffenden made introductions, and told Sacco that Lanza was going to help them around the waterfront, and with the fishing fleets.

Haffenden then turned to Lanza and asked, "Is that correct?"

"Yes," Lanza said. "But I'll need a few days to think things over." Then he clarified that he meant he'd need some time to think about how to get what Haffenden wanted.[6]

Guerin had stayed silent during the entire conversation, and was given no instructions whatsoever on any further involvement. Just as with Guerfin, what would follow was to be limited to only the parties concerned in the unholy alliance between the navy and Mafia.

Haffenden's relationship with civilian agent Dominick Sacco stemmed from his involvement in the Executives Association, as Sacco had previously worked for Ray Schindler as a private investigator. Aside from the fact that he was a good investigator and an Italian American, Haffenden wanted Sacco as one of his civilian agents because they were best friends.

MacFall and Haffenden had developed Sacco and dozens of other civilian agents who were as much a part of B-3 section as the sailors under Haffenden's command. They received a paycheck from the US government and mostly comprised men with investigational experience who wanted to aid the war effort but were too old to enlist in the military. But there were also other agents recruited for special skills that made them indispensable.

A man who fit all of those descriptions was Dominick's younger brother, Felix. Felix Sacco looked almost exactly like his older brother, except that he was completely bald. He was also an investigator and had known Haffenden since the early 1920s. Felix had previously worked for the Customs Intelligence Bureau, during the First World War. At that time he'd taught himself something that made him indispensable and Haffenden knew would come in handy—lockpicking.

But Felix Sacco was also a flawed man; years earlier a judge decreed that he had to move out of his house because he was beating his wife Anna. When Felix came back home, Anna called the police, and Felix was hauled in front of the judge. When the judge ruled against him again, Felix rushed the bench and punched the judge in the face. As Felix pummeled the judge with kicks after he fell to the ground, Felix yelled that it was repayment for the last time the judge had kicked him out of his own house. Three policemen then rushed Sacco, and he managed to best all of them. Sacco became exhausted from delivering so much trauma that a fourth officer was finally able to subdue him. If there was one thing that Haffenden was sure of, it was that if it came to it, Felix Sacco could handle himself.

After Lanza and Guerin left at 3:05 p.m. on March 30, 1942, Haffenden invited Dominick Sacco back into his office. Sacco had been meeting with Haffenden for a couple of weeks already about a new operation the commander was presently concocting. The flow of information between them was free because they trusted each other—Haffenden had even told Sacco about the baked bread that was found on a German U-boat.[7] He also trusted him with the most important of assignments.

Now Sacco's assignment, as Haffenden explained to him, was to join Squad #2 under the command of Lieutenant Treglia. Squad #2 was one of six active squads (with two in reserve) in B-3, under Haffenden's command. Affectionately, he called all of them his "ferret squad"—for their ability to find the enemy, no matter how hard these enemies burrowed into the city. Out of 142 investigators that Haffenden had under his command, 19 of them were on Squad #2.[8] Presently, Squad #2 had the most important job in the section—use Socks Lanza to infiltrate men into Fulton Fish Market, and then, hopefully, the rest of the Port of New York.

As Haffenden explained this to Sacco, he turned behind him to open a safe that was mounted inside the wall. After Haffenden spun the dials and opened the safe, he reached for his little black book. Inside the book was a collection of ciphers and codes that Haffenden used to designate his informants and civilian agents. Sacco, as one of Haffenden's civilian agents, unofficially a "specialist" employed by the navy, was given a letter designation.

Haffenden usually used the first letter of the person's last name to identify his civilian agents, but because the Saccos had the same last name, he designated Dominick as "Agent X," and his brother Felix as "Agent Y."[9]

While civilian agents were given letter designations, informants were given numbers. Haffenden made a new entry in his little black book, as Joe "Socks" Lanza was given the number designation "63."[10] "Informant 63" is how Haffenden would refer to

Lanza in all reports that he shared with the rest of ONI. Only he knew the identity of 63, and the only place that information could be found was in Haffenden's little black book.

Haffenden and ONI had a rating system for the reliability of informants and the information they provided. It was too early to rate the reliability of Lanza's information and promises. Plus, he still had to get Captain MacFall and Captain Howe to sign off on the mission, now that he had an informant on the waterfront. Captain Howe still had his reservations about using underworld informants, and that meant that he wanted to meet Haffenden's new informant before he allowed him to proceed.

Joe "Socks" Lanza didn't get his nickname because he wore special hosiery—"Socks" referred to his oversized mittens. Socks Lanza had enormous hands, and when he delivered the full weight of his body into a punch, the target suffered devastating consequences. Lanza didn't climb his way to the top of Fulton Fish Market—he "socked" anyone who got in his way, disagreed with him, or was foolish enough to make him mad. And if Lanza's hands weren't intimidating enough, he was happy to "sock" people with other things—like brass knuckles, or a giant fish.

As tough as he was, though, when he went home, the "Socks" veneer rubbed off, and he was a devoted family man.

On the evening of March 30, 1942—after his meeting with Haffenden—Lanza went home to his three-and-a-half-bedroom apartment at 101 West 65th Street on the Upper West Side. He shared the apartment with his second wife, Ellen Connor. Connor had light hair, was very pretty, and was nine years his junior. At thirty-two years old, she was a divorcée—just like Lanza—and considered Lanza an ideal husband.[11]

They had only been married for a year. The wedding had been particularly lovely, and Lanza's best man was the acting boss of the Luciano family—Frank Costello—whom he was close to. Costello was *the* boss as far as Lanza was concerned, even though the hierarchy of the Luciano family (to which they both belonged) was currently in a state of limbo. The founder of the family—Charles "Lucky" Luciano—was in prison, and his underboss, Vito Genovese, was a fugitive who was on the run in Italy. That left Costello in charge of the Luciano family at the moment, as acting boss.

Should Lanza tell Costello about the navy?

Definitely, but not yet. Lanza would have to tell Costello eventually, lest he find out about Lanza's actions later and become suspicious of him working with authorities. Lanza was under indictment, after all, and he couldn't have Costello thinking that he might be trading a reduced sentence for cooperation with the DA. That would lead to a terrible outcome for Lanza.

There were other consequences of Lanza's pending trial—he and Ellen decided to not have kids. As a repeat offender, Lanza was looking at doing hard time in prison, maybe even fifteen years. If he was acquitted, then they could try to start a family. For now, marriage was good enough, and they loved each other deeply. But both of them lived with the notion that their days together were probably numbered.

Lanza's latest indictment was a result of something he'd initiated five years ago. Back then, he was firmly in control of Local 359, and he was trying very hard to exert his influence, if not complete control, over Teamsters Union Local 202. Where offloading cargo from fishing smacks was one end of the transportation racket, the other end landed the fish in trucks or wagons operated by teamsters. Local 202 was responsible for operating the trucks that came in and out of Fulton Fish Market. Lanza wanted one of his men, Nicholas DeStefano, to be installed as the secretary-treasurer of 202, but the president of 202, Sol Schuster, was defiant in the face of Lanza's effort to muscle in. First, Lanza asked Schuster and was shockingly rebuffed. Next, Lanza sent DeStefano to Schuster's office.

"Stick me in that secretary-treasurer job!" demanded DeStefano.

"I can't do anything about it," replied Schuster.

Then DeStefano socked Schuster on the chin. Schuster, a bit shocked, gathered himself, took off his glasses, and stood up.

DeStefano wasn't expecting a fight, and he ran like a coward back to 359 and told Lanza what happened.

The next day, Lanza and DeStefano, along with James Carlo—who was the leader of Lanza's enforcement gang—and Carlo's nephew, went back to Schuster's office. This time Lanza had a gun and tried to make Schuster an offer he couldn't refuse. But Schuster proved to be one tough nut as he told Lanza to go ahead and shoot him. Schuster was adamant that there was no way he could place DeStefano in the secretary-treasurer position, and he did such a good job of arguing his case that eventually, Lanza agreed with him. Instead, they worked out a $120-a-month tribute, paid by union dues from Local 202's workers to Lanza and his gang.

Shortly after, Lanza was given a two-and-a-half-year sentence for a completely different crime. He did his time all the way over in Flint, Michigan, and all the while he kept his hold over Fulton. In fact, Carlo even collected 202's $120-a-month extortion money for Lanza while he was jailed. When Lanza was released from prison in 1940, he came back to Fulton and reclaimed his presidency of Local 359. The American Federation of Labor (AFL) then promptly pulled 359's charter and would only reinstate it if they elected a business agent who wasn't a notorious criminal.

So 359 did something that was typical of "pistol locals"—so named because their meetings were brought to order by a gangster banging the butt of a gun instead of a gavel—and took Lanza off their books (other "pistol locals" simply rechartered so their Local became a different number), only to pay him off the record. He maintained his hold on everything in Fulton except the title of business agent, and moved to expand. Lanza harassed other industries, such as the fruit and vegetable market, and he even started extorting taxicab unions. That expansion included Local 202, which Lanza wasn't finished with yet. Even years later, he still wanted DeStefano placed as 202's secretary-treasurer.

Just months after being released from prison, he and his men crashed a Local 202 meeting, and a brawl erupted. Several men would have been killed when gunfire erupted in the room, but they saved themselves by jumping out the windows. This time, the leadership of Local 202 relented, and DeStefano finally became secretary-treasurer.

But the real trouble for Lanza started when Schuster, the president of 202 whom he'd threatened, was himself given a ten-to-twenty-year sentence for racketeering. This put Schuster in the mood to talk, and talk he did. He told the man prosecuting his case—Thomas Dewey—about the extortion money he was paying Lanza and his three companions. On Wednesday, January 8, 1941, police came to Meyer's Hotel and arrested a "nattily" dressed Lanza, who somehow knew they were coming. Minutes later he was arraigned, looking like the best-dressed man in court.[12]

Despite Dewey's objections, Lanza's lawyer, Joe Guerin, was able to convince the judge that Lanza wasn't a flight risk. His bail was set at $50,000, which Lanza promptly paid. Since then he had been out on bail, and had continued his criminal activity. He hated thinking about going to jail and being taken away from his beloved wife and fish market. Now what "the commander" was asking for was a welcome distraction from the impending trial that hung over his head like a black cloud.

That evening of March 30, Lanza was oddly distant from Ellen, as he began to replay in his mind the conversation he'd had with Haffenden.

Lanza was upset that the DA, and the commander—he still wasn't sure how to pronounce Haffenden's name—kept asking him if he was a patriot. Of course, he was! Lanza was active in local politics. He was friends with some of the highest-ranking Tammany Hall members, such as Albert Marinelli, and his sister was married to Tammany leader Prospero Vincent Viggiano. Did they not know who Lanza was? He was sure that he would show them how much he loved his country.

Lanza also thought about what Haffenden said he needed. Lanza could handle talking to the fishing boat captains, but what did he know about rumrunners? That had never been his business. For all the different rackets that went on at Fulton Fish Market, smuggling was not really one of them.

Who did Lanza know that was a rumrunner?

Who knew the New York, Long Island, and Jersey coastline like the back of his hand?

The name he came up with was Ben Espy. Since Carlo wasn't able to pay his bail money, he was waiting in prison while Lanza's lawyers dragged the case out as long as they could. That meant that Lanza needed a new leader for his enforcement gang in Fulton Fish Market, and that job came to Espy.[13]

The next day—March 31, 1942—Lanza went to work like he did every day at his office in Meyer's Hotel. Meyer's Hotel was at the corner of South Street and Peck Slip, and right across the street from Fulton Fish Market. It was a low-rise brick building of a kind referred to as a "humpback," which were common at the southern end of Manhattan. At nearly seventy years old, the building, including the interior, was pretty run down, but it suited Lanza just fine. When he got to his office—a hotel room, just like Haffenden's—he immediately called Espy and told him to come to his office.

Espy was in charge of the Patrol Association and was responsible for shaking down fishing boat captains, their crews, and teamsters. Members of the patrol forced captains to pay tribute (about $10 a load) if they wanted their fish unloaded and sold at Fulton. Then they charged the teamsters for loading their trucks and wagons. The patrol was the muscle of the fish market and made sure no one loaded or unloaded fish except for Local 359 members. Lanza was not only a founding member of Local 359, but he was also the one who had started the Patrol Association nearly twenty years earlier. If the fishing captains didn't like being shaken down, the Association was happy to let the fish rot in the cargo holds of their boats.[14]

Espy arrived at Lanza's office and was more than a bit surprised about what Lanza told him. Espy was balding, with a high forehead, and was bug-eyed. He was a little lost in the criminal world,[15] as his rap sheet, which was long, didn't have any arrests for violent crimes. He was a thief, hustler, and smuggler first and foremost, and despite being head of the Patrol Association, not so much of a strongman. Espy was just a fill-in for the role, as Lanza's chosen leader for the Patrol Association was currently in jail for the same extortion charges that Lanza was facing.

As soon as Espy arrived, Lanza didn't hold back that he'd met with the DA who was prosecuting him, and with Naval Intelligence. This came as a shock to Espy—meeting the DA in the middle of the night was a red flag that Lanza might have been turned into an informant. But here Lanza was, admitting that he was an informant, only not for the DA, but for the navy. And then Lanza started to complain.

What the hell would make them think that Lanza wasn't a loyal patriot? Didn't everybody know that? Every election year, Lanza campaigned hard for Tammany Hall, after all.

Espy had no choice but to agree, though deep down he didn't know what to think. He also didn't really have a choice if Lanza asked for his help.

Espy asked if there would be any monetary compensation.

"None whatever," Lanza stated.[16]

Would Espy help?

"I would be glad to," he said.

As promised, Haffenden called later that day. He asked Lanza to come down to his office the following day, but this time he meant his office at 90 Church Street. Lanza told Haffenden that he was going to bring someone with him—a friend who could help. Haffenden thought it was a good idea. After all, he had to sell Captain Howe on the feasibility of his mission, and it would be smart to show that he had not one, but two new informants on the waterfront.

Ninety Church Street was a short building (by New York standards) with deco architecture and an enormous base that covered the entire block. It was nearly exclusively made of concrete, and if it hadn't had some shape to the ten-floor towers above the first five floors, it would have looked every bit a dull government building. Haffenden's office and the rest of B-3 section were on the fourth floor, and on April 1, 1942, Haffenden sat there ready to receive his first visitors.

He was nervous, as Captain Howe was going to decide if Haffenden was taking the right approach. Howe needed assurances that he wasn't about to approve an operation that empowered the Mafia, or worse, that the Mafia might make them look foolish. Howe was in the office next to Haffenden's, and was called in when Haffenden received his first visitor of the day.

Haffenden's visitor was assistant DA Murray Gurfein. After all, who better to explain to Captain Howe how underworld informants could benefit the navy's operations? Plus, it was Gurfein who had vouched for Lanza, and given the two men's conflict of interest, Gurfein's endorsement carried strange but heavy weight. Gurfein seemed enthusiastic about the whole setup, and believed in what the navy was doing.

The mood was different at Church Street than the Hotel Astor, and so too was the protocol. Gurfein arrived there and signed in at the desk just beyond the front door. He was given a badge and escorted all the way up to Haffenden's office by an armed guard.

At the far end of the hallway were two desks occupied by two of Haffenden's men who handled communications and administrative tasks. They were against the back wall, so each man using the desk could watch anyone coming toward Haffenden's office. To their left were two offices occupied by O'Malley and Haffenden's orderly, Louis Wade. Haffenden's office was adjacent to them across the hall, and in front of Haffenden's office was another yeoman at a desk whom Haffenden used as a stenographer.[17] The guard escorting Gurfein knocked on Haffenden's door and waited outside the office. Haffenden then greeted Gurfein and called in Howe.

After Haffenden introduced Howe, as always when Gurfein was in the room, the assistant DA did most of the talking. Howe was quiet and didn't say much as Gurfein addressed all his concerns. When Howe felt like he had heard enough, he excused himself and went back to his office. Haffenden was satisfied, but

Howe was still uneasy, and Haffenden knew it. Haffenden was close friends with Howe, and their families knew each other well. Haffenden even went golfing almost weekly with Howe. So even though the captain looked like he was about to be seasick, Haffenden let him leave the room, knowing that Howe needed to gather his thoughts.

Haffenden then thanked Gurfein and let him go. Just as Gurfein shut the door behind himself and his guard got ready to escort him out, he saw two familiar faces walking toward him—Socks Lanza and Ben Espy.

The last two meetings between Lanza and Gurfein had been in the middle of the night, and a secret office, respectively; now it was broad daylight with dozens of people all around. Each man saw the other, then averted his eyes and continued on his way without acknowledgement. Espy was confused but said nothing. The guard led the two men to the end of a hallway past the stenographer and knocked on Haffenden's door.

In Haffenden's office, Socks introduced Espy, and not as a fellow racketeer or business associate, but as an "intimate friend" of his.[18] Haffenden asked how Espy could help, and Lanza told the commander that Espy could help with supply houses and ship captains. He was also the most knowledgeable about trucking in and out of Fulton, as it was part of his job to procure new trucking contracts. This meant that he was privy to all the places the trucks traveled, which included strategically important locations such as Long Island. This was particularly interesting to Haffenden, as securing the Long Island shore was also of vital importance to the navy.

Could Espy help get Haffenden's men onto these trucks?

Absolutely, no problem.

Haffenden was elated, so he called Captain Howe back into the room.

Howe came in, but he didn't sit down. Instead, he stood at attention, and listened to Haffenden as he explained how Lanza could help at Fulton, and how Espy could help with trucking and contacts in Long Island and throughout the Third Naval District.

All the while, Howe stared at the two men who looked out of place, and certainly were out of place.

These were the guys that the navy was going to use to get information?

The US Navy, with its centuries of proud tradition, couldn't do any better than two lowlife criminals? Howe believed that these informants were beneath the navy.

Then Haffenden was finished. Howe was still standing at attention, as he gave Lanza and Espy one last look. After a few tense moments, he finally shook his head and said, "All right."[19] Then he left without excusing himself. It seemed like Haffenden was the only one in the navy who was in a good mood about the whole idea, as doubt permeated the minds of the other officers.

But that mattered very little, as his and MacFall's brainchild had just gotten the green light. Haffenden reached into his desk, grabbed a piece of white bond paper, and wrote the words "Underworld Informants." He wrote a message bound for the spymaster in Washington, DC, that he had established contact with two underworld informants on the New York waterfront, and shared their number designations. Now he was going to send his own men to the waterfront at Fulton to find out if there was any enemy activity going on.

Operation Underworld had officially begun.[20]

CHAPTER 3

Operation Underworld

Within days of meeting with Haffenden, Lanza and Espy visited all of the supply houses between Fulton and John Street, and on Peck Slip. The supply houses had records of supplies purchased by fishing crews, and Espy was extremely well versed on what each fishing boat could and should take on. If any fishing boats were taking on extra fuel or supplies, Espy would be able to see it. Then they made sure that the men who ran the supply houses would inform them about any fishing boats taking on extra supplies. Now that that had been accomplished, it was time for Lanza to introduce Haffenden's men to the fishing captains themselves.

To join Lanza on this mission, Haffenden chose two of his most trusted members of Squad #2—Lieutenant Treglia and Dominick Sacco (aka Agent X). Apart from being trusted and able, Treglia was also chosen for his knowledge of the high seas, Sacco for his experience in surveillance, and both men because they spoke fluent Italian.

In the first week of April 1942, Treglia and Sacco met Lanza at his office in Meyer's Hotel, and then the three men headed to the corner of Peck Slip and into a sea of chaos. Pushcart peddlers selling everything from fruit to cigarettes to a myriad of fish were haggling with buyers, yelling to attract new customers, and smelling up the street something awful with fish scales and melting ice on an unseasonably warm day.

The group crossed Peck Slip and into Fulton Fish Market. Fulton Fish Market had been a stylish building until it literally fell into the East River in 1936. Since then, a new building had been constructed, and was a gleaming white that made the place look new. It was one of three new buildings added recently, as all along South Street there were upgrades happening. The white building was square-shaped like a warehouse, and its exterior walls were sheet metal painted white. Above the ground level, which was all garage doors for vendors, there was a strip of windows to air out the pungent building. Above the glass, there were giant letters that read, "Fulton Fish Market."

The stalls of wholesale fishmongers in the market itself sold over fifty different kinds of fresh and saltwater fish, brought in from all over the country and the world. Inside, hundreds of men scurried about negotiating the best prices as fish were stacked on large hanging scales.

Haffenden wanted general observations from Sacco, so Sacco spent some of his time in the stalls at first, looking for anything and everything suspicious. He passed a man who made a batch of New York City's finest turtle stew. The man, just like everyone else who ran a stall at Fulton, kicked back some of his earnings to Lanza for the privilege of selling his product. His stew was one of the rare welcome smells in the market, as most people smoked some form of tobacco—a cigarette, cigar, or pipe—to save them from the stench of fish and brine.[1]

After stepping out of the stalls and back into the open air, Sacco, Treglia, and Lanza navigated trucks, wagons, and men on their way to the giant pier at the end of Beekman Street. Haffenden had given orders to Treglia and Sacco to find specific types of boats, so Lanza guided them to boats that fished for mackerel and had Italian captains.[2]

At the pier off Beekman Street, members of Lanza's Patrol Association were off-loading mackerel and squid from the fishing boats and onto scales that were bolted into the pier. The fish were then dumped into ice-loaded barrels and made ready for transport aboard a truck or horse-drawn wagon.

Boat after boat was tied up to the pier, as they were mostly single-masted smacks that had gaff rigs that supported a four-sided sail (though all sails were down on boats that were tied up). The smacks were around fifty feet long, with booms that stretched forward to the bow and aft to the stern. Some of the newer versions of smacks had a short exhaust tower for their engine, where the mast would've been.

Lanza made introductions to the Italian captains and told them that Treglia and Sacco were friends of his. Glaring, Lanza made it clear that the captains needed to answer any questions that Treglia and Sacco asked.

What was the status of their fuel and supplies?

What waters had they just come from?

Did they see any U-boats while out at sea?

Before moving on to the next crew, they left the captains with instructions that if they saw any U-boat activity, they were to alert Lanza immediately.

When they were finished, Treglia and Sacco reported back to Haffenden that the sea captains were talking and actively working for them, which was a major step in the right direction. Over the course of the next week, Lanza, Sacco, and Treglia talked to hundreds of Italian fishing crews, and all were given the same orders to contact Lanza if one of them saw a U-boat.

Prior to the first week of April 1942, fifty more Allied ships had been sunk in the Atlantic during the month of March alone. The Germans had sunk another eleven ships in the first week of April—including a handful of oil tankers—and in just a week the US had lost nearly 125 lives to drowning, burning, crushing, and many other terrifying and unfathomable ways to die at sea.[3] And Haffenden still couldn't answer if the enemy was being aided by people on the mainland.

The US military were suffering horrendous losses wherever they engaged the enemy. The US also had yet to go on the offen-

sive anywhere. The US garrison at Bataan in the Philippines
would fall in early April and prisoners would begin a weeklong
death march. It looked like the Soviets weren't going to lose their
capital, for now, but they were still suffering horrific losses and
had a massive German army occupying the entire western portion
of their country.

President Roosevelt admitted to the press that there "have been
losses," but he was mum on the details. The federal government
told the press that they would be censoring the information that
they shared with the American public, and the press, for their
part, cooperated. The only time they did report on a sunken ship
was when the enemy reported it in their press. They also reported
attacks like the one on *Coimbra*, which was an oil tanker. *Coimbra* had held over 450,000 gallons of fuel in its hull when it was
torpedoed just twenty-seven miles off the coast of Long Island.
People who lived near the shore in the Hamptons, on the eastern
end of Long Island, called the Coast Guard as they witnessed a
650-foot-tall conflagration rising in the distance like a volcano
that had just opened up at sea.

There were very few warships to escort the tankers and merchant ships, and as much as the Royal Navy implored the
US Navy to invoke a convoy system, the American navy simply
didn't have enough ships. Transport ships operated independently and were sitting ducks for the first wave of Operation
Drumbeat—Germany's U-boat assault on Allied shipping around
American ports. The Germans were having extraordinary success, and some of their U-boat captains didn't even bother sub-
merging when they made a kill, knowing that there would be no
response from the US Navy to their attacks.

Haffenden knew that if the U-boats could operate on the surface with such confidence during an attack, then a resupply rendezvous also carried little risk to the enemy. The high command
was still pressuring ONI to find out who was supplying the
U-boats from the mainland, and it was proving a difficult threat
to combat. Haffenden had no ships or aircraft to patrol the waters,

and neither did the US Navy, for that matter. But what he did have was a determination to establish a network of informants that could do the navy's work for them. If he could get information about resupply missions to U-boats, then maybe he could shut them down, and the threat to US coastal waters would subside, or perhaps even disappear.

The thought that he could win the battle based on a single piece of intelligence was his driving force. Haffenden believed that he could tip the scales in the Battle of the Atlantic by himself. And that thought excited him.

In early April 1942, as Haffenden began exploring the boundaries of total war all by himself, this thought started to grow in his mind. Then, an important piece of information finally came through Lanza's contacts: A fishing boat captain had spotted a U-boat on the surface off of Montauk Point, on the far eastern end of Long Island, just 115 miles due west of Manhattan.[4]

Haffenden immediately sprang into action, and alerted Captains MacFall and Howe. All three men had the same question: What was a U-boat doing on the surface so close to the shore?

German U-boats had been torpedoing their prey in American waters while beneath the surface. They typically surfaced only after an attack for various reasons. If this U-boat was on the surface that close to shore, and it wasn't tracking an Allied ship or convoy, then it was doing something else. That something else, as Haffenden knew, could have been a resupply launched from Long Island itself. And if that was the case, then whoever rendezvoused with that U-boat might still be on the island.

But there was also an even more terrifying possibility—the U-boat was making a reconnoiter of the beach and the enemy was thinking about landing troops on Long Island. Or maybe the enemy was thinking of landing a team of commandos who could covertly infiltrate the East Coast, with intentions of sabotage. If that was true, there might be little Haffenden could do before the enemy blew up their first target on mainland US soil.

As terrifying as these thoughts were to the lieutenant commander, the notion of finally being able to do something to contribute thrilled him. He believed it could be an opportunity to make his own mark and prove that the navy's investment in Operation Underworld was worth the risk.

Haffenden thought about what resources the navy had on Long Island. There was already an outpost there, which was under the command of the Third Naval District. But Haffenden had no intention of passing the buck to anyone at the outpost—this was his moment. He remembered what Lanza and Espy had told him about trucks from Fulton Fish Market driving just about everywhere, including Eastport, which was about fifty miles east of Montauk Point. Trucks ran supplies—mainly fish and fuel—in and out of the fishing port, and it was possible that the enemy could be using them or their resources to ferry supplies. It would be difficult to hide purchasing and ferrying enough oil to supply a U-boat. Anyone who could pull off such a mission had to have access to large amounts of fuel.

Haffenden called Lanza and told him that he wanted to get his men onto the fishing boats that operated out of Eastport. Haffenden said that they would need union identification so as to not be exposed as navy agents. Lanza said he had a contact that could get Haffenden's men onto trucks that went out of the port. His name was Hiram Sweezey, and he owned a fleet of twenty trucks that operated in and out of Eastport daily. Lanza then called Espy to his office. Reticent to talk about something illegal on the phone, Lanza instructed Espy to procure at least two union identification cards from the United Seafood Workers Union and one Teamsters Union card. Done—it was that easy.

Then Lanza got in touch with Sweezey.

"Listen," he said. "There's something going around on the island, and I want to try and get some men on your trucks. Will you put 'em on?"

"Sure, Joe," Sweezey replied. "Anything you want."

By the next morning, Haffenden had the union cards, and he sent Lieutenant Treglia, Dominick Sacco, and another civilian agent, named Charles Hoyt, to Long Island. Beyond Haffenden's interest in finding out if anyone on Long Island was helping the Germans, the navy also focused a lot of attention on the island itself. For centuries, American war planners had seen Long Island as the most likely site of a foreign invasion from a European foe. It had ports and plenty of sandy beaches to land troops and equipment, and its proximity to New York City made it the perfect staging area to launch an assault on America's biggest and most important city.

At the farthest end of Long Island was the Montauk Lighthouse, which was the most significant navigation point for both Allied shipping and German U-boats in the Eastern Sea Frontier. The navy had even begun beefing up an old World War I fort out there that they called Fort Hero, and were able to hide sixteen-inch shore guns by building a fake town that looked like an innocent fishing village.

The northern coast of Long Island was sparsely populated, with some of the most beautiful and expensive estates in the country. On the island's south coast and west of the Hamptons, things were rural, and very different.

The Montauk Highway ran seventy-eight miles along the southern shore of the island and passed through the half-ritzy estates, half-fishing communities that made up that side of the island. Then there was a lot of nothing—sandy beaches without visitors, and a landscape that was 80 percent potato farms. Plus, the category 3, once-in-a-century storm that became known as "the Great New England Hurricane of 1938" had previously thinned out the already-sparse population.

Almost eighty miles from the Montauk Lighthouse, the Montauk Highway ended and Highway 27 started. After another forty miles of farms and shoreline, drivers could find themselves in Queens to the north and Brooklyn to the south.

On the morning of Friday, April 10, 1942, Lieutenant Treglia, Dominick Sacco, and civilian agent Charles Hoyt began a one-hundred-mile drive east from Queens along Highway 27 and the Montauk Highway. Hoyt was a retired investigator for the Alcohol Tax Unit. MacFall had sent Hoyt to Haffenden earlier in 1942, as MacFall was high on Hoyt. Haffenden had wanted Hoyt to join the regular navy, but he was too old (already in his mid-fifties), so Haffenden and MacFall agreed to hire him on as a civilian agent. MacFall held him in higher regard than other civilian agents, and even paid him with checks that he wrote personally. Hoyt was about five feet, six inches tall and a little overweight, with a stocky build, and was from a German family.[5] Haffenden named Hoyt "Agent H" in his little black book, and placed him in Squad #2.

It was unseasonably cold that day, as spring had arrived, but New York City and Long Island had seen a snow flurry hit the day before.[6] There was no traffic along their route, as the road was wet and the car passed in and out of rain. As the men looked out at sea just beyond the sand, the visibility was poor, which was a good thing, or else they may have been able to see the signs of wreckage washing up all over Long Island's beaches—including oil, debris, life rafts, and bodies. When they got to Eastport, they stopped at the head offices of the H. E. Sweezey and Son trucking company, which was one of the largest trucking companies on the island.

Sweezey—whom his friends called "Chet"—had founded the trucking company with his father back in 1921, in Riverhead, and moved it to Eastport in 1926. They were following the duck trade, as duck farms on Long Island were making handsome profits from raising and killing their own ducks and providing delicious duck eggs. Sweezey's father died in 1936, and since then Sweezey had been running the company with the help of his son-in-law, Duke, and all the while shipping fish and barrels of ducks to Fulton Fish Market, among other places.

Sweezey had never actually driven a truck in his life, as he had been blind since age seven. But he'd worked hard to get to his current position—even learning how to read and write despite having had no formal education—and honed his senses along the way.

When the three men got to H. E. Sweezey and Son, they were

met by Duke, who walked them into Sweezey's office. The company grounds had plenty of flat land and were surrounded by open duck farms. His trucks were mostly out for the day, picking up their loads at the Eastport Duck Packing Plant.[7]

The office was a small room, and the three men sat down in front of Sweezey, who was seated behind a desk. Treglia would've normally started by asking Sweezey if he was "ready to do his patriotic duty." But Treglia skipped that after observing that over Sweezey's shoulder, as the man sat at his desk, was an unmistakable Distinguished Service Cross, awarded to his brother during World War I—posthumously. When he was younger, Sweezey couldn't go to war because he was blind, so his brother went, and didn't come back alive. This was Sweezey's chance to do *his* duty for his country.

Treglia informed Sweezey that the navy's concern lay in rumors that fishermen disembarking from Long Island were supplying German submarines out at sea. Treglia was also concerned that there might be German agents around the island, and they might be procuring supplies for a U-boat rendezvous.

There were fishing ports and coastline all over the east end of Long Island, and Treglia asked if the fishing boat captains in the area could be trusted. Sweezey offered to take the three men to meet the captains, and they could go right now if they wanted to. Treglia said they most certainly did want to meet the captains, and also asked Sweezey if there was anyone in Montauk who could help, particularly someone who had access to large amounts of fuel. Sweezey called up a friend of his named Charles Bonner, who operated a gas station near the Montauk coast where the U-boat had been spotted.

They set up a meeting for that evening.

Treglia checked in with Haffenden, who reported that there was nothing coming in anywhere about German agents on Long Island. That meant that either the U-boat hadn't landed any saboteurs, or that they hadn't been spotted yet. If they were there, and hadn't been spotted, then the likelihood that they already had a contact helping them on the island went up profoundly.

Treglia, Sacco, and Hoyt then followed Sweezey and Duke, and drove thirty miles west to Greenport, at the northeastern end of Long Island. It was a strategically important spot, as it was the farthest eastern railroad junction on the island, and the navy had a shipyard there building minesweepers and tugboats. The area was mostly covered by Greenport Village, which was a community completely devoted to the fishing industry. Once they arrived, Sweezey rounded up as many captains as he could find—about a dozen—for lunch at Claudio's restaurant.

Claudio's restaurant had been built in 1870, right on the water, between two piers. The interior was mostly open and was dominated by a large Victorian bar. During Prohibition, rumrunners used to deliver booze through hidden trapdoors behind the bar. It was a popular place with both the fishermen and the pilots from the nearby airstrip.

Rum and a hearty lunch made the atmosphere lively and loud. Sweezey introduced his three new companions as "friends," and made them out to be big shots. After all, anyone from New York—Fulton was considered the mecca of the fishing world—was someone important. He told the captains that if these three men came around and asked for something, they should cooperate—no questions asked.

The fishing boat captains had a great time, and Sweezey even footed the $30 bill. He was good and drunk by the end, and confessed to Sacco that one of the captains present at the table, a man named Eddie Fiedler, had previously been interrogated by the FBI in connection with an allegation that he supplied meat to an enemy ship. Sacco wrote down the name of Fiedler's ship. Though Fiedler had been cleared by the FBI, he was still under suspicion.

From Claudio's, the five men set out for a fuel station by Lake Montauk, way out on the tip of the longest finger of Long Island, to speak with Charles Bonner. Bonner was in a different class than Sweezey; he was a yacht club member and sailed in circles of high society that Sweezey was not privy to. When they arrived, Sweezey introduced the men to Bonner, and then Treglia and Sacco took Bonner outside to talk.

They told Bonner that they were in the navy; Sacco wanted to know if boat captains out this way could be trusted, and would they ever consider helping the Germans by providing fuel or water for money?

Bonner was in a great position to know. Not only was he the operator of the farthest eastern fuel station on Long Island, but he was also a financier and had guaranteed loans for many of the fishing boat captains.

Bonner, just like Sweezey, was given the phone number to the local Naval Intelligence branch office in Riverhead. Bonner was told to report any fishermen that showed signs of "prosperity." If someone had just made a deal with a German U-boat, they would have made a lot of money doing it, and they might be foolishly flaunting their cash. Bonner was adamant that there was no one there that he knew of colluding with the Germans.

Treglia also asked if Bonner could get one of his men on board a fishing smack. Bonner said he could do it. Haffenden then ordered Treglia and Sacco to come back to Manhattan—they needed to continue their work at Fulton Fish Market. As for Hoyt, he stayed on Long Island, readying himself for a day at sea.

On Thursday, April 16, 1942, Bonner spoke with William de Waal, captain of the fishing boat *Margie Lou*. Bonner told de Waal that a man—Hoyt's name was not given—would join him on his boat the next morning. Bonner even lied and told de Waal that Hoyt was a good friend.

De Waal was a salty lobsterman of Dutch descent, tall, with dark hair and eyes and a medium build, and a forty-year veteran of the high seas. He was also a veteran of World War I, having served in the army, and was sharp as a tack—nothing got by him. He was suspicious of taking anyone aboard whom he didn't know, and Hoyt, or whoever he was, certainly fit the bill.

"Just take him out for a day's fishing and do him good," Bonner insisted.

"Does he get sick?" de Waal asked.

"No," Bonner assured him. "And he has a day off."

"This is war," de Waal objected. He knew better than to take just anybody out with him amid the U-boat threat. And though he finally relented, when he met Hoyt at the dock the next morning at 4 a.m., he was still suspicious.

Margie Lou was a "beam trawler" that had a wood hull and a prominent bow. The wheelhouse followed shortly after, and de Waal perched himself on top of it to have a view of Hoyt. Aft of the wheelhouse on the beam trawler was the mast, and then the boat sloped slightly downward while a large beam that was fixed up in the air at a forty-five-degree angle, which made it ideal for trawler fishing. Underneath the beam, Hoyt and three others busied themselves on the deck of the ship that was about thirty feet from bow to stern, and almost ten feet at its widest. As *Margie Lou* disembarked, heading south by southwest for two miles out to sea, Hoyt found it very difficult to escape de Waal's watchful eye.

The weather was good that day, warm because of the overcast. Not only that, but the waters around Long Island were always relatively warmer than surrounding areas, and typically this meant milder weather on colder days. For twelve hours Hoyt toiled aboard *Margie Lou*, to the point of near-complete exhaustion. Even a young man would have found the day hard. As de Waal dropped the net and kept the boat moving forward, they pulled up lobsters off the seafloor. After that first load arrived, the crew never stopped packing lobsters into the hull. Load after load was dropped until the ship was full, and all the while, de Waal kept a close eye on Hoyt. The more Hoyt talked, the more de Waal was sure he detected a German accent. And he still didn't know his name.

At 4 p.m., *Margie Lou* got back to port, and Hoyt was met by a Coast Guard officer de Waal was familiar with. De Waal kept watching Hoyt, and when Hoyt left, de Waal approached the guardsman. De Waal asked who Hoyt was, really, and the guardsman told de Waal that Hoyt was from Naval Intelligence.

"Oh," said de Waal, as it all suddenly started to make sense. "I can understand it."[8]

Hoyt had good news for Haffenden, and he was eager to make his report. He hadn't found the enemy, nor did he gain any intelligence of value, but he was positive that Captain de Waal would be a valuable asset to the navy in the future. Hoyt had taken extra steps and asked around about de Waal. Everything he heard was good. De Waal could be trusted to scout the waters off Long Island, bring agents out to sea, and keep an eye on fishermen in port.

Haffenden wanted to get more men onto fishing boats from Long Island, so he sent another one of his civilian agents for the job—Joe Maculitis. Maculitis was a Greek-American, with a dark complexion and a medium build, standing about five feet, eight inches tall.[9] Haffenden had previously designated him "Agent M" in his little black book.

Before dawn on Saturday, April 18, 1942,[10] Maculitis pulled up to the Blue Marlin Inn in Montauk. He had instructions from Treglia to meet Ellis Tuthill, who was another contact of Bonner's and captained a boat called *Adelaide T*. Tuthill arrived ten minutes after Maculitis, who had already woken up half of the people staying there because he got upset that he had to wait.

Maculitis was a temperamental man and was ill-suited for undercover work. Tuthill had already been informed that Maculitis was from Naval Intelligence, but the rest of the crew of *Adelaide T* didn't know this. Hoyt may have been put to work aboard *Margie Lou*, but on *Adelaide T*—another beam trawler—Maculitis wasn't interested in doing anything. The crew found him dreadfully unpleasant, as Maculitis spent most of the day in a bunk, trying very hard to not get seasick. The weather had been cooling a little bit, but it was good on that day and the sea was not particularly rough. Maculitis still couldn't stomach it.[11]

Maculitis was an embarrassment to B-3, and after his day on *Adelaide T,* his role in Operation Underworld was over. Even though two of his civilian agents had basically had their cover blown, Haffenden couldn't help but observe that his team had indeed accomplished their mission. The enemy, it appeared, wasn't on Long Island, and if they were there, Haffenden had drastically expanded his network of informants to meet them if and when they came out of hiding. He now also had two fishing boat captains who were in the know about the navy's mission on Long Island, and could be trusted to help in the future. Bonner had done such a good job for the navy that Treglia brought him to New York City the next week and introduced him to Haffenden and MacFall.

Soon, Sweezey, Bonner, de Waal, and Tuthill weren't the only ones who were making calls to the station at Riverhead, as one by one, they brought nearly all of the local fishing boat captains into the fold. Dozens, even hundreds, of fishing boats were now actively observing the Eastern Sea Frontier for enemy activity. Another section of Naval Intelligence began arming these fishing boats with radios powerful enough to call to shore. Captains de Waal and Tuthill of *Margie Lou* and *Adelaide T* began taking these radios with them out to sea. Hoyt made another half dozen trips with de Waal, as the two were now getting along better.

With US fleet strength in the Atlantic still floundering, and insufficient to protect its merchant fleet on not only the high seas, but their own home waters, the navy was now using Long Island's fishing fleet as the first line of defense against the enemy. It was desperately needed, as over the week when Haffenden's agents were infiltrating Montauk, another fifteen Allied ships had been sunk in the Atlantic. Long Islanders, for their part, were doing a lot to combat enemy U-boats. The US high command had issued orders to commission civilians all over New York to watch the shores. Coastguardsmen called "sand pounders" paced every inch of beach on Long Island. Also on Long Island, private yachts began making up what was called "the Hooligan Navy." They patrolled the water for enemy U-boats—some of them were even armed with machine guns—and were joined by other civilians who flew their private planes for sub watch patrols.

US merchant ships had already been told a month ago not to operate with their lights on at night, but back in New York City lights still made them perfect, dark silhouettes for U-boat captains who observed them through their periscopes. In April 1942,

New York City finally decided to turn out the lights. However, the "blackout" that was desired by Admiral Andrews never materialized, as Mayor La Guardia argued for a compromise—New York City would institute a "dimout."

The Statue of Liberty's torch was extinguished. The Wrigley's fish and neon bubbles in Times Square were taken down. However, at night, the Camel man kept smoking, and blowing smoke rings over a dark street. Street lamps and traffic lights were dimmed, and cars either ran with just their parking lights on or had their lights painted over so light could only escape through a slit. Gasoline and rubber shortages saw fewer and fewer cars were on the road, and most cars running were yellow taxicabs that were exempt from rationing. Floodlights that illuminated the facades of New York City's most recognizable structures—the Empire State Building, the Chrysler Building, and Rockefeller Center—were turned off, making them look like "giant mausoleums." In late April, sporadic blackout drills made the city even darker.

Also in late April, Alfred Hitchcock released his latest film—*Saboteur*. The movie was a cinematic version of Haffenden's worst nightmare, and even featured footage of the Third Naval District's most epic failure—SS *Normandie*, used in the movie to show the aftermath of a plot carried out by a saboteur. Frightening thoughts infected the people walking the dark streets of New York City, and nightmares of enemy spies lurking in the pitch black were burrowing into people's psyches.

In late April 1942, Commander Haffenden's men were conducting missions to develop numerous contacts and were producing valuable intelligence. Haffenden had officers meticulously tracking all of the supplies taken on by fishing boats at Fulton Fish Market to see if there were any discrepancies. Treglia and the Sacco brothers were still visiting Fulton and Lanza nearly every day, along with a number of other officers and civilian agents.

Dominick Sacco would take agents down to meet Lanza, and Lanza was instrumental in the entire process that followed.

Sometimes he would have a drink with the agent at the Paris Café below Meyer's Hotel, but in any event, Lanza would then walk them across South Street, onto the pier at the end of Beekman Street to the docked fishing boats. He'd find the boat he was looking for, and all he had to say to the captain was "Put him on," and the captain always complied.[12] These agents were also bringing radios aboard so they could immediately communicate to the navy if they spotted a U-boat.

By the end of April 1942, Haffenden saw the opportunity to expand his operation in response to the navy's problems all up and down the East Coast. He called upon Lanza and Espy again, seeking to take advantage of their reach. And their reach into other states along the East Coast had little to do with the criminal empire that they were a part of and more to do with their membership in the United Seafood Workers Union, which was a nationwide organization.

Haffenden and Lanza were now talking and meeting regularly, sometimes at the Hotel Astor or Church Street, and other times at bars or restaurants in Manhattan. During this time, Haffenden had learned a lot about Lanza and the reach of his business dealings. The lieutenant commander told MacFall that Lanza and Espy could make contacts in all the major fishing ports on the East Coast.

There was only one problem—Lanza was on parole, and it was a crime for him to leave the state.[13] If he was caught, he would not only lose his $50,000 bond, but he would be thrown in prison until his trial began, and his role in Operation Underworld would be over. Lanza brushed off any worry about leaving the state, confident that whatever trouble found him, he'd be able to handle it. For Haffenden, losing Lanza would be a big blow, but it was worth the risk.

Over the course of three-and-a-half days, Lanza and Espy took a road trip in a borrowed car that saw them driving nearly the entire time. They went as far north as Portland, Maine; and stopped in Boston, Nantucket, and New Bedford in Massachusetts; and Providence and Block Island in Rhode Island. They also went to

Connecticut; and Wildwood, Cape May, Manasquan, and Brielle in New Jersey. Then they went south, and visited Virginia Beach and North Carolina. All in all, over a dozen stops.[14]

In each of these locations, Lanza found the union delegates he'd known for a long time and told them the same thing—sometime in the future he might be sending a "fella" to them, and they'd be able to recognize this "fella" because he would be carrying a union identification card from Local 359. If they encountered such a man, they were to give him whatever job he requested. Then he added his personal touch.

"You will be doing me a favor, and I'll get you one back down [in] the city."[15]

Socks and Espy returned to New York with a list of names that Haffenden could contact for any reason. It was an incredible achievement—if the Germans infiltrated just about any major port on the East Coast, Haffenden would be able to respond immediately with undercover investigators. The irony was, though, for all the reach that Lanza now showed up and down the Atlantic coast, he was still struggling to secure the Port of New York. Despite his and Haffenden's early successes, there were still two locations that were not under the navy's control, and they contained the most strategically valuable piers in all of the mainland United States. Those locations were the West Side of Manhattan and Brooklyn.

The West Side of Manhattan was where hundreds of thousands of troops were loaded onto transports, and where *Normandie* was now laterally recumbent. One of the reasons Lanza was struggling on the West Side was that it was dominated by the Irish. The Dunn-McGrath gang had staked their claim there years before, and they were firmly entrenched. The Irish and the Italians in New York City had been feuding since before the Civil War, but Lanza also had a personal, infamous history with the Irish. Not only did he have an Irish wife, which the Irish hated, but Lanza had also murdered an Irish gang member fifteen years earlier.[16]

And the men who controlled the longshoremen on the West

Side—President of the International Longshoremen's Association (ILA) Joe Ryan and his right-hand man, Jerry Sullivan—were also Irish. Their power extended to other ILA members all over the Port of New York (and the entire East Coast), and Lanza had zero ability to influence their actions.

Then there were the Brooklyn piers, which were responsible for the majority of war supplies sent to Britain, and the Brooklyn Navy Yard was starting to send troops too. The problem that Lanza faced in Brooklyn stemmed from the fact that he was under indictment. He tried to reach out to the Mangano family that ran Brooklyn, and he attempted to contact the "pistol locals" over there that were dominated by the Camarda brothers. He even reached out to his imprisoned boss's longtime friend Joe Adonis, but Brooklyn wanted nothing to do with Lanza. It wasn't so much a problem of not knowing him, or that he was not high-ranking, but the fact that Lanza was currently under indictment and facing a very stiff prison sentence meant that he was a perfect candidate to become a police informer. Asking for the Brooklyn longshoremen's help while the indictment hung over him was a fool's errand. Brooklyn was ruled by the most ruthless gangsters of New York, with an iron fist soaked in blood. When Lanza came calling, they nearly laughed in his face.

And so too did the Italians. Not the Italian-Americans, or even the Italians who came from Italy as children. These were the Italians who had only recently fled Italy and Benito Mussolini's Fascist government. These Italians would not bow to or cooperate with Lanza, as they were too attached to the Padrone System and their own bosses.

The other problem that Lanza had, and perhaps the most significant, was that he was not a very powerful gangster. Sure, in the Luciano family, he was a high-ranking soldier, he had his own territory, and his influence stretched across the country. But that influence stopped cold when it came to the territories dominated by the other four families in New York City.

This was by design—the design of his imprisoned boss, Lucky Luciano. Perhaps it was time to talk to the acting boss of his family—Frank Costello—but even he would have trouble exerting influence over the other families. It had been purposely set up that way to maintain a balance of power and keep the peace in the underworld.

Lanza was in a bit of a bind, and in turn, so too was Haffenden. They both tried to come up with solutions, and at the end of April 1942, their efforts were starting to reach their limits. Forty-nine Allied ships had been destroyed in the Atlantic that month, just one fewer than the month before. To make matters worse, Haffenden's men were in position, but had yet to uncover an enemy plot, find any tangible leads on enemy agents, or assist in any arrests. For now, Lanza had gotten Haffenden's men in position in some fantastic spots, but the mission was far—very far—from complete.

Haffenden and Sacco were meeting with Socks Lanza so often that sometimes Lanza would come to them in coveralls stained with fish guts.[17] As Lanza's liaison, Dominick Sacco often visited him at Meyer's Hotel, but just like Haffenden, Sacco was also becoming accustomed to having dinner or drinks with Lanza out on the town. One night in late April 1942, Lanza, Espy, and Sacco were having dinner at Shine's Restaurant in the Garment District of Manhattan, just two doors down from bustling Penn Station. Shine's was known for its seafood, which apparently, Lanza couldn't get enough of. As Lanza and Espy were speaking, Sacco took notes that he intended to share with Haffenden.

The topic that night had to do with contacts that Lanza and Espy hoped who could help Operation Underworld. Lanza and Espy mentioned a man named James Piccarelli, who was a member of the National Union of Stevedores. They were also trying to reach out to a man named Tommy Green, who lived and worked at the Seaman's Institute in Brooklyn. Also, they were trying to contact someone called "Scotty," who was English, and was "very much in the know."

These names didn't ring any bells for Sacco. Who were these people?

The answer was that they were nobodies. It was clear that Lanza and Espy had exhausted their contacts. Haffenden needed contact with Mafia leadership in Brooklyn—Vincent Mangano and Joe Adonis, for example—and not some guy who worked at the Seaman's Institute.

Was there someone high enough up in the food chain who could get Lanza access to everywhere in the Port of New York? Lanza jumped at the opportunity to answer this question.

"You know," Lanza started. "There is someone who could snap the whip on the entire underworld."[18]

Sacco's ears perked up.

Lanza continued and told Sacco that if this "someone" was brought into the fold, he would have no problem gaining access to anywhere, or anybody. He also told Sacco that this "someone" would want to meet Commander Haffenden. But this "someone" would also need assurances that he would not be double-crossed, and any promises made by Haffenden would have to be honored.

Sacco could see that Lanza had already put a lot of thought into this. So who was this "someone?"

Lanza told Sacco that his name was Charles "Lucky" Luciano—former public enemy number one and head of the Luciano family.

Sacco knew who Luciano was, and actually, he even knew him personally, from his years as an investigator. He knew that Luciano was a leader—maybe even *the* leader—in the Mafia. But Sacco also knew that Luciano had been imprisoned six years earlier at Dannemora Prison. Dannemora was way up north by the Canadian border.

How could Luciano possibly help while he was in prison way up there?

Lanza told Sacco that arrangements would have to be made for someone to contact Luciano. If this person was able to tell Luciano what the navy needed, perhaps he would give his blessing to the operation and spread the word.

Sacco wondered what would change if Luciano's cooperation was secured.

"Why, I'll go to town," Lanza said.

But Sacco still wondered if Luciano was as powerful as he once was now that he was in prison.

"Yes," replied Lanza. Luciano still held tremendous power in the underworld.

Lanza concluded by saying that if Luciano said it was okay to cooperate with Naval Intelligence, then the underworld would most certainly comply. By now Lanza had talked to Costello, and Costello knew that Luciano was the person who could benefit the most from helping the US government. Lanza, for his part, felt like he owed Luciano, as Luciano had gotten him out of so many jams during his youth, when he was constantly being arrested during his rise to power in Fulton Fish Market.[19]

Sacco immediately told Haffenden about Luciano. Haffenden knew who Luciano was, and though he was surprised that his name came up, he was not shocked, as he had been pushing Lanza for weeks about the extent of his contacts. Haffenden followed up by calling Lanza into his office in room 196 at the Hotel Astor. Once Lanza arrived, the two hatched a plan to bring Luciano into Operation Underworld.

How could Luciano help?

Lanza explained that there were a lot of people who were in a position to help who were friends of Luciano's. He explained that people in the unions whom they needed had a lot of respect for him too. Lanza also explained that Luciano was the only one who could cross the racial divide between the Irish and the actual Italians on the waterfront.

"The word of Charlie," Lanza said, "may give me the right-of-way."

Haffenden knew that recruiting the man who was believed to be the country's top criminal to help the navy could never reach the light of day. None of his fellow officers would try something so audacious and risky, that could damage the reputation of the navy so badly. But his qualms about recruiting Luciano for the navy's interests only went so far as whether or not Luciano could help him accomplish his mission. If it was going to succeed, nobody outside of MacFall, Howe, and the spymaster in DC could know about it. If the main branch of the navy heard about it, they'd be shut down and possibly reprimanded. Whatever information or contacts they developed would also have to be controlled, and sworn to secrecy, if that was even possible. Haffenden knew that bringing in Luciano would mean they were going to develop dangerous contacts that went way beyond fishing boat captains and low-level gangsters. These informants would represent the top echelon of Mafia leadership.

"I'll talk to anybody," Haffenden said at the time. "A priest, a bank manager, a gangster, *the devil himself,* if I can get the information I need. This is a war."

CHAPTER 4

"The Devil Himself"

In late April 1942, Commander Charles Radcliffe Haffenden undertook the unlikely task of trying to recruit Charles "Lucky" Luciano to become an informant for Naval Intelligence. It was complicated in that he would have to successfully move through a number of government and bureaucratic hoops without causing a stir. It was a delicate dance filled with imagination, the kind only a man like Haffenden could conceive; a circus of go-betweens, all of whom had to understand the necessity of secrecy.

Keeping it quiet was only one of Haffenden's problems. There was another hitch: Lanza had communicated what Luciano would probably expect if he became involved, but Lanza hadn't even spoken with him yet, so the actual specifics of Luciano's demands remained an unknown. And furthermore, the DA was adamant about there being no deals cut to criminals for helping their country, so what could Haffenden possibly offer him anyway?

And how did Lanza know for sure if Luciano would be willing to help in the first place? There were so many open questions that it gave Haffenden pause. The first contact with Luciano had to be handled delicately. A man like that only trusted a handful of people, not to mention he had a very long history of not cooperating with authority figures. Whoever Haffenden sent to meet Luciano needed to be a trusted friend, and someone that the mob boss held in high regard.

But before Haffenden could even make a choice of go-betweens, he had to recruit an inspector in the Westchester District, who then made clear to Haffenden that there was yet another hurdle: In order to set up a meeting with Luciano in prison, Haffenden would have to get the approval of the New York Commissioner of Correction, John Lyons.

Haffenden had reservations about contacting Lyons directly. The way Haffenden saw it, he needed to convince Lyons to let the navy send someone to meet Luciano, but he also needed to convince the commissioner to give Luciano special privileges, such as access to his bosses, capos, and other underworld leaders. This in and of itself was going to be an extremely difficult objective to accomplish, made more complicated by the fact that Haffenden didn't even know the commissioner.

Haffenden's first move was to bring Assistant DA Murray Gurfein back into the mix. Haffenden invited Gurfein to his office at the Hotel Astor for a meeting where they would be joined by Socks Lanza. In the circus of go-betweens to get to Luciano, the meeting between Lanza and Gurfein would be perhaps the oddest of all. After all, now, strangely in the interest of national security, Lanza found himself meeting face-to-face—and not in a courtroom—once more with the very man who wanted to put him behind bars. There was a mutual understanding that put the age-old game of good versus evil on the sidelines, and in its place they were playing another ancient game—warfare.

In the third week of April, the two men on opposite sides of the law sat next to each other in front of Haffenden's desk in room 196 of the Hotel Astor. Lanza found himself revealing secrets about the waterfront that confirmed suspicions that Gurfein had had for a long time. Lanza wasn't divulging the secret to the wide scope of his own power; instead he was revealing the limits of his influence with the Italians and other gangs and families. As much as he was having trouble on the West Side and Brooklyn, Luciano, Lanza told Gurfein, could open the door for the navy to accomplish all of its goals. Gurfein agreed with Lanza's assessment, and the three men came to the understanding that Lanza would be the "inside man" to contact Luciano and convince him to cooperate.

Then Gurfein insisted that one person who could help Lanza convince Luciano, and perhaps assist in the process, was Moses Polakoff, Luciano's attorney of record. Not only was Polakoff Luciano's attorney, but he was also a seaman second class, as a veteran of World War I, and a former member of the DA's office. When the meeting in room 196 ended, Haffenden and Gurfein had several moves to make, while Lanza waited for the door to Luciano to be opened.

First, Gurfein approached his boss, Frank Hogan, for the go-ahead. Hogan always liked to be "in the know," and as long as that was being respected, he was happy to let events proceed. Hogan permitted Gurfein to contact Polakoff and enlist his help to get to Luciano.

On the phone Polakoff balked at the idea. "As far as [I'm] concerned," he told Gurfein, "the case [is] closed." Polakoff had just recovered from surgery a few weeks back and was not in the mood for nonsense.

But Gurfein pressed the issue, and convinced Polakoff to come in for a meeting.

The attorney arrived at Gurfein's office the next day. He was forty-six years old, had a long nose, and thick, wavy dark hair. He may have represented his fair share of underworld figures, but he believed in the law, and that everyone—no matter how sinister— deserved a legitimate defense, and their day in court. He was devoted to his country, and his Jewish faith.

Polakoff had no interest in reopening Luciano's case. The DA's office had creamed them back in 1936, and then they lost again when they appealed the conviction. But when Gurfein started talking about the threat of sabotage and U-boats, and how Luciano could help, the former sailor changed his tune.

Gurfein told Polakoff the details of what he knew about Operation Underworld. He also told Polakoff that helping the navy was in his client's best interest.

"If I [can] be of service to [you] or the navy I [will] be glad to do so," Polakoff told Gurfein.

Gurfein said that he believed that Polakoff was the man best suited to convince Luciano to help. As a former member of the DA's office, he was also perfect for Gurfein's peace of mind.

"If Luciano made an honest effort to be of service in the future," Gurfein said, "[the DA's office] would bear that in mind."

Polakoff expressed that he hoped that Luciano would want to do his part too. But he disagreed with Gurfein, and said, "I don't know Luciano well enough to broach the subject to him on my own. But I know a person whose patriotism, or affection for our country, irrespective of his reputation, [is] of the highest [order], and I would like to discuss the matter with this person first before I [commit]."

Gurfein said he was open to the idea, so Polakoff told him he would call this "intermediary," as Polakoff put it.[1]

Gurfein had no idea who Polakoff was talking about, but he did have faith that Polakoff understood perfectly how the underworld was organized and knew what he was doing. Socks Lanza was happy to be Luciano's contact. But from what Haffenden had learned about underworld hierarchy, he had his reservations about sending in Lanza to meet Luciano, so when Gurfein reported back that Polakoff had someone else in mind, the commander was more than receptive to the idea. Another dancer was thus added to the circus.

Interestingly, Polakoff's choice wasn't Frank Costello—Luciano's acting boss—or anyone from the Luciano family, for that matter. Polakoff knew Luciano well after spending so much time defending him—albeit unsuccessfully—during his trial. So he knew that the person who held the most sway with his client was his business partner, current accountant, and best friend, Meyer "Little Man" Lansky.

Meyer Lansky had been born Maier Suchowljansky, on July 4, 1902, in Belarus, but identified as Polish-American. In response to a wave of anti-Semitism gripping Eastern Europe in the early twentieth century, the Suchowljansky family had immigrated to the United States in 1911. Lansky's father, mother, and younger brother Jacob eventually settled on Grand Street, on the Lower East Side of Manhattan.

At the beginning of the twentieth century, the Lower East Side was the embodiment of America as a "melting pot." Jews, Irish, and Italians all lived packed into the neighborhood, and most lived with birds of their own feather. Five-story brick tenements, affording one room per family, stretched from block to block, while the sidewalks were crowded with people living on the streets and pushcarts peddling everything from fish to fruit.

Lansky's father got a job as a garment presser and tried in vain to get his son to be more immersed in the Jewish faith. This pressure created a weird dichotomy in Lansky, in that he rebelled against his father by displaying a lack of faith, yet when confronted by anti-Semitism, Lansky became militant. As a boy, he was smart, and something of a mathematical genius. He was also small for his age and was a target for older Irish and Italian kids.

One day as he walked to school, a gang of older Italian boys came after little Meyer Lansky. The leader got in Lansky's face and said, "If you wanna keep alive, Jew boy, you gotta pay us five cents a week protection money." Lansky was having none of it.

"Go fuck yourself!" Lansky told the kid.

The Italian kid laughed. He respected this boy who wouldn't flinch. He put his hand on Lansky's shoulder and said, "Okay, you got protection for free."

"Shove your protection up your ass. I don't need it!"

The encounter between the two boys would become the stuff of lore, as it was the first time Meyer Lansky and Lucky Luciano met. Luciano was shaking down kids for protection, which was his first venture into racketeering. It was an encounter that would be the start of a friendship that lasted a lifetime.

In eighth grade, despite Lansky's fantastic aptitude, he dropped out of school and joined Luciano's gang. By then, Luciano had already made friends with Frank Costello (known then by his real name, Francesco Castiglia), and Lansky brought into the gang his fellow Jewish friend Benjamin "Bugsy" Siegel.

A year later World War I started,[2] and though Lansky was just fifteen years old, the four boys were having success as stickup men and thieves and making more money than they could deal with. Luciano was the brains and the leader, Costello made important connections, Siegel was the brawn, and Lansky was the accountant.

It was a fruitful partnership, and the four of them were sitting on a pile of cash just waiting to invest in something. Then, after World War I, the US government solved that problem for them when they passed the eighteenth Amendment, which started Prohibition.[3]

Soon after, Lansky split off and started his own gang with Siegel called the "Bugs and Meyer Mob." Lansky was ambitious, and while the Bugs and Meyer Mob worked with Luciano and Costello frequently, the gangs of New York were still largely divided along racial lines. Lansky recruited other Jews from the neighborhood, and together they provided trucks and protection for the movement of alcohol. They also shook down Jewish moneylenders and made them pay tribute. But of all the rackets that Lansky ran, the most notorious was his murder-for-hire business that the press called "Murder Inc."

Lansky was no stranger to guns, but he was not a triggerman. For all their street credibility, and all their exploits, Luciano, Costello, and Lansky were not killers (Siegel was the exception). They didn't, however, shy away from giving orders, or paying out death contracts. Over the course of the next decade, Murder Inc. would grow, and be responsible for the killing of nearly one thousand souls.

Lansky got married to a woman named Anna Citron in 1929, and she gave birth to their boy, who would be disabled his entire life—Anna was certain it was God cursing them for her husband's crimes. Lansky locked himself away for a week and drank himself into oblivion. But wherever he went in his mind he shook off the demons, and in the ensuing years, Lansky would be a good father to the boy, and the couple would successfully grow their family with a healthy boy and girl.

As much financial success as Lansky had in the underworld, anti-Semitism was alive and well in the realm, and put a ceiling on his rise. Sicilians were at the top echelons of underworld leadership, and they were stuck on old world ideas that precluded them from working with gangs of differing races. In a time when the gangs of New York each destroyed the mountain that they were all trying to climb, anti-Semitism was a hurdle that Lansky could not negotiate. Luciano's association with Lansky and other Jews even got him into trouble with the Sicilian old-world guard.

Lansky had dealt with anti-Semitism all of his life, and when Nazism found its way across the ocean and into New York City, he was there to meet it. In 1935, an associate of his telephoned him about a rally that was taking place in Yorkville—a German neighborhood in Manhattan, where Brownshirts, Silver Shirts, the German American Bund, and Friends of the New Germany flourished.

Lansky rounded up fifteen of his toughest, who arrived to a scene that would have fit perfectly in Nuremberg—swastikas lined the stage, and there were photos of the Führer, Adolf Hitler. Hundreds of Brownshirts were waiting in heavy anticipation for a speech that was about to be delivered by the American Führer, Fritz Kuhn.

Though he was heavily outnumbered, Lansky lit firecrackers, threw them into the auditorium, and as they exploded, his gang charged into the Fascist mob with clubs and bats. It was complete chaos, and the Brownshirts were taken by such surprise that they dispersed, and Kuhn was unable to give his speech that night. Nights like this happened on more than a few occasions, with Lansky leading the charge.[4]

These events spotlighted the weird dichotomy that Lansky felt about his faith, as he was willing to risk his life to bust the heads of anti-Semites, yet he would not yield to his father's wishes that his children be bar mitzvahed. His lifelong rejection of his father's ways, even in the face of his faith, was a trait that he shared with his friend Luciano. It was also a trait that was responsible for many decisions that shaped both men's lives. Deep down, their need to blaze a trail for themselves in America—the land of opportunity—was the driving force behind their criminal activity.

Despite being known for his brains, Lansky was also the toughest man Luciano ever knew. Even when he was a fully grown man, he was barely five-foot-four and somewhere in the neighborhood of 150 pounds, but Lansky was as hard as they came. He had brown hair and eyes, and a long scar down the right side of his face.

Moses Polakoff didn't know where Luciano's allegiance lay, but he had every confidence that Lansky was a loyal American. In late April of 1942, Polakoff summoned Lansky to his office and told him about Operation Underworld.

"I [will] be happy to help in any way that I can," Lansky said without hesitation.[5]

Polakoff picked up the phone and told Gurfein that his intermediary was willing to help and was ready to meet him to learn more about what he needed to do.

The next morning, Polakoff and Gurfein took a cab to Longchamps restaurant just a couple of blocks south of Central Park, on West 58th Street, between Fifth and Sixth Avenues. Longchamps had a chain of large restaurants, and each had a row of stools and a counter that looked into the serving area, and a giant art deco design on the wall. Tables and booths filled the rest of the large dining area, as Longchamps restaurants were known for seating hundreds, if not over a thousand, patrons at a time.

To this point, the identity of Polakoff's intermediary was still a mystery to Gurfein, and when Gurfein and Polakoff got to their booth, a short, smartly dressed man sat there sipping coffee. Gurfein didn't know Lansky by sight, but once he was introduced, the head of New York City's rackets bureau knew exactly who he was having breakfast with. Polakoff opened the discussion and introduced the two men, and immediately followed with why Lansky was there.

"I don't know Charlie well enough," Polakoff stated. "I have confidence in this fellow," he added, referring to Lansky. "I am willing to put the responsibility in his hands."

Lansky didn't say much during the meeting, but he indicated he was willing to take the "responsibility."

But Gurfein didn't fully understand what that meant, since he was not there to vet Lansky. He was there under orders from Haffenden to get this "intermediary" to cooperate and tell him whether Luciano would cooperate or not. Gurfein then revealed to Lansky most of the details of Operation Underworld. For the better part of an hour, the young prosecutor laid out the entire problem as if it were the facts of a case. All the while, Lansky ate, quietly, and voiced at least one concern: "We have to be very careful making any moves because . . . Mussolini [is] popular with some Italians in New York."

Then Gurfein finally asked if Luciano could be trusted. Would Luciano help the government that incarcerated him? Or was Luciano sympathetic to the regime in his native Italy?

Lansky put any doubt about Luciano's loyalty to bed, and he reminded Gurfein that Luciano's family was in America, including his nieces and nephews. Plus, Luciano was Sicilian, and they considered themselves as part of a different country than Italy.

Gurfein was satisfied that Luciano was more likely to help if Lansky was the inside man. It was agreed that Polakoff would accompany Lansky to visit Luciano. But Polakoff complained that the trip to Dannemora was too far, and it was cold, as snow was still on the ground up there. He also remembered his last visit with Luciano three years ago—how the prison authorities looked at him with hawk eyes, as they did every stranger.[6] They needed a place that was closer, and where discretion could be practiced, so he suggested that Luciano be moved to Sing Sing prison. Gurfein told him he would see what he could do.

The attorney for the most notorious gangster in prison, the

most notorious gangster not in prison, and the man who was busting crime bosses all over the city left together and took a Sunshine taxi the dozen blocks to the Hotel Astor.[7] Through the
Broadway entrance and up the stairs to the mezzanine level, they
arrived at room 200 and checked in with Mrs. Schwerin. Room
198 was bustling with activity. There were several navy agents in
civilian clothes all over the place. Haffenden received the three
men in room 196, and this time he wore civilian clothes as his
uniform hung in the closet.

The meeting was brief. Haffenden was introduced to Polakoff,
and explained to him that the Hotel Astor was his "off the record
office," and it was resolved that Polakoff and Lansky were on
standby until Gurfein got permission from Commissioner Lyons
to make contact with Luciano, which was certainly going to be
the toughest performance in Haffenden's circus.[8]

Haffenden got to work on a move for the next person in his circus
of go-betweens, Commissioner Lyons. On April 29, 1942, Gurfein met Lyons in Albany, New York, and in typical fashion didn't
leave any details out. He happened to be aided by the day's newspaper, which had an article that told the story of fourteen Merchant Marine sailors who had just been rescued after spending
eight days adrift in the Atlantic Ocean. Lyons was intrigued by
what Gurfein had to say, and concluded the meeting by telling
Lyons that he would be contacted by the navy with details. After
the meeting, Haffenden the ringmaster made his most theatrical
move.

Two men suddenly confronted Lyons—one of Haffenden's
lieutenants, named Cowen, and a yeoman. They demanded Lyons
read a letter they provided. The lieutenant gave the letter to
Lyons, who read it quietly, and without asking any questions. The
letter was addressed to Lieutenant Cowen and signed by Commander Haffenden. In the letter, Haffenden instructed Cowen to
show it to Commissioner Lyons, have him read it, and then burn
it. The commissioner read the letter, which was less than a page,
and processed the request from Naval Intelligence that Luciano

be moved to Sing Sing prison to aid in the war effort and be given access to some of his associates. When Lyons was done, he didn't nod or smile—in fact, he didn't even say a word—he just handed the letter back to Lieutenant Cowen and walked away. Cowen later carried out his orders and burned it.[9]

The move had the desired effect on Lyons, and if there was any doubt as to whether Lyons would allow contact with Luciano, it was certainly quashed by Haffenden's letter. In early May 1942, Lyons got to work on moving Luciano to another prison. Haffenden sent another one of his men to check in on Lyons, and when Lyons informed one of his confidants about the situation, a "man . . . from Naval Intelligence" stood in the room quietly.[10]

The only problem was that Lyons didn't feel good about Sing Sing. Neither did Gurfein, who suggested that moving Luciano to Sing Sing would cause "suspicion, talk, and furor." To keep a low profile, Lyons chose a different prison. It was the newest of the four maximum security New York prisons and was considered a great improvement to Dannemora. Evidently, "Lucky" Luciano was indeed "lucky," and soon he'd be headed to Great Meadow prison, and far closer to New York City. Still, Lyons had more work to do to figure out how to move Luciano without causing suspicion.

CHAPTER 5
A Deal with the Devil

O n his bed in his prison cell in B Block of Dannemora prison, Charles "Lucky" Luciano lay silent in the dark, and breathed in fresh air as it blew through his bar-clad cell gate. As he stared at his cell gate—eight thick round bars so close together he couldn't even grip them, then five more across with exactly thirty-eight rivets holding it all together, and certainly more interesting to look at than the other three concrete walls[1]—he fantasized about sleeping next to a window and sticking out his hand so he could grab the air.[2]

April 1942 was warmer than previous years in New York, but that far north, just miles from the Canadian border, the air blowing in from the outside was still cold—cold enough to freeze the condensation on the walls where the wind hit. Thus, the common nickname for Dannemora—"Little Siberia." During the summer, the entire penitentiary smelled like sweat and human waste, but at least for now, in the cold, the air was fresh.

The air had not been fresh where Luciano was born, in Lercara Friddi, a small mining town that was slightly inland on the island of Sicily. Lercara Friddi was near a sulfur mine, where Luciano's father, Antonio, toiled hard for his family. Antonio and Rosalia were his parents, Bartolomeo and Giuseppe were his big brothers, and Filippa and Concetta his younger sisters. Back then he wasn't "Charles 'Lucky' Luciano"—he was Salvatore Lucania.

And the way it was looking for young Salvatore, he was going to spend the rest of his life like his father did—working hard for scraps to feed his family, and never having enough for life's little extras.

In April of 1906—when Luciano was eight years old—Mount Vesuvius blew its top and sent a plume of ash skyrocketing into the atmosphere. Dark dust rained down upon the Italian countryside to the south, and Sicily. Antonio and Rosalia had already been dreaming for years of relocating their family to America, and the eruption was the last straw, lest they spend the next couple of years breathing in sulfur-tasting ash. Like so many millions of other Sicilians and Italians during the time, they booked passage for their entire family to go to a new world full of promise and leaving behind an untenable past.

The Lucania family settled in a crowded tenement on the Lower East Side of Manhattan, at 265 East 10th Street. Their one-room apartment was tiny and dingy, and the building was in a state of decay. Much to Antonio's and Rosalia's chagrin, when they arrived, the Manhattan air was as rancid as Lercara Friddi's.

A citywide garbage strike had caused rubbish to pile up, rot, and offend every functional nostril in the city. Kids even played in the garbage, and rats had a field day, causing outbreaks of terrible consequence. But Salvatore's teachers understood why it was happening, singing the praises of the garbagemen's union that called the strike and teaching their students about the power and the good of labor unions. Young Salvatore didn't learn many lessons in school, but he did learn that one.[3]

As far as Luciano's parents were concerned, the schools were the best part of America. They were free, and they weren't Catholic schools like in Lercara Friddi. The only problem was, Luciano rarely attended. Rosalia looked after the home as Luciano's father worked as a day laborer, and barely made enough to support his family. Luciano looked upon his father's hard work in disgust—referring to him as a crumb—so he started hustling to make his own money.

He ran errands for businesses, and every once in a while he

stole something, but eventually he found his way to his first racket. The Lower East Side was filled with Irish, Italians, and Jews, and he watched the Jewish kids with envy, as they excelled at school in a way he never thought possible for himself. He also watched the bigger Italian kids whale on them and shake them down on their way to school every day. So Luciano started shaking them down too, except that he offered something in return—protection from the other bullies.

It worked, and not only did he make money, but he also met his best friend, Meyer Lansky, that "Mighty Mite," as Luciano used to call him because of his temper. For a moment there in Dannemora, Luciano wondered what Lansky was up to. He hadn't seen his best friend in six years, and he missed him.

As he lay on his bed, Luciano fought the urge to urinate. He put off peeing in his bucket as long as possible, knowing full well that once he did he'd have to smell it for the rest of the morning. Hopefully, he could hold on to what was in his bowels until after sunrise, and right before he'd join a troop of prisoners to the bucket house, where they'd empty the contents as fast as they could before the stench clung to their clothes. In the freezing winter, the prisoners feared the walk to the bucket house, as small spills of urine and excrement combined to form one giant, putrid sheet of ice. It made the ground so hard that it was common for inmates to slip and break bones when landing in their neighbor's frozen shit.[4]

Prison was a place for Luciano to reflect on his life, and he truly hated this inevitable exercise. He was mixed up and confused about his choices. He figured he had made the choice to be a gangster long ago, and thinking about doing it differently was a waste of time. "So why am I still upset?" he'd ask himself over and over, and over and over again he'd tell himself he was mad because he had been stupid—stupid for getting caught, and stupid for ever getting mixed up in racketeering in the first place.[5]

"What if I'd done it differently?" he thought. "Then I'd be a crumb, and if I hadda wind up a crumb, I'd rather be dead."[6]

Over and over again, he was locked in this angry loop of thoughts, and unable to free himself from it.

Luciano's first racket had been extorting the Jewish kids, but the first crime he got in trouble for was truancy. By the time he was fourteen years old, he had missed so much school that he was only in the fifth grade.[7] While he had promised his mother that someday he'd finish school, he couldn't keep himself away from the streets. He couldn't compete with the other kids in school anyway, but on the streets he excelled. He even ran his own gang. He had stature, and he had respect among his peers. Knowing that Luciano was up to no good, the New York Board of Education gave him the maximum penalty for truancy, which was four months in Brooklyn Truant School.

At Brooklyn Truant School, Luciano received an education in pickpocketing and the art of thievery from the other kids. What formal lessons the instructors tried to cram down his throat he would never swallow, and he vowed to never return to school ever again. He also hated the experience so much that he vowed to never return to Brooklyn again.

When he was released at the age of fifteen, Luciano returned to his family, who still lived in the same tenement on the Lower East Side. He got an honest job and worked for an honest man— Max Goodman. Luciano was an errand boy for Goodman's garment company. But all the while, he moonlighted as a jewel thief.

He only earned $5 a week as an errand boy, but he was making a lot more than that stealing. Luciano was already done with school, but now he was growing wary of an honest living, as he was disillusioned by all the "honest" people he observed. Goodman was an exception, but everyone else who was supposed to be honest was stealing from somebody—dirty cops, shady landlords, and crooked storekeepers, for example.

And the people who drove fancy cars and wore nice clothes weren't day laborers like his father, or his teachers—they were crooks and gangsters. One of these crooks came to his family's apartment one day, as Antonio had borrowed money to pay for a mattress for Luciano's sisters. The man took one look at a beautiful prosciutto ham that had been drying in the kitchen and took it for himself.

"I'll take this," the man said. "You don't want your girls to sleep on the floor."

Antonio did nothing, and Luciano could've murdered the son of a bitch. But Luciano was a man who only used violence when he had to, which was something of a novelty for ambitious criminals in New York City. Instead, he got his gang together, and two months later they knocked off the crook's apartment. The $400 they stole was divided evenly between Luciano's gang members. Luciano was adamant that the whole gang pool their money, so nobody got jealous of the others. It was a move with deep foresight, and a philosophy that would shape the underworld in the future.[8]

Luciano started coming home looking different. He wore new clothes and nice shoes, all procured from his wages as an errand boy, he assured his father. Then one day Luciano was able to get his hands on a pistol. He was showing it to a friend when the gun went off, and in an extreme stroke of luck it only grazed Luciano's leg. Amazingly, it was the only time in his life that he ever got shot. When his father found the gun, however, it was not a pleasant scene. Antonio pointed the gun at his son and told him that he should shoot him because he was a disgrace to the family.[9]

After that Luciano stopped coming home, at night anyway, and slept wherever he could find a bed. Eventually he got a one-room apartment that he shared with a friend. He kept his job as an errand boy for four years, and all the while Goodman tried in vain to teach Luciano the ways of civilized life and working for an honest dollar—Luciano even had dinner with Goodman's family at their home. But their closeness only made for one of the lowest moments of Luciano's life.

Luciano had put two-and-two together and figured out that his job as an errand boy was a great cover for moving contraband, namely drugs. He started moving heroin for a local dealer, and after only a month he got busted with a half dram of heroin, hidden in one of Goodman's hats. Luciano was making a drop to what turned out to be a police informant.

Even an impassioned plea from Goodman, and a hysterical outburst from Rosalia in court, didn't save Luciano. In 1915, when he was eighteen years old, he was sent to New Hampton Reformatory Farms. Still pimple-faced and acne-scarred, the skinny Luciano was a target for other inmates who came at him ravenously. They teased him about his name (Salvatore) and called him an effeminate "Sallie," as they made advances to try and rape him.[10]

Six months at Hampton Farms were enough to convince Luciano that he never wanted to go back to prison. It was also enough of being called "Salvatore." When he arrived at home, back in the Lower East Side of Manhattan, on Christmas Eve 1916, to a pair of disappointed parents, he announced to them that he was no longer Salvatore, but "Charles" (he liked the American sounding name)—Antonio spit on the floor and left the room while Rosalia wept.

Prison had given Luciano clout and respect on the streets, because he had done his time, and did it without squealing on anybody. He was ready to leave behind any semblance of an honest life, and fully commit himself to racketeering. In case there was any doubt, he won $244 in a craps game shortly after coming home, which would've been a year's salary working for Goodman.[11]

Unlike the other Italian gangsters in New York City, Luciano worked with other ethnicities—chief among them Jews. Luciano and Lansky had hit it off after their first encounter, and Lansky introduced Luciano to another Jewish kid—Benjamin "Bugsy" Siegel. He was a boy of violent temperament, and some of the kids in the neighborhood called him by another nickname than "Bugsy"—"*vilda chaye*," which was Yiddish for "wild animal." Siegel hated that nickname too.

But there was also an Italian that Luciano respected, and his name was Francesco Castiglia (later changed to Frank Costello). When Luciano met Costello, the latter was the leader of the 104th Street Gang. Castiglia was a little older and sounded like a full-grown adult because of his scratchy voice. It wasn't from smoking, but the result of a botched adenoid and tonsil surgery he got as a child, when a surgeon's knife slipped and cut his vocal cords.

Costello was something of a revelation to Luciano, as he was the first person to make him realize that there were Italians who were just as smart as Jews. He might have combined forces with Costello right when he met him, had Costello not gotten caught with a gun and sent to jail for ten months. After his release, Costello never carried a gun again, and he hadn't seen a prison cell since.

The four of them really raised hell together, and Luciano looked back fondly when he thought about his first "real" gang. He smiled—from that point on, he never once thought about going back to an honest life. Antonio had disowned Luciano, and then Luciano lost both of his parents in the same year he went to prison. Outside of his brothers, Bartolomo and Guiseppe, and sister, Fanny, Lansky, Siegel, and Costello were the closest he got to having a family of his own.

Now they were just a memory, as life for Luciano was mostly his prison cell, where he spent fourteen to sixteen hours every single day. Dannemora was designed for prisoners to reflect—a form of torture for most.[12] But while he wallowed in his fate, sometimes Luciano reflected on his rise to power, other times he thought about his reign as king of the underworld that followed, and these days, he thought very little about what he'd do if he ever got out.

To make matters worse, and what kept him silent most days, was the shame he felt for what had actually got him caught—running a massive prostitution ring.

Luciano was embarrassed beyond belief. He would have rather been convicted of anything else, as he maintained that it was a lie, and a big conspiracy concocted by the district attorney at the time, Thomas Dewey.

Sixty-two counts of compulsory prostitution and accusations of human trafficking got Luciano a sentence of thirty to fifty years in prison. After a brief stint in Sing Sing, he had been at Dannemora since July 2, 1936.

That son of a bitch Dewey. Luciano now thought that he should have killed him when he had the chance. And he did have the chance prior to his incarceration—twice. But Luciano had insisted on leaving the high-powered prosecutor alone.

What a mistake that was.

Now Dewey was taking the year off, and word had it that he was eyeing the governor's office, thanks to Luciano's orders that kept him alive. At the time, Luciano had believed that killing Dewey would have caused an extreme reaction among law enforcement that might bring down everything he'd built. But what was worse than what he was experiencing now? Over and over, he said he'd rather be dead than at Dannemora, but he wasn't about to take his own life. So he did what other Dannemora inmates did—he adapted, and he thought about the past.[13]

Luciano was silent during quiet hours, and never made a sound while working his job at the library. Even his fellow inmates noticed how little he spoke.[14] In his cell in Dannemora prison, bewildered, and with no hope—his last appeal had been denied years earlier—Luciano was far more comfortable being mute.

By April 1942, Luciano was breathing the cold Canadian air for his sixth winter, and even if he was able to get out of Dannemora the next time he was up for parole, he'd be there for at least another fourteen winters.[15] That would be the longest time he'd ever spent in one home. Now only a miracle would spring him from his current hell. In his dark hole of a cell on B Block, he waited for something—anything—to happen to get him out of there.

When a high-profile inmate like Lucky Luciano was moved from one prison to another, there had to be a reason. Lyons then came up with a plan to conduct what would look like a routine prisoner swap. Along with Luciano, eight lucky souls were chosen at random from Dannemora, and nine unlucky souls were chosen from Great Meadow, to be swapped in a single day. Lyons contacted the warden at Great Meadow, Vernon Morhous, and told him that Luciano was coming to his prison, and there were special provisions that needed to be granted.

He told Morhous that Luciano was going to be receiving visitors, and that these visitors were not to be recorded in the traditional manner. Instead, Morhous was told to waive registration requirements, and given instructions that every time Luciano received a visitor, the warden was to send Lyons a letter stating who the visiting parties were. It was seldom permitted for an inmate to be visited by what were believed to be his fellow criminal conspirators, but Morhous nevertheless agreed to Lyons' terms.

On the morning of May 12, 1942, inmate number 24808—Charles Luciano—said goodbye to his piss bucket and Dannemora prison. Flanked by eight other shackled convicts, he was headed by truck 112 miles directly south via the New York 22 Highway to Comstock, New York, and Great Meadow Correctional Facility.

That afternoon, he endured the usual protocols of intake. First was a medical exam. The senior physician at Great Meadow found a forty-four-year-old man in mostly good health. He had short brown hair, brown eyes, scars on the left side of his face and chest, and most distinctive of all was the ptosis in his right eyelid—the result of a savage beating that had almost killed him years earlier. The physician also detected a distant murmur. The same heart ailment had taken his mother just after he arrived in prison years earlier, and the doctor noted the family history.

Luciano also seemed to be devoid of venereal diseases, as his Wassermann test was negative, and even though he had arrived at Sing Sing back in 1936 with gonorrhea, he had finally gotten past it. Luciano was generally in poor health back then. Prison put an end to his nightlife—his "midnight jamborees," as he called them—and ultimately saved his life. Not only was his heart in trouble back then, but he also had kidney problems, and at least seven sinus surgeries prior to his incarceration.

After being looked at by the physician, Luciano was turned

over to the chaplain, who administered Communion and noted that Luciano had previously been both baptized and confirmed. Luciano didn't currently practice Catholicism—he was confirmed all the way back in Sicily—but every single month he donated between $10 and $20 out of his commissary account to the Church.[16]

After receiving the sacrament, Luciano and the other eight inmates were told by the education supervisor that both the chapel and the school were available for their use. This was great news to Luciano, who had become something of a bookworm when he worked in the library at Dannemora. There, he also practiced his penmanship, as his early departure from school had left him with atrocious handwriting and grammar. He also read history books, mostly about the United States and Sicily. His newfound love of books was a result of the influence of his friend, Lansky.[17]

Luciano got to his cell just before lights-out. When he entered his cell, which was only five by eight feet, his spirits were instantly lifted. He had a clean cell, all to himself, that had running water—both hot and cold. Not only that, but he had decent toilet paper for the first time in six years. Even he was surprised at how happy that made him.

At 10 p.m. all the light in Great Meadow was extinguished, and for the next two days Luciano got used to his new surroundings. He caught himself looking at the tattoo of a horseshoe on his arm[18] and wondered what lucky twist of fate had landed him there.

On the morning of Friday, May 15, 1942, just before 9 a.m., two guards approached Luciano's cell and informed him that he had visitors. In utter bewilderment—not only was he not expecting anyone, but it wasn't visiting hours—Luciano spruced himself up at his new sink and followed the guards into the corridor, where they frisked and shackled him, then escorted him toward the warden's office. Luciano walked obliquely, lurching a little to the side, and this was exacerbated by the chains around his ankles.

But by now, he was an expert at avoiding being tripped. He wore his standard prison uniform, which consisted of blue jeans and a blue chambray work shirt.

The two guards placed him in a room that was right next to the warden's office. The room was about twenty by ten feet, with a long table and chairs, and was typically used for interrogating prisoners. Luciano had previously been paid a visit by investigators back at Dannemora in a room just like this. They turned out to be narcotics agents, and the moment Luciano had seen them he shook his head and said, "Take me out of here. I won't talk to these people."[19] Now, if that's what was waiting in the warden's office for him, he was prepared to say the same thing.

The guards sat him down in a chair in front of the table and unshackled him. Then they stepped out of the room, locked the door behind them, and stood at attention outside.

What was going on?

Then Luciano smirked, thinking maybe there was a broad for him in the warden's office. He knew it was wishful thinking, but he hadn't had one in so long he couldn't help but think about it. Finally, the side door that led to the warden's office opened. Two men appeared in the doorway, and after a moment of sheer disbelief, Luciano jumped up and stretched his arms out wide.

"What the hell are you guys doing here?!" Luciano exclaimed to his lawyer, Moses Polakoff, and his best friend, Meyer Lansky. "I never expected to see you [fellas] here!"[20]

He hadn't seen Polakoff since his last appeal, some three years prior, and with Lansky it had been twice as long. Luciano was so happy to see them that he embraced them both. Luciano's friends called him "Charlie," and Meyer Lansky was certainly a friend to Luciano, and Polakoff knew him well enough to also call him by his preferred name. But the pleasantries and happiness that came with their reunion was very short-lived, as they were not permitted much time together.

For the first time Luciano learned the reason for his transfer to Great Meadow. He learned that the District Attorney's Office had contacted Polakoff, and that the navy was behind the whole thing. He heard about Operation Underworld for the first time, and about Socks Lanza and the help he'd given. They also told him that the navy felt he would be extremely useful in bringing "prominent Italians" into the operation, and the difficulty Lanza was facing trying to do it without Luciano.

When he was listening intently, Luciano had a habit of closing his eyes as if he were asleep and nodding his head. As Lansky laid it all out—a lot to consume in one sitting—Luciano did exactly that. When they were done explaining everything to him, he opened his eyes and revealed that he wanted nothing to do with Operation Underworld.

Why not?

"Look, I'm going to be deported," Luciano said. Luciano's prison file had a deportation warrant in it that would send him back to Italy, and it was to be executed in the event he ever got paroled. "When I get out—nobody knows how this war will turn out."[21]

Not many people knew about it, but that deportation order hung over Luciano's head like an anvil. He had never gone through the trouble of becoming a US citizen, so technically he was still Italian. If it became a known fact that he had aided the US Navy, Luciano felt it was highly likely that Mussolini's regime would have him lynched if he returned to Italy, especially given Il Duce's policy against *mafiosi*.

At present, Luciano's bets were hedged. His underboss was already in Italy—Vito Genovese—and Genovese, amazingly, was friendly with Mussolini's government. That could come in handy if Luciano were deported.[22]

Why would Luciano burn that bridge?

Polakoff said that Gurfein had mentioned to him that it might help get him out of prison. Lansky then put his personal touch on trying to convince Luciano. The two had their own language— Lansky had a talent for coming up with odds on the spot. That's why Luciano had another nickname for Lansky—the "Human Adding Machine."

"It's 10 to 1 they'll be after you next," Lansky had said to

Luciano seven years earlier, warning him about the District Attorney's Office coming after him with their next case. Lansky turned out to be right; the DA targeted Luciano, and now he was in jail.[23]

Lansky gave Luciano a betting nugget that if he helped the navy, it could only improve his odds of getting out. Not only that, but Lansky "had a way of thinkin' around a corner,"[24] as Luciano once put it. Lansky then told Luciano that in the future—if he decided to help—he could ask for anyone he wanted to come and visit him. Lansky implored him to think about what they could put in place—what they could plan together.

Luciano then thought about how they planned on keeping this whole thing a secret.

"Whatever I do I want it kept quiet," he said. "Private so [if] I get back to Italy I'm not a marked man."[25]

Lansky retorted by telling Luciano about Commander Haffenden's insistence on secrecy, and that he and Lanza had been given number designations to keep their names out of government files. They only needed Luciano to talk to a few key people, not the entire waterfront and city of New York.

Luciano then told Polakoff and Lansky that he could probably assist in recruiting the right Italians to help if he wanted to. Lansky then told Luciano they thought it was a good idea to bring Socks Lanza up to visit him so he could tell Luciano exactly what he needed and where he needed it.

Luciano finally came around. "Bring him up," he said.[26]

The meeting in the office next to the warden's only lasted half an hour. The men then said their goodbyes, and agreed that Lansky and Polakoff would come back up in a few weeks with Lanza. Luciano was searched by the guards again and escorted back to his cell. As for Lansky and Polakoff, they were driven back to Albany by chauffeur, and boarded a train that arrived in New York City before 8 p.m. They'd be back in less than three weeks. In that time, another twenty-one Allied ships would be lost to the enemy in the Atlantic.[27]

*   *   *

"Everyone [will be] protected," Haffenden assured Lansky. "Names [will] not be revealed. . . . Everything [will] be done by numbers." The ciphers for all of their names were kept in Haffenden's little black book, in his safe in room 196 at the Hotel Astor. But the participants—Haffenden, Luciano, Lansky, and Lanza—understood that Luciano's involvement precluded total secrecy, as the purpose of recruiting him was to use his name. But Haffenden agreed that he would keep Luciano's name under wraps at ONI. As for secrecy in the underworld—Lansky and Lanza were in charge of that.

Meanwhile, Luciano was left alone with his thoughts. For three weeks he thought about his last visit from Lansky, but he didn't think much about Operation Underworld. Of course, he could see, as Lansky saw, that his participation would really help his chances for parole. But because his parole could mean deportation, he would have to come up with something to get him out of it. And if he did end up getting deported, he had to have things set up so that he would have a path back to New York City.

Lansky was looking after his money at the moment, and visiting with him to relay orders was essential. There were also others that he needed to make contact with to get set up—friends, trusted allies, business partners, and other stakeholders in various rackets.[28] He'd need to rely on Lansky to get the right people to come to him and go along with his orders.

On the afternoon of Wednesday, June 3, 1942, Lansky, Lanza, and Polakoff boarded a train bound for Albany. Once there, they spent the night and woke up early to have a chauffeur drive them seventy more miles north to Great Meadow. The prison was an extremely long, three-story building housing two giant cell blocks. It was mostly made of brick, with regimented high arches from end to end that were filled with glass, bringing in a lot of natural light.

The three men were let through the gate that was the only opening in the formidable concrete walls that surrounded the twenty-one-acre prison grounds. They got out of the car at the entrance to the prison itself and were escorted through the main doors by a guard. No stranger to prisons, Lanza was amazed at the lack of adherence to protocol—they didn't fingerprint him, and his name was left out of the registry. Only Polakoff had to sign. After that, they were led through more doors, and then into the prison proper. Just before 10 a.m. they arrived at Warden Morhous's office, and waited for Luciano. Luciano went through the same routine as before—searched, cuffed, and escorted by two guards, who took him to the room adjacent to the warden's.

Just after 10 a.m., Luciano greeted Lansky and Lanza warmly, and the three men made small talk. Lanza was Luciano's subordinate. In the hierarchy of the Luciano family, there was a boss—Luciano—and an underboss—Vito Genovese. With Luciano in jail, and Genovese on the run, Costello had been designated "acting boss." Below that were his *caporegimes*, and underneath the capos were soldiers, like Lanza, and then finally associates.

When the three men got down to business, Polakoff took one of the chairs to the far corner of the room, opened a newspaper, and did his best not to listen to anything that was being said. If his client was making plans outside the scope of Operation Underworld, Polakoff didn't want to hear it.

"[I'm] having a little difficulty," Lanza said to Luciano. Lanza explained that he had a pending trial, and his case didn't look good. The people he had approached thought he was an informant.

"I know that if [you send] out word that [you're] interested in this thing," Lanza said to Luciano, "and when I go to meet people in these locals and union[s] I would be very respected and they would all look up to me."

"Joe, you go ahead," Luciano said. "I will give word out, and everything will go smoother."[29]

Luciano's tune had changed since the last visit. Realizing the access Operation Underworld could give him to his family, and what his participation could mean for his freedom, he was all too willing to help. Then they started naming people who could help both Operation Underworld and Luciano directly.

The first name to come up was the most difficult, in Lanza's mind. The banks of the Hudson River on the West Side of Manhattan—where *Normandie* still bobbed on its side like a buoy—belonged to the strongest Irish gang in the city—the Dunn-McGrath gang. Lanza's history with them made it difficult for him to contact them, and he didn't have any sway with the Irish longshoremen union bosses.

Who did Luciano know over there?

The answer was the president of the ILA, Joe Ryan, and his right-hand man, Jerry Sullivan. These two men cooperated with criminal elements all over the city's waterfront. If Lansky could contact Ryan and Sullivan and tell them that Luciano wanted them to help the navy, they could have most of the longshoremen in the city cooperating.[30]

What about Brooklyn?

Brooklyn was not always a friendly place for the Luciano family, and Lanza certainly wasn't making any headway there. Not to mention the fact that ever since truant school, Luciano had hated Brooklyn, and had actually managed to not set foot in it since then. Brooklyn had some feelings about Luciano too, as the boss there—Vincent Mangano of the Mangano crime family—didn't like how close Luciano was with some of his capos.

What about the Camarda brothers?

The Camardas owned the Brooklyn waterfront in the Red Hook district—where the US military was highly active—and their family of Camarda brothers, fathers, sons, uncles, nephews, and cousins had divided up the longshoremen and stevedores on the docks into what were called "the Camarda Locals." But there were other, even more notorious gangsters who ran some of the other locals. To button up the Brooklyn waterfront, they'd need the "Lord High Executioner" himself—Albert Anastasia. Anastasia was a good friend of Luciano's.

The only problem was no one had seen Anastasia for almost two years (no authorities, anyway). He had resurfaced just two weeks ago; evidently, he'd been hiding out in Utica, New York. Previously, one of his former assassins, named Abe "Kid Twist"

Reles, turned on him. When Reles started singing to the police, they filled twenty-five notebooks with details of hundreds of some of the most horrific murders imaginable, including two that were committed by Anastasia.[31]

But Luciano and just about every other gangster in New York City had wanted Reles dead. He knew too many secrets as a former member of "Murder Inc." Originally started by Lansky and Siegel, "Murder Inc." was later taken over by Anastasia and a Jewish gangster named Louis "Lepke" Buchalter. When Reles flipped, Buchalter was one of the men who was targeted. Buchalter was now in the Sing Sing death house, waiting for his turn with the electric chair there, named "Old Sparky." Anastasia had no intention of suffering the same fate. Then he pulled off a miracle.

His trial was meant to start with Anastasia in absentia, but just hours before opening arguments, Reles was thrown out of a fifth-story window while he was under guard at a hotel in Coney Island. It looked like a suicide, and while several of the guards were demoted, none was prosecuted. Brooklyn District Attorney William O'Dwyer, who was bringing the charges (because he had to with Reles's testimony), even mockingly declared that the case had gone "out the window."[32] He subsequently dropped the charges. Anastasia was off the hook, but he was still feeling pressure from investigators, who were irate that he was going to get away with murder. To combat this threat, on May 18, 1942, just over two weeks ago, he had become Recruit Anastasia when he joined the army. It was an ideal place to lie low. Operation Underworld would need someone else to help in Brooklyn.

That person was someone very close to Luciano, and another one of Mangano's capos—Joe Adonis.

Adonis was a self-given nickname, as his vanity knew no bounds, and neither did his ruthlessness. Adonis and Luciano went way back to the days of the Bugs and Meyer Mob. Back then, Adonis ran the Broadway Mob, and frequently worked with Luciano and Lansky during Prohibition, even introducing Luciano to some major bootlegging players. Now Adonis was not only a capo in the Mangano family but also a big-time investor in the gambling racket in Jersey, which was certainly something that would come in handy for Luciano. The two even had a joint investment, which was a casino called the Piping Rock Club in Saratoga Springs.

"You go up and mention my name," Luciano told Lanza.

What about Harlem?

Harlem wasn't on the waterfront, but Haffenden and Dominick Sacco had mentioned to Lanza that they wanted a contact there. It was a hotbed for radical political activity, and it was thought that some of the groups there were fifth columnists—subversives who were undermining or aiming to attack the United States war effort.

"Tough" Willie McCabe was Luciano's guy in Harlem, as McCabe ran the numbers racket there, had union connections, and also ran a legitimate vending machine company in midtown Manhattan. Luciano gave Lanza instructions to go meet McCabe

What about Frank Costello?

"Go and see Frank," Luciano ordered Lanza. "And let Frank help along. This is a good cause."[33]

If Luciano was going to carve a path for his reentry into the underworld, he'd need access to Costello. Not only was Costello his acting boss, but he was also the most well-connected gangster ever to grace New York City, as he had countless policemen, judges, and politicians in his pocket. If anyone needed to be bribed or influenced to let Luciano out of prison, Costello was the man for the job. He was also working on creating and running a national sports book from his casinos, and there were loads of money to be made.

Between Meyer Lansky, Joe Adonis, and Frank Costello, Luciano had brought into Operation Underworld most of what he referred to as his "board of directors." Only Bugsy Siegel in California was absent, and of course, Vito Genovese in Italy.[34] Luciano had put together various "combinations" throughout his criminal career, usually in relation to organizing specific rackets—such as drugs, booze, numbers, and prostitution—and this was the combination that he put together to aid the navy in Operation Underworld.

Before the clock reached 10:30 a.m., the three men had discussed everything they needed to in regard to helping the navy. The list of names they'd come up with was formidable, but it was short, and for the next three hours they talked about other matters.

Luciano oscillated between English and Sicilian; Lansky didn't fully understand the language, but since Lanza was born in Sicily, just like Luciano, he understood perfectly. Every so often, one of the guards would poke his head in the door, but they heard nothing of consequence. But there was at least one conversation that would have a deadly outcome.

What about Tony Spring? And the Other Guy?

Anthony "Tony Spring" Romeo was a former union boss in one of the Camarda Locals and also an accomplished assassin who used to do work for Anastasia, and by proxy, Luciano and Lansky. Romeo was hiding somewhere, as it was known that the Brooklyn District Attorney's Office was hot on his heels, trying to turn him into a government witness. They knew that because Brooklyn DA O'Dwyer was in their pocket, courtesy of Costello's influence. O'Dwyer had even run for mayor last election with Costello's backing, and lost to La Guardia only by a thin margin.

Was anyone gonna take care of this guy Romeo? And the Other Guy?

Lansky said it was already being looked into.[33]

Lanza then asked for permission to come back up to Great Meadow for a meeting in about a month, to follow up on everything they'd set in motion.

"All right. Fine," Luciano said with reserved glee.

More meetings were fine with Luciano. Luciano told Lansky that he wanted to see a friend of his during the next meeting—Michael Lascari. Lascari was a low-level gangster in Jersey, but he was a friend of the Lucania family (Luciano's actual family). He was such a close friend that he even lived with Luciano's siblings in the early 1940s.

The three men left Luciano around 1:30 p.m., with their marching orders in their heads. And all the while, while the three gangsters were plotting and planning, Polakoff read his paper, front to back and back again, playing the part of a deaf-mute to perfection.

Back at Fulton Fish Market the next day, Lanza felt like a brand-new man. He brought Espy in to meet just to tell him that he'd been up to see "Charlie." Now Lanza would be able to contact anyone he wanted to help the navy.[34] He was an important man for Haffenden, again, and he was elated that he could now report to him that the entire waterfront of the Port of New York was within the navy's grasp.

PART II

CHAPTER 6

The Enemy Arrives

It was just after midnight on Saturday, June 13, 1942, when Commander Charles Haffenden and his wife, Mary, woke up to a phone call. Details were sketchy, and not much was said over the phone, but there was a report from the Riverhead outpost that enemy soldiers had landed on the Long Island coast near Montauk, and their whereabouts were unknown. Haffenden quickly got dressed, hopped in his car, and then drove the ninety-five miles from his home in Flushing, Queens.

Haffenden had been directed to stop at the Naval Intelligence Branch office in Riverhead, where a yeoman directed him to the private estate of Lieutenant Philip Dater. Dater was an ONI officer who worked out of Church Street. His Easthampton estate had been temporarily turned into a makeshift headquarters. When Haffenden arrived, the place was buzzing with activity, and most of it was centered around a lonely, young Coast Guardsman named John Cullen, who sat in Dater's living room, surrounded by navy officers, who peppered him with questions like AA guns.

Haffenden got a crack at Cullen too. He learned that Coast Guardsman Cullen had been on sentry duty as a "sand pounder," and was pacing his section of Amagansett Beach, when he saw four men in the dark and pointed his flashlight at them. Cullen could barely make them out, as the moon was almost nonexistent, and the fog was so thick he couldn't even see his shoes. But he was able to see that the men were wearing civilian clothes, and one of them was actually in swimming shorts. When Cullen got closer, he shouted, "Who are you?!"

Cullen then told Haffenden that one of the mysterious men had approached him and said they were fishermen. The man was of average height with slicked-back blond hair and a long, skinny nose. He told Cullen that their boat had run aground. This was satisfying enough for Cullen, as the man had spoken like he was an American. But then one of the "fishermen" had slipped up, and shouted something in German. The man confronting Cullen suddenly changed his tone. He asked Cullen if he had a mother and a father, and then chillingly added, "I wouldn't want to have to kill you."

Cullen was shaken, as he was alone, outnumbered, and armed only with his flashlight and a flare gun. But the man didn't linger on his threat for very long, and offered Cullen $300. He asked Cullen, "Why don't you forget the whole thing?"[1]

Cullen accepted their money and pretended to play along. The four men then disappeared into the night, and the Coast Guardsman ran to alert his commander. Cullen's actions were under a microscope as officers were still deciding if Cullen should be praised or keelhauled.

Regardless of what happened to Cullen, Haffenden knew that the whereabouts of the four men on the beach had to be ascertained, and speed of action was of the utmost importance. In the hours that followed, as men from the Third Naval District descended on Montauk, there had been one noteworthy exception— Lieutenant Lindsay Henry. Lieutenant Henry was the commander of Zone 9, which included Easthampton and Montauk, but Haffenden had made no effort to contact him. Oddly enough, the two were actually friends; Henry was a part of a foursome that Haffenden golfed with every weekend. Instead of contacting his friend, who would've been the ranking officer, Haffenden took charge and had no intention of anyone else doing so.[2] This was his battle to fight and win.

After dawn, Haffenden had Cullen lead him and a few other investigators to the beach. There they found a trove of clues precisely where Cullen had reported seeing the men. The Coast Guardsman had disrupted their plan, to be sure, and as a result, the four men had failed to bury or sink their landing craft. It was an eerie sight on the sand—a rubber boat with wooden oars and the passengers gone. It was clear to Haffenden that these men had come ashore after launching from a German U-boat. It would've had to surface very close to the beach, much like the one spotted in the area two months ago.[3]

It was an audacious move by the enemy, and it was exactly what the officers and men and women of the Third Naval District feared the most. No one knew where these men were, as they could be in New York City by now, getting ready for their first attack. Haffenden's eyes combed the beach, looking for clues. As luck would have it, his group did find something.

Partially buried in the sand were four cases that included primers, incendiaries, and enough weight in explosives to carry out operations within the United States for years. There was no mistaking the invaders' nationality either, as they found a pile of four German uniforms. The men had worn them during their paddle to the shore. It was a bit of a mystery, but apparently the men had come ashore wearing them. That way, if they were captured immediately, they could be classified as soldiers and would be protected under the articles of the Geneva Conventions. When they thought the coast was clear, they decided to change into civilian clothes. Cullen just happened to come upon the men while they were doing this and making the transformation from soldiers to spies.

It looked like Cullen's presence had forced the men to hastily hide everything, and they had done a terrible job doing it. It was an extreme stroke of luck that this equipment hadn't been properly buried. But that didn't matter, because Haffenden knew that this cache meant one thing—the Germans would eventually come back for their explosives.

Haffenden's hand-selected team from B-3 arrived later in the afternoon. The first of Haffenden's men to arrive at Dater's estate were the Sacco brothers, Lieutenant Treglia, and Charles Hoyt (notably absent was Maculitis). Back in April, these men from Squad #2 had already infiltrated the boats, trucks, and supply houses in Riverhead, Easthampton, Eastport, and Montauk.[4] Each man had little to no knowledge of what was going on, so Haffenden pulled them aside and briefed them.[5] The enemy had arrived, and it was up to them to find the spies before they carried out an attack. Haffenden felt that these men—these saboteurs— were likely receiving help from a contact nearby, and even if they weren't, he had to be sure. Haffenden's ferrets got to work contacting the network of informants that they had previously established.

The FBI also arrived by Saturday evening, and when they got to Lieutenant Dater's estate, it was very clear to the agents who was in charge. Haffenden began organizing them as they streamed in, and all the while he still hadn't contacted Lieutenant Henry.[6] Hoyt was given a team of four agents, and then Haffenden gave him his orders.

"You were here before," Haffenden said to Hoyt. "You know the roads. Take the four men and see what is going on in Montauk Point. Try to get information as to where the [four] men are."[7]

After searching for a former rumrunner that led to a dead end, Haffenden then ordered Hoyt to spend Sunday in a Coast Guard tower on Amagansett Beach. Hoyt spent nearly the entire day there, observing the coast and looking for any follow-up activity, but he saw none. Then Haffenden ordered Hoyt to visit the Long Island Railroad station at Amagansett. Hoyt spoke with the stationmaster and made a startling discovery—at least three suspicious-looking men had visited the station the previous morning, and had boarded the 6:57 a.m. train to Penn Station in Manhattan. The stationmaster had thought they were fishermen, but something about them seemed off. Hoyt rushed back to Dater's estate and told Haffenden that the saboteurs were probably somewhere in the heart of the New York City.

For the rest of the weekend and the start to the week, Haffenden went back and forth between Manhattan and Long Island. He was running multiple operations on the waterfront and in New York City proper in conjunction with his manhunt on Long Island. Even though the Germans were last known to be in Manhattan, he knew that they'd come back for their explosives on Long Island.

On Monday morning, June 15, 1942, Elizabeth Schwerin came into work at the Hotel Astor to find Haffenden absolutely exhausted. He told her he'd been "chasing saboteurs almost all night." He even showed her a German button that he'd taken from one of their discarded uniforms.[8]

Haffenden then went back to Long Island, where he was overseeing efforts to keep the area under observation. Haffenden enlisted the help of Charles Bonner and Hiram Sweezey. These two men had proven essential to Haffenden last spring in setting up a surveillance network on Long Island, and they could certainly help now.

Two days later, on the evening of Wednesday the 17th, Haffenden drove back to Amagansett. He needed to see Sweezey immediately. Sweezey was a little reluctant to meet, as June 17 was his wedding anniversary. He and his wife were headed for dinner at Millie's Inn at Napeague Beach off of the Montauk Highway, between Amagansett and Montauk. But since Haffenden insisted it was important, Sweezey invited him to join them.

Millie's Inn was the equivalent of a modern-day bed-and-breakfast on a mostly unpopulated beach. It was painted white and looked like a house, with a white picket fence surrounding the building. Any notion of romance that Mrs. Sweezey had hoped to have at her anniversary dinner was replaced with Haffenden's explanation of what amounted to one of the biggest spy hunts in US history. Sweezey told Haffenden he would do what he could, as the commander asked for his help getting some of his ferrets into various positions.[9]

Haffenden got Hoyt a job as a waiter at a different inn. Evidently, Lieutenant Dater was suspicious of some of the people who were patrons at the restaurant.

Felix Sacco was placed in the filling station that was owned by Bonner. It was a strategic location, as it operated along the only road off the island. As for Dominick Sacco, Sweezey got him aboard one of his trucks delivering ice. Sacco used a Teamsters Local 202 union card—"Frank Arico" was his alias—which was furnished by Socks Lanza.[10]

Lieutenant Treglia was sent back to the waterfront, and replaced by Lieutenant Tony Marzulo and a new civilian agent, Paul Alfieri. Alfieri was in his mid-forties, and a little too old for active duty, but he was distinguishing himself well as an investigator. He had dark hair and a smile that put people at ease. He was a family man with a wife, and hopes of having a child. He was an eager learner, and ready to take on any and all challenges that were put in front of him.[11] Alfieri and Marzulo started receiving reports from Hoyt and the Sacco brothers via dead drops. They'd take the reports to a small cottage that they set up as a safe house. If informants or contacts needed to be interrogated, the safe house was the designated spot. The team widened their net on the island and lay in wait for the moment the Germans surfaced for their explosives.

On June 15, 1942, Lucky Luciano received two more visitors. But this time it wasn't any part of his new combination, or a friend from his past, but his older brother Bartolomo Lucania, now called "Bart," and his younger sister Filipa, now called "Fanny." Both Fanny and Bart visited Luciano often, and it was common for them to be together when they saw their brother. They were still loyal to their brother Salvatore, and though Bart was no gangster—he was the secretary-treasurer of a local chapter of Master Barbers—he certainly helped his brother out of a jam once upon a time.[12]

In 1923, Luciano had gotten arrested again, and with heroin again. With his previous drug charge, he was looking at years, if not decades in prison. He'd tried to bribe the men who arrested him, but they were not for sale. Instead of calling his lawyer, Luciano had called Bart and, speaking in Sicilian, had asked him to move a small trunk from one location to another, and he was by no means to look inside.

Turns out, the trunk was filled with more heroin, and in exchange for his freedom, Luciano gave up the stash—$75,000 worth of drugs. Cooperating with authorities to save himself was a violation of the *omertà* code of secrecy established by Mafia leadership. But since he paid the money back and didn't snitch on anyone, his associates were able to look past it. It was the only time he got Bart mixed up in any of his rackets, and Bart's visit made him think about that, because technically cooperating with the navy was an equally egregious violation—cooperating with authorities was not permitted.

Luciano loved the visits from his siblings, but they often had a terrible psychological effect on him. To see his brother—legit and prosperous—made him go into that same old vicious loop where he questioned his choices. At Dannemora it had been especially hard, and oftentimes when Luciano had been taken back to his cell after their visits, he'd bang his head against the wall. One time he needed stitches because he split his head open.[13]

Now at Great Meadow, with Bart and Fanny in the room, Luciano alluded that he had something cooking to get him sprung from prison. He smiled when he thought about the combination he was putting together—his board of directors—and certainly remembered how they all had previously come together.

Salvatore Lucania, Giuseppe Doto, Francesco Castiglia, and Maier Suchowljansky had something in common—they desperately wanted to be Americans, but they were not born in the United States. They came from places like Lercara Friddi, Montemarano, Cassano allo Ionio, and Grodno, Belarus, but in their youth, after they came to the United States, they called New York City—not their birthplaces—their home. Then, they changed their names to fit their new country—Charles Luciano, Joe Adonis, Frank Costello, and Meyer Lansky.

Their partnership came into fruition in the early 1920s, during Prohibition. In those days, Luciano and Costello, the Bugs and Meyer Mob, and the Broadway Mob run by Adonis were trying to establish themselves as leaders in the underworld. But Sicilian mafiosi from the old world had their regents in the United States. They acted like kings and took advantage of the incredible moneymaking opportunity delivered with the passage of Prohibition. Hijackings of booze shipments were commonplace, making Luciano, Lansky, Costello, and Adonis very busy in an extremely dangerous environment.

That they hated the old-world bosses[14]—the "Mustache Petes" with their old rules and mistrust of anyone not Italian—was beside the point. These four young men were influenced by the likes of Rockefeller and Ford, and had been backed by stylish gangsters like Arnold "the Bankroll" Rothstein. They wanted money and power, and certainly not racial violence and gang warfare. Because Luciano and his associates were trying to make money in bootlegging—a time that should have meant prosperity for anyone involved in the racket—the amount of killing was atrocious.

As much as Luciano and the young gangsters wanted to run their own outfits, they had to take orders from the most powerful Italians in New York City. For Luciano, that meant working for Joe "the Boss" Masseria, a particularly vile Sicilian whom Luciano hated.

Eventually, all the bad blood erupted in 1930 into what became known as the Castellammarese War, and bloodletting replaced counting dollars. The two belligerents were Masseria and Salvatore Maranzano, who was from the Castellammare del Golfo, just sixty miles from Luciano's birthplace of Lercara Friddi.

Luciano already had his problems with Massaria, as his old-world ways were unshakeable, and Luciano constantly caught hell for working with Jews like Lansky. Furthermore, Masseria ignored Luciano's pleas to end the war and get back to business. Masseria was unrelenting, solely focused on winning the war and becoming the boss of all bosses.

With all of the killing going on, one of Masseria's assassins was rising in power—Vito Genovese.

Genovese had a square jaw and thinning brown hair. His right eyebrow looked like it was cocked at all times, giving his face an asymmetric look. He and Luciano were about the same height, and had been born within days of each other, and like Luciano, Genovese had ambition and wanted to see the old-world order toppled. The two became allies, and a mutual respect began to grow. But one of the two biggest differences between them was that Luciano was a Sicilian and Genovese was a Neapolitan. Luciano, Costello, and others in the family teased Genovese about that, because they knew it bothered him, and called him "Don Vitone" behind his back.

The other big difference between them was that Genovese was a stone-cold killer, and Luciano was not. Luciano ordered countless murders but was never comfortable with killing. Genovese was so comfortable with killing that once upon a time, he fell in love with his cousin, and not only did he murder her husband, but Genovese married her just weeks after his death.

Luciano and Genovese thought of ways to kill Maranzano, but then Luciano caught wind of a plot against him by his own boss. Massaria was growing wary of Luciano's rise, and having at first made him a top lieutenant, the Sicilian began to see him only as a threat.

Luciano learned that Massaria was going to kill two of Maranzano's capos, but for some reason Massaria didn't tell Luciano about it. That's when he realized that these two specific capos had been targeted so it would look like Luciano was the one who did it. Then all of Maranzano's revenge efforts would be focused on Luciano, and not his boss. The Sicilians were turning on each other and masking their movements with skillful treachery.

Luciano used to say that it took a Sicilian to outsmart a Sicilian. But even still, Luciano gathered his board of directors—Costello, Lansky, Adonis, plus Genovese and Siegel—and the men plotted how they could turn the situation around to their advantage.

Each of them thought carefully and bounced ideas off of the others. That is, except for Siegel, who said, "We're always wastin' time. You Italian bastards are forever chewin' it over and chewin' it over until there's not a fuckin' thing to swallow!"[15] Siegel would not be disappointed with all the killing to come.

First, Luciano ordered Genovese to murder the head of a family that Massaria was courting as an ally.[16] It was made to look like a Chicago outfit had carried out the killing. One by one, Luciano's board of directors started killing people to make it look like their enemies had done it, and pitting them against each other. Luciano's board was preparing for peace during war, and targeting people who would cause problems when notions of peace were presented. Then, when the moment was right, they reached out to their enemy—Maranzano and his capos.

Luciano and Maranzano met at the Bronx Zoo, and in front of a lion's cage, they made an agreement—if Luciano saw to it that Massaria was killed, Maranzano promised to end the war and give Luciano control over all of Massaria's territory and rackets.[17] Luciano was no fan of Maranzano—in fact, Luciano may have hated him more than he hated Massaria. But killing Maranzano could wait, for the time being, as Luciano had the patience of a saint.

As a final stroke, Luciano met with Massaria and told him about a bold strategy to have Maranzano and his capos killed. For the final touch, he told him he'd target the very capos that he knew Massaria wanted dead, and that would put Luciano in a terrible position. Massaria ate up every word of it, and after that, they had lunch.

At noon on the ides of April 1931, Luciano sat for lunch at the Nuova Villa Tammaro restaurant on Coney Island with Joe "the Boss" Masseria. Luciano had trouble eating. Luciano's stomach was often upset when he was stressed out. Masseria, on the other hand, was in a mood to celebrate, and he had antipasto and spaghetti with red clam sauce, lobster Fra Diavolo, and chianti, followed by a cannoli and coffee.[18] After about an hour, Luciano suggested a game of cards. When the first cards had been dealt, Luciano asked for permission to use the bathroom, and he left the table.

Luciano leaving the table was a signal—suddenly, Genovese, Adonis, Albert Anastasia, and Siegel emerged loaded for bear from a parked car. Masseria was something of a bullet dodger, but never before had he been confronted by such skilled and audacious killers. The four men unloaded their pistols on him and his unsuspecting bodyguards. As Luciano took his time micturating in the bathroom, the better part of his board slammed three bullets into Masseria's back. The boss absorbed the bullets and turned to confront his assassins. Two more bullets were fired into his neck, and a fatal shot hit him right above the eye. Masseria slumped over the table facedown, as his blood soaked the white tablecloth. Just as the shooting stopped, Luciano emerged from the bathroom, slipped an ace of diamonds—the suit of greedy merchants—into Masseria's left hand, and fled with his board.[19]

That was the end of the Castellammarese War.

Little by little, Luciano's board, now an integral part of Operation Underworld, had been killing the old-world order, with their eyes on creating something new in America. In 1931, all that stood in their way from doing just that was their new boss, Salvatore Maranzano. Luciano didn't like taking orders—not from his father, Massaria, Maranzano, or the navy. He also always figured out an angle to get ahead. With the unprecedented access he now had to his board of directors, Operation Underworld had just become that angle.

On June 20, 1942, Haffenden and the men in B-3 section of Naval Intelligence caught a break from one of the saboteurs himself. His name was George Dasch—team leader of the German spies—and the one who had threatened and bribed Coast Guardsman Cullen a week ago on Long Island.

Dasch had served in the German Army at the conclusion of World War I, only to make his way to the United States as a stowaway in 1923. He served a year in the US Army and gained citizenship when he married an American woman. He then deserted, left her and their son, and went back to Germany, where he'd been recruited by the elite German Abwehr force for his knowl-

edge of the United States. But his encounter with Coast Guardsman Cullen on the shore had spooked him. Dasch calculated that
his cover had probably been blown, and that going back to get
their explosives would be suicide. Given that Haffenden's men
were waiting for him there, Dasch was probably right.

On June 14, 1942, fearing he'd be caught, Dasch called the
FBI field office in Washington, DC, mentioned "Pastorius," and
told them he'd see them in Washington in a week. This referred to
Operation Pastorius, which was the German code name for the
mission. Over the next five days Dasch and the three other saboteurs in New York sweated it out in two separate hotels just ten
blocks from the Hotel Astor. They spent a total of $352 of the
nearly $200,000 they'd come ashore with, on food, clothing, and
hotel rooms, plus a train ticket for Dasch to the nation's capital.

On June 16, 1942—a few hours after Haffenden concluded his
dinner with the Sweezeys—four more German saboteurs launched
from a U-boat landed with explosives and cash, at Ponte Vedra
Beach in Jacksonville, Florida. Unlike the saboteurs on Amagansett Beach, these men were not detected and successfully
buried their explosives. Two of them then began making their
way to New York City to link up with the other team.

On Friday, June 19, Dasch called the FBI again, this time from
the Mayflower Hotel in Washington, DC. He gave himself up,
and the FBI quickly apprehended him. Then they put him under
the lights for eight days. Dasch spilled the beans on the entire operation. He told them that the German Abwehr (German special
forces) had devised a plan to terrorize and strike fear into the
hearts of the American people. Several of their targets were in the
Port of New York, including the Hell Gate Bridge in the East
River.

Dasch and his seven co-conspirators had been recruited for
their knowledge of the United States and had been trained as
commandos to deploy explosives at vital points on railroads and
bridges, aluminum and magnesium plants, canals, and locks. They
had also trained in the chemistry of incendiaries and explosives,
timing devices, and tradecraft. They were given fake identifica-

tion and birth certificates. Their money and the number of explosives were enough to sustain them for at least two years' worth of sabotage activity. Since all of his instructions had to be memorized, Dasch had plenty to tell the FBI.

While Dasch was sweating it out with the FBI, all seven of his co-conspirators had been rounded up and arrested. On June 27, 1942, FBI director J. Edgar Hoover announced that the Bureau had taken eight German saboteurs into custody. Hoover loved the spotlight and relished his opportunities to tout the FBI's success, while Haffenden and his ferret squad happily preferred to be, and remained, in the shadows.

CHAPTER 7
Surreptitious Entry

By the end of spring 1942, New York City had begun to rise from a gloomy run of months. The United States Navy had won its first major victory at the Battle of Midway. Losses in the Battle of the Atlantic were horrific and still being censored, which was a good thing, as the Allies lost 213 ships in May and June alone. In New York City, however, business was beginning to boom, as a major boost in government spending cut unemployment in half. Servicemen from all over were beginning to filter through the city and spend their government paychecks on local entertainment.

Soldiers were also disembarking from the Port of New York in increasing numbers, as were weapons and other war materials. On the waterfront, the swelling of materials meant more men were working on the piers, and the need for security was greater than ever.

In mid-June 1942, Joe "Socks" Lanza and Ben Espy were sitting together at Carmine's restaurant, just a block from Meyer's Hotel, at the corner of Beekman and Front Streets. Carmine's was an old restaurant, having been opened forty years earlier. The interior was dark, as it had very few windows, and there was dark wood everywhere from the bar to the booths. There were fishing nets hung for décor, but even though it was very close to the Fulton Fish Market, savvy eaters knew to stick to the Italian dishes on the menu.[1] As it was too early in the day for a cocktail, Lanza and Espy had coffee, and waited for one of Luciano's closest friends and business partners—Joe Adonis.

Adonis was indeed a good-looking man, and nobody thought he was more handsome than himself. He had big lips and boyishly soft olive skin. He made sure he always looked his best; manicures and pedicures were part of his daily routine.

The three of them knew each other, but they weren't close. So Meyer Lansky had sent word to Adonis first, and asked him to meet with Lanza. When Adonis arrived at Carmine's, Lanza and Espy greeted him cordially, and Adonis sat down with the two men.

"I've just been up to see Charlie," Lanza said to open the conversation. He loved being able to say that.

Lanza then told Adonis what he was doing on the waterfront for Naval Intelligence. Lanza told him about "the Commander," as Lanza was still having trouble saying the name "Haffenden." He also told Adonis that he needed some help from him with the longshoremen in Brooklyn.

Adonis was a *capo* in the Mangano family, and though Mangano was frequently perturbed by Luciano's constant partnering with Adonis without his permission, Adonis knew he could handle whatever flak he received. His friend Charlie needed his help, and he was happy to give it. So Adonis asked how he could assist.

At this point in the conversation, Lanza asked Espy to step out. Espy left the table, and Lanza and Adonis talked in private.

Luciano wanted to know about "Tony Spring," and the Other Guy.

Luciano wanted to be told that it was being taken care of.

Luciano also wanted to talk to Adonis about the Piping Rock Club in Saratoga, and some casinos that Adonis was an investor in, in Jersey.

No problem.

Lanza also told Adonis that he'd need help getting a direct line to the Camardas in Brooklyn. It used to be that you just needed to know one Camarda—Emil. He was their leader, until he was shot to death during a petty dispute just a year ago. Then there was Anastasia, but he was busy training longshoremen in Pennsylvania for the army. So Adonis was the man whom Lanza needed to contact the Camardas. Between their six locals in Brooklyn, there were thousands of longshoremen loading war supplies onto Allied merchant ships, making control of their territory of vital strategic importance.

When Espy returned, Lanza told Adonis that he would act as the liaison between him and Haffenden, and that Lanza would contact Adonis directly for anything he needed. Haffenden now had the contact he had been looking for in Brooklyn, and thanks to that, Luciano was back giving orders.[2]

While Lieutenant Treglia ran Haffenden's units on the waterfront, Haffenden had another officer in B-3 who ran an entirely different squad, and operation. Lieutenant Maurice Kelly had been a cop for over a decade in New Rochelle, New York, prior to the war, and joined the navy in April of 1941.[3] Haffenden recruited Kelly for his hard-nosed investigational skills, and his stop-at-nothing energy to get any job done—whatever job he was ordered to carry out.

A born leader, Kelly was almost forty years old and tall, with dark hair and a prominent chin. He had been working with Squad #2 previously, connecting with Lanza for missions in Fulton Fish Market. Now he was the leader of the special team of ferrets that comprised Squad #3. Squad #3 didn't work on the waterfront, but inland, on Haffenden's ship—SS *Concrete*, which was his name for New York City.

Haffenden recruited the agents in Squad #3 by looking for candidates with very specific and finely tuned skills. One of these recruits was a civilian named Willis George—"Agent G" in Haffenden's little black book—and not only was George trained in investigating and undercover surveillance, but he was also an expert at cracking safes and picking locks. He was a self-

Commander Charles Radcliffe Haffenden (date unknown)— Lieutenant Commander Charles Radcliffe Haffenden was the commander of B-3 Section, and later "F" Section Third Naval District Office of Intelligence. While the date of this photo is unknown, it seems to be from Haffenden's days as a Reserve officer, and as much as a decade prior to Operation Underworld. *(Courtesy Steve Lansdale, Public Relations Specialist at Heritage Auctions)*

Dominick Sacco (Agent X), circa early 1942—Up until now, Dominick Sacco's face and identity have been withheld from the public. He was Felix Sacco's older brother, and Commander Haffenden's best friend. Sacco was an accomplished private investigator with expertise in surveillance. *(Courtesy Steve Lansdale, Public Relations Specialist at Heritage Auction)*

Felix Sacco (Agent Y), circa early 1942—Up until now, Felix Sacco's face and identity have been withheld from the public. Sacco was Dominick's younger brother, an accomplished private investigator, and an expert lock picker.
(Courtesy Steve Lansdale, Public Relations Specialist at Heritage Auction)

Ensign James H. Murray, circa early 1942—Murray worked the B-7-I desk for the Third Naval District out of 90 Church Street. He's one of four Italian-American officers from New York City recruited by Naval Intelligence to participate in Operation Husky, which was the Allied invasion of Sicily.
(Courtesy Steve Lansdale, Public Relations Specialist at Heritage Auction)

Lieutenant Maurice Kelly, circa early 1942—Kelly was a cop before and after the war, distinguishing himself during Operation Underworld in surreptitious entries and on the waterfront. *(Courtesy Steve Lansdale, Public Relations Specialist at Heritage Auction)*

Lieutenant j.g. Paul Alfieri, circa late 1942—Alfieri joined the war effort in February 1942 as a civilian agent under Commander Haffenden. He was used on the waterfront and during surreptitious entries. He's one of four Italian-American officers from New York City recruited by Naval Intelligence to participate in Operation Husky, which was the Allied invasion of Sicily. *(Courtesy Steve Lansdale, Public Relations Specialist at Heritage Auction)*

Captain Roscoe MacFall (date unknown)—MacFall was Commander Haffenden's superior and commanded over all Naval Intelligence sections in the Third Naval District. *(Courtesy Steve Lansdale, Public Relations Specialist at Heritage Auction)*

Captain William B. Howe (date unknown)—Howe was Captain MacFall's Executive Officer, and presided over all sections of Naval Intelligence in the Third Naval District. *(Courtesy Steve Lansdale, Public Relations Specialist at Heritage Auction)*

Willis George (Agent G), circa early 1942—George was a professional safecracker who was hired by the federal government, and later used by Commander Haffenden during several surreptitious entries. He wrote a book about his exploits titled Surreptitious Entry, published in 1946.
(Courtesy Steve Lansdale, Public Relations Specialist at Heritage Auction)

Joseph "Socks" Lanza (date unknown)—Lanza was the "Czar of the Fulton Fish Market," and a soldier (and later capo) in the Luciano crime family (later the Genovese family) who ran all racketeering in the Fulton Fish Market from the mid-1920s to the late 1960s. This mugshot was taken in New York City, most likely sometime in the 1930s. From 1937 to 1939, he spent two years in prison, all the while collecting profits from various rackets at Fulton Fish Market.
(Courtesy of the New York Police Department)

Meyer Lansky, mugshot circa 1928—Lansky was one of the country's most notorious and successful gangsters from the early 1920s to the early 1980s. During Operation Underworld, Lansky was "Lucky" Luciano's liaison, as he carried out Luciano's instructions in service of the navy and the mafia. *(Courtesy Municipal Archives, City of New York)*

Frank Costello, mugshot from May 31, 1935—Costello was "Lucky" Luciano's acting boss, running the Luciano crime family during Luciano's ten-year incarceration. He served as underboss during Vito Genovese's absence. Costello didn't actually provide much direct help to Operation Underworld, but he did allow it to proceed in Luciano's territory, which included most of Manhattan. *(Courtesy Municipal Archives, City of New York)*

John "Cockeye" Dunn, mugshot from 1939—Dunn was one of the bosses of the Dunn-McGrath Gang, who dominated racketeering on the waterfront on the Upper West Side. As ruthless and violent as Dunn was, prominent politicians and US military leaders in the army and navy deemed his work invaluable during the course of World War II. *(Courtesy Municipal Archives, City of New York)*

Ferret Squad by Art Bartsch, completed February 6, 1942—This piece of art is a bit a mystery, but what we do know is that it was completed by Art Bartsch, who was a rytoons artist at the time, in gouache, and just days before the Normandie caught fire. kely resided in the office of either Commander Haffenden, Captain Howe, or Captain Fall at 90 or 50 Church Street. It depicts a snow-white ferret (Haffenden's nickname his team was "the ferret squad") from the Third Naval District ferreting out rats in v York City that depict Japanese Emperor Hirohito, German Führer Adolf Hitler, Italian Prime Minister Benito Mussolini. The 19.5" x 10" image area is surrounded photos of Haffenden's Ferret Squad, including several civilian agents that are his day still unidentified.

urtesy Steve Lansdale, Public Relations Specialist at Heritage Auctions)

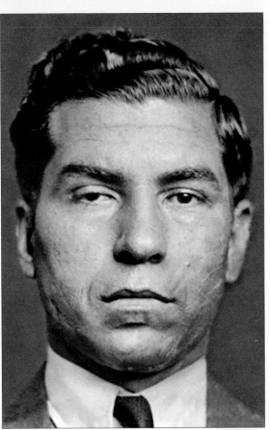

Charles "Lucky" Luciano, circa 1935—
Luciano was arrested in 1935
(his twenty-fifth time) and was sentenced
to thirty to fifty years in prison the following
year (note the scars on the left side of his face
and ptosis of his right eye). After being moved
to Great Meadow prison in May 1942,
he was given unprecedented access to his
criminal associates, as he met with his
"board of directors" regarding
Operation Underworld and mafia business.
(Courtesy of the New York Police Department

Vito Genovese, circa 1946—Genove
was on the run from a murder charge a
hiding out in Italy during World War
Though he played no part in Operati
Underworld, he was constantly
"Lucky" Luciano's mind during the tin
Deep down, Luciano could sense Genovese
lust for power, and that he was the o
standing in the way of Genovese's desir
After World War II, they would clash
number of times, leading to a power strugg
within the Luciano crime fami
(Courtesy of the New Yo
Police Departme.

described "professional burglar," and something of a character, who liked to joke around. In his mid-forties, he had a receding hairline and held a facial expression that made it look like he was always on the verge of busting out laughing.

George had been recruited to Squad #3 when Haffenden had targets for him to enter. Those targets came courtesy of Socks Lanza. In the spring and early summer of 1942, Lanza used his contacts within the building unions to get Haffenden's ferrets into the offices of suspected enemy spies.

Kelly, George, and several other agents were spread out all over the city. Haffenden had already had George rummaging through the trash of a dozen different buildings in Midtown Manhattan. The trash that George was looking at belonged to foreign consulates that were suspected of having friendly ties with Germany, Italy, or Japan. New York City had nearly sixty different consulates. While Axis nations didn't have their consulates in the country anymore, some of these countries hadn't officially declared their allegiance to the Allied cause. It was possible they could be spying for the enemy.

Wastebaskets full of discarded papers were analyzed—even the doodles in the margins could reveal a person's mindset. They were mainly looking for anything that didn't fit the profiles of certain foreign diplomats. Haffenden even had their mail intercepted sometimes, and had Agent George use a tiny flashlight with a powerful bulb that illuminated writing through an envelope. The printed words were somewhat inconsequential, as George was really looking for writing with invisible ink. He was looking for the message within the message.[4]

Operationally, Squad #3 was small, until one day when a particularly troublesome piece of intelligence reached Haffenden from ONI in Washington, DC.

When information was passed from ONI in Washington to the Third Naval District, it typically arrived at Captain MacFall's, Captain Howe's, or Haffenden's desk. It came in the form of a three-by-five chit that they called a "flimsy" because it was such a thin piece of paper. A letter from A to Z would be used to rate the value of the informant who supplied the intelligence (A being the most accurate), and a numeral between 1 and 4 indicated the accuracy of the information (1 being the most accurate).

The flimsy that Haffenden received on this occasion indicated "A-1" intelligence—the most reliable. And not only that, it came on a blue "flimsy," which of the three colors was the most urgent (white = routine, yellow = semi-dangerous, blue = dangerous).[5]

Haffenden, Howe, and MacFall read the flimsy, and it said that the "attachés" of a Spanish-speaking country's[6] embassy in DC had been burning papers the previous day. Naval Intelligence had a job for Haffenden—was this country's consulate in New York City also burning papers?

It wasn't Haffenden's job to analyze intelligence (though he frequently did so anyway), but to collect it. But suffice to say even he realized that diplomats burning papers with sensitive material was a common practice as a prelude to war. Was this country about to declare war on the United States? What were they trying to hide?

Haffenden sent Agent George on a solo mission to find out if the country's consulate was burning anything. Haffenden reminded George "that consulates are foreign territory. Breaking into one of them is a serious matter. If you should get caught, it would be extremely embarrassing to the Navy."[7]

George set out for the designated building in midtown Manhattan.[8] Lanza had set up a meeting with the night superintendent of the building. To gain access to the building required no special spy trickery or burglar's trick, as the night superintendent was a navy veteran from the First World War and was more than happy to help.

George procured a set of janitor's coveralls. The superintendent showed him the consulate's special elevator, and rode with him two floors above the consulate's office. The men then walked down two flights of stairs, and the superintendent used his passkey to open the consulate's office.

George didn't have to walk two steps into the office—the odor of burned paper permeated the entire suite of rooms. Just about every wastebasket in the office was empty, which was further evidence that paper had been destroyed.

George then combed the office but touched nothing. He made note of locked file cabinets, safes, and a main vault, and then reported back to Haffenden. Haffenden filled out one of his own blue flimsies and reported back to Washington that the same country's consulate in New York was also burning paper.

Then, the flow of information from Washington stopped. He had accomplished his mission, but he hadn't provided the reason that this was happening. Without a directive from the high command, Haffenden decided to act on his own. Perhaps he could provide more intelligence that could help, and at the same time inflate his stature.

For this mission, Haffenden added men to Squad #3.[9] Lieutenant Kelly was assigned as its leader; Felix Sacco[10] was added for his expertise as a lock picker; and his brother Dominick joined the team too, because Lanza had given Dominick a legitimate elevator operator's union card that could come in handy.

Haffenden also needed other specialists. His men couldn't steal anything, such as documents and envelopes, so they would have to photograph them. Then the problem arose of which documents to photograph? They would need a linguist—someone who spoke Spanish—to read the papers and tell them which ones were worthy of being photographed.

For this aspect of the mission Squad #3 grew to include civilian Agent Alfieri, who was a talented linguist. He had distinguished himself during operations on Long Island and was becoming one of Haffenden's best men. There were others too, as they also needed security in the form of armed sailors dressed in civilian clothes who would be stationed at various locations within the building. Sixteen men, including Kelly, George, the Sacco brothers, and Alfieri, readied themselves for their first "surreptitious entry," which in law enforcement terms was a fancy way of saying "burglary."[11]

"I only make one condition," Haffenden said to the team. "You must do your stuff in such a way that no one will know you did it."

"Make sure that no one catches us, you mean?" joked Agent George.

"I mean much more than that," Haffenden said in a serious tone. "I mean that every paper in those safes and files must be left in exactly the same place and condition they were in when you found them. . . . And we want codes if there are any—and I suspect there are—but no one must know we have them or suspect that we've even seen them."[12]

In the months of May and June 1942, the combined navies of the Allies in the Atlantic were experiencing their heaviest losses to date. In just those two months alone, they lost 213 ships, compared to 170 from December to April. With extremely limited resources, the navy high command devoted all of its convoy defense to troop-carrying ships. The lives of tens of thousands of GIs were so greatly valued compared to tonnage of fuel and supplies that not one troop-carrying ship had been sunk in the Atlantic. By the summer of 1942, there had been only one exception—SS *Normandie*.

The troop-carrying ships that were ferrying men to Britain were being loaded from the piers on the Hudson River. Seven operational embarkation piers (one pier, Pier 88, was out of action, where *Normandie* still reclined) loaded the armies that would fight the Axis legions. And the people who loaded equipment onto these troop-carrying ships were civilians—longshoremen and stevedores.

Presiding over these men at the top were President of the ILA Joe Ryan and his organizer Jerry Sullivan. Of all the gangsters now involved in Operation Underworld, Meyer Lansky knew them the best, so it was he who made contact with them, and told them two things: what the navy wanted, and that Charlie Luciano also wanted the same thing.

Ryan and Sullivan offered limited help, as they knew that as much as they represented the longshoremen unions, many of the unions operated quite independently, with criminal gangs and bosses dominating certain areas. If Lansky wanted boots on the ground, and to be able to gain eyes and ears among the longshoremen, he needed the help of the boss who dominated the West Side of Manhattan. They recommended the most ruthless and terrifying Irish gangster in New York City—Johnny "Cockeye" Dunn.

"Cockeye" had gotten his nickname because of a deformity that made his left eye look like it was cocked all of the time. It had a terrifying effect, as he always looked mad, and like he was about to kill someone. He was just thirty-two years old, but he was already the chief enforcer of the piers south of 14th Street. He was only five-foot-seven and 135 pounds, but he was deadly with a pistol, which was something he had proven many times over. Dunn had been arrested for robbery, assault, and homicide, with an added gun charge for each. But his days with petty crime stopped when he teamed up with his brother-in-law, Eddie McGrath.

The two were full of ambition, and after Dunn spent a long stretch in Sing Sing, they formed the Dunn-McGrath gang, and set their sights on running a pier. Once in control, they could run the "shape ups"—the deplorable system that saw longshoremen get shaken down for their right to work—and make a fortune off of the loading and unloading of cargo.

Just a year ago, in September 1941, Dunn had shown everyone—that being the army, the navy, the DA, and the ILA— who was the power broker on the West Side piers. With a firm hold on the piers of Hell's Kitchen, Dunn made a move that showed his reach extended much farther south, to Pier 51 in Chelsea.

There, an ILA local elected a business agent who was anti-union, and unwilling to take orders from the Dunn-McGrath gang. But shipping companies loved this business agent, because he hired "short gangs"—too few employees for a job—and often undercut union contracts. In protest of his actions, the longshoremen of his local conducted a strike. For five days in September 1941 the strike delayed the shipment of vital war materials to the English, who at the time were fighting the Germans by themselves. This was a huge problem, as England was hanging on by a thread, almost completely reliant on America's influx of supplies arriving via merchant ships. The navy high command thought the strike was inconceivable, but they stood powerless to confront a labor dispute.

So it was Dunn who confronted the business agent in a bar, and after demanding that he give in to worker demands, Dunn landed a hail of fists on the man's face. The man grabbed at Cockeye, who kept punching him until the crowd in the bar broke up the fight. The men then threw the business agent out the front door.

Dunn was arrested the next month. The details of the case came out, and a few things happened—the US government got a glimpse of who was actually in charge on the waterfront, and Dunn got charged with coercion (which was very similar to Lanza's charge). Dunn was given an indefinite sentence, and imprisoned at Rikers Island.[35]

The US government might have been content leaving Dunn there had the US not been thrown into World War II two months later. Dunn took advantage of the situation and directed an ingenious letter-writing campaign to the Parole Commission—letters came from the biggest trucking firms in the country, even from a congressman, all on the same day of January 29, 1942. Dunn was released less than a month later, with his trial eventually set to resume in a year. He was simply too valuable on the waterfront to prosecute. McGrath, for his part, was also currently under indictment—charged with murder out of the state of Florida. Somehow, all of this did not bother Lieutenant Commander Haffenden.

Haffenden might have never come into direct contact with Dunn if it had not been for an incident that made Dunn furious. He stormed into Moses Polakoff's office and started screaming about what he saw from the loaders. Polakoff had been designated as Lansky's liaison between the ILA and the navy, and at this moment, he found himself in a very uncomfortable situation and just had to listen as Dunn barked at him. Polakoff was powerless to do anything about what Dunn was describing, so he immediately reached out to Haffenden, and Haffenden didn't really have a choice but to meet Dunn in person.

Lansky then brought Dunn to the Hotel Astor to introduce him to Haffenden, but Lansky didn't stick around.

Dunn was incensed, and Haffenden was a little scared. This man was violent, and a conniving murderer, and yet Haffenden gave him a look of calm as Dunn explained that the security at the piers was absolutely abysmal. The way cargo was being handled and loaded onto ships seemed to have little to no oversight. Dunn pointed out how easy it would be to stash a bomb in some of the cargo, and how that could just as easily doom an entire ship.

Haffenden listened to every word that Dunn had to say and assured him he would do whatever was possible to address his concerns. Dunn even spoke to high-ranking officers in the army shortly after, and schooled them on the precautions they should be taking.

Haffenden kept in contact with Dunn, and put his cockeye and ears to work on the piers, using Dunn as his enforcer for the popular warning "loose lips sink ships." He became the "watchdog"[14] of the piers on the West Side of Manhattan, and recruited men from his gang to help.

In the bars around the piers, and in New York City proper, enemy spies could be just waiting to hear some loudmouthed drunks reveal the time of a ship debarkation, or their route. If a spy obtained this information, they could relay it to someone who had the ability to transmit the information to a foreign government that could route it to the Germans. This information could then be routed to a U-boat commander at sea, so he would know exactly where and when to find his prey.[15]

Dunn's gang and closest companions were told to report anyone mouthing off about ship cargo, or especially any ship's destination, or debarkation date. Dunn had the bartenders at various

watering holes along the waterfront listening for drunken longshoremen blabbing about classified information. More often than
not, Cockeye Dunn took care of matters himself.[16] He would
never waste an opportunity to punch out a loud drunk, especially
with the backing of the US Navy.

However, if anyone was capable of sabotage, or was suspected
of being a spy, Dunn would report it to Haffenden. Some informants and suspected enemies needed to be questioned thor-
oughly, and Haffenden needed a place to conduct such inquiries.
In case they were hostile, he certainly couldn't bring them to his
office at the Hotel Astor. So MacFall and Haffenden had a separate office on Greenwich Street. Its location was almost perfectly
an equal distance from Dunn's territory and Lanza's. The room
was operated by Lieutenant Treglia, and frequented by Dominick
Sacco, among others. If an informant or suspected spy was brought
there, then whatever transpired was kept a secret.[17]

During the daytime, Haffenden was meeting with various underworld informants and administering his section. He was upbeat
and liked to keep morale high by showing constant enthusiasm
for his job. But outside of his section his enemies were growing.
B-5 section was supposed to oversee the piers and docks of the
Port of New York, but Haffenden made little to no effort to cooperate with this section. Lieutenant Commander James Coddington, who headed B-5, hated Haffenden, as Haffenden showed
absolutely no regard for the job Coddington was supposed to be
doing. Whenever Haffenden had a job to do, he was not interested in sharing responsibility.[18] That included his oversight of
extremely risky top-secret missions.

Surveillance of the consulate's consul general himself hadn't
even begun prior to the first surreptitious entry. His habits, his
comings and goings, were entirely unknown. This put Haffenden
on edge, and to add to the tension, he told Lieutenant Kelly that if
someone tried to detain them at the consulate, they were to use
whatever means necessary—even if that meant violence—to pre-

vent being apprehended. Haffenden was freelancing, after all—he had no official clearance from the navy for what he was about to do.[19] So only the officers were armed, some with small revolvers, and others with single-shot pencil-type gas guns.[20]

The night of the first mission, Haffenden could only wait a couple of blocks away at the Hotel Astor as his team made their surreptitious entry in the dark. On nights like these, his heart raced, and he felt a pain in his stomach that made him think he had an ulcer.

Gaining access to the building came care of the night superintendent, who left the door unlocked, but did have a condition—the elevator had to be operated by a member of the elevator union. Thanks to Socks Lanza, Dominick Sacco carried just such a credential, as he had been designated by book 33529 issued by the Building Service Employees International Union, Local 32B, with a current stamp for the month of June.[21]

Two junior grade lieutenants named Boynton and Smith stayed in the lobby, while the rest of Squad #3 filed into a freight elevator. Boynton and Smith had orders to intercept the consul general if he were to suddenly arrive. Two more lieutenant j.g.s joined Kelly, Alfieri, the Sacco brothers, George, two other civilian agents, two chief yeomen, and three boatswain's mates as they entered the consulate's office and immediately began hanging blackout shades over the windows.[22]

Felix Sacco had an easy time using a metal pick that was flat at the end to bypass the four-pin file cabinet and desk locks.[23] Sacco took the time to show his methods to Alfieri, who was an eager learner. Cabinets and desk drawers were opening up all over the office. Soon a number of men were sketching pictures of the inside of drawers so everything could be put back like it was found. Once this was accomplished, the photographer became busy snapping photos of documents.

Alfieri had an equal interest in lock picking as he did in safe cracking. As Agent George took a crack at the main vault, he also took the time to show Alfieri how to do it. Finally, after a long process George actually managed to open the safe. In it, there was an envelope that looked important, with writing on the outside.

Alfieri read, *"Secreta, solo para ser abierto en caso de guerra."*

Translation: "Secret, only to be opened in case of war."

They dared not open it, lest they leave evidence that they had been there, so they took a picture of the envelope, put it back, and closed the safe. George then spun the dial counterclockwise to clear it, and placed the dial on the exact number it had been on when he arrived.

Haffenden was thrilled with the outcome of the mission. Not only had Squad #3 managed to operate undetected, but they also came back with a vital piece of intelligence. Haffenden then relayed to Washington that he had located an important document inside an envelope, and also noted that the information was obtained from a "confidential informant," saying nothing of his team's surreptitious entry. ONI in Washington was happy with the information, and then did what Haffenden was hoping for: They asked Haffenden for more information. Could his confidential informant find out what was inside the envelope without disturbing the envelope or its contents?

Haffenden, MacFall, and Howe used their network of resources, and despite all the law enforcement agencies and intelligence outfits in the United States, it turned out to be MI6—British Intelligence— who were going to fly in a specialist to help.

Meanwhile, Felix Sacco and Willis George were spending more and more time at the Central Lock Shop in Manhattan. It was a modest shop, but it had all of the necessary equipment to cut keys. Alfieri started spending a lot of time there too, as Sacco and George continued his education in the art of lock picking and safe cracking.[24] Perhaps these skills would come in handy for him in the future.

When it was mission time again, the specialist from MI6 joined Squad #3. The men were surprised to learn that not only was this agent British, but she was also a woman. She was in her mid-fifties, with an athletic build, and she was not one for con-versation. Agent George wasn't impressed with her personality but her gear certainly made an impression on him, as it took two sailors to carry her incredible assortment of electric burners, pots, pans, and teakettles.

The men wondered what the hell this equipment was for.

After the team had entered the consulate's office a third time, the specialist from MI6 waited patiently until Agent George had opened the safe once again.

The agent from MI6 heated up water in one of her electric tea-kettles, which had a long, thin spout. As the water reached a boil, the spout began to emit steam, and she was then ready to take it to the envelope. Calmly, she brought the steam into contact with the envelope flap and began the slow process of melting the glue that held the flap down.

Once a part of the flap was separated from the rest of the enve-lope, she moved the spout in and out of the void, but not for too long, so as to avoid damaging the contents or the envelope itself. After thirty agonizing minutes the envelope was open, and the men breathed a collective sigh of relief.[25]

As one of the agents photographed every word of the message, MI6's finest brought out glue to seal the envelope shut. She then resealed the envelope to look like it had never even been dis-turbed and used an iron to flatten some wrinkles.

When the photographs made it back to Haffenden, he was jubi-lant, and soon so was the navy high command. Only a handful of people ever got to lay eyes on the photographs that were devel-oped and provided to ONI. Among a treasure trove of informa-tion, Squad #3 provided ONI with diplomatic codes, an index of pro-Axis residents living in the US and abroad, and other infor-mation linking the consulate to espionage activity within the US itself. But the contents of the envelope were never used against anyone, as ONI found it far more valuable to have Haffenden keep spying on the consulate than confront them and force their hand. Surveillance of all involved also began

Surreptitious entries became a common occurrence for Squad #3, and it was causing Haffenden to become stretched to the farthest length of his abilities. While he waited up nights at the Hotel Astor for his squad's report, he was still holding appointments during the day. Little sleep was becoming commonplace, his blood pressure was constantly on the rise, and he was coming home to Flushing less and less. He loved the thrill, which was almost a nightly occurance since Squad #3 carried out no fewer than fifty operations. He was finally running Operation Underworld the way he wanted to, and it only emboldened him to take on more challenges and many more risks.

Under orders from Luciano, and at Haffenden's request, Tough Willie McCabe was brought into Operation Underworld. McCabe was a good-looking man, so much so that he had another nickname—"the Handsomest Man on Broadway."

In the case of McCabe, Luciano's influence was unmistakable, as he was already part of the Luciano family. He was about equal in stature to Socks Lanza, as each man had his own territory and controlled all the rackets that came with it. In McCabe's case, his territory was Harlem, and his chief racket was the numbers game (a lottery). Lanza introduced Dominick Sacco to McCabe and told him that Luciano was in favor of helping the navy.

"Anything the boss wants," McCabe said. "We'll do anything for him."

Intelligence reports from the FBI were pouring in about Mid-town Manhattan and Harlem. Radical groups were distributing subversive literature directly aimed at undermining the United States' war effort. Some groups were also starting to hold rallies, and the FBI and the navy needed to know if any of these rallies were turning into a full-on political movement, or a coup against the country. Haffenden resolved that his ferrets needed to adopt a wide net for eavesdropping, and the best places to focus on were where people gathered and talked—bars, restaurants, nightclubs, and hotels.

Together, Haffenden, McCabe, and Lanza came up with a brilliant plan to use Luciano family resources to aid Operation

Underworld. In just about all the bars and restaurants in Midtown Manhattan and Harlem, McCabe had a vending machine or a kinetoscope. They were very popular among patrons, and had to be serviced almost daily. So when Haffenden asked McCabe how they could eavesdrop on conversations occurring in so many establishments, McCabe suggested that the servicemen listen for subversive conversations, report them to McCabe, and then to the navy.

But McCabe's help didn't stop there, as his hold over the numbers game was another resource. He had taken over the numbers racket in Harlem in the mid-1930s after Luciano had Dutch Schultz—a member of his own family—assassinated. Since then, McCabe had run a fair lottery—illegal, to be sure, but after Schultz was gone, the game was seldom rigged, if ever. And the numbers runners stopped at just about every bar and restaurant in Harlem and Yorkville, taking bets and collecting money.

"What better informants can you have than the collectors?" Lanza asked rhetorically.[26]

Haffenden liked what he was hearing, but what if they located a person or a place of interest? How could he get his men inside to spy on any targets?

The questions were posed to both McCabe and Lanza, and they both came up with a man named Ben Jacobs. Jacobs was the secretary-treasurer of Checkroom Attendants Union Local No. 135. Lanza called up Jacobs, whom he'd known for twenty years, and while meeting with him, Lanza told him that he could be helpful to the war effort. Lanza also asked Jacobs if he would be willing to meet someone from the navy. Jacobs was more than willing to help but was still very unclear about how he could do that.

They decided to meet for dinner at Roger's Corner restaurant on Eighth Avenue, at West 50th Street in Manhattan, which was perpendicular to Madison Square Garden. The two men walked into the giant corner restaurant that stretched down both streets. They sat at a circular booth with upholstered seats in the middle of the dining room, rather than in one that lined the back wall. Roger's Corner also had a big circular concession stand at the corner of the restaurant that was open to people on the street. Steaks, veal, and seafood were on the menu, and the bar was popular, so the two men had a drink while they waited for Haffenden and McCabe. The pair showed up a half an hour later, and the four of them had dinner.

Haffenden explained the situation to Jacobs, and then Lanza and McCabe filled in the blanks, and told Jacobs how he could help. There were a few places that their informants had identified that needed better surveillance. That meant that navy agents needed to be placed in a few specific places, such as a Harlem cabaret; the Commodore Hotel, which had two thousand rooms and was located right by Grand Central Station; and one other place.

What other place?

As the four men sat in a circular booth in the middle of the dining room of Roger's Corner, in full view of everybody, Haffenden told Jacobs that he intended to surveil the very restaurant where they were dining. He then turned the group's attention to the concession stand at the corner of the restaurant. On both sides—on the street and in the restaurant—there were soldiers of all stripes gathered. It was a location that would afford them thousands of conversations to eavesdrop on.

"Would you do me a favor," Lanza asked Jacobs, "and issue union books for navy agents?"

"I'd be happy to," Jacobs said enthusiastically. "How many do you need?"

"We need 10 or 12," Haffenden told Jacobs.

"Men or women?" Jacobs asked.

"Both," replied Haffenden.

"There's already a labor shortage with the war on," Jacobs started. "That shouldn't be a problem."

"Can we get four guys in here, soon?" asked McCabe.

"Why, sure," Jacobs answered. "Come by my office tomorrow."

The next day, McCabe came to Jacobs's office, and paid him $60 to balance the books, and in turn, Jacobs gave McCabe four legitimate union cards with phony names. Haffenden sent four of his agents to Jacobs, who found them jobs at the concession stand at Roger's Corner restaurant.

"They are very close friends of mine," Jacobs told the manager of the restaurant.[27]

Haffenden sent Jacobs more of his ferrets, and soon, at the cabaret in Harlem and the Commodore Hotel, waiter and bathroom and cloakroom attendant jobs were staffed by Haffenden's agents, listening to anything and everything people were saying. If anyone spoke out against the United States when the agents were listening, they'd soon find themselves in the unchecked crosshairs of Operation Underworld.

CHAPTER 8

Thick as Thieves

On Friday, July 17, 1942, at 9 a.m., a delegation of Lansky, Lanza, and Polakoff visited Luciano at Great Meadow prison. But this time, as per Luciano's request, they walked into the room adjacent to Warden Morhous's office with someone else—Michael Lascari.

Luciano was so happy to see Lascari that the guards outside could hear the commotion when he walked in the room.[1] They were hugging, joking around, and laughing; Luciano was jovial that he was about to spend time with two of his best friends. And not behind bars or in a room where someone was listening. They could hug, shake hands, and talk about whatever they wanted.

Polakoff had his edition of the day's newspaper, and he sequestered himself in the corner like before. Lansky and Lanza then gave Luciano a rundown of everything they had accomplished. Adonis had been contacted and Brooklyn was in the process of being contained. Lansky had aided on the West Side of Manhattan, and now it was most certainly being watched. In Harlem, Lanza was working with Willie McCabe and doing everything Haffenden asked of him. The report about Operation Underworld was good, and Luciano was happy.

"Continue and do everything possible, everything you possibly can," Luciano instructed Lanza. "And don't let me down."

By now Luciano firmly understood that the success of Operation Underworld and his best chance of getting out of prison were inextricably linked. His men on the ground had to come through for him. Motivating them was the only part that he could really control, and he made sure that Lanza understood how important his job was to him.

The conversation about Operation Underworld was once again a brief one—very brief—leaving Luciano hours of uninterrupted and unchecked time with his men. There were no listening devices in the room—he was free to talk about whatever he wanted.

Had Luciano heard about "Tony Spring," and the Other Guy?

Yes, he had—Luciano read about it in the newspapers.

On July 2, 1942, it was announced that Anthony "Tony Spring" Romeo had been shot to death in mid-June, and his body had been discovered—riddled with bullets—weeks later in Delaware. The Brooklyn District Attorney announced that Romeo was about to cooperate with authorities before he met his demise. Had he cooperated, it would have been a calamity for Luciano and Lansky, and especially Anastasia. As a former contract killer, Romeo knew about dozens, if not hundreds, of murders that had been contracted over the past decade. If the Brooklyn District Attorney's Office got to him first, the DA could've brought cases down on all of them. It had happened before, after all, with Abe "Kid Twist" Reles.

For over a year now, Brooklyn was no longer the sanctuary it once was for murderers. The fact that they had DA William O'Dwyer in their pocket didn't save some of their friends from Reles's testimony—O'Dwyer could only do so much. There were plenty of honest men in O'Dwyer's office, and they didn't know that their boss was actively working against them. And now O'Dwyer was gone. Fearing that he might get in trouble for all the things he had been doing for the Mafia behind the scenes, he had done what Anastasia did, and joined the army to avoid investigation. Had Romeo been apprehended by the Brooklyn DA now, the Mafia didn't have O'Dwyer there to feed them information or sabotage the case.

That fear was suddenly muted, however, as Romeo was now

dead, so it didn't matter whether O'Dwyer was around or not. As for the Other Guy, in late June 1942, a burning trunk was found on the Brooklyn waterfront. Inside was a body so badly charred that it was never identified. Investigators concluded it was a gangland murder.[2]

With that bit of good news, the conversation shifted to Luciano's plans for post-prison life. He had been thinking about them a lot, and they were beginning to take shape in his mind. However, it was complicated, and there would be a lot of pieces to move in order to get him set up for success.

And success would be defined as taking back his seat at the head of the family and running his empire like before. After speaking with Lansky a few times now, he knew that the gambling racket was going to be the key to his future. With cash he could buy anything, and Lansky was already well on his way to creating a coast-to-coast gambling racket; if he played his cards right, it could go international with the additions of the Bahamas and Cuba.

But there was also plenty of action nearby. New Jersey was a kind of gambler's paradise. Also nearby was Saratoga Springs in Upstate New York, where Luciano used to spend every August when the horse races were running there. The summer sports book at his places near Saratoga Springs had been so busy back in the early 1930s (even during the Depression) that he had to step in and run the operation himself.

That task had since been taken over by his underboss, Frank Costello. Saratoga Springs was very close to Great Meadow— just thirty-five miles south. Luciano knew that Costello would be in the vicinity soon.

Luciano wanted to see Frank next month.

Costello was at the forefront of gambling in the United States, and he was friends and business partners with the people who could take their sports book national. And if anyone needed to be paid off to make that happen, or bribed to get Luciano out of jail, Costello was the man to see. Lansky agreed to come back next month to facilitate a summit of Luciano family bosses.

It was decided that Lanza would come back too. Lanza had already been given all the contacts he needed from Luciano, but having Lanza present gave the meetings a sense of legitimacy. If Lanza came to meet Luciano, as far as Warden Morhous, Commissioner Lyons, and Commander Haffenden were concerned, they were conversing about Operation Underworld.

Luciano also had Lascari memorize a number of instructions. Luciano was shaking up how his future visits would go—Lascari would be his new liaison for Operation Underworld, not Lanza. In practical terms, it made sense, since it looked like Lanza was headed to jail soon. But in terms of Luciano's plans for postprison life, if Lanza wasn't in prison, then he had no place except for right where he was—Fulton Fish Market.

Luciano's plans were beginning to take shape, and he was bringing in his closest and most trusted associates, one by one, using Operation Underworld as a cover for his true intentions.

In the late summer of 1942, Luciano's acting boss, Frank Costello, was on a roll, and given all of his political connections, he probably slept better at night than any other boss. When Luciano and several other high-level gangsters were given long prison sentences, many of the underworld bosses scattered, but Costello didn't budge an inch. He walked around in public like he didn't have a worry in the world, and he looked damn good doing it.

He got a haircut and a manicure daily in the barber shop at the Waldorf Astoria. He wore fine bespoke silk suits and had his hair slicked back like it was painted on his head. His nose was long and fat, and his hairline was just starting to recede. He also had a special power—an equal number of people thought he was Irish as knew he was Italian. It was Luciano's idea to give him an Irish name—Frank Costello. It stuck, and oftentimes his close friends jokingly hailed him by saying, "Hey, Irish." He didn't have an Italian accent, after all, as the surgeon's scar on his vocal cords back when he was a child made him sound American.[3]

This special power manifested itself in an ability to schmooze and rub shoulders with New York's various sources of power.

When the Bugs and Meyer Mob kicked off, Costello was responsible for keeping law enforcement away from their operations. So Costello collected $5,000 from Luciano, Lansky, and Siegel, for what they called the "Buy-Money Bank."[4]

Within ten years, each man had contributed millions of dollars. Costello started small by bribing policemen, and eventually worked his way toward politicians. His aim wasn't largely meant to sway legislation, at first, as he had a more specific purpose—keep law enforcement away from the various bookmaking operations he was buying a stake in. Gambling was illegal in New York (and most of the country), but Luciano and his board calculated that the public was willing to look the other way on certain vices, and those were the safe, illegal enterprises to pursue out in the open. It was a lesson they'd learned from Prohibition. This philosophy was something that Lansky and Costello held very close to the chest, and one that Luciano paid dearly for not respecting, as prostitution was not one of those publicly accepted vices.

Costello now had Tammany Hall—the Democrat powerhouse of New York City politics—in his pocket. The previous April (when Operation Underworld was getting started) he had successfully delivered district votes to get his man—Michael J. Kennedy, a former two-term congressman—elected leader of Tammany. And because he was a criminal chameleon, Costello also had plenty of Republicans in his pocket too.

He was also expanding his gambling interests and was making a fortune. He was partnered with Lansky on several ventures, but the one that was making him money hand over fist was his slot machines. At first he operated his "one-armed bandits" in New York City, but in 1934 he got caught. Though he escaped any criminal charges, Mayor La Guardia smashed about a hundred of the machines with a sledgehammer, and then threw them out to sea.[5] Since then, all the bosses had pulled their gambling interests (with the exception of the numbers racket) out of the city, and begun to branch out nearby, and all over the country. As for Costello, he moved his slot machine racket to Louisiana.

Now he was being summoned by his boss, Luciano, and he was looking forward to the visit. The timing was good for Costello, who spent every August in Saratoga Springs, watching the horse races and raking in the dough at his, Lansky's, Adonis', and Luciano's sports book in the Piping Rock Club.

On the morning of August 25, 1942, Costello was looking his best, and was all smiles, as he prepared to meet his boss. He had been able to remove himself from the action at Saratoga Springs (races were scheduled for the afternoon) on that Tuesday morning, and had his daily manicure appointment moved to accommodate his early meeting.[6] Gambling action was down over the weekend; betting had reached a paltry $656,503 on Sunday, versus $837,616 the previous year. War rationing was the reason behind lower earnings, and that was to be expected.[7] Despite this small setback, Costello had made some incredible moves recently, and there were a lot of good things to report to Luciano.

This visit to Luciano was different, however, from the previous ones by Lansky and Polakoff. Instead of traveling to Albany, as per usual, Lansky, Lanza, and Polakoff took a slight detour, and stayed the night near Saratoga, at Lake Lonely, where the Piping Rock Club and Lansky's Arrowhead Inn were located.[8]

Saratoga brought about a feeling of nostalgia for Luciano, Lansky, and Costello. They had been regular habitués during summers at the Saratoga Springs racetrack, and Luciano and Lansky had even had Arnold "the Bankroll" Rothstein finance them to open one of their first joints nearby—the Chicago Club. It was more like a speakeasy, but a modest gambling den nonetheless, complete with two roulette wheels, a birdcage, and a craps table, but most of the space was dedicated to the sports book for the horse races. It took three men to run the sports book in the summertime, and when it got really busy, Luciano stepped in and personally ran the operation.

A similar setup emerged in 1932 when Luciano, Lansky, and Costello opened up the Piping Rock Club in Saratoga. There were seven "Saratoga Lake Houses," and the Luciano family had two of the best—the Piping Rock Club and the Arrowhead Inn. The two casinos and attached entertainment halls and hotels dwarfed the Chicago Club, as Piping Rock had as many as a dozen roulette wheels and three craps tables, and also featured lavish entertainment. From the outside, it looked like a country club, but the inside was where the Piping Rock set itself apart from previous casinos. The ballroom was large and gorgeous with crystal chandeliers and a larger central one. A stage and a small dance floor were encased by two-foot-high Greek columns, with a much larger surrounding space for tables and dancing. No expense was spared in the summertime, as Lansky paid a $25,000 retainer fee every month just for the entertainers alone.

Lansky also operated a beautiful restaurant at Arrowhead Inn that had an entire back wall covered in glass, so patrons could take in a gorgeous view of Lake Lonely. In the 1930s, Luciano, Lansky, and Costello were experimenting with this new formula— providing entertainment for the rich gamblers, to keep them spending money while they weren't at the tables or the horse track. It was a formula that worked, and was being brought to every corner of the country. They also tried to portray themselves as legitimate businessmen as they broke a law that very few seemed to care about enforcing. This way, they attracted New York City's and the country's legitimate wealthy elite, such as Walter Chrysler.

As Lansky, Costello, Lanza, and Polakoff set out for Great Meadow from Saratoga to visit Luciano, they were joined by three other men. Two of them were associates who gave Warden Morhous fake names—M. Einsberg and John Martini. The third man who joined the group from Saratoga was Willie Moretti, the big-time owner and operator of gambling establishments in Up-state New York and New Jersey. Aside from being Costello's underboss, he was also Costello's cousin and his right-hand man.[9] He grew up in New Jersey and started working with Luciano, Costello, Lansky, and Siegel back in the early Prohibition days. He was in his late forties and handsome, with beautiful white, straight teeth that beamed when he smiled. He was also balding, and usually wore a hat to hide it. His appearance was important, as he was an unapologetic womanizer. He was also always good for a joke, and liked to talk—a lot—and brag.

The seven men arrived at Great Meadow prison around 9 a.m., and Warden Morhous was a bit alarmed at the size of the group. He didn't make them sign in, as per usual, but he told them there was no way that all these men would be allowed to see Luciano at the same time.

Morhous insisted that they split themselves into two groups, so only three people (plus Polakoff) at a time could see Luciano. The first to go see him were Lansky, Costello, and Moretti, plus Polakoff.

When Luciano laid eyes on Costello, the two erupted in elation. Jokes and obscenities flew through the room, and they laughed like drunken sailors.[10] They made small talk, and at no time during their discussion did Operation Underworld even come up.

Lansky had been counseling Luciano for months that gambling was the future, and he was happy to let Costello explain to him how this was taking shape. Costello reported that the Luciano family's interests had extended way beyond New York, and with a combination of investors—Costello, Lansky, Siegel, Adonis (Luciano's board of directors), and Willie Moretti—they covered much of the country (and beyond). Lansky had the longest reach, as he also had interests in casinos in Hallandale, Florida; Council Bluffs, Iowa; and Havana, Cuba.[11] Every single one of them was connected to a horse track, and Costello held interests in several of them too. Siegel was out West in California, running floating casinos in the Pacific Ocean and building a sports book off of races at the Santa Anita horse track. Costello revealed that Adonis was cashing out his share in the establishments at Saratoga Springs and would be moving his money into several successful casinos in Jersey that were operated by Moretti. It would be best if Luciano did the same with his money. And then Costello offered the real prize.

Of course, he had his slot machines and the Beverly Club in

Louisiana, but it's what he had in New York that really interested Luciano. Costello told Luciano that he spent much of his leisure time with a specific group. At least once a week, he golfed at Pomonok Country Club in Queens, or other courses, with three men. The foursome was always the same: Costello, George Morton Levy, Frank Erickson, and a former tax revenue agent named Schoenbaum.[12] In the world of sports gambling, these might as well have been the Four Horsemen.

Erickson was fat—fat with cash and a robust waist size. His jolly good nature belied his street credentials, as he worked his way up from crooked back-alley dice games to becoming the biggest bookmaker in the country. He went so far back that he was one of Rothstein's original partners, and was so important that he was never touched through the entirety of the Castellammarese War, or all the murdering that took place after.

The reason is because Erickson was connected to every high-level gangster in the country. He had gained that status early, as he was responsible for changing sports gambling forever when he created a wire service that gave up-to-the-minute results on sporting events.[13] Erickson also loved prizefights and was the official bookie at Madison Square Garden. In fact, that's where he met Michael J. Kennedy for the first time, and told him that he knew a guy who could deliver votes for him. Later, Erickson introduced Kennedy to Costello. Shortly after, Erickson and Costello spent so much time together they became known as the "two Franks."

Erickson also liked horse races, and that was certainly the forte of George Morton Levy. Levy was something of a Renaissance man, as he was a pioneer and innovator for horse racing, and yet previously he had been a criminal attorney.

Levy invented harness horse racing, and in September of 1940, he raked together his life savings, lined up investors, and opened the Roosevelt Raceway. But horse racing was tough to make a profit on during the Depression and the war, and Levy was even selling shares to the bettors for $1. He offered shares to his staff too, as payment, but they refused. He had also been getting strong-armed, as rival bookmakers set up shop at his track. He wanted them out, so he made an agreement with Costello. Weekly payments that amounted to $15,000 a year made sure that Costello would keep rival bookmakers out of the Raceway.[14]

Luciano was happy to hear about Levy. Once upon a time, Luciano had been one of Levy's clients. In fact, Levy and Polakoff also knew each other well, as they had been part of the legal team that defended Luciano during the trial that put him in prison. Levy had even previously visited Luciano at Dannemora.[15]

Should the Allies win the war, Luciano, Lansky, and Costello were calculating that gambling was going to be big business, and Luciano had finally learned his lesson—only engage in rackets where the moral lines were blurred. Prostitution and narcotics were black-and-white with both the law and the public, and responsible for all of the prison time he had ever served. Lansky and Costello had almost never even touched those rackets, and both had avoided long prison sentences as a result.

With access now to Lansky, and Costello put in motion, combined with Lascari in Jersey to work with Adonis and Moretti, Luciano was forming the combination that was going to set him up for his return to the throne of the underworld, and expand his operations nationwide and beyond. He could come back even bigger than he was before.

The only mention of Operation Underworld in the August 1942 meeting at Great Meadow was about the fact that Costello had met Commander Haffenden.

What did Costello think of the commander?

Costello had had drinks with Haffenden and Lanza at the Madison Hotel over the summer. Costello liked Haffenden—he was a Tammany man, after all. Maybe he could be useful down the line.[16]

What about Dewey?

Thomas Dewey—the man who had put Luciano away—was running for governor of New York, and if he won, it wasn't lost on any of them that he would have certain special powers, and one of those was that he'd be capable of giving Luciano a pardon.

What if Costello gave Dewey a campaign contribution? Would that influence him to help Luciano? Dewey owed Luciano, after all. Luciano saved Dewey's life, twice.

Costello agreed he would present the opportunity to Dewey. The dollar amount decided on was a lot of money—$90,000. Lansky would arrange to make this money available to Costello, who would in turn provide it to Dewey.[17]

For nearly five hours Luciano talked about his plan, and communicated it to Costello and Moretti in Sicilian, and Lansky in English, as he dreamed about all the dough he was about to make, just as long as he got out of that godforsaken place.

Bringing Willie McCabe into Operation Underworld was a brilliant move by Haffenden and Lanza. The East Side and Midtown Manhattan—McCabe's territory—was a haven for the disenfranchised and radical thinkers. At the time the US military was still segregated, but they allowed black people to serve. This was not the case, however, in defense plants around New York City, which hung signs that read, "HELP WANTED, WHITE." Of all the neighborhoods in New York City, the Depression had been hardest on Harlem, and the neighborhood never really experienced the wartime boom of other locales.

There was an exception, however, as cabarets still hosted great musicians such as Louis Armstrong during lively shows that mixed music with dancing. Swing jazz had already been around for a while in Harlem, but visitors from around the country, and the world, were seeing it for the first time. Harlem's culture was still rich as its economy was recovering, but there was plenty of unrest in the summer of 1942, and thus it became the location of a proposed revolution against the United States of America.

The FBI was all over neighborhoods like Harlem and Yorkville, the latter of which was where they had successfully indicted and prosecuted Fritz Kuhn, the American Führer. And while the German American Bund was still being surveilled, a nearly unbelievable plot against the United States was unfolding in Harlem.

But it wasn't the Germans, or even the Italians, who were plotting—it was a Japanese cell.

In late August 1942, Haffenden received a piece of intelligence from MacFall's contacts at the FBI. They told MacFall that they had nabbed a Filipino-American in New York City named Mimo de Guzman.[18]

The FBI picked up de Guzman under the guise of draft dodging, but they knew he was up to something else. They pummeled him with questions until he admitted everything. He told them that he was a part of the infamous Black Dragon Society. The Black Dragon Society was created by a Japanese nationalist who was trying to spread ideas of imperialism in the United States. Along purely racial lines, he believed that the Japanese people had a common history and future with the colored people of the United States—specifically, Negroes. Given that there was a large population of black people in Harlem, de Guzman and others had targeted this disenfranchised group, but hadn't gotten the response from his listeners that he was hoping for.[19]

De Guzman held rallies and told listeners that his organization had a hundred thousand members in the United States alone. De Guzman also told them that the Japanese were procuring firearms to equip an army, but that they should try to arm themselves with whatever they could. In the meantime, an army of allies would be storming the southern border from Mexico soon and would link up with them in New York City.

When being interrogated, de Guzman told the FBI about others in New York City. Specifically, he mentioned four names, including Robert O. Jordan, who was the president of the Ethiopian Pacific Movement of the Eastern World, which held that Japan and the Japanese people were the liberators of all non-white people from the rule of Western governments. Jordan spoke out against the United States and embraced the Axis cause. In certain circles, Jordan was known by another name—"the Black Hitler."[20]

Three of the four identified by de Guzman had already been rounded up, but the FBI came to MacFall and Haffenden for help with Jordan. Jordan was in violation of the Smith Act passed in 1940, which held that it was illegal to "advocate the violent overthrow of the government or to organize or be a member of any group or society devoted to such advocacy." Haffenden immediately called Lanza and McCabe and summoned them to his office at the Hotel Astor.

As Lanza and McCabe sat in front of Haffenden's desk, from his chair, the commander explained to the men the situation—Jordan might be at the head of a movement against the United States. Haffenden implored them to find Jordan quickly. He then produced a photograph that had been given to him by the FBI. Lanza and McCabe leaned in closely as the commander pointed to one man in particular. There were several people in the photo, in rows, but specifically Haffenden wanted them to focus on the man who was seated second from the left and wore a striped suit with a polka-dot tie. He was Robert "the Black Hitler" Jordan. Jordan had dark skin, but upon closer inspection they could see his biracial Japanese roots.[21]

"We need to find this man immediately," Haffenden said.

Then Haffenden gave Lanza the photograph.

Lanza and McCabe were excited—even thrilled—to help. They made their way to Harlem and sought out McCabe's partner in the numbers racket—a black gangster named "Big" Joe.[22] Lanza and McCabe showed Joe the photograph. Joe told them that he'd try to find the man.

Joe got back to McCabe directly. McCabe went to Haffenden without Lanza, as his work in Harlem had been proving extremely valuable, to the point where the two men were now having personal meetings. McCabe reported to Haffenden that Joe knew who the man in the photograph was, and more importantly, he knew where to find him. He told Haffenden that Jordan was hiding out on the Upper West Side, at a hotel at 166 West 87th Street.[23]

Haffenden relayed this information to the FBI. There was never any fanfare for Naval Intelligence, and Haffenden's role was never acknowledged when Jordan was arrested in early September 1942 and charged with sedition.[24] Haffenden was more than satisfied with the outcome. Assisting in having an agitator arrested prior to pulling off something big was in the highest traditions of Naval Intelligence. But Haffenden was starting to wish that he could receive at least some sort of merit or commendation that showed everyone how good a job he was doing. Didn't Haffenden deserve some of the spoils of victory?

At Great Meadow, in the early fall of 1942, Luciano didn't mind his job in prison. As a cell hall porter, he had a lot more freedom than other inmates. He may have been a glorified janitor—a position unbecoming of an underworld kingpin—but the job got him out of his cell longer than other jobs. As long as he stayed in his designated area, he roamed as he pleased. It was a psychological game that Luciano was playing with the other inmates: They saw him working, and it prevented him from looking like a "big shot," which could make him a target.

Inmates and guards alike sought him out often, and asked him for favors. Luciano was happy to grant favors to keep him in good standing with everyone, and he was also content to listen. But he didn't talk much to anyone—and he missed his friends.

His near vow of silence was one of the reasons why the library at Dannemora had been a great place for him to work—it had been quiet. He could read and practice his penmanship without anyone bothering him. When Luciano had arrived at Sing Sing back in 1936, he told authorities that his occupation was "barber." After all, his brother was a barber, and someone told him that it was a good job to have in prison. Prison authorities didn't believe him, however, so they assigned him to the laundry. That was hard work, but it didn't last long, as he was taken off that duty because of his heart murmur.[25] What a stroke of luck.

There was no question about it—Luciano was "Lucky." But depending on whom he was talking to, his telling of how he got that nickname might be different. Luciano had a loose relationship with the truth, and if there were stories circulating about him, he was just as likely to embrace them as he was to cry foul. Always an opportunist, if he thought a story would increase his stature in the underworld, he embraced it wholeheartedly. With all the stories that swirled around him, and all the violence that was associated with them, when he looked at you with a cold stare, and with his right eye only half-open, even the most hardened criminals thought he looked nothing short of sinister.[26] It was all intentional.

His sister Fanny and brother Bart hated seeing him looking like he'd gotten hit in the face with a bat wrapped in barbed wire. Each of them visited Luciano in September 1942, and witnessed Luciano's right eye lose its white color and be replaced with a blood red. The muscles in his right eye weren't functioning properly, and the inability of his pupil to adjust made bright lights blast his retina, resulting in extraordinary pain.

In the dark in his cell, after lights-out, it wasn't as much of a problem—just when he was outside, breathing fresh air, or doing his porter duties during daylight hours. The headaches got worse, and eventually he couldn't do his job anymore. He was admitted to the hospital at Great Meadow, where they treated him for iritis.[27]

Stories of how Luciano's right eye had been damaged, and how he'd gotten the terrible scars on the left side of his face and chest, varied. The popular version—which was an out-and-out lie—was the one he liked to repeat, and it not only explained the state of his right eye and his face, but also his nickname—"Lucky." He said that the trauma he endured had been caused by Salvatore Maranzano.

The way Luciano told it, he was summoned by Maranzano to meet on Staten Island. Once he was there, Maranzano set a trap for him—he demanded that Luciano himself kill his rival, Massaria. In the Sicilian mafiosi, this was almost a death sentence for Luciano. If he killed Massaria, it was likely that he would also be killed in an act of vengeance, or he would have to accept a tertiary role after the assassination, as old Sicilian mafiosi rules dic-

tated that a king could not replaced by a kingslayer. Luciano, as
he told it, told Maranzano, "You're crazy," then everything went
dark, as one of Maranzano's men clubbed him from behind.

Luciano said that he was rudely awakened when water was
thrown in his face. His wrists had been bound, and he was hanging with his arms over his head, while ligatures suspended him
from the rafters. He said that six men, all with handkerchiefs hiding their identity, went to work on Luciano with clubs and belts,
and they even burned him with lit cigarettes. All the while,
Maranzano pleaded with him to come to his senses.

"Charlie, this is so stupid," Luciano recalled Maranzano saying. "You can end this now if you will just agree. It is no big thing
to kill a man, and you know he is going to die anyway. Why do
you have to go through this, Charlie? . . . If you do not do it, then
you are dead."

Then, when Maranzano drifted a little too close to him, Luciano managed to kick his feet, and caught Maranzano in his
groin. Maranzano keeled over, and in a fit of pain he demanded
that his men, "Kill him! Kill him! Cut him down and kill him!"
Maranzano went to work on Luciano with a knife—slashing his
face, and slicing a deep gash into his chest. One of the men put a
gun to Luciano's head, and that's when Maranzano, according to
Luciano, decided that he'd let Luciano live. It was a lucky break,
and when Lansky and Costello visited him in the hospital, according to Luciano, Lansky called him "Lucky," and the name
stuck. People loved Luciano's story, but that's just what it was—
a story, and it had no truth to it.[28]

The truth, which he revealed only to his closest friends, such as
Costello, was far less dramatic, but no less painful. The truth was
that Luciano had been called "Lucky" long before his scars became part of his face,[29] and the nickname had more to do with his
gambling ability than his talent for escaping death. In fact, Luciano was growing very tired of his nickname—he felt that he
didn't ascend to the top of the Mafia out of luck. It took brawn
and skill.

But Luciano had been lucky, thirteen years earlier, on Staten

Island, when he was lucky to survive. The real story of how he got his scars came from when he was nabbed outside of his home as he waited for a date, and was forced into the backseat of a car. There were four armed men in plain clothes who said they were cops. They handcuffed him and then wrapped tape around his eyes and mouth as they took Luciano "for a ride." When the car stopped, Luciano could tell that he was on a ferry. The men left the car, and to attract attention, Luciano kicked out one of the windows, but only managed to catch the attention of one of his abductors.

The cop beat him senseless. Not only that, but the son of a bitch had a big ring on his finger, and it tore through the flesh of Luciano's face like a dull razor blade with every blow. Luciano still couldn't see on account of the tape over his eyes, but he could feel blood pouring from his cheek all over the rest of his face. That's when he passed out.

When he came to, the men threw him out of the car. They were well off the road, in a muddy field. They tore the tape off his face and put a gun to his head. The cops were after a man Luciano knew well—and the cops knew that Luciano knew him—Jack "Legs" Diamond, who was Arnold Rothstein's enforcer in chief. Diamond had just committed a murder, and the cops were dead set on finding him. Luciano was not only unwilling to talk to these policemen, but he had "no goddamned idea where [Diamond] was." They beat him senseless, again, and when they decided he was telling the truth, they left him there to die in the mud.[30]

Luciano—blood-soaked and less than half-conscious—crawled his way through that muddy field until he came upon a road and tried to get a car to stop and help him. His eyes were so swollen shut that he thought he'd hailed a cab riding by, but instead he actually hailed a police car. Fortunately, this was a different kind of cop, and he took Luciano to a hospital. During the ride, Luciano passed out again, and when he awoke in a hospital bed, he couldn't believe he was still alive.

In that hospital bed, he had felt lucky to be alive, but now in a hospital bed at Great Meadow—agonizing in pain for weeks—he hated every minute of life.[31] He still bore the scars from that cop's ring, and his right eyelid had only opened halfway ever since. But the story he told, and the scars he bore—like badges of honor in the underworld—he certainly used to his advantage. It wasn't, in truth, the way he had earned his "Lucky" nickname, but really it *was* when his name officially changed from Lucania to Luciano.

Sicilian street toughs had no problem pronouncing "Lucanya," as it was pronounced phonetically, but no one in high society ever got it right. He had given many aliases in the past, and he noticed that when he told people his last name was Luciano, they had no trouble repeating it.[32] When he had woken up in the hospital thirteen years ago, he told them his name was "Lucciano" (he'd later drop a "c") and it stuck. As for the cops who beat him, he told the police to "forget about it."[33]

The story of Luciano's "ride" made its way to the press. The publicity was a problem, as it painted him as a gangster, which was an image he had been trying desperately to hide. It was an important part of his business that legitimate people with money would deal with him—like they did Costello—if he played the part of a high-society gentleman.

For many years Luciano played that part well enough, but any notion of that was certainly wiped away when he was convicted of compulsory prostitution.

That son of a bitch Dewey.

Dewey broke the rules, as far as Luciano was concerned, when he set up Luciano and charged him with such a scummy, low-life crime. Prostitutes like Cokey Flo Brown fingered him as the head of a prostitution combination.

On the witness stand, Brown testified that Luciano had said, "I'm gonna organize the cathouses like the A&P. We could syndicate the places on a large scale same as a chain store system."

Luciano often asked himself if he had really said that, and deep down, he knew the answer. Whore after whore took the stand—

forty in all—and fingered Luciano as the boss of his co-conspirators. It was absolutely shameful, getting done in by a bunch of hookers.

During Luciano's appeal in 1937, Polakoff found out that a handful of those hookers had been paid off by Dewey. They were even willing to change their testimony, but Dewey and Judge McCook shut the door on that too. Polakoff's appeal failed.[34]

Now society thought Luciano was a pimp, and all his work toward creating his reputation had been flushed down the toilet. Luciano believed that if Dewey didn't owe him before—for saving his life—Dewey certainly owed him now.

But the word from Costello was not good. Dewey rejected the payment of $90,000 and wouldn't hear about any monetary exchange for Luciano's freedom. Dewey was not privy to Luciano's work for the United States war effort, and Luciano wondered how the hell he'd get pardoned if Dewey didn't accept his money. Luciano also knew that if Dewey didn't play ball, but pardoned him anyway, then it was highly likely that Dewey would have him deported.[35]

Everything Luciano was planning, and setting up for life after prison, hinged on the graces of a governor who had made his career by convicting him. It was a long shot, and Luciano hated that he needed to get "lucky" to get out of there. The way it was looking at the Great Meadow prison hospital, while he could barely see, was that his luck had already run out. And at these moments, Luciano hated the nickname "Lucky"—he made his own luck, and came out on top because he was smart, and not lucky. He couldn't rely on luck with Dewey—that attitude had landed him in prison—so he would have to explore other ways to get himself out.

CHAPTER 9

Spying on Spies

The summer of 1942 was a blur for Commander Charles Radcliffe Haffenden. After a spike in Allied shipping losses in May and June, July and August returned to normal (albeit still horrible), which was about fifty ships lost each month. But there were signs that the tide was starting to turn, as the US Navy introduced more warships into the Atlantic Ocean. The Soviets and the Germans had started a new battle, as both were locked in what sounded like an all-or-nothing attack on a city called Stalingrad. In New York City, New Yorkers cheered on the Yankees, as it looked like they were going to make another run at the World Series.[1]

Haffenden had never been busier in his entire life. His heart was being tested to the extreme, his stomach hurt often, and he slept fewer hours every night. His ferrets were producing good intelligence, and the waterfront was nearly safe from the threat of sabotage.

But every time one of those blue flimsies came into his office, his heart rate spiked, and he loved it.

There was that directive that came in on July 16, 1942, about Governor's Island that read: "Information has reached this office that the U.S. Coast Guard has discovered inflammable or incendiary discs on certain dock property in the vicinity of Savannah, Georgia, and at Jersey City, New Jersey."[2]

Evidently some of these incendiary discs were missing from Governor's Island, which was just a few miles from Manhattan and Brooklyn. Haffenden remembered that directive. He placed Dominick Sacco in the armory on Governor's Island to find out if someone there was a double agent, and then he told Lanza to spread the word on the waterfront. Lanza managed to alert the entire Port of New York. In the end, no one found anything, but that had Haffenden up nights.

There were other times too, where he'd have to send his men all over the place. When they helped nab Robert "the Black Hitler" Jordan, they had to follow up on the threat about an army coming in from Mexico. Haffenden briefed Lieutenant Maurice Kelly, who took up the assignment. He reached out to Lanza, who brought him a contact in Texas through the United Seafood Seafoods Union.[3] Nothing ever came of that either, despite the fact that Japan's largest concentration of spies against the US resided in Mexico.

By the fall of 1942, the threat of sabotage by a foreign agent in the Port of New York had decreased dramatically, thanks in large part to the cooperation and orders of Lucky Luciano. And also thanks to Luciano's cooperation and influence, Haffenden's men were nearly everywhere in New York City. Between Socks Lanza, Meyer Lansky, Johnny "Cockeye" Dunn, Willie McCabe, and Joe Adonis, there was seldom a place in the city where Haffenden didn't have eyes and ears.

Hundreds of thousands of servicemen and -women passed through New York City on weekend leave, or on their way to disembarking from the port. Every night Times Square was a madhouse, even without the lights on. Parties of people piled into bars like the one in the lobby of the Hotel Astor, and drank until the early hours of the morning. Military police attempted to keep order in the streets. Restaurants swelled with patrons, and nightclubs like Costello's Copacabana were making money hand over fist.

Lansky had gotten Haffenden's ferrets into the Pierre Hotel about ten blocks south of Yorkville. The building was forty-one stories of blond brick and limestone and capped with a sloping copper roof. Haffenden's men worked as waiters in the restaurant in the extravagant rotunda and in another restaurant in the hotel that promised diners unrestricted views of Central Park. The waiters eavesdropped on conversations from visiting military personnel and spied on the staff.

Dunn helped get waiters into the Great Northern Hotel on West 57th Street. This eight-hundred-room hotel was once the most profitable in all of New York City. Its recently remodeled restaurant was also referred to as the "back room," a private place where businessmen of varying stripes could chat. Haffenden's spies knew of its reputation, and started listening in on the conversations of patrons and staff.[4]

But of all the valuable pieces of New York real estate where Haffenden inserted his ferrets, the waterfront was the jewel. Longshoremen touched and handled nearly 100 percent of warfighting materials loaded onto boats embarking for Europe from the Port of New York.

Hordes of "hookers"—the longshoreman's nickname because of the twelve-inch metal heaving hooks they used to pierce and move cargo—gathered in the dark every morning on piers of the Hudson and East Rivers. Piers typically had warehouses built right on top of them, or at land's end, from which longshoremen moved crates and boxes of material—with cranes and their heaving hooks—to the ships. In the morning when the dock bosses arrived at their respective piers, the hookers huddled around and waited to see if their names got called for work that day. Typically, it wasn't a mystery, because the first ones chosen were paid up with the dock boss. Kickbacks were at the heart of what was called the "shape up" system, and nobody worked without kicking up a portion of his already dismal pay.

But now there were other kinds of men who were successfully navigating the "shape ups"—navy spies. Thanks to Dunn and the ILA, Lanza and Adonis, and the Camardas, all Haffenden had to do was call one of them up, and one of his agents would be placed and chosen in the "shape up." Haffenden even shifted all of the men in B-3 with Irish names to Squad #1. They were then assigned to work on the piers of the West Side, where the Dunn-McGrath gang and their dock bosses reigned over the Irish long-shoremen.[5]

As far as the navy was concerned, any activity that inhibited the loading of supplies onto ships in the Port of New York could be classified as an act of "sabotage."[6] That included the activity of longshoremen who performed work strikes in the name of ex-panding their rights as workers. In September 1941, the strike on the West Side delayed war fighting material bound for England. In February 1942, a similar strike occurred in Boston Harbor. Haffenden (along with the navy) wasn't concerned about labor rights, or the power the Italian and Irish gangs exerted over the longshoremen—he was concerned about preventing "sabotage," and therefore not letting strikes like those occur on his watch.

But the navy interfering with labor rights was something more akin to what was happening in Nazi Germany, where the Fascist government controlled all facets of production and commerce. If Haffenden was going to walk this line, he had to keep the navy's involvement a secret. The fallout from such an exposure would seriously harm the reputation of the navy and bring serious ques-tions as to the right of the federal government to spy on its citi-zens.

On Thursday, October 22, 1942, at 11:15 a.m., Moses Polakoff, Meyer Lansky, and Socks Lanza met with Lucky Luciano. Luciano was far less welcoming this time. He asked Lanza to give him the rundown on Operation Underworld, and Lanza de-livered a great report. Luciano reminded him, as he had before, that Lanza was to do everything possible to help the navy. After a few minutes, the conversation shifted to other topics more press-ing on Luciano's mind.

This time, Luciano wanted to talk to Polakoff. That was fine by Polakoff, who was beginning to question why he needed to be there in the first place. He was busy running his law office, and he was tired of taking entire days out of his practice to play watchdog over a bunch of crooks. The last visit had been weird—they hadn't even talked about Operation Underworld. So yesterday, Polakoff had phoned Commissioner Lyons and asked if he could sit this visit out, along with future visits.

Even though both men agreed that Luciano probably wouldn't try anything that would embarrass prison officials, Lyons insisted that Polakoff's presence made him feel better about the situation. Polakoff agreed to keep visiting Luciano, and chaperoning his guests.[7] And on October 22, that was a good thing, because Polakoff was the man Luciano wanted to talk to the most.

Luciano could not rely on Dewey setting him free. There needed to be another way out.

Lansky agreed.

Polakoff reminded his client that all their appeals had already been settled, and he wasn't eligible for parole for another fourteen years.

There had to be another way. What could Luciano do?

Polakoff didn't know.

Luciano demanded a solution, and he told Polakoff he was willing to pay for it. Lansky was then ordered to restore Polakoff's retainer for Luciano, and Polakoff told Luciano he'd do his best to find a solution. If there was a legal way to get him out of prison, Polakoff would find it.

Luciano excused his guests just after 2 p.m. Out of the five visits during which Luciano received guests under the guise of Operation Underworld, this was the shortest. Luciano conveyed a clear message that he wanted out, and that it was time to explore all options on how he could accomplish just that.

Warden Morhous noted the time when the men left and wrote his usual letter to Commissioner Lyons regarding the visit. But Morhous was getting lazy, and he was starting to leave the names of the visitors out of his letters. DA Frank Hogan was also getting suspicious that Luciano might be misbehaving, and he started to wonder if Operation Underworld was progressing according to plan. He wrote a letter to Warden Morhous demanding a list of all parties that had visited Luciano. When he got the list back, it only made him more concerned that Luciano was taking advantage of the situation.

On November 12, 1942, Haffenden was alarmed to learn that his ace in the hole, Lanza, was in jail. The timing was terrible, as the commander was receiving reports from the FBI that a dangerous Communist labor agitator was coming to New York City to stir up trouble.

Of course, Haffenden had long feared that Lanza's indictment for conspiracy and extortion would result in prison time, but Lanza had now managed to get himself imprisoned for another reason entirely—voter fraud.

Evidently, Lanza—active in local politics—had been campaigning prior to the 1942 midterm elections held on November 3. For Socks Lanza, however, campaigning was a bit different than for the average supporter, as people witnessed him intimidating voters as they tried to cast their ballots at the local elementary school across the street from his mother's house on Staten Island. Word of this reached the mayor's office, and La Guardia himself assigned two detectives to stop Lanza, and also make sure that he didn't vote.[8]

Lanza managed to escape the detectives' surveillance, bully his way into a voting booth, and cast his ballot—for all Democrats, except Thomas Dewey for governor. Casting his vote was a crime, according to the prosecutor, as Lanza had previously been convicted of a felony, thereby disqualifying him from voting.[9]

While Lanza was sorting that out from the Tombs prison in Manhattan, Haffenden was receiving reports about the Communist threat emerging on the waterfront in both Manhattan and Brooklyn. An Australian-born man named Harry Bridges—the president of the International Longshoremen and Warehouse Union (ILWU)—was an idealist and labor rights activist. He was also an outspoken Communist, had been behind one of the only general strikes in the nation's history (which had shut down nearly every port on the West Coast), and was currently fighting his own deportation order. The FBI had been after him for a long time—tapping his phones and keeping him under constant surveillance—but he was out on bail awaiting appeal for deportation, and free to do what he liked.

Out of California, the ILWU reigned over longshoremen on the West Coast, while the East Coast was run by Joe Ryan and the International Longshoremen's Association (ILA). Bridges wasn't a big man—saved from a shipwreck by a mandolin case, they said—but he was a giant when it came to rousing "hookers" into strikes. If that happened in the Port of New York, it would be Haffenden who would have to provide answers to his superiors about why it had been allowed to happen. Not only that, but the choking of supplies for days or weeks would inevitably result in the loss of American lives.

With Lanza out of the picture, Haffenden went to Meyer Lansky's liaison, and recently retained lawyer, Moe Polakoff. Polakoff and Lansky were both Jewish, both working in Luciano's interests, and had been forced to spend a lot of time together, riding to and from Albany six times now. The two had formed a bond, and Lansky had decided to hire Polakoff as his lawyer—should he ever need one. For now, if Haffenden wanted to get in touch with Lansky, it was best to go through Polakoff.

Haffenden wanted to know if Luciano or Lansky could do something to stop this threat. Polakoff couldn't contact Luciano about this. It could get him in trouble. Couldn't the navy just intervene themselves?

"The navy can't butt in," Haffenden said.[10]

Polakoff did tell Haffenden that he would get in touch with Lansky. Lansky was the one who had introduced the ILA to Operation Underworld in the first place, and if ILA leadership was needed, he was the one to reach out. Lansky then came to Haffenden's office at the Hotel Astor. After Haffenden explained the threat, Lansky was confident that his friends in the ILA would

help. West Coast longshoremen leadership was filled with ideal-
ists, while East Coast longshoremen leadership was filled with
gangsters—the two mixed like oil and water.

Lansky reached out to ILA President Ryan, who went to the
Hotel Astor himself to visit Haffenden. Ryan assured Haffenden
that he would help in any way he could. Haffenden told Ryan that
he wanted to up his presence on the waterfront and get more of
his men into the shape ups. If his agents caught wind of a rally, or
even a strike, perhaps they could get that information to one of
Ryan's watchdogs on the waterfront—like Cockeye Dunn—who
were notorious for breaking strikes.

Around the same time Haffenden was meeting with Ryan, Lanza
was freed after spending over a week in the Tombs. It wasn't
Guerin that had argued for Lanza's exit, and it wasn't Assistant
District Attorney Murray Gurfein—who had recommended Lanza
to the navy—who got him out either. The person who freed Lanza
this time was the district attorney himself, Frank Hogan.

On November 19, 1942, Hogan told the judge that the police
had made a mistake, and that Lanza's previous convictions had
been recorded as misdemeanors and not felonies. Therefore, he
was eligible to vote, and should have never been detained in the
first place. Hogan even gave the prosecutor a rebuke, saying that
if the District Attorney's Office had been consulted, this would
never have happened. The prosecutor, who knew nothing of Operation Underworld, called Lanza a "terrible citizen."

Seeing Lanza in court made Hogan even more curious about
how Operation Underworld was proceeding. Gurfein had left his
office shortly after Haffenden recruited Luciano, as he had been
commissioned as an officer in the Office of Strategic Services
(OSS). When that happened, Hogan lost his connection to Operation Underworld, and since then, it had been running without any
oversight by his office.

But what could be done?

Hogan found a way. A known criminal associate of Lanza's
was on the run. To catch the fugitive, Hogan convinced a judge to
let him install wiretaps on phone numbers—WOrth 2-7624 and

WOrth 2-7625. The phones connected to these numbers were in Meyer's Hotel.

On November 23, 1942, without warning Commander Haffenden, and four days after Lanza was released from the Tombs, two police officers managed to install the taps in Meyer's Hotel undetected, including one in Lanza's office. Hogan had just lifted the lid that would uncover the inner workings of Operation Underworld.[11]

Upon learning that Lanza was out of jail, Haffenden immediately contacted him for his help with the Harry Bridges situation. On a cold and rainy Tuesday, November 24, 1942, District Attorney Frank Hogan received his first transcript of recorded phone conversations originating in Meyer's Hotel. At 2:40 p.m., Haffenden called Lanza from his office at Church Street, reached Lanza at the number WOrth 2-7624, and had the following conversation:

"Hello," said Lanza.

"Commander Heffner. How are you?" Even after seven months, Lanza still couldn't pronounce Haffenden's name. Haffenden, for his part, had grown tired of correcting it, and though he told himself "Heffner" was his code name, really, he went by whatever Lanza could pronounce.

"[I'm] okay," replied Lanza. "Listen, I've got that for you." "That" was some seafood.

"I'll send down for it," said Haffenden.

"Okay."

"Now," started Haffenden. "On that Harlem thing, do you think that Meyer Lansky knows anything there?"

"You mean the Italian section?" asked Lanza.

"No," replied Haffenden. Then he explained what that "Harlem thing" was: "The Negroes—the two factors up there are the browns."

"I think Willie is your best," Lanza said, referring to Willie McCabe.

"On that new cabaret in Harlem, is that some of Brown's stuff?" asked Haffenden, referring to a publication coming out of

Harlem. Rumor had it that a fifth columnist movement had its headquarters somewhere in New York City. "Brown" was allegedly the owner of that cabaret.[12]

"We'll get some of your people in on that." Lanza was referring to using Tough Willie McCabe's connections to get some of Haffenden's agents into the "new cabaret in Harlem."

"Anything doing at the DA's Office?" continued Haffenden, referring to Lanza's case.

"No, nothing," replied Lanza.

"I had a visit with Ryan the other day and I thanked him," said Haffenden. "Have you heard anything around the waterfront?"

"No," replied Lanza.

"How about that Brooklyn Bridge thing?" Haffenden and Lanza had previously worked out a code name for Harry Bridges—"Brooklyn Bridge."

"Nothing on that," said Lanza.

"I don't want any trouble on the waterfront during the crucial times," Haffenden cautioned.

"You won't have any," Lanza assured him. "I'll see to that. I'll give you a ring, we'll get together."

"Okay, Socks."[13]

On the same day, November 24, 1942—Lucky Luciano's birthday—Luciano didn't celebrate the fact that he had just turned forty-five years old. He was permitted a phone call, and he reached out to one of his closest friends—Joe Adonis.

But Luciano was all business, and used the excuse of a birthday phone call to tell Adonis that he wanted him to contact Willie Moretti in Jersey about some of the casinos that he was buying a stake in.

The next day, at 2:07 p.m., Adonis called Meyers Hotel.

"How are you?" Adonis started.

"Oh, Guy," answered Ben Espy, who answered the phone first. "Guy" was their code for Adonis. "How the hell are you?"

"I was away and came back. Say, how can I get Willie?" asked Adonis.

"Wait a minute," Espy said. "Jersey or the Bronx?"

"The fellow in New Jersey," replied Adonis, referring to Willie Moretti.

"Call up the place opposite Dukes," said Espy. Dukes was a restaurant in Cliffside Park, New Jersey, and Moretti was there nearly all the time. "It's Cliffside 6-1799."

"Okay, kid, see you Friday," said Adonis.

"Wait a minute. Here's Joe," Espy said, as he passed the telephone to Lanza.

"I had a talk with you about a big fat guy," Lanza said cryptically about his associate whom Hogan was looking for.

"Year," Adonis said as he scuffed the receiver.

"He's not in the country," Lanza added.

"No?" Asked Adonis.

"Follow me?"

"Yes."

"Definitely out," Lanza said.

"All right see you Friday or Monday."[14]

Lanza and Haffenden both celebrated Thanksgiving with their families on Thursday, November 26, 1942. A couple of days later they chatted on the phone, but there were no updates about Bridges or Harlem. The only real update that Lanza had for Haffenden was that he'd have some lobster ready for him next week. Then on November 30, 1942, at 11:50 a.m., Haffenden called Lanza with something important.

"How are you?" asked Lanza.

"Fine," replied Haffenden.

"We got all the data for you," Lanza informed him. "Willie could come up or call you up and give it to you."

"I'm very busy right now," answered Haffenden. "I have a million things on my mind. Suppose you call [Sacco] and give it to him?"

"Will you have him call me?"

"Yes."

The next day, Haffenden left New York City, and spent a week in Washington, DC, at ONI Headquarters. He went to Washington once a month, and this was a routine visit. In the meantime, he had his men trying to find the headquarters of another fifth columnist movement known as the Spanish Falange.

The Spanish Falange was a Fascist group that originated in Spain and was plotting against the United States. They were trying to recruit black people in Harlem, just like the Pacific Movement of the Eastern World. The FBI wanted to know if Haffenden might be able to find out where they could find their headquarters.

Lieutenant j.g. Paul Alfieri was already heading up the case. Working with him was Dominick Sacco, who had made contact with an informant in Harlem—a black owner of a cabaret with the last name Brown—thanks to Willie McCabe.[15] Charles Hoyt even helped from time to time, but his task was mainly to use Haffenden's car to drive Sacco around.

Over the course of the next week, thanks to information that was relayed to Alfieri through McCabe, Haffenden was able to learn that the headquarters of the Spanish Falange was the El Chico restaurant in Greenwich Village,[16] and there was another satellite headquarters in Ramapo, New York.

On December 7, 1942,[17] Haffenden got back to town, and at 12:30 p.m., Lanza called 2-7100 and reached Haffenden at Church Street.

"Hello, Socks," Haffenden said in greeting. "How are you?"

"Okay, how did you enjoy your trip?" Lanza asked.

"I had a swell time," replied Haffenden.

"How about having dinner with me?" asked Lanza.

"Joe, I'm busy," Haffenden replied. "Some other time. On that Spanish thing," he said, "I want that fellow to get in touch with me. He did some splendid work." Haffenden was referring to Willie McCabe's work on the Spanish Falange.

"That could be arranged," said Lanza. "When will I see you?"

"I'm leaving now. I'll be in my office at the Astor around 1:30 p.m. Come up to see me."

"Okay," Lanza agreed.

"Listen, Joe. I'd like to get some crab meat and scallops," Haffenden requested. "To go" orders were fulfilled all the time at Fulton Fish Market. Behind the white building, row after row of sawed-off half barrels lined with butcher paper were filled with fish and waiting for someone to pick them up. Haffenden never went to pick up his own orders, which were becoming frequent; he would either have Lanza deliver them or have one of his yeomen pick it up.

"I'll have them ready about three o'clock," Lanza said.

A little over two hours later, Lanza called McCabe.

"Listen," said Lanza. "Remember that spic we took out that one time?"

"Yeah," replied McCabe.

"Well, that's the fellow," Lanza said, referring to a cafe owner. "We want to straighten him out. You get in touch with him and tell him to see the big fellow in Brooklyn and then he'll see the other guy, and get that license straightened out."

Evidently, McCabe was having trouble getting Haffenden's men into a certain cafe. Lanza wanted the owner "straightened out," and that meant getting physical if necessary. The big fellow in Brooklyn was Adonis.

"Now on the other thing," McCabe said, changing the subject.

"Don't see Wade," Lanza said, referring to Haffenden's attaché, Lieutenant Wade. "You see him, you know, the commander."

"Okay," McCabe said.

"And don't see the other guy," Lanza ordered. They had a union identification card that they wanted to go directly to Haffenden, and not be handled by any of his subordinates.[18]

Lanza was growing in confidence about his upcoming case, but even still, he decided to level all his weapons in order to keep himself out of prison. That meant using a weapon that he had neglected up until December 1942—Haffenden. Assistant District Attorney Murray Gurfein had told Lanza to expect no quarter from the courts just because he was doing his part as a citizen of the United States by helping Operation Underworld. But wasn't he doing more than his part? Wasn't he doing great things for the country and the war effort?

Guerin, his attorney, certainly thought so, and the two men agreed that Lanza should talk to Haffenden about helping.

On December 15, 1942, Haffenden called Lanza.

"Oh, hello, Commander, how are you?" asked Lanza.

"Okay," replied Haffenden. "I'm very busy."

"Anything new?" asked Lanza.

"Oh, yes," started Haffenden. "I spoke to the other fellow. I'm to come in before the case goes to the jury. I don't think you'll need me anyway."

Haffenden was about to speak to Judge James Wallace, who was presiding over Lanza's case. The problem was that Haffenden had no clearance from the navy to take such an action. If he had asked his superiors, they would've given him a stern rebuke, but Haffenden wasn't afraid to freelance. Not even MacFall knew he was going to have a chat with Wallace.

"Gee that's fine," Lanza said excitedly. "How about having dinner with me?"

"Well, I don't know, Joe. I've got a lot of work here."

"Try and have dinner with me, yeah?"

"Okay Joe."[19]

Lanza's requests for dinner were constantly being rejected by Haffenden. It wasn't what it was like just a few months ago, when Operation Underworld orbited around Lanza. Haffenden was even busier than before, and Lanza had less to offer now. Not to mention Lanza wanted his help now for the first time. Lanza had a few more moves to make before his case went to trial.

Lanza had been tracking Harry Bridges since he arrived in New York City almost a month prior. Jerry Sullivan, the ILA's chief organizer, informed Lanza that Bridges was speaking at a gathering in Webster Hall on East 11th Street, just north of Lower Manhattan. Lanza headed over there immediately.

Bridges didn't announce the meeting to the press, and nearly held it without any ILA leadership noticing. He had invited a number of rank-and-file longshoremen to hear his words, and that was enough to alert someone who was working undercover for the ILA. In Manhattan and Brooklyn, the underworld had so many ears to the ground that any rumor about a strike found its way to Lanza.

Bridges successfully held his meeting, and as he and his men were packing up, Socks Lanza came charging in out of the freezing cold.

Lanza didn't go about explaining what he was doing for the navy, or the navy's interests in avoiding strikes, or even how it related to the war effort as a whole. Instead, Lanza did what Lanza does—he socked Bridges in the face.[20]

Bridges was tough but not a big man, as one of Lanza's fists was the size of his head. It only took one punch and a threat: If Bridges didn't get out of town immediately, it would get a whole lot worse. Bridges left New York City shortly afterward.

On December 22, 1942, Haffenden followed up on the "Brooklyn Bridge" situation.

"How about the waterfront condition in Brooklyn?" he asked Lanza.

"Bridge's men were stopped," said Lanza proudly. "We saw to that. Everything is under control."

"Swell," Haffenden replied approvingly.

Lanza again requested that the two eat together, but Haffenden was too busy. Besides, he was taking a few days off to spend Christmas with his family. It was time to reflect and look back on a year of a job well done. But before then Haffenden caught up with Polakoff.

"Gee, you sure did a swell job," Haffenden said when he saw Polakoff. "The strike was stopped."[21]

CHAPTER 10

When You Dance with the Devil . . .

Haffenden spent his Christmas with his wife, Mary, and his kids, Charles and Mary Adelaide, and his mother, while Lanza spent the holiday with his wife, Ellen, and his brothers and sisters. For Christmas breakfast Haffenden ate lobster that had been provided by Lanza. Mary cooked it up in the morning, which was becoming common, as Haffenden was receiving weekly seafood deliveries.[1]

Lucky Luciano, on the other hand, spent Christmas alone at Great Meadow prison. His brother Bart had usually made the journey north in the past, but this year he couldn't make it.

Last year—in 1941—it had been a decent Christmas for Luciano. At that time, every prisoner in Dannemora was waiting for their annual Christmas package. They were being put together through charitable donations and were to be distributed by the prison's minister. But given that the war had only started a few weeks prior, everybody's charity went to the war effort, or the Red Cross, and the packages never materialized.

This was deeply concerning to the minister, who knew that many in his congregation were only there because of packages like these. They had food in them—good food—and with the war on, good food was becoming increasingly scarce.

The minister was given the recommendation to visit Charlie

Luciano and see if he could help. Luciano liked to do favors for people. He had, after all, been extremely charitable to other prisoners in the past, even paying legal fees for a desperate guy he didn't really know who was up for an appeal.[2]

So when the minister came calling, Luciano happily gave him the names and phone numbers of people who could help. On December 25, 1941, three trucks loaded to the maximum with packages full of food, fruit, candy, and cigarettes showed up at Dannemora prison.[3] Nineteen forty-one—at Dannemora—was the year that Luciano saved Christmas.

In the words of one of his fellow cons, "It was not a bad Christmas."[4]

Just like all of Luciano's moves in prison, and his previous decisions on how to run the underworld, the packages were a way to make sure that no one had a reason to come after him. It was that attitude that had allowed him to rise as high as he did and hold on to the crown of the underworld for so long.

The end of the year is typically a time of reflection, but life in prison lends itself to that activity year-round. Luciano was feeling particularly nostalgic in the week between Christmas 1942 and New Year's 1943. He was getting ready to receive several special guests. There was the usual crew in Polakoff, Lansky, and Lanza, but this delegation was also going to include his good buddy Mike Lascari, and another man from his past, Michael Miranda.

Michael Miranda—"Big Mike," on account of the irony in how short he was (five foot five)—was about the same age as Luciano, but he was a Neapolitan, just like Vito Genovese. Miranda was very close with Genovese, in that they shared the same passion—murder for hire.

Miranda was one of the most lethal killers that Luciano had ever met. He was a valuable asset back in the early 1930s, after the Castellammarese War had been won. Miaranda even helped Luciano take the throne of the underworld.

After Luciano had Joe "the Boss" Masseria killed, the war

ended, and Salvatore Maranzano declared himself the winner. To him, and him alone, went the spoils, which Luciano knew even then was a mistake.

Brazenly, Maranzano called together every boss from just about every major city in the United States to meet him in the Bronx for a declaration of *Pax Romana*. The Julius Caesar–loving Maranzano packed five hundred underworld leaders in a banquet hall and had them sit before him. He sat in his chair—a throne—while Luciano and a handful of others sat right next to him.

In dramatic fashion Maranzano rose and delivered an address in Italian, mixed with Sicilian, and even Latin. He declared that all past disputes were to be quashed, and a clean slate granted to everyone. He made rules too, such as that none of them could fight with each other, that they couldn't court each other's wives, and that they had to do anything their leader told them.

Then Maranzano made history—for the first time in America, someone organized crime.

He declared himself *Capo di Tutti Capi*—"the Boss of All Bosses." The Caesar-loving Sicilian had become the self-proclaimed ruler of the underworld, and then he explained his vision for the future. He envisioned peace, but fealty. Profits for all, but tribute to him. And he told everyone that his chief lieutenants—his capos—were to run the "Five Families" of New York. Charlie Luciano would run the Luciano family in Manhattan; Vincent Mangano would run Brooklyn, and Tom Gagliano, Joe Bonanno, and Joe Profaci were also to run their own families.

Luciano gathered his board of directors shortly after the meeting in the Bronx. He was tired of bowing to old world leaders and was convinced that there was a better way to run things. His board agreed—they would kill Maranzano. But like always, they waited for the right moment and made sure that the assassination would not start another war. To that end, Luciano, Lansky, and Michael Miranda went on a trip.

The three of them visited some key underworld leaders who had been present at the meeting in the Bronx. They went to the bosses in Pittsburgh, Detroit, Chicago, and Cleveland. Each stop had the same message—Maranzano had to go, and once that was accomplished, Luciano would take over, and either cut himself out, or gave them a better deal on whatever they were doing. Luciano was a Sicilian with American ideas, and he felt that the best way to maintain power was to make sure that nobody wanted a piece of what he had, and nobody was jealous about what he was taking from them.

Miranda, for his part, wasn't brought along to help Luciano and Lansky convey their message.[5] Miranda was around in case any of them decided to not go along with their plan. The people they visited knew who Miranda was, and his presence made an effective deterrent to going against Luciano and Lansky. It worked, as all of the bosses Luciano spoke to agreed to go along.

Soon, Maranzano became apprised of Luciano's treachery, and he put a contract out on Luciano's life. Then, thinking that Luciano didn't know about the contract, he invited him and Genovese—now Luciano's underboss—to his office for a meeting. Luciano quickly gathered his board of directors, and they all agreed that Luciano and Genovese would not walk out of the meeting alive if they went.

So they told Maranzano they'd follow orders and meet him at his office. But when the anointed hour struck on September 10, 1931, Luciano and Genovese stayed away while four hit men arrived at Maranzano's office. They were Jewish—handpicked by Lansky and Siegel—because they knew Maranzano wouldn't recognize them.

That came in handy, because the four of them came disguised as revenue agents, and were able to disarm Maranzano's bodyguards and get Maranzano alone in his office without even firing a shot. Maranzano had tried to live like Julius Caesar, so Luciano's board of directors ordered that he die like the Roman dictator. Two of the hit men began stabbing him repeatedly. But his exit was anything but abrupt, as the forty-five-year-old had plenty of fight in him. They stabbed him six times, but when this failed to kill him, they shot him four times and then finally slit his throat.

Upon receiving confirmation that Maranzano was dead, Luciano and his board unleashed a countrywide purge of the underworld that became known as "the Night of the Sicilian Vespers." Luciano had wooed key allies, but he also knew that some of the bosses would not go along with him. Killers like Vito Genovese, and his friend Michael Miranda, and another killer named Anthony "Tony Bender" Strollo, had a field day.[6] After that, everyone fell into line, and peace reigned throughout the underworld—sort of.

Miranda was technically part of the Luciano family, but he was also part of a faction within the family headed by Genovese. When Genovese was coming up in Greenwich Village, he had been one of Maranzano's top hit men. In the process of committing so many assassinations, he traveled in a trio of non-Sicilians that included himself, Miranda, and Bender. The three had no problem making moves without Luciano's consent, and that had only increased since Luciano went to prison. They were a powerful faction within the Luciano family. So powerful that Luciano had to make Genovese his underboss to appease them.

Just over eleven years after they took out Maranzano, on December 29, 1942, Michael Miranda was to be Luciano's guest at Great Meadow prison. Luciano had no idea why Miranda was coming to see him—it was Lansky's idea, after all.

Was there word from Genovese in Italy?

Did someone need to be killed?

On December 29, 1942, at 10 a.m., Luciano received Moses Polakoff, Meyer Lansky, Michael Lascari, and Michael Miranda in the office next to the warden's, at Great Meadow prison.[7]

Socks Lanza was a late scratch to the meeting, as he was now completely embroiled in his case, which was to be brought before the court in just six days. That was no matter for Luciano, as Lanza had been a nonfactor in the last two meetings. Operation Underworld was becoming less and less of a priority for Luciano.

They all greeted each other warmly with laughter, hugs, and wishes of Merry Christmas and a Happy New Year.

The first order of business for Luciano involved Polakoff. He wanted to know if he had come up with any ideas about how to get him out of prison. Polakoff said that he had thought of something.

What had Polakoff thought of?

The sentence Luciano received had been severe—overly severe. Whoever heard of a thirty-to-fifty-year sentence? Polakoff felt that they could take a shot at appealing the sentence. After all, he argued, the severity of Luciano's crimes should have dictated that he receive ten years in prison at a maximum.

Luciano was enthusiastic. What was the plan?

Polakoff wanted to bring in an expert, someone who was better suited than himself to challenge the sentence.[8] His recommendation was a lawyer named George Wolf. Wolf had been an attorney for thirty years and had tried many criminal cases, Polakoff told Luciano, and he would take care of retaining him personally.

What did Luciano need to do?

Polakoff told Luciano he'd have to sign a letter that said Mr. Wolf was allowed to represent him, but other than that, Polakoff would handle all other arrangements.

Luciano didn't even get to meet this guy?

Polakoff vouched for Wolf and told Luciano that this was his best shot at getting out. And as an added benefit, an appeal right now was great timing, because they could tell the court about Luciano's contribution to the war effort. The judge was a veteran, after all.

Absolutely not!

Luciano reminded everyone present that he still had a deportation order to deal with. If he got booted to Italy, the government there could have him killed for helping the Americans. After all, the war wasn't going so great for the Allies. They had made strides with an invasion of North Africa, but had yet to put a single boot on the ground in Europe. Who knew what could happen? Mussolini could still come out of this thing on top.

It was agreed—Luciano's help to the navy was not to be used in his appeal. However, Polakoff was given the green light to retain Wolf. Polakoff then excused himself to the corner with an edition of the day's newspaper.

Now, what was Miranda doing there?

Lansky took the floor. Evidently, Commander Haffenden had told him something that couldn't leave the room.

It was considered "top secret."

Haffenden had requested that Lansky ask Luciano to do what he could to get Italians to come to his office.

Italians?

Like people from Italy, who'd lived there, especially recently. Why?

The Commander wouldn't say, but Lansky thought maybe the navy was planning an invasion.

Where did Miranda fit in?

Lansky told Luciano that he was going to bring up a delicate subject, and it would require his patience. Luciano's curiosity was piqued, but he prepared to get upset. Lansky continued that they all knew that in the past, Miranda and Anthony "Tony Bender" Strollo had managed to smuggle drugs into New York City from Vito Genovese's European connections. Before Luciano could say anything, Miranda assured him that he was not doing that anymore (not because he didn't want to, but because he couldn't, as Mussolini had shut it down). Then Lansky got to the point: Maybe Miranda still knew some of the Italian and Sicilian smugglers, and maybe some of them were in New York. And they were probably in Brooklyn.

Miranda was friends with several Italian criminals from the old days, and that included Vincent Mangano of Brooklyn. Mangano wasn't the most ardent supporter of Operation Underworld, but there were two things Lansky knew about him—out of all the underworld bosses, he did the most business with Italy, which mainly consisted of legitimate importing and exporting of olive oil and wine as a front for smuggling drugs and contraband. Also, out of all the underworld bosses, Mangano hated Mussolini the most. Mussolini had shut down this operation altogether. Mangano might be looking for some payback, and since Miranda knew the valuable people in Mangano's territory, perhaps he could convince Mangano to provide them to Naval Intelligence.

It was agreed, Miranda would approach Mangano about bringing Italians to the commander.

Now Miranda, speaking in Italian—his English was very poor, and he didn't speak Sicilian because he was a Neapolitan—told Luciano that Genovese had reached out to him from Italy. Genovese also reached out to another mutual friend, Tony Bender. Since Genovese fled to Italy, he had mainly relied on Miranda and Bender to communicate messages to the US. Whatever business brought the three of them together meant one of two things—drugs or death.

Genovese, as it turned out, was requesting permission to have someone taken out. This someone was causing problems for him over in Italy, and . . .

Luciano cut Miranda off. He didn't want to hear another word. Genovese did not have his permission. He didn't want to know about it. Whatever Genovese ordered Miranda, or their other murdering friend Tony Bender, to do was not okay. Miranda said that he didn't think he would be able to stop it from happening. Luciano, knowing that he needed Miranda and realizing that his own power was very limited given his status as an inmate in Great Meadow prison, could only tell Miranda that he didn't have his permission. There wasn't much else he could do to prevent it from happening. This faction within his family was formidable, and Luciano would never forget it.[9]

After three hours and forty-five minutes, the men prepared to leave Luciano.

Then Luciano told Lansky and Lascari, "Tell Joe [Lanza] to keep working the way he is doing, and work goddamned hard."

They wished each other a Happy New Year, and Luciano was less than thrilled, knowing that New Year's in prison was no holiday. He went back to his cell knowing that it would be another New Year without a broad to kiss at midnight.

Another transcript from District Attorney Frank Hogan's wiretap on Meyer's Hotel came through before 1942 came to an end. On New Year's Eve at 1:05 p.m., Hogan received confirmation that Operation Underworld was indeed functioning, albeit on a violent level he had never expected.

"Hello, Guy," Ben Espy said. "Guy" was none other than Joe Adonis.[10] "There's a guy over in the Brooklyn Navy Yard by the name of Jack Gilbert," continued Espy. "That's the name he fought under, he's a special operator over there, I think his real name is Ed Strand. He got in some difficulty over there and got very mouthy and he said he knows you very well and can do anything with you. A fellow was here yesterday who knows all about the questioning and we told him the guy is a loon. It would be very advisable to kick him in the ass."

Then Espy passed the phone to Lanza. "Hello, Guy, how are you?"

"Okay, Joe," Adonis responded. "I'll catch up with you Saturday, then I can talk to you."

Hogan couldn't believe his eyes when he read the transcript. The navy was using underworld muscle on the waterfront to keep things under control.

And that wasn't all. The transcripts seemed to reveal that Haffenden was beginning to act like the gangsters he was interacting with daily. After all, Haffenden was regularly taking free gifts in the form of expensive seafood, which was taboo in law enforcement (and counterintelligence). Accepting gifts from informants made the person receiving the gift want to do something to pay it back. Now Haffenden was meeting with a judge—without permission from the navy—in an effort to influence his decision on a known criminal. It was also evident that Haffenden was using thugs to beat up people on the waterfront who were out of line, and others who were trying to advance the cause of labor rights.

Haffenden was winning the battle on the home front to be sure, but it appeared that he was in a dangerous dance with the devil.

What other lengths could Haffenden go to?

It wasn't his intention, but Haffenden's actions were ensuring that the Italian and Irish gangs were being empowered to strengthen their hold on the waterfront. The well-being of the longshoremen who toiled on the docks and piers by loading America's ships for war was an afterthought, if even that.

As for "Jack Gilbert," or "Ed Strand" as he might've been called, nobody knew what happened to him.

PART III

CHAPTER 11
Black January

At midnight on January 1, 1943, a crowd of four hundred thousand soldiers, men, women, and teenagers gathered in Times Square to celebrate the New Year. But because the lights had to be out at night to protect Allied ships in the harbor, they weren't there to watch the ball drop at midnight. For the first time since 1908, the ball was not going to be used to ring in the New Year. Instead, New Yorkers and visiting soldiers packed the subway and taxicabs to Times Square and came armed with every kind of noisemaker they could find. At midnight, after observing a few moments of silence for the fallen, a choir of noise: trucks, and people with rubber "blurpers," cowbells, and horns erupted in the night. Air raid searchlights crisscrossed the sky. It was a weird ode to the old New Year's tradition, "ring out the old, and ring in the new." The whole event was a sign that the world still had a long way to go before normalcy returned.[1]

In January 1943, the Allies took stock of their accomplishments and failures, and taken together, things could have been better, but they also could have been a lot worse. The Battle of the Atlantic was now, thankfully, raging farther out on the high seas, as the United States had finally launched enough warships to successfully defend its own waters. However, German U-boats were still having tremendous success in the middle of the North

Atlantic—so much success that at the beginning of 1943, Britain was down to just two months' worth of its oil supply.

As it turned out, the Allies learned that U-boats were not receiving aid from mainland North America. There were no rumrunners running fuel and water to U-boats. Instead, big German "milk cow" U-boats were refueling and resupplying the submarines out at sea. As for the intelligence that reported fresh sliced bread aboard a U-boat, no one was able to explain that one.

Victory on the waterfront, and the home front as a whole, was all but complete by January 1943. Lieutenant Commander Charles Haffenden and the men of B-3 had successfully brought any and all subversive activity toward the United States in New York City to its knees. Every section of the Port of New York was under their control, just in time for a massive influx in men and supplies as the Allies prepared to launch another offensive.

Operation Torch—the Allied invasion of French West Africa in November 1942—was moving along, though at a snail's pace. The Germans and Italians clung to Tunisia, while British forces from the east and American forces from the west closed in. Most of Vichy French West Africa had been taken by the US Army, and in a power move, on January 14, 1943, Allied leadership planned to meet in newly conquered territory—Casablanca.

There, President Franklin Roosevelt; England's prime minister, Winston Churchill; and their respective joint chiefs were going to decide where to allocate their resources for their next invasion of Axis territory. And while the site of the invasion had yet to be determined in the lead-up to the Allied meeting at Casablanca, Commander Haffenden had already received orders to begin collecting information on possible targets. During the previous month, the Third Naval District started devoting sections of their command to collecting data on different countries in Europe.

Haffenden's own command was divided, as he kept many of his agents on the waterfront, and in the bars, hotels, nightclubs, and restaurants in New York City, but now he also devoted men to a new "target" section.

"Target" section was to develop intelligence—through informants or any other means possible—about prospective targets that the Allies might attack in Europe. As the United States high command and military planners began to look at what intelligence they had gathered about possible battlegrounds overseas, they realized that they had next to nothing to help them plan an attack—no charts, no maps, no idea about topography, infrastructure, local economies, or local mores and customs. Anything they could've used from WWI was nonexistent.

Naval Intelligence, which had been the only intelligence outfit in the military between the two world wars, was not given any resources to develop information about possible foreign enemies until 1942. It left a large enough void in the high command's planning that they had to resort to other methods of gaining the information they needed. So for ONI target section I (the "I" in which stood for "Italy"), the high command realized that the United States had a unique advantage over every country in the world—there were more Italians in America than anywhere else, save Italy itself.

At the beginning of the war, the fact that the United States was a nation full of immigrants had been deemed a threat by the high command and federal government. By early 1943 it had been realized that the immigrant population was actually a potent weapon to combat the enemy. In just a year's time, Italian-Americans had gone from "enemy aliens" to "allies." As Haffenden began to carry out orders to develop intelligence on possible target areas, he first contacted two of his most important informants—Meyer Lansky and Socks Lanza.

As a result of this need for Italians and Sicilians, Lansky had contacted Michael Miranda and brought him to see Luciano. Lansky told Haffenden that Miranda would help with Vincent Mangano to gain access to the Italians working in Brooklyn. There were a lot of Italians working on the docks there too, and when Haffenden contacted Lanza, he also came calling to Brooklyn.[2]

Lanza knew of two Italians in Brooklyn who had recently come to the United States. Lanza reached out to the Camarda brothers, and Lanza brought the two men to see Haffenden at the Hotel Astor. Fortunately, these men spoke English. The two Italian men then went inside Haffenden's office in room 196—more than a little confused as to why they were there—while Lanza waited in room 198.

The two Italians took seats in front of Haffenden, and Haffenden began asking them questions.

What kind of work had they recently done in Italy?

The two men explained that they had been performing maintenance on ships that came into port.

Where were these men working?

These two men were extremely valuable because they had last been working in a port in Sicily. In fact, they had visited many ports on boats that went in and out of various Sicilian harbors. Haffenden was pleased, as Sicily was one of the priorities of target section I.

Haffenden spent hours with these men, talking about everything from the kinds of ships that went in and out of certain ports, to Italian customs in the areas they had worked.

What kind of infrastructure? Where was the local government? Was there a German garrison there? Were the Italians there friendly to the Mussolini regime? Was the Sicilian mafiosi there?

When the two men emerged from Haffenden's office, Lanza escorted them out. He asked them how the meeting went.

"Well," one of the Italians started, "he wanted to know an awful lot about Italy."

"That's what you went there to tell him," Lanza reassured the man.[3]

On January 4, 1943, Socks Lanza arrived at general sessions court, and listened as the prosecutor—Sol Gelb, who was a man who worked directly under Frank Hogan—laid out a scathing argument for Lanza's and his four co-conspirators' guilt. Over the next three days, Gelb thundered away, and had the five defendants shifting in their seats.

On January 7, 1943, he delivered the kill shot. Sol Schuster—

the former president of Teamsters Local 202 that Lanza had threatened and pointed a gun at—took the stand for the prosecution. Schuster arrived shackled, and had made a deal to turn over Lanza and his co-conspirators in exchange for time off of his sentence. He was embroiled in a plot of his own and was happy to "roll over" on Lanza to save his own skin.[4]

After Schuster's damning testimony, Gelb rested his case. He had done such a good job of presenting the case, and Schuster's testimony was so convincing, that Lanza and his attorney, Joseph Guerin, knew they had absolutely no chance at mounting a defense to disprove the charges.

On January 12, 1943, Guerin told the judge that Lanza and the codefendants wanted to change their plea to guilty on all counts. Lanza was to turn himself over on January 27, and would wait for his sentence in the Tombs, which would be his second visit in two months.[5]

Amid the fighting, genocide, and chaos of World War II, Vito Genovese was in Italy, enjoying himself as a guest in the Fascist Party's court. Despite his Mafia ties in America, he contributed funds to the party, and succeeded in charming the ruler of Italy—Benito Mussolini. But his true value came to Italy's foreign minister Galeazzo Ciano, who was Mussolini's son-in-law.[6]

Ciano had a cocaine habit, and Genovese's talent for smuggling drugs fed the addiction. Since Genovese left the United States in 1937, he'd been setting up drug networks that flowed through the veins of Axis-occupied Europe. Ciano even supplied a plane for Genovese so he could pick up contraband in North Africa and the Middle East and bring it back to Italy for distribution.

What had caused him to flee the United States was a case that had been building against him for years. Back in 1934, in a power grab, he targeted another gangster named Ferdinand Boccia.

Genovese; Michael Miranda; Tony Bender; and three others ambushed and shot Boccia to death at a coffee shop in Brooklyn. They then took his body, drove it all the way across Manhattan, and dumped it into the Hudson River. Shortly thereafter, one of the gunmen—a man named Ernest "the Hawk" Rupolo—was picked up for attempted murder on a different crime. At the time, District Attorney Thomas Dewey, it was rumored, was trying to turn Rupolo against Genovese.

Miranda, for his part, stuck around and tried to lie low, as charges hadn't actually been filed against any of them in the Boccia murder. He ran a legitimate business as the owner of the Progresso restaurant in Manhattan. But Genovese was a boss, and was right in the crosshairs of a very determined Dewey. He had no intention of going down like Luciano did. Fortunately for Genovese, he had been stashing hundreds of thousands of dollars in Swiss bank accounts for years as a contingency plan for escape. The threat from Dewey made him skip town, and of all the other countries he could've gone to, he chose Italy, where he had previously made contacts with drug smugglers in Naples (where he was originally from).

There were no formal charges against him—no outstanding indictment. Yet he remained in Italy, hedging his bets and seeing which side was going to come out of the war on top. To remain in the good graces of Mussolini himself—to show off—Genovese ordered a hit on a man in New York City.

On January 11, 1943, a man named Carlo Tresca—an anticommunist and anti-fascist who wrote for the Italian-American publication *Il Martello* ("The Hammer") and had personally insulted Mussolini years prior—emerged from his office on 96 Fifth Avenue, in the heart of downtown Manhattan. Tresca was an idealist of the highest degree and was extremely outspoken about his hatred for the government in his native Italy. To his readership, he was a hero, but to Mussolini, he was a very public nuisance, and Il Duce had a personal vendetta against Tresca, to boot.

At 9:45 p.m. Tresca was walking beside a coworker when a black Ford sedan pulled up behind him. A psychopathic but skilled killer named Carmine Galante opened the back passenger door and aimed a small .32-caliber pistol at Tresca.

Galante fired three shots, and one of them struck Tresca in the lung and spun him around. Now looking squarely at his killer, Tresca departed instantly when one last bullet struck him in the face. Galante then got back in the car while another man—Tony Bender—drove him away.[7]

When Luciano found out about the Tresca murder, he was furious. It was an unauthorized assassination, and an extremely public one at that.

Was Genovese still in the Luciano family?

Was Genovese signaling that he was now a part of the Fascist Italian government?

Was Genovese still loyal to Luciano?

If Luciano did end up in Italy, could he even trust that Genovese would help him—let alone let him live?

If word got out that Genovese had carried out the murder of Tresca without Luciano's consent, that would weaken his position with the other bosses who were part of *El Unione Council*—"the Commission"—that Luciano had previously established. If it looked like Luciano couldn't control his own family, then it might embolden the others to go after his business.[8] The Commission was what governed the five families of New York (families in Chicago and Buffalo were also a part of the Commission). Luciano was the one who created and oversaw it, and he knew that Genovese wanted control of it. They established it together, after all, right after they had Maranzano killed back on September 10, 1931.

On September 10, 1931, at the moment after Maranzano's assassination, Charles "Lucky" Luciano—who was only thirty-four years old—had become king of the underworld. He had not only bested and toppled Joe "the Boss" Masseria, but also Salvatore Maranzano, who was the *Capo di Tutti Capi*—"the Boss of All Bosses." After the "Night of the Sicilian Vespers," the heads of the five families of New York and the heads of crime families all over the country stood ready to bow to Luciano and swear their fealty.

Luciano may have been a Sicilian—who constantly clashed

with others for power—but when he stood atop the underworld, he did a most American thing: He gave up his power.[9] Luciano knew that if he sat at the top of that criminal juggernaut, it was only a matter of time before one of his own tried to kill him in an effort to take the throne. Plus, the heads of a hydra are far more difficult to decapitate than a single snake.

Maranzano had done the hard part—he organized the five families and the others around the country. Luciano was fine with that structure. Luciano was also tired of the ultimate goal of Sicilian bosses' old thinking: Rise to the top. This was America, and there was so much money to be made that it could be spread around to more than accommodate everyone. It was a model he created when he was a child.

Why should they devote their time and resources to going to war with each other?

Luciano was a hybrid gangster, with Sicilian cunning and foresight mixed with American ambition and dreams. If he could get all of the other gangsters in the underworld to focus on their business, then he figured they would stay the hell out of his. And as long as he was running things, he would run them like a corporation, complete with a board of directors.

In place of *Capo di Tutti Capi*, Luciano created *El Unione Council*—"the Commission." An equal say in mutual business was given to the heads of seven crime families—the five heads in New York City, plus Al Capone (who was originally from Brooklyn) in Chicago and Stefano Magaddino in Buffalo. They were to clear all major decisions with each other *before* acting, to prevent any bad blood that might start a war.

Some other old traditions were done away with, such as the ban on doing business with non-Italians. To preserve the peace among the seven families of *Unione Sicilione*—the "Mafia"— Luciano kept the Commission to Sicilians only, but there was no longer an embargo on Italians from the mainland becoming members, which was in part a nod to Vito Genovese. Membership in each family could still only be Italians, but it was now permissible to do business with anyone they saw fit to—Jews, Irish, and other Americans.

In the end, not many of their traditions were done away with. The Commission maintained the utmost secrecy and still adhered to the old world *omertà* code. *Omertà* precluded them from ever talking to authorities, or even their spouses, about what they called *Cosa Nostra*—"this thing of ours." More often than not, the punishment for violating *omertà*, especially in the case of dealing with authorities, was death.

Omertà was put to the test when the district attorney picked Joe "Socks" Lanza to be a part of Operation Underworld, and also presented a gray area for Luciano. It wasn't like the *Unione Sicilione* to choose their country over their code. This generation of criminals were different, however, as Luciano and *Cosa Nostra* Americanized organized crime.

When Luciano got back to business late in 1931, with all of the families in the country doing the same, he began enjoying the best years of his life. Unfortunately, they were abruptly followed by the worst years of his life.

From his prison cell in Dannemora, and then Great Meadow prison, he still held his seat on the Commission, and with limited communication, he had to rely on others to make most of the decisions. Costello and Genovese—as his underbosses—represented his interests on the Commission. When he got out, if the two men had a problem with him being the boss of the family again, he would confront them with whatever it took.

Costello wasn't a worry, but Genovese certainly was. When Genovese left for Italy, Luciano gave him his blessing because, even back in 1937, he knew that he had a deportation order, and Genovese could help him if he ever went to Italy. But trouble followed when Genovese wanted to appoint Tony Bender as the Luciano family's acting boss. Luciano believed that it was not Genovese's call to make, so he forcefully installed Costello as his acting boss. Plus, this recent Tresca murder was a clear show of force against Luciano. Luciano had long suspected that Genovese desired the crown—not just of the Luciano family but to bring back the title of *Capo di Tutti Capi*.

If Genovese got back to America and managed to stay out of jail, Luciano had to get out of prison to prevent being muscled out. Something in his gut—his *intuizione Siciliana*—told him that however everything played out, Genovese was going to be a problem for him.

"Socks" Lanza was a busy man in the final days of January 1943. He was attempting some last desperate measures to keep himself out of prison. He met with Costello on Wednesday the 20th, at the Madison Hotel. Then he met Costello again at the Madison that Saturday at 5 p.m.[10] They were trying to influence the judge as much as possible, but they weren't getting anywhere.

On January 26, 1943, Willie McCabe talked to Murray Gurfein about Lanza's case. Gurfein didn't want to hear it and reiterated that there were no deals for criminals. McCabe then called Espy at Meyer's Hotel at 3:45 p.m.

"I called that party up and I'm afraid it's no good," McCabe started, referring to Gurfein. "I told him all, and he seems to know everything. The reaction was completely different." McCabe had brought up Lanza's involvement in Operation Underworld to Gurfein, and Gurfein was unimpressed.

"His mind is made up?" Espy asked.

"Definitely," answered McCabe. "I said Colonel, look back fifteen years—the same thing happened to me." "Colonel" was Lieutenant Colonel Gurfein. "Geez, in a way I'm sorry I started the whole thing but you know how much I like Joe," McCabe said, referring to Lanza. "Christ, I would go out and beg, borrow, or steal for him."

"Yeah, I know, Bill," said Espy. "How about the fellow across town?" he asked, referring to Commander Haffenden.

"Church Street?"

"Yeah."

"I called him and he's the same," McCabe said. "He knows

about me and I got a rebuke. Joe should've started that a long time ago." "That" was referring to talking to Gurfein and the judge.

"Oh, he's like a child," Espy said about Lanza, taking full advantage of his first opportunity to vent about his boss. "First he believes one and then the other. The last one to get his ear is the winner. I could see through him all the time. They can say what they want but I got plenty of respect for the little fellow downtown," he added, referring to Assistant District Attorney Sol Gelb. "He presented such overwhelming evidence in such a dignified manner that defense counsel was floundering. He was very fair and I know he gave them a break. He could have refused plea and continued right along and they would have been in a worse fix."

"Well, they're on the other side of the fence," McCabe said. "I'm sorry what I done, but Benny, after tomorrow night I'm going away for two weeks. When I come back everything will be different."

"I hope so," said Espy.

"After tomorrow night I'm leaving," McCabe repeated. "I'm sick and tired of fucking around."

"Okay, Willie," Espy affirmed.

On January 27, 1942, Lanza was taken into custody and remanded to the Tombs. He was to wait there for three days, until sentencing. But he had one last hope to get himself freed—Commander Haffenden.

Later on the 27th, at 4:15 p.m., Espy called Haffenden at his Church Street office.

"Commander Hefferman?" Espy started. Espy, like Lanza, still struggled with Haffenden's name.

"Yes."

"Ben Espy."

"How are you, Ben?" Haffenden asked.

"Very well, thanks," Espy replied.

"No word today," said Haffenden.

"No, that party was sick," Espy said, referring to the judge in Lanza's case.

"Yes," affirmed Haffenden.

"I wonder if I could fix up a little something for tomorrow," Espy offered.

"Okay," Haffenden said. "I don't like to bother you, Ben."

"It's no bother, Commander, it's a pleasure."

"Well, it's always welcome," said Haffenden.

"Joe's brother saw him today and he feels swell," Espy informed Haffenden.

"That's swell."

"He wants to let you know how much he appreciates everything," Espy said.

"That's quite all right, Ben."

"I'll make up a package for you tomorrow," Espy offered.

"That's swell, Ben. I could eat them every day in the week. My wife cooks them for breakfast," said Haffenden, referring to the lobster that Lanza gave him.

"In that case I'll make up an extra package."

"Oh, Ben, that's too much."

"It's been a pleasure, Commander," said Espy. "I'll have them ready when the yeoman comes for them tomorrow, say at five o'clock."

The next day Haffenden went and visited the judge in Lanza's case. Haffenden told the judge about the help that Lanza had given the navy in the war effort. Haffenden would have been in deep trouble if anyone found out that he had talked to the judge on Lanza's behalf, but Haffenden was never afraid to go off the reservation and do as he pleased. He also saw value in doing favors for the Luciano family, in case down the road a relationship with them could come in handy. He was beginning to think that after the war was over, there would be some position of more power that might open up for him.

Unfortunately, the judge was not receptive to Haffenden, who tried to deliver as few details as possible while also praising Lanza. The lack of detail hurt Lanza's chances, but Haffenden was only willing to go so far and disclose so much. Later in the day, two packages of lobster were delivered to him at his office in the Hotel Astor.

The following day, on January 29, 1942, Lanza appeared in court shackled with his four co-defendants and waited for the judge's sentence.

Lanza's lawyer, Guerin, explained to the judge that Lanza was the sole support for his wife, widowed mother, and eight younger brothers and sisters. Guerin also tried to tell the judge that Lanza was a great organizer and a union champion. He said that Lanza was an "asset to the community." The judge cut Guerin off right there.

"He was an unmitigated nuisance to the community!" the judge interjected.

Because of Lanza having previous convictions on his record, the fact that his record indicated that he had never even attempted to have a legitimate job, and the judge's prediction that when he got out of prison Lanza would go right back to what he had been doing, the judge said, "I am doing my bit." Then he gave Lanza a seven-and-a-half to fifteen-year sentence in Auburn state prison. Lanza was then taken away.[11]

Later in the day, at 4:30 p.m., Haffenden heard the news about Lanza and called Espy at Meyer's Hotel.

"Hello, Commander," said Espy.

"That's a damn shame," Haffenden said, referring to the outcome of Lanza's case.

"Yes, it is," Espy agreed.

"I just dictated a letter to Albany," Haffenden told Espy. "And my man up there is going to see the commissioner." Haffenden was referring to Commissioner Lyons.

"Very good, Commander."

"I was speaking to Joe Guerin and I told him the way the judge spoke to me; he made no promises, he gave him the book."

"Yes," Espy agreed.

"He couldn't give him any more," said Haffenden.

"Sweezey came in and spoke to the judge for three-quarters of an hour," Espy told Haffenden. Lanza had been courting Hiram Sweezey from Long Island for about a month to speak with the judge. Sweezey was an honest businessman and was something of a character witness for Lanza.

"He did?" Haffenden asked, a bit surprised about Sweezey's involvement.

"Yes, he was very much interested in Sweezey," said Espy about the judge. "He asked him all questions about money."

"He certainly is a son of a gun," Haffenden said about Sweezey, smiling. Haffenden really liked Sweezey.

"Yes," Espy agreed.

"Well, listen, Ben," Haffenden started, "I'll have my man go see the commissioner, and then see what happens. I'm sorry. I feel like I let him down. I could have taken more belligerent steps; the judge is very dramatic. If I knew he was going to do this, I would've handled him different."

"We're all very grateful for you, Commissioner," Espy said, getting the "commissioner" and the "commander" mixed up.

"Well, if I'm here five years from now I may be of more help," Haffenden said.

"Thank you, sir," Espy said.

"Keep in touch with me, Ben."

"Thank you, sir, I will. Goodbye."

"So long, Ben."[12]

Joe "Socks" Lanza and Ben Espy's role in Operation Underworld had come to an end. Losing Lanza was a blow to Haffenden's operations around New York City, and if that wasn't enough, Haffenden also lost another one of Operation Underworld's most valuable gangsters—Johnny "Cockeye" Dunn. His coercion case was settled within days of Lanza's case, and Dunn was remanded to Rikers Island prison after being given a three-year sentence. With the added death of Tresca—rumors were flying about Mafia involvement in the murder—January had been a very dark month for Operation Underworld.

But Haffenden lost Lanza and Dunn at a time when the mission for Operation Underworld was changing, as his new target section was just getting going. As bad as losing those two men was to Haffenden, he didn't really need them anymore, as the Port of New York was very much under the control of the Mafia and the navy. Haffenden was still armed with the word of Lucky Luciano and had his support for Operation Underworld, which was more than enough to keep target section humming.

CHAPTER 12
The Devil's in the Details

Commander Charles Haffenden had created thousands of informants during his time at B-3 section of Naval Intelligence. To some of the people within Haffenden's section, his use of underworld informants to gather intelligence was a known fact. But after Captains MacFall and Howe, and a few need-to-knows at the District Attorney's Office, the only person outside of B-3 that knew about Operation Underworld and Lucky Luciano was the spymaster in Washington.

It had been an incredible accomplishment for Haffenden, as while he protected the identities of his informants, they also produced valuable intelligence that was forwarded to Naval Intelligence in the nation's capital. The passing of flimsies from New York City to Washington and vice versa was a success. Hundreds of thousands of small blue, yellow, and white pieces of paper were responsible for the flow of information that kept military planners apprised of the situation on the ground, while the commanders in those home-front battlegrounds ran their missions, and kept their sources a secret.

By February 1943, the process for gathering, communicating, and analyzing intelligence had been perfected. And while the process was certainly not going to change, the mission of B-3 section did change to something else.

After US naval high command identified several targets to

focus on, Haffenden's target section was ordered not only to secure information, but also to process that information. Furthermore, if it was determined that the information was accurate, Haffenden was to indicate on a map where and how this intelligence was applicable. It was a massive reorganization of B-3, and required Haffenden to bring in new specialists, including mapmakers and artists.

But for the process of gathering intelligence, not much changed for Haffenden, as he already had a massive network of Italians at his disposal. If the target of the next Allied invasion turned out to be in Italy, Haffenden knew he was in a fantastic position to provide intelligence that might be read by the top echelon of battle planners. It was another—even better—opportunity to shine.

The Luciano network of informants was a great resource for Haffenden, and thanks to Luciano, Haffenden was receiving cooperation for target section. Michael Miranda had done his part in talking to Vincent Mangano in Brooklyn. He told him that the purpose of providing Italians to the navy was to gather information that would lead to an invasion of Italy. Mangano—no fan of Mussolini—jumped at the opportunity, and even decided to meet with Haffenden.

When Mangano came to the Hotel Astor, Haffenden informed Elizabeth Schwerin that their adjoining door was to remain locked, and she was not to disturb the meeting. Sometimes, when Haffenden had important meetings, he sent her away, but this time, she was only told to get rid of the receptionist in room 200. In an effort to be discreet, Haffenden was going to have his guests enter through the main door of his office and bypass Schwerin.

Mangano didn't come alone; he had three of his bodyguards and advisors with him. Mangano had chubby cheeks that made his face look round. He was in his mid-fifties, with a receding hairline, droopy eyes, and a cold stare that made him look angry. The group entered Haffenden's office in room 196 and listened as the commander told them what he needed. He offered them drinks, and they accepted.

Haffenden made a call to the Hotel Astor bar and told them that he wanted cocktails delivered to room 200. When they arrived, the waiter left them in the room, and Schwerin called Haffenden via their interoffice communication to tell him that the drinks were there. Haffenden told her to bring them in, and she did so. Haffenden was happy that his visitors were having a drink, and happy because he needed one himself to steady his nerves.

The navy was looking for Italians, and Haffenden had been informed that there were a lot of Italians working as longshoremen loading the ships in Brooklyn. But there were others too of all professions, and someone like Mangano, who knew a lot of Italians, could be very helpful. Especially because he had been able to conduct business with Italy even during the war, which meant he might know people who'd been to Italy recently. Those people were the most valuable to Haffenden, as they could give him a current and accurate picture of the places they had visited.

Haffenden reminded Mangano that Luciano wanted him to go along, and then Haffenden held his breath. Haffenden had already established contacts within Mangano's territory. Given Mangano's negative feelings about Adonis working with Luciano, telling him that Luciano was making this request could've gone both ways.

But Mangano told Haffenden that he hated Mussolini, and that he was happy to help the navy. With Lanza gone, Haffenden had lost his link to Brooklyn, so he was happy that Mangano would bring the navy any Italians in Brooklyn who could help.

Then, the men left out of room 196 into the hallway of the mezzanine level and out of the Hotel Astor. Haffenden was so giddy that he just had to tell someone. In exuberant fashion, he called Schwerin into his office and told her that these men were close associates of Luciano.

"Did you recognize who that was?" asked Haffenden.

"No," Schwerin answered.

"Do you know who [Vincent Mangano] is?"

"Oh, yes I do," Schwerin said in a state of disbelief.

"He's a very important underworld figure, and it's a name you might read about in the papers," Haffenden told her, gloating.[1]

* * *

Mangano's cooperation led to a more involved presence by Joe Adonis, and to show it, six Italians were rounded up and led by Adonis to meet with Meyer Lansky.[2] Lansky, Adonis, and the six Italians went to 50 Church Street, where Haffenden was waiting for them. Fifty Church Street—just down the street from the giant Third Naval District Headquarters—was smaller and was under much heavier security given the highly sensitive material behind its doors.

As they were waiting, one of the Italians expressed to Adonis that he was nervous and had changed his mind about talking to the navy. These men had been schooled in the Padrone System, and talking to the navy felt like a violation of that code.

"Lucky Luciano is giving you an order to talk," said Adonis.

But the Italian was still nervous and said he wouldn't go in.

The soft features on Adonis's handsome face dropped. He looked angry and stared the Italian man in the eyes and said, "Lucky will not be pleased to hear that you have not been helpful."[3]

The Italian man changed his mind and decided he would talk.

Adonis didn't want to go in, and having delivered the Italians to the navy, he felt he had done his part.[4] Lansky stayed with the Italians as they checked in with the armed Marine guards and were escorted through the front door. A quarter of one floor had been opened, as the interior walls and partitions had been jettisoned in favor of an open-office concept.

As Haffenden escorted the men to a far wall, they passed a series of other men hard at work, drawing on drafting tables and creating visual images based on the words printed on flimsies, books, and photographs.[5]

When Haffenden, Lansky, and the six Italians arrived at the correct spot, they were introduced to Lieutenant Anthony Marzulo,[6] who they were told spoke Italian and Sicilian and would serve as a translator if needed. Haffenden also introduced them to Lieutenant J. E. Jamison. Lieutenant Jamison had been an aide to Haffenden for nearly a year, and though he was no expert, he was being used as a mapmaker.

Prior to their arrival, Haffenden had been able to get word to Adonis through Lansky to make sure that the six Italians brought any photographs, books, or documents they had that had anything to do with Italy.

Each man produced various photographs, books, and even postcards from coastal towns. Of particular importance were any photographs that might show the terrain of the coastline, the inlet to channels, or the layout of ports.[7] Haffenden collected all of this intelligence and held on to it with the promise that each man would get back what he had provided.[8]

The conversation then shifted to their personal knowledge of Italy. It was important to establish when the last time was that they had been to any town or city. If it was a long time ago, then Haffenden would ask them only about terrain and topography, but if they had been there recently he also asked about the strength of German garrisons and fixed fortifications.

Through these conversations that were going on between Haffenden, Marzulo, Jamison, and the Italians, they learned that one of these men was formerly the mayor of a town in Sicily.

Jamison walked to a wall cabinet that held dozens of maps that were three feet wide and four feet long. Each map was contained in a drawer and had a plastic overlay that could be written on with a wet-erase pen. The maps were framed in wood and could be removed from the cabinet very easily. Jamison looked for one of these maps in particular, and placed it on a table.[9] There on the map was the island of Sicily.

The mayor was part of the Masonic order, as it turned out, and one of the other Italians—who was actually Sicilian—was a mason as well. Haffenden got very excited about these two men and directed Marzulo to ask them questions about the accuracy of the map in front of them.

Was the mayor's town in the right place?

Were the surrounding towns and larger pieces of terrain in the right places also?

Then Jamison began bringing over more maps of Sicily. They were just as big as the other map, but zoomed in to fixate on smaller portions of the island.

What did these men remember about the coastline?

Could they identify which parts of the coast were rocky and which parts had sandy beaches?

Haffenden also asked the two Sicilians about German troop strength in the area and if there was any enemy infrastructure in town.

Did they know of any German fortifications or command centers in any other parts of Sicily?

Haffenden was determined to squeeze every piece of information out of these two men about Sicily. If Sicily turned out to be the next target for the Allies, then this information would be solid gold. Haffenden and Marzulo extracted enough information to keep Jamison and his men busy for weeks, as they compared it to everything else they knew and did their best to determine if it was true or not.

Haffenden kept their contact information and excused the six Italians, and a very impressed and stunned Meyer Lansky. He couldn't wait to tell his friend Charlie about what he'd just seen.

On Monday February 1, 1943, Charles "Lucky" Luciano's lawyer, George Wolf, who was aided by Luciano's other lawyer, Moses Polakoff, submitted a motion to the Supreme Court of New York County to modify Luciano's thirty- to fifty-year prison sentence. It wasn't like this effort by his lawyers would get him sprung tomorrow, but Luciano would be happy with any time taken off of the twenty-three years—at a minimum—he had left on his sentence (though he would be eligible for parole in thirteen years).

The next day, Luciano penned a letter to Wolf declaring that Wolf was going to represent him in the motion challenging his sentence. Polakoff had done his part to convince Luciano that Wolf was the right man for the job, as Wolf was able to find several legal precedents pertaining to improper sentencing guidelines. It was a delicate and difficult strategy, as they had to convince the judge he was wrong when he sentenced Luciano.

As Polakoff and Wolf were discussing the best strategy for Luciano's motion, Polakoff told Wolf all about Luciano's involvement in the war effort. He told Wolf about how Luciano had used his influence to help the navy control the waterfront and stop any sabotage activity in the Port of New York. Wolf found what Polakoff was telling him compelling, and insisted that this information be included in Luciano's motion.

Polakoff told Wolf that that was impossible, and that Luciano would not allow it.

Why not?

Because Luciano's family—his brothers and sisters and their children—would be put in danger, and the same went for Luciano himself, Polakoff told Wolf.

Wolf was frustrated and didn't fully understand. He told Polakoff he was "disappointed," because Wolf knew that Judge Philip McCook—who had given Luciano his original sentence, and upon whose authority the motion was to be decided—was a veteran himself and would look upon any service to the war effort favorably. But Luciano had been insistent and told Polakoff that the only way he'd go along with this motion was if his involvement with the war effort was omitted. But Wolf persisted, and Polakoff finally broke Luciano's rule by permitting Wolf to write in the motion:

"[Luciano's] conduct has been mostly exemplary; he has given affirmative indications of a repentant spirit; *has been cooperative in the war effort* [emphasis added] and has demonstrated the ability to redeem himself."[10]

Wolf didn't stop there either, as he was able to convince Polakoff to reach out to two men who knew all about Luciano's involvement in Operation Underworld—former Assistant District Attorney Colonel Murray Gurfein and Commander Charles Radcliffe Haffenden. Gurfein was stationed nearby, and agreed to meet, while Haffenden, this time, consulted Captain MacFall.

Haffenden had spoken to the judge in Socks Lanza's case as a favor to Lanza, but in Luciano's case, he felt it necessary to inform his commanding officer. If he slipped up here, Operation Underworld could go public, and if that happened, everyone would know about how the navy had stooped to the level of making an alliance with the worst criminal in the country. Everything that B-3 had done had been kept out of the press, and it needed to remain that way. In the end, MacFall allowed Haffenden to see Judge McCook, but gave him very specific instructions on what to say, and what not to say.

On February 8, 1943, Luciano's motion came before Judge McCook. The press was in the courtroom, even though Luciano wasn't. At 10 a.m., Wolf began delivering Luciano's case. He was suggesting that Luciano's minimum sentence be reduced from thirty years to ten years. Judge McCook and Wolf exchanged arguments as McCook tried to make Wolf get to the point while Wolf insisted what a model prisoner Luciano had been.

Then, sensing that his case was floundering, Wolf got desperate. With court reporters typing his every word and journalists in the gallery taking notes, Wolf said that Luciano was cooperating with "high military authorities" and was providing "a definite service to the war effort."[11] Judge McCook stopped him right away.

"Where are these people?" McCook asked, referring to Haffenden and Gurfein.

"I have the names of those two individuals," answered Wolf.

"I told you to have them here, as I recall it," McCook said.

"I have since been advised, Your Honor," Wolf started, "that these two are available to Your Honor at any time you see fit."

"But now is the time!" McCook demanded. "I told you to have them here."

"I gave those instructions," Wolf said, shrinking. "But they asked me to ask Your Honor if they could not arrange for it at a later date, any time that Your Honor sees fit."

"I saw fit to do it today," McCook snapped back.

"I understand," Wolf relented.

"Can't they come today?" McCook asked.

"I think they may be able to come today," Wolf responded.

"That is not the point at all!" McCook exclaimed. "I am very busy, and if I set a time, they must come in."

Then Wolf made one last, desperate gasp. "Could I arrange then to have them come in today to Your Honor, in chamber?"

"I want it finished now," McCook said stubbornly. "I have other things to do. If you want to telephone and tell them to come immediately, all right."[12]

The motion had gone about as badly as possible, and it wasn't about to get any better. The call went out to Haffenden and Gurfein, who each dropped what they were doing and headed to the courthouse. After hearing arguments from the district attorney, Judge McCook retired to his chambers and waited for the two officers.

When the two men arrived, they were ushered into McCook's chambers while they were still catching their breath. They didn't even meet with Luciano's lawyer.[13]

Haffenden and Gurfein were reluctant to give the judge any facts on the case. Gurfein, for his part, had been recruited by the OSS, as evidently he had a knack for intelligence work. It also meant that he understood "top secret," and the details of Operation Underworld most certainly fell into that purview.

The two officers told Judge McCook that Luciano had aided the war effort, but they didn't really go beyond that. Gurfein made no recommendation as to whether or not Luciano's sentence should be reduced.

Then Haffenden added a notion that carried serious weight with the judge. Under instructions from MacFall, Haffenden told McCook that the navy "had no interest one way or the other in the question of whether Luciano's sentence should be reduced."

Wolf had correctly concluded that Luciano's involvement in the war effort would be the determining factor in the motion, but because neither man would elaborate on just what that meant, it became the nail in Luciano's coffin. McCook excused the two men and informed counsel that he'd make a decision within two days. Then Wolf had a conversation with reporters.

On February 9, 1943, both Commander Haffenden and Lucky Luciano got most unwelcome news in the *New York Times*—the press published word of Luciano's involvement in the war effort.

How could this have happened?

Haffenden's heart raced as he read about himself in the newspaper: "[Wolf] said he would call two 'high ranking military officials' to appear privately before the court, and declared later that they had met with Judge McCook, but that their testimony could not be made public."[14]

Haffenden and MacFall both breathed a sigh of relief. It was close—it was too close—but they felt confident that Haffenden's meeting with Judge McCook in camera would not be revealed to the public. And while the article said he may have helped with the war effort, it did not single out the navy. As for Luciano, he was very upset that his instructions had been ignored.

The next day, on February 10, 1943, Judge McCook denied Luciano's motion for a modification of his prison sentence. Luciano was floored. He wasn't going to be up for parole until 1956 at the earliest. The motion had been a complete failure, and not only that, Polakoff had outed him, and now it was public. The next time he saw Polakoff, Luciano wanted answers.

After the article was published in the *New York Times*, Haffenden and MacFall held their breath, and waited to see if anyone from the navy wanted answers about their actions. Then word reached MacFall that Washington was indeed sending an investigator to New York to ask some questions.

MacFall was upset, and Haffenden knew that they were both in a highly compromising position. Haffenden had rubbed more than a few officers in other sections the wrong way. His methods seldomly followed protocol and it angered the people around him. Many of Haffenden's men loved him for his free spirit, while others questioned his judgment, and others were just waiting for a scandal so they could justify getting rid of him.

An investigator coming up from Washington was information that MacFall was not supposed to know. The investigator—a

lieutenant colonel in the Marine Corps named Angelo Cincotta—
was given instructions to find out if Luciano had worked with the
navy, and if he had, what information had been obtained.

Cincotta worked in the B-7 section of the Office of Naval Intelligence in Washington, DC, and actually had a passing ac-
quaintance with Commander Haffenden. He worked on the
B-7-I desk, and the "I" stood for "Italy." He collected intelligence about that Axis country, and during Haffenden's monthly
visits to Washington, the lieutenant commander had stopped by
his desk often.

"One of these days I'm going to give you a lot of information,"
Haffenden had said to Cincotta.

"About what?" Cincotta asked.

"About your desk," Haffenden replied, referring to "Italy."

Cincotta had been a bit perplexed by Haffenden. When he had
seen him in DC, he witnessed Haffenden meeting with the spymaster, and yet Haffenden never seemed to give the spymaster
any written reports. That was odd.[15]

News of Luciano's reported contribution to the war effort had
also been picked up by newspapers in Washington, and Cincotta's superiors expressed concern that if it was true it was a bad
look for the navy. Because he was the head of the B-7-I desk in
Washington, Cincotta's superiors wondered if any information
provided by Luciano had ever come through his desk.

"Did you get any information from New York?" asked his superior.

"No, sir," replied Cincotta.

"Well, I want you to go back and check."

Cincotta was then ordered to New York City with explicit in-
structions not to contact either Captain MacFall or Commander
Haffenden. So Cincotta called his shipmates in B-7 section in
New York City and scheduled a lunch with two officers.

MacFall and Haffenden got word of this visit, and were able to
talk to the two officers prior to their scheduled luncheon with
Cincotta. They told the officers to tell Cincotta the truth—that

they had never seen any intelligence come across their desk that indicated Luciano was an informant. But therein lay a lie, as all intelligence gathered by informants provided by Luciano had been passed through B-3 section, and B-3 section only. If they told Cincotta that nothing about Luciano had come across their desk at B-7, then they'd be telling the truth.

The lunch went off without a hitch, and even though Cincotta spent over two hours with the two officers, they never disclosed any connection between the navy and Luciano.

Haffenden and MacFall were tickled with their subterfuge. Cincotta went back to DC and reported to his superiors that Luciano had provided absolutely nothing to the war effort, and that the story in the press was without merit. If Luciano had helped the navy—Cincotta was sure—then Cincotta and the other men in B-7 section would have known about it.

Not only had Haffenden dodged another bullet, but his and MacFall's ruse now ensured that if they were asked again in the future, there was an officer who had investigated this very matter—the Luciano connection—and could testify under oath that no such connection ever existed.[16]

A little before 9:45 a.m. on Wednesday, February 17, 1943, at Great Meadow prison, Lucky Luciano was escorted to the office next to Warden Morhous's. He sat down in a chair and was unshackled by two guards as he worked himself up to explode with anger at his visitors who would arrive in minutes.

Polakoff brought reinforcements that day in the form of Luciano's two closest friends—Meyer Lansky and Michael Lascari. The three men greeted Luciano, who was decidedly less than enthusiastic about their presence.

Luciano family business was typically the first topic of discussion during these visits, but today it was Polakoff's turn to tell Luciano what had happened, and why it happened. As Luciano raised his voice, Lansky and Lascari tried to calm him down. Eventually, Polakoff was able to explain that Wolf had thought it was best to include his involvement in the war effort as he thought it would appeal to the judge.

Luciano reminded Polakoff that that was not part of the agreement.

What about the two "high ranking officers" that were mentioned?

Polakoff explained that one of the men was Commander Haffenden, whom Luciano had never met. No one had any idea what the commander had said to the judge, but Polakoff was very pleased, and impressed that Haffenden would do that for him. And actually, it was the officers' testimony that left the door open for Luciano in the future. Maybe Luciano even owed Haffenden after he did him a favor like that.

Owed him for a favor? What had either of the officers done to actually help Luciano? Their effort was commendable, but what had it amounted to?

Then Polakoff shared that he had what he considered good news.

What good news?

Polakoff produced a copy of Judge McCook's ruling and brought Luciano's attention to the penultimate paragraph. In it, McCook wrote: "Finally we reach the argument that the defendant has assisted the government in the war effort. Following the precedent in the Metropolitan matter, the authorities have been interviewed, privately, in the public interest. As a result, the Court is able to conclude that the defendant probably attempted to assist them, and possibly with some success. Again, we are presented with a situation far from justifying the Court in granting the present application. If the defendant is assisting the authorities and continues to do so, and remained a model prisoner, Executive Clemency may become appropriate at some future date."[17]

What was "Executive Clemency"?

Therein lay the good news—McCook was suggesting that Luciano might be a good candidate for a pardon from the governor.

A pardon from Governor Dewey? Luciano wasn't excited

about that, especially because they had already tried to bribe him into giving him one.

But Polakoff now had McCook's recommendation as a weapon. All Luciano had to do was sit tight, and keep behaving well, and when the time came, they'd make a motion for Governor Dewey to pardon him. In light of all the help Luciano had rendered to the navy, Dewey would probably let him out. Lansky agreed; it was better than a long shot, and he told Luciano his odds were really good that McCook's decision would help with Dewey. Dewey was a "by the book" man to a fault, after all.

Luciano was starting to feel better, but the devil's in the details. He had to know what "appropriate at some future date" meant.

Polakoff told Luciano tough news—it meant "when the war was over."[18]

When the war was over?! That could take another decade!

Again, Lansky and Lascari tried to calm Luciano down, and again Polakoff explained himself. He and Wolf, and even Haffenden, all agreed that when the war was over, the details of Operation Underworld, and Luciano's aid to it, would likely not be as heavily protected. Perhaps then the navy would be able to speak about Luciano's involvement freely.

What happened if the Allies lost the war?

Then nobody knew what would happen. But for Luciano, as had been evident for a while, as went the war, so went his freedom. If freedom meant being deported to Italy, the war had to turn out in favor of the Allies.

Luciano then wondered if there was anything even left to do for the navy.

Lansky informed him that he was recruiting another friend to help the operation—Vincent "Jimmy Blue Eyes" Alo. Luciano was happy to hear Alo's name, as Lansky and Alo were currently partnered in casinos in Florida and were working together on Cuba. And as for Operation Underworld, Alo knew several native Italians in Brooklyn, and would be assisting the navy by bringing forward any that were deemed valuable.[19] Mangano was on

board with it too. Lansky thought maybe the next target was
Sicily, as Haffenden kept asking him specifically to bring people
to him who'd lived or spent time there.

Sicily? That certainly was a coincidence. Luciano could provide the Allies with whatever they needed about Sicily. Hell, he
could even tell them the best spots for an invasion. Lansky agreed
that he'd tell Haffenden that Luciano was willing and able to provide information about targets in Sicily.

Luciano couldn't help thinking that if only there was something he could do to be more directly involved in the Sicily invasion, it would help his cause. Even in prison, maybe he could do
something to hasten the end of the war. Because if he didn't, he'd
be anticipating the day the war was over like it was the end of his
sentence, and in the meantime he'd do what he'd already been
doing for seven years—wait. He was getting awfully tired of that.

Over the course of the next two months, Haffenden continued
using Luciano's connections to bring in more Italians to tell him
about Italy and Sicily. Haffenden's office at the Hotel Astor was
now flooded with books about Italy and the Mediterranean Sea.
Even Elizabeth Schwerin had provided titles from her own library.

Men were constantly poring over this material in rooms 196
and 198. Books were coming in by the dozens through their network of informants. And there were also brochures and pam-
phlets, which were printed by travel companies and featured
photos of sandy beaches and other geographical landmarks.

Haffenden also had most of his Italian officer corps now devoted to target section. Paul Alfieri, who had distinguished himself during several surreptitious entries, and undercover work in
Harlem, had been rewarded by a commission as a lieutenant j.g.
in August 1942. Now working for target section, Alfieri brought
Haffenden a few particularly valuable pieces of intelligence.
Through his network of informants, he was able to obtain maps
of the Italian coastline, and also charts and hydrographic reports
of the waters directly surrounding parts of the country.[20]

In pooling all of his resources, Haffenden even had Polakoff bring him a number of Italians who could help. With Socks Lanza out of the picture, the Brooklyn locals, aided by Mangano and Vincent Alo, began sending their Italians and Sicilians to meet at Church Street through Polakoff and Lansky. Once there, they would be met by a translator, usually either Lieutenant Marzulo or one of the Sacco brothers. The two brothers had each just finished undercover work at various industrial plants around Brooklyn and New Jersey, and were once again available to Haffenden in full support of target section. Polakoff brought at least six delegations to the Sacco brothers[21] and the special office of mapmakers at 50 Church Street.

Lieutenant Jamison had been in way over his head for what the navy needed, so Haffenden brought in a specialist—civilian agent George Tarbox. Tarbox was in his late forties and had twenty-five years of experience as an investigator. He was an invaluable addition to target section, as he was not only an exceptionally skilled mapmaker, but he was also a gifted illustrator.

Haffenden's search for information had expanded beyond topography and beach conditions to include the locations of enemy installations, communication centers, sources of supply, technicians, naval bases, industrial plants, airports, and public service facilities. Reports of these facilities, taken from Haffenden's translators, inundated Tarbox. In the absence of a photograph that showed what the informant was talking about, Tarbox would use written or verbal descriptions to draw what had been articulated. These drawings were filed away and could be located by a series of corresponding symbols on the maps.

Tarbox was adding exceptional skill to the mapmaking room at 50 Church Street. The twelve-square-foot maps were becoming enormous indexes for information. Plastic overlays had symbols on spots of the maps and arrows that pointed to the margins. There, tables of what reports were available, and how many of them there were, showed anyone who wanted to look where they could find the information they sought.

The flimsies that were provided by informants to target section were copied in quadruplicate, and sometimes quintuplicate. Some of these copies were then made available to Naval Intelligence in Washington.[22] With all the reports available to the military high command in DC—millions of flimsies and thousands of reports—it became obvious to some of them that a map would provide a single visual reference that could otherwise take hundreds of pages of information to communicate.

Haffenden soon became consumed by this constant need for information from target section. He was visiting 50 Church Street every single day. He was more than happy to bring in officers from all over the country to show off Tarbox's work. The United States' military planners feasted on the work provided by Haffenden's target section, and used it to develop their battle plans.

By May 1943, Haffenden had distinguished himself with his leadership of target section, and as a reward, when another shake-up of the Third Naval District came, he was promoted and given a new command.

Haffenden was no longer lieutenant commander, but a full commander, and was appointed as the new head of F section. "F" stood for "foreign targets" and was an expansion of target section that would now consume all of B-3.[23]

In May 1943, F section's (formerly B-3 and target section) mission on the waterfront, and New York City proper, was over. The battle for SS *Concrete* had undeniably been won by the navy, as at no time had there been a disruption due to sabotage to the flow of supplies between the Port of New York and Europe, no ships or infrastructure had been destroyed as a result of sabotage, and enemy spies and subversives had been uncovered and thwarted. Not only all of that, but Haffenden had also been able to keep his connection to Lucky Luciano a secret from the high command, the FBI, and the press.

F section could now devote all of its resources to fighting the enemy abroad. With his promotion and his new command, however, Haffenden felt a bittersweetness. Soon, he knew, he would become irrelevant in the fight against the enemy. Once boots hit the ground in Europe, troop reconnoiters and aerial reconnaissance missions would certainly be of more value to planners than the word of a gangster who hadn't visited the battleground for over three decades.

Haffenden knew that he had to come up with something to remain relevant, and to keep working at the feverish pace that he had grown accustomed to and fallen in love with.

CHAPTER 13

Desperate Measures

On May 11, 1943, Meyer Lansky, Michael Lascari, and Moses Polakoff woke up in Albany, and by 10:30 a.m. they had arrived at Warden Morhous's office at Great Meadow prison to meet with Charles "Lucky" Luciano.

Over the past couple of months, both Lansky and Polakoff had become increasingly aware that the navy's next target was most likely somewhere in Italy. And from the questions Haffenden and his interpreters asked, and the kinds of people they were interested in, they believed that an invasion was probably going to occur on Luciano's home island of Sicily. They were absolutely correct, as the decision to invade Sicily had been made months ago by Allied leadership at the meeting in Casablanca.

When the four men were brought into the room next to Warden Morhous's office, Luciano got straight to business. For the past two months—at Lansky's suggestion—he had been trying to remember everything he could about Sicily.

What type of stuff did the navy want to know?

Lansky told Luciano about the maps he had seen at 50 Church Street. They were asking these Italians everything about their homes, and especially about the coasts, ports, and harbors. They were also asking about people that these Italians might know in Sicily.

Luciano reminded Lansky that to a Sicilian, an Italian from the mainland was like a foreigner. Luciano felt that it took real Sicilians to get real Sicilians to speak about things. On the waterfront in New York City, this had also proven to be true.

Who did Luciano know in Sicily?

Luciano hadn't actually been to Sicily since he was eight years old. But during his rise to power and his time on top, he had done business with a number of Italians and Sicilians. And the mafiosi there knew all about Charles "Lucky" Luciano—Salvatore Maranzano came to America from the Castellamarre del Golfo, after all, and Luciano had been responsible for Maranzano's murder.

But that was a long time ago. Luciano had patched up old wounds, and he was highly regarded among the Sicilian mafiosi—what was left of it. When Mussolini began his crusade against the mafiosi back in the late 1920s, many of them had ended up immigrating to the United States. They kept their old-world ties, as their families remained behind, waiting for the day when the Fascist plague in Italy would be cured, and the mafiosi could rise again.

Luciano knew of many Sicilian mafiosi who had ended up in New York City, and he gave Lansky their names. If only Luciano knew someone who had gone the other way—from New York City to Sicily. Then there'd be someone there for US troops to contact. But he hadn't sent anyone that way for a long time. Not since at least fifteen years ago.

Luciano remembered that he had previously helped his cousin's boy escape a murder charge. His mother begged Luciano to get him out of New York City. He was a "cop killer," they said, and there would be no mercy despite the fact that he was only a teenager. So Luciano smuggled him out of the city and sent him to Sicily. What was his name? Luciano told Lansky that he should look up his cousin, as she still lived in New York City. Lansky said he'd look into it.

Then Luciano switched subjects and started relaying information about Sicily to Lansky. He had Lansky memorize every detail about his recommendations to the US Navy. Luciano—like Commander Haffenden—felt that maybe he could tilt the scales of battle in the direction of the Allies.

Luciano said that the Allies should definitely invade the Castellammare del Golfo—where the American Mafia was born (not far from Lercara Friddi), and where there would be the highest concentration of people friendly to Luciano. Hell, Luciano thought that maybe there was even some way that they could get him out of jail and have him go with the invasion force to make contact with the mafiosi.

Lansky thought Luciano was kidding, but Luciano persisted. He wanted Lansky to tell Commander Haffenden that he was willing to go to Sicily with the invasion force. He'd need a pardon in exchange, of course, but Luciano felt he could have the battle won within a week if he went along.

Lansky agreed that he would take Luciano's idea—crazy as it was—to the commander.[1]

In the lead-up to what became known as Operation Husky—the invasion of Allied forces on the Italian island of Sicily—the United States high command discovered a fatal flaw in their plan of attack. Intelligence had indicated that Sicilians were wary of Mussolini, and were especially tired of the presence of their German allies, who were beginning to feel more like invaders.

Even though the Italian garrison in Sicily was nearly two hundred thousand strong, it was believed that they had little appetite for a fight. If the Allies got lucky, most of the garrison would defect, or perhaps even surrender. It was also thought that the local populace of Sicily might be willing to help the Allies, given their disdain for the fifty thousand German troops on the island.

With this intelligence in hand, Allied planners suddenly realized that they didn't have anyone in their invasion force who would be tasked with making overtures to Sicilians. If the Allies were to exploit Sicilian hatred toward the Germans, they would need soldiers who could make contact with the locals. For this mission the high command decided they needed soldiers who were in shape for combat, had counterintelligence training, and were fluent in Italian.

On May 15, 1943, on orders from the highest echelons of military leadership, a Commander Thayer from Washington, DC, came calling to Commander Haffenden's F section looking for his best officers.

Haffenden rounded up all of the officers in F section and the other B section desks that fit the navy's requirements. Haffenden himself was disqualified because he was too old, unfit, and couldn't speak Italian. He couldn't help feeling a little miffed, watching his younger officers get chosen over him.

Commander Thayer then explained to all of the officers who fit the requirements that he was going to select four of them for a top-secret assignment that would involve combat duty. They would also have to leave the moment this conversation was over.

Did anyone want to volunteer?

Every single officer volunteered.

To narrow the field, Thayer conducted interviews with the men to see which ones were the best fit.

His first choice was Lieutenant Anthony Marzulo. Marzulo was young and fit, and the most talented linguist of all the men in F section. He had distinguished himself in operations on Long Island, on the waterfront, and in the past few months he had also become apprised of Sicilian mores and customs, and learned to speak multiple dialects of the island's languages.

Thayer's next choice was another F section veteran—Lieutenant j.g. Paul Alfieri. Alfieri also spoke Italian, and thanks to his work during Squad #3's surreptitious entries, he had a special set of skills that included lock picking and safecracking. He wanted his chance at combat, and since he was already in his mid-forties, this would be his only opportunity. Despite the fact that he had a pregnant wife at home, he decided to do his part for his country. Like Marzulo, Alfieri had also recently been educated about the details of Sicily and had even obtained the names of a few mafiosi there that he could try to make contact with. Alfieri didn't mention it to Thayer, but his contacts were courtesy of one Lucky Luciano.

Thayer's third choice was a man from the B-7 desk—Lieutenant j.g. Joachim Titolo. Titolo was in his early thirties and had previously worked at the District Attorney's Office. He also spoke Italian, and had been working on developing information about Italy since early 1942. He had made informants and passed information to and from Haffenden often.

The last of Thayer's choices was an officer from the B-7-I desk, Ensign James Murray. Murray may have had an Irish father, but his mother was Italian and she had taught him the language. Like Titolo, he had spent the last year developing intelligence about Italy.

The four men were plucked right out of the Third Naval District, and within two hours they were on a train bound for Washington.[2] By the end of the day, they were on a plane to Newfoundland. From Newfoundland they flew to Iceland, from Iceland to Scotland, and then finally to Mers-el-Kebir, the location of an Army Counterintelligence school on the Algerian coast in West Africa.

Once there, the four men were indoctrinated into intense commando training and given the latest reports from British and American intelligence units. Over the course of the next two months, in nearby Tunis they even began developing informants for details about the upcoming target areas. Marzulo and Alfieri distinguished themselves during this time as they used the skills they had developed in New York City to gather intelligence.

Fishermen out of Tunis were still able to make smuggling runs between Axis-occupied Sicily and Allied-occupied North Africa. The fishing boats were running supplies to the enemy—just as Haffenden, MacFall, and the navy had feared was happening with German U-boats on the East Coast of the United States. From their experience in Fulton Fish Market and on Long Island, Marzulo and Alfieri had advanced knowledge of the operations and capabilitiesof fishing fleets, and made it their mission to target fishing boat captains for intelligence. Alfieri even obtained a particularly vital piece of information—the location of the Italian Navy Headquarters in Sicily. He made a drawing of the building as his informant described it.

The four men were being hustled through their training as fast as possible, as D-Day for Operation Husky was fast approaching.

In late May, 1943, Commander Charles Haffenden traveled to Washington, DC, and was as excited as he'd ever been in his entire life.

Haffenden had been affected by two of his best officers being plucked right out of his command. The expediency of it told him that the invasion was coming fast. If he was going to play a part in it or provide a piece of intelligence that would drastically tip the scales in favor of the Allies, the time was now.

He had been speaking with Meyer Lansky, who told him about the idea that Lucky Luciano had come up with about sending him into Sicily with the invasion force. When he told Haffenden the idea, Lansky was shocked for a second time, as Haffenden absolutely loved it. Over the past couple of weeks, Haffenden had been thinking about the finer details that would need to be addressed to make this complex mission happen. If he figured it out, then this trip to Washington would be his best one yet.

Haffenden arrived at Naval Intelligence Headquarters in the State, War, and Navy Building, which was located at 17th Street and Pennsylvania Avenue, just kitty-corner to the White House. The architecture of the sprawling four-story building, which consumed the entire block, tried very hard to make it not look like a square, but only succeeded in giving it the reputation for being the ugliest building in America.

Haffenden was received by the spymaster—Commander Wallace Wharton.[3] Wharton had been in the navy as long as Haffenden, having begun his naval career as a seaman in the Oregon Naval Militia. Then he was given officer's training at the US Naval Academy, and in 1920 he became a part of the Naval Reserve. In April 1941, he became active in the navy, and by February 1942 he had been assigned to be the spymaster in the Chief of Naval Operations' Office. Since then, he had been neck-deep in the most secretive homeland intelligence operations in the war.

He had busied himself with German sabotage in industrial plants, and reports on the internment of Japanese-Americans. His knowledge was boundless, and he oversaw spies all across the country, and the world, as the head of counterintelligence. He was also one of the only navy personnel outside of F section who knew all about the Haffenden-Luciano connection.

Haffenden's energy on that day was palpable. He started by telling Wharton that his section had many names of mafiosi who would be willing to help the invasion force. His section had already developed dozens, if not hundreds, of names. Haffenden felt that there was someone in the United States who could get them to come out of hiding and convince them to help the Allies. This man was Charles Luciano.

But Luciano was still in prison.

The way it would work, Haffenden explained, was that they'd have to secure a pardon for Luciano from Governor Dewey. Haffenden expressed that he was positive he could obtain it, especially for the mission he had in mind.

After Luciano was pardoned, Haffenden continued, he could be smuggled out of the country, and arrive close to the battlefield via a neutral country, such as Portugal. From Portugal he could make contact with the invasion force. Once he joined up with Allied forces, he could then join the advance wave of paratroopers and be dropped into Sicily undetected.

From behind enemy lines, Luciano could direct Allied forces to the local inhabitants—particularly mafiosi contacts that he already knew—and use them to help expel the Germans from the island.

In fact, Haffenden told the spymaster, Luciano was willing to go at a moment's notice. And not only that, but Luciano had intelligence on the best place to make an amphibious landing—Castellammare del Golfo.

Did Luciano know the German troop strength there?

Luciano did not know the German troop strength, but Haffenden insisted that he could help the invasion force. Luciano knew several people there who would talk to him.

Did Luciano know about German fortifications in the Castellammare del Golfo?

Luciano didn't know that either, but once on the ground, he could find that information out.

Wharton was skeptical of this plan. He didn't think it was a good idea and he turned Haffenden down. But then Haffenden pleaded with him to make sure that Wharton would discuss this plan with his superior.

When Wharton did this, Haffenden's plan was categorically denied. Wharton thought the idea was crazy, and Haffenden was lucky that Wharton's rebuke didn't come with a punishment. The spymaster was now sure of it: Sometimes Commander Haffenden's judgment was off. What Wharton and his superior knew, and Haffenden didn't know, and Luciano couldn't know, was that there was an enormous German garrison in the Castellammare del Golfo, and landing there would be suicide.[4]

Haffenden was crushed. There had been a momentum building that had him thinking his connection with Luciano was going to help him win the war all by himself.[5] Now there was nothing he could do to get himself involved in the invasion of Sicily. He knew it was a golden opportunity blown, because there would never be another target where his section would have so much more knowledge than all of the other intelligence outfits in the United States military.

Haffenden went back to New York City with his tail between his legs. The reality was beginning to set in—his war was coming to an end. The war on the home front had been fought and won, and he was too old for combat. That meant that after the Sicily invasion, he would be confined to a desk for the remainder of the war. Nothing—not even death—sounded worse than that to Haffenden.[6]

On D-Day, July 10, 1943, at around 2:30 a.m., Lieutenant Anthony Marzulo, Lieutenant Paul Alfieri, Lieutenant j.g. Joachim Titolo, and Ensign James Murray rode landing craft to the shores of Sicily with the first wave of assault troops. A freak summer storm had struck the previous day, and a strong crosswind mixed with rain jeopardized the approach. Combined with rough seas, the wind pushed landing craft off course, while others ran aground on unseen sandbars, causing them to capsize and spill their men into the dark ocean. The bad weather did bring one advantage, though—the enemy didn't think a landing was possible.

Operation Husky's American invasion force was led by the Seventh Army commander, General George S. Patton. His plan was to land over fifty thousand troops in the first wave of the attack. The four officers from New York City had been split into two teams, as there were two landing sites that General Patton intended to establish into beachheads. The first was Gela, on the southern side of Sicily, and the second was Licata, about thirty-five miles to the west. To maximize their success, Alfieri and Titolo went ashore at Gela, while Marzulo and Murray landed in Licata.

Much depended on the four men, as their mission was deemed imperative to success. General Patton and the navy had decided that a shore bombardment from their heavy guns was not a good idea. Not only would it alert the defenders that an attack was coming, but it might also offend the populace, who they were hoping would help them out. But that decision also meant that the minefields in the sand would still be intact. Of the 150,000 Allied troops that were set to land on Sicily on D-Day, there were only the four officers from New York City, and two more army officers, who were responsible for making contact with Sicilian civilians and finding out where they could locate enemy minefields on the beaches.

It was still dark when the first landing craft hit the sand on Gela and Licata. Pillboxes on the beaches opened up with their machine guns, and tracer bullets suddenly illuminated the night. Searchlights attempted to zero in on Allied troops and quickly became targets for navy guns. As American troops stormed the beaches, many of the Italian defenders abandoned their positions, running up through town and all the way into the inland hills. Amid the chaos and confusion, Alfieri and Titolo, and Marzulo and Murray, ran ahead on their respective beaches and went into town.

In both Gela and Licata, the four Italian-American officers from New York City began shouting in the streets, urging the people to come out of their hiding spots, telling them that the Americans were here, and they were not going to shoot them. The streets were deserted, as the beautiful two- and three-story buildings offered shelter for frightened civilians and pockets of resistance. As Alfieri and Titolo entered the town of Gela, a group of Italians fortified the cathedral in the town square. Then an explosion from back on the beach broke almost every piece of glass in town—the Gela pier, which had been lined with demolition charges, had been blown up by the Italian defenders.

As advance units moved through the streets in columns, the four officers successfully convinced a few brave Sicilians to emerge and talk to them. With another wave of invasion forces coming shortly, they asked the people of Gela and Licata where they could find enemy minefields. Before daylight hit, and the next wave arrived, the four officers were able to mark many of the minefields and indicate where it was safe to land. As tens of thousands of Allied troops arrived on the beaches in the first hours of the invasion, their actions saved hundreds of lives.

Once the beaches were deemed safe, the four officers immediately made their way to the closest harbors and began talking with the local fishermen. They found out where the Germans had placed booby traps in the harbor, and the location of the safest sea passages that were free of enemy mines. The navy also wanted to use the harbors to land more ships and supplies. Out at sea, they were locked in a desperate fight against German bombers, who turned night into day when one of them dropped a bomb on the destroyer USS *Maddox*.

By midmorning Gela and Licata had been taken. Italian garrisons in the area had mounted sporadic resistance, and as the day progressed, Italian armored units supported by artillery began arriving at Gela. Tanks and infantry clashed as Italian reinforcements arrived from the northern road leading into Gela and the inland hillside. US Navy ships hammered them with their giant deck guns, as army infantry prepared to defend Gela without the support of tanks.

Amid the Italian counterattack, Alfieri then turned his attention to a special assignment that he had been given prior to the invasion—find the Italian Navy Headquarters and raid it for intelligence.

Back in New York City, through the Luciano connection, Alfieri had been given the name of a local mafioso who might help. He successfully found this man, and at the mention of Luciano, the man became eager to help.

Some years back, Luciano's cousin's son had murdered a police officer. At his mother's begging, Luciano had smuggled the boy out of New York City and had him sent to Sicily. This boy became head of a mafiosi family in Gela. The very mention of Luciano's name was like a password. Now Alfieri not only had the help of a man who would tell him the location of the Italian Navy Headquarters, but he and his soldiers would show him.[7]

Alfieri had been told by his informants in North Africa that the headquarters was not in an official building in the harbor, but an inland villa meant for vacationers in the hills near Agrigento. Alfieri produced his drawing of the villa, and Luciano's Sicilian mafioso contact said he knew where it was.

As the Italian advance poured down gunfire on US positions from the inland high ground, Alfieri and a group of Sicilian mafioso charged inland and attempted to circumvent the battle. The group managed to get behind enemy lines, and successfully located the villa. They found that the two-story building was protected by two guards standing outside the front door. The mafiosi quickly gunned them down. The villa was then deserted, as the officers there ran out the back the moment they heard the gunfire outside.

The group stormed the building and went up the stairs to the second floor and into an Italian admiral's office. In the corner of the room Alfieri located a safe. He had been told through his informants in Tunis that the contents were invaluable, and bringing them back to the beach was his primary objective. And that's why Alfieri had been chosen for the mission in the first place—he had been taught how to open safes by Willis George (Agent G) and to pick locks by Felix Sacco (Agent Y) back in New York City.

But Alfieri's adrenaline got the better of him. He feared that the fleeing Italians might be alerting more troops, causing them to launch an attack on the building itself. He knew the precision and calm that was necessary to successfully crack a safe by hand, and the way his heart was pumping made his hands shake, and such an effort impossible.

Alfieri opted instead to use high explosives. He was in such a rush that he rigged a fuse for "zero," which would give him no time to hide from the explosion. He connected the tiny fuse to TNT and attached it to the hinges of the safe. When he lit the fuse, he only had time to turn away and plug his ears as the explosives detonated while he was still in the room, nearly killing him.

When the smoke settled his ears were still ringing, and he found that the contents of the safe were intact. He grabbed a trove of documents and everything else in there. He then ran down the stairs and directed his mafiosi companions to take him back to the beach. The men braved more enemy fire as they passed through Italian lines of advance again. Alfieri made it back to the beach safely, and immediately went about finding Lieutenant Marzulo so he could help him decipher what they had.

When the two Italian-American lieutenants from F section of New York City's ONI met between Gela and Licata, they embraced and were thrilled to see each other alive after enduring a long day of combat. The two men then went through the material and found that they had discovered a treasure trove of information— Italian and German tactical ciphers and codes among them. If they could get this information to their commander, then they could break the German communication codes and listen to the enemy's orders in real time.

Alfieri and Marzulo demanded an audience with the highest-ranking admiral on the scene, and were taken out to sea, to Admi-

ral Connolly's flagship. Connolly immediately realized what he
had, and since the battle was still unfolding, he put it to use right
away. They also discovered that Alfieri's haul of documents included not only codes, but also maps with plastic overlays that
showed the safe-conduct routes for ships around the entire island.
Admiral Connolly spread the word, and US Navy and British
warships were diverted to avoid destruction.

The two officers—Commander Haffenden's finest—were heroes. Their value to the invasion force was undeniable to their
commanders. Their joy in victory would have to wait, however,
as the Battle of Sicily was still raging. Their exploits of the day
had their origins in New York City, and thanks to the Luciano
connection they had saved the lives of hundreds, maybe even
thousands, of men.

For Luciano, news of the invasion of Sicily was bittersweet. On
the one hand, the Allies had finally attacked Fortress Europe, which
was essential for their winning the war. But on the other hand, the
fact that the Allies had invaded Sicily meant that any chance of him
being placed there ahead of the invasion was gone. Another chance
at getting out of prison had slipped through his hands.[8]

Right before Charles "Lucky" Luciano was sent to prison, he had
been living the best years of his life. By the time he was thirty-
five years old, in 1932, he had conquered all of his foes, organized crime, and sat at the head of the Commission that oversaw
crime in most of America. Of course, Luciano didn't like to think
of himself as sitting at the head of anything, but the respect that
he commanded made everyone outside of the Commission think
that he was king of the underworld.

Room 39C, high up in the tallest hotel in the world—the Towers of the Waldorf Astoria, which was one of New York City's
finest hotels—was the best place he ever lived. It was a place that
was friendly to a man like him. He'd been in the press plenty, but
the Waldorf didn't ask him questions about who he was, no one
went in without being screened, and Luciano had several members of the staff on his payroll. The hotel catered to a rich market;

it was decorated with marble columns, giant Persian rugs, luxurious furniture, and lavish entertainment venues fit for a king.

Luciano certainly looked the part of a king with his fancy clothes, but he didn't get a daily manicure, massage, shave, and haircut at the hotel barbershop like Frank Costello—Luciano would never let someone get that close to him with a razor[9]—and the only reason he was in the Towers was because he figured he needed to live on a higher floor than Costello.

Luciano tried to be low-key, as he was officially checked in as "Mr. Charles Ross," which was an alias he commonly used to avoid attention. His "office" was two unassuming, conjoined rooms off of Broadway and 51st Street—just a few blocks from the Waldorf. There wasn't even a name or a number on the door to the street, and inside were just a sofa, two chairs, and a desk—no money, weapons, or financial records. All instructions and orders were repeated and memorized so nothing was written down. And as for the cops, they knew all about Luciano's office—Luciano even told them where it was so that they would help protect him. Everyone within his orbit was in his pocket.

Violence often wasn't necessary, as Luciano was happy to give people leeway—sometimes. While he had the appearance of a man who didn't use violence, his Commission signed off on countless murders. But public executions of the sort orchestrated by Al Capone in his Saint Valentine's Day Massacre brought too much attention.[10] So Luciano got killers who traded their Thompson submachine guns for garrote wire and ice picks—more intimate, and quieter, methods of killing.

Luciano was living the good life, with so many fancy clothes—bespoke suits, silk underwear, and embroidered initials ("C.L.") on his shirts. Oftentimes he had to give them away on account of not having enough closet space. He slept until noon and then ordered room service. He'd hold court in his room while in his bathrobe, eating breakfast as various members of his board came by. Sometimes he'd go to the barbershop and meet Costello and his bookmaker Frank Erickson, who were there every morning.

As much as Luciano never really had a permanent home, he

was a homebody. Oftentimes he'd waste away the afternoon with a girl from Madam Polly Adler—$20 for a romp, plus $5 for a tip.[11] But if the horses were racing, then that's where you'd find Lucky Luciano. Anywhere the ponies were running—Saratoga Springs, the Aqueduct Racetrack in Queens, Belmont Park, or Hialeah Park in Miami during the winter—Luciano rarely missed a race.[12]

But on typical days, in the evening he'd start what he called his "midnight jamborees," and do a tour of his favorite speakeasies, nightclubs, and cafes—all of which he had a stake in. His friends came out, and they talked business as they listened to the best musicians of the day perform for an audience of celebrities, high society types, and gangsters. And on his arm for some of the time was the Broadway dancer and actress Gay Orlova.[13] She was a beautiful Jewish blond from Eastern Europe—just Luciano's type. She had big lips, a doll's face, and a devilish stare—like Luciano. She also had a showgirl's body, and Luciano liked to say that "Gay Orlova" was "gay all over."

Orlova may have been the love of his life up until then, but in his business Luciano never understood the rush of some of his men to make their own families. It was a dangerous business that they were in, and life wasn't normal, with odd hours that made it hard to raise a family.[14] Plus, Luciano was having too much fun. His nights always ended back at the Waldorf with another girl, or Orlova, and then he read the first editions of the day's paper in bed as the sun rose, until he finally dozed off.[15]

When he woke up, he was in Great Meadow prison, and it was 1943. Dreaming about the past was like a curse, but when he thought about his future, he longed for those wonderful times back in the 1930s at the Waldorf. And now, to get back to this life, he would have to rely on the grace of the man who had taken it away—*ain't life rich*. When thinking in a loop irony prevails.

The late summer of 1935 was when it had all come crashing down. After Luciano returned to the Waldorf from Saratoga Springs, he met with the Commission. This meeting was dominated by a discussion about the fate of a man named Dutch

Schultz, who ran numbers in Harlem (prior to Willie McCabe) and muscled in on a number of other businesses. He made them a lot of money, but he was also outwardly hated, and the first in the crosshairs of Mayor Fiorello La Guardia's specially appointed prosecutor on crime—Thomas Dewey.

Dewey had just unsuccessfully prosecuted Schultz twice, after Schultz influenced the juries of both trials. La Guardia then effectively banished Schultz from New York, and Schultz sought revenge against his accusers—he wanted permission from the Commission to assassinate Thomas Dewey.

Luciano expressed that if Schultz took out Dewey, the reaction from law enforcement would amount to nothing short of a crusade against *Cosa Nostra*. The Commission sided with Luciano, as they were unwilling to risk their futures to save Schultz. Schultz stormed out of the meeting and declared that he would kill Dewey anyway, Commission be damned.

As easy a decision as it had been, Luciano was now in a bind. The Commission had another meeting—this time without Schultz—to decide if they should kill Schultz or let him live. Luciano wanted Schultz dead, but then Meyer Lansky told him something he didn't want to hear. Lansky pulled Luciano aside and said, "Charlie, as your Jewish consigliere, I want to remind you of something. Right now, Schultz is your cover. If Dutch is eliminated, you're gonna stand out like a naked guy who just lost his clothes. The way La Guardia and the rest of them guys've been screamin' about you, it's ten-to-one they'll be after you next." Lansky and Luciano always had their own language.[16]

A cold shiver went down Luciano's spine. A vote to kill Schultz would save the Commission but wasn't in his personal interest, while a vote to let him live might lead to the destruction of the Commission. To prove his devotion to the Commission that he had started, he used his one vote to save it. Dutch Schultz was to be eliminated immediately. It became a race against time to get to Schultz before he got to Dewey. While Schultz was gathering with his co-conspirators in the plot to assassinate Dewey, Luciano's hit men shot and killed Schultz in a bar in New Jersey just thirty-six hours before they were going to carry out their attack.[17]

Then, it played out just like Lansky had said, and Dewey came after Luciano next. Somehow an anonymous letter had tipped Dewey off to Luciano's involvement in the prostitution racket.

It was very difficult for Luciano to live with—saving Dewey's life was directly responsible for his present stay in prison. Luciano felt that he had chosen legacy and principle over personal gain, and now he was paying a very heavy price for that choice. It was time for Dewey to do right by him, Luciano felt. Luciano had certainly already taken his licks, after Dewey made a fool out of him in court, and made it sound like he was a pimp and a human trafficker. Luciano felt that Dewey owed him his life. And Dewey owed Luciano his life back.

CHAPTER 14

Unfinished Business

Commander Charles Radcliffe Haffenden was receiving news of Lieutenants Paul Alfieri and Anthony Marzulo's war exploits through the naval grapevine and was starting to feel a little jealous. It was rumored that Alfieri had been nominated for a medal after only one day in combat. And from the sound of it, they were bringing all kinds of things that they learned while in B-3 section to the battles that were occurring in the Mediterranean Sea and up the Italian boot.

As General Patton's Seventh Army advanced northwest along the Sicilian coast, the lieutenants from New York City were charged with reestablishing control of the harbors and ports. Remembering what he had learned from Haffenden about the waterfront in the Port of New York, Alfieri taught Lieutenant Titolo how to organize the Sicilian fishing fleet to work for Naval Intelligence.

They got the Sicilian fishing fleet up and running to feed the locals, and soon after, fishing boats from Gela and Licata were running reconnaissance missions and providing vital intelligence to Allied command.[1] To organize these fishing boat captains, Alfieri and Titolo's first steps were to contact local mafiosi.

The Italian Army in Sicily crumbled within days, just as Allied planners had hoped. And with the German garrison on the run, mafiosi were emerging from hiding all over Sicily. When the Italian-American officers greeted these men and said the right things, and mentioned the right people, the mafiosi let their guard down.

When asked if they were mafiosi, they'd respond with "*E cosa mia*," meaning "It is my thing."[2]

"*Gli amici*," answered Alfieri and others, meaning "Friends of friends."

Alfieri plunged into his work with little regard for his own safety. His mind was in turmoil, as he had received terrible news from back home. In late July 1943, his wife Nellie gave birth to a baby girl. The girl did not survive, and there would be no child waiting for him when he made it back home—if he made it back home. Receiving the news during the unfolding campaign gave him no time to grieve, and no time to process, so he focused his energy on his mission.

If he could forget about bad news from home, he could forget about producing an unintended result of partnering with mafiosi. The lieutenants from New York noticed that mafiosi who leaped forward to help were all too eager, because using their influence to restore order was also empowering them to fill the power void left by the fleeing Fascists. Once mafiosi were installed as the harbor masters, the dock bosses, the foremen, and town leadership, they were not going to just hand their power back to the new Italian regime. They had been waiting over two decades for this moment. And while there were mafiosi who helped the Allied Army and risked their lives on the front lines, they were also picking the pocket of Allied supply lines and selling American goods on the black market to a starving populace.

On August 17, 1943, Alfieri, Marzulo, Titolo, and Murray celebrated as Operation Husky came to a close. Sicily had been conquered by the Allies as the last German troops escaped back to mainland Italy. Not even a month later, the Italian government gave Benito Mussolini a vote of no confidence and he was placed under arrest. Just as Allied planners had hoped, the new Italian government then promptly signed an armistice with the Allies. But Italy was far from conquered, as Hitler sent half a million troops into the country and ordered that Italy be defended at all costs.

On September 9, 1943—the day after Italy surrendered—Lieutenants Marzulo and Alfieri landed with the first wave of landing craft on the beaches of Salerno, Italy. Their mission in Sicily had been so successful that military planners vastly expanded their group. The four from New York City were among six officers that landed on Gela and Licata, and this time there were forty other specially trained Italian-American officers to join them.

Alfieri and Marzulo braved enemy fire from German shore fortifications and ran into town. Once the beachhead was established, the battle died down for a moment, and the officers were able to contact local mafiosi and fishermen to point out the minefields on the beaches. Then, just hours into the landing, a massive German counterattack slammed into the American Fifth Army as they were occupying the town of Salerno.

Over the course of the next week, Salerno became a dangerous battleground as gunfights erupted in the streets. Advances were measured in city blocks, and buildings were taken one contested room at a time.

Through this whirlwind, Lieutenants Alfieri and Marzulo went from building to building contacting the local inhabitants, braving enemy fire to interrogate prisoners and find any mafiosi they could speak to. Thanks to contacts with the local mafiosi, the two officers made some incredible intelligence discoveries.

They were shown the location of a secret Italian naval facility that had an intact torpedo that had homing capabilities. They were also instrumental in helping locate enemy artillery positions that were pounding away at the Allies. Those positions included an Italian Navy armored train that was thundering away at Salerno with a six-inch gun. The artillery coming into Salerno, however, got its revenge on Marzulo, as a piece of shrapnel nearly killed him when it hit him in the face just below his right eye.[3] Marzulo recovered so fast that he was back in action at the end of September 1943 for the Allies' next target—Naples.

*   *   *

On Tuesday, September 28, 1943, at 11 a.m., Meyer Lansky, Michael Lascari, and Moses Polakoff arrived at Great Meadow prison to meet with a depressed Charles "Lucky" Luciano. There were smiles, but no laughter when they greeted each other in the room next to Warden Morhous's office. Luciano hadn't been sleeping and was reading news about the war constantly. He was buying and drinking more and more milk from the prison commissary, which was what he drank when his stomach was upset. Following the war was becoming an obsession. It was taking too long, he felt, and he was starting to complain that the Allies needed to open a new front in France to defeat Hitler.

Defeat Hitler. That was the answer. To Luciano, the name of the game had always been to kill the king.

Over and over again, Luciano went through scenarios in his mind that transported him beyond the walls of Great Meadow prison and into a fantasy land where he had the power to influence world events.

But before Luciano got to his plan about how to end the war sooner, he needed to know what the fuck what was going on with Frank Costello. Luciano demanded answers from both Polakoff and Lansky.

Evidently, District Attorney Frank Hogan had installed another wiretap, only this time his target had been Costello. Hogan caught Costello in a whole slew of conversations with Tammany Hall's delegates, trying to influence them to appoint a DA named Thomas Aurelio to a judgeship. Hogan even had Costello on the phone with Tammany Hall leader Michael Kennedy. Hogan learned from listening that Kennedy was loyal to Costello because Costello was the one who got him his position. Aurelio then conveniently got appointed.

If that wasn't enough, Hogan even had Judge Aurelio recorded as saying to Costello, "I want to assure you of my undying loyalty for all that you've done—it's undying."

Now Hogan was talking about disbarring Aurelio, and Luciano wanted to know from Polakoff if Costello was going to be indicted. Polakoff assured Luciano that it was unlikely that Costello would be indicted, but he also said that it was possible that Costello would be called as a witness in a disbarment proceeding for Aurelio. That was a problem, because Costello couldn't hide behind the Fifth Amendment, as he would likely be given immunity, and since no charges had been filed against him, he'd have to answer or go to jail.

Luciano said that he wanted someone really good to represent Costello. The articles Luciano was reading in the newspapers suggested that Costello had lifted the lid on all of Luciano's efforts to influence New York City's political establishments. And if the DA got curious about all of his backdoor dealings, that could spell doom for Luciano's entire empire, and certainly hamper his abilities to prosper if he got out of prison.[4]

Polakoff suggested George Wolf for the job, and told Luciano that he'd arrange for Wolf and Costello to meet.[5] Luciano just hoped that Wolf would do better for Costello than he'd done for him. Then Luciano excused Polakoff to his corner to read the newspaper, and got to the topic that he really wanted to discuss.

"Somethin's gotta be done with this guy Hitler," Luciano said to Lansky and Lascari.

Lansky and Lascari listened closely as Luciano continued.

"If somebody could knock off this son of a bitch, the war would be over in five minutes."

Lansky and Lascari laughed and looked at each other like Luciano had just made a joke. But Luciano was dead serious and continued.

"What the hell are you laughin' at?!" Luciano said. "We've got the best hit man in the world over there—Vito Genovese."

Just as Luciano, Lansky, and Lascari were having this conversation at Great Meadow prison, Alfieria, Marzulo, and Titolo were in the process of taking Naples. There, a man who spoke English, and whom nobody knew, came out of hiding and offered to become a translator for the US Army. To get his job, he gave his commanding officer—who just happened to be a former governor of New York—a 1939 Packard Sedan. The man was hired, and was placed in charge of a goodwill mission distributing Red

Cross and Allied supplies to Italian civilians. But he double-crossed the Allies and smuggled these vital supplies to other locales and sold them on the black market. The man who did this was well known to Charles "Lucky" Luciano, as it was none other than his underboss, Vito Genovese.

Genovese had found himself on the winning side once again, as his ally in the Italian government—Italy's foreign minister and Mussolini's cocaine-addicted son-in-law Galeazzo Ciano—turned on Mussolini at just the right moment. Genovese then turned his attention to getting into the good graces of the Allies and continuing his treachery. Genovese, ever the opportunist, had turned war into wine.

"He's so fuckin' friendly with Mussolini and that punk son-in-law of his, that Count Ciano," Luciano said. "He oughtta be able to get close enough to Hitler to do it."

Lansky objected and tried to calm Luciano down, which only made him more upset.

"That dirty little pig owes his life to me," Luciano said about Genovese. "Now it's time for him to make good on it."

Then Luciano reminded Lansky that their buddy Benjamin "Bugsy" Siegel once had an opportunity to kill two of Hitler's top guys—propaganda chief Joseph Goebbels and Luftwaffe chief Hermann Goering. In the mid-1930s, Siegel had happened to be in Rome staying at the same hotel as the two Nazi chiefs. By then, their anti-Semitism was a known quantity, and Siegel nearly came at them, guns blazing. His girlfriend at the time dissuaded him, but he always regretted not going after those two war criminals.[6]

If Siegel could get close to them, then maybe Genovese could get close to Hitler too.

At that moment the guard came in to find Luciano standing up and yelling at his guests. The guard told them to keep it down, and his appearance sobered Luciano for a moment. Then Lansky saw his opportunity.

Lansky reminded Luciano that as a Jew, he had more reason

than anybody to want Hitler dead. In fact, he did want Hitler dead, but this idea was insane.

Wasn't Hitler the most hated man in the world? Had Luciano thought about how hard it would be to get to Hitler, given that there was a war on? If there was a way to get to Hitler, don't you think the millions of people fighting him would have come up with a way to kill him?[7]

Luciano came back down to earth, and could see that Lansky—a man he was always on the same page with, and who could read Luciano better than anyone—was looking at him like he was crazy. Luciano knew what both Lansky and Lascari were thinking—that he was losing his mind. He calmed down, and actually started laughing with his friends at his insane idea. After two visits in a row when he had come up with impossible notions, he realized he needed to get a grip on reality if he was going to see his plans through.[8]

On January 22, 1944, as Alfieri and Titolo were fighting in the battle against the German-occupied monastery at the top of Monte Cassino, Marzulo participated in his third combat landing, this time at Anzio. As the battle dragged on for months, Marzulo was plucked by the high command and given a special assignment.

He was promoted to lieutenant commander—Haffenden's rank just a few months prior—and became part of "S" force, which was a special group tasked with planning the final assault on Rome itself. As the Allies finally moved past Monte Cassino and broke out of Anzio, the way was paved for the attack. Ahead of the Allied advance, Marzulo entered the city and located two VIPs, including an Italian admiral who was a spy for the Allies, and brought them to safety.

By June 6, 1944, which was D-Day for the Allied landing at Normandy—the biggest amphibious landing in military history—Rome fell, and Alfieri, Marzulo, Titolo, and Murray became decorated heroes. For his actions in Sicily, Alfieri was awarded the Legion of Merit. Marzulo was recognized for his exploits with seven battle stars and a Legion of Merit of his own. The four of them received countless positive citations from their commanding officers and several medals from the Italian government.

As far as Commander Haffenden was concerned, their exploits and the Normandy invasion were the last straws. One of his former lieutenants had even landed on Omaha Beach. And Lieutenant Lindsay Henry—the Zone 9 commander Haffenden had previously golfed with weekly, and left in the dark when the German saboteurs arrived on Long Island—received a Silver Star for his actions in command of a landing craft.

When Haffenden was coordinating Operation Underworld, he was a very busy man, and so caught up in the moment that he hadn't had much time to think about his future. But over the last year he'd had plenty of time. He was no longer the president of the Executives Association, and thus he no longer had access to his secret office in the Hotel Astor. Haffenden had been confined to his office at 90 Church Street, and it did not suit the style he had grown accustomed to.

His battle had been fought and won, and he had proved all the naysayers wrong. The only problem was, outside of a few need-to-knows in Naval Intelligence, no one would ever be aware of what he had done to defend the Port of New York.

This was extremely troubling to Haffenden, who over the course of the previous year had indulged in developing grand plans for himself—perhaps even political office. After all, he had long been a Tammany Hall supporter, and now, thanks to Operation Underworld, he had the support of Tammany's influencer in chief—Frank Costello. The two were even golfing buddies from time to time at Pomonok Country Club in Flushing, where Haffenden lived.[9]

But there were three things vexing him that he hadn't resolved. The first was that he had a problem with his war exploits as they pertained to his future. He couldn't talk about them, he couldn't brag about them, and if he ran for office, he couldn't speak to voters about his bravery and his genius in orchestrating them. It would be difficult if he faced an opponent who was a decorated war hero.

Secondly, the navy was where he got his greatest sense of pride and purpose, and he felt a sense of duty to lend his services to the war effort as long as the fight endured. He had done his job, to be sure, but there were more jobs that needed to be done, and if men like him could help the navy, then he should do his best to volunteer to help.

The third thing that was vexing him was that he knew how old he was—now fifty-two, an age when many men like him were closing in on retirement. Captain MacFall, after all, who had delayed his retirement years earlier to stay on for the war, left the Third Naval District in December 1943 to accept an assignment in sunny San Diego, California. Captain Howe took his place, and then he was gone four months later, as the two friends had always planned on retiring in Southern California. But Haffenden wasn't interested in that—not yet.

After all, he had been operating his section day and night, and working with an officer corps that was half his age. Alfieri wasn't that much younger than him, and Haffenden thought he could keep up with him. Haffenden had the energy, he felt, that if an opportunity for combat came up, he could do it.

He started complaining to his wife, Mary. He was home more, and she loved it, but over the course of the last year there had been an energy missing from her husband. When he was excited, his energy was electric and irresistible, but now the job that had given him such validation as his place in the world was no longer providing that satisfaction. As he insisted more and more that he had unfinished business and wanted a job in a forward zone, Mary Haffenden didn't stand in the way of her husband going for it.

In the days after D-Day, Haffenden learned that there was a combat position that would accept men in their fifties. The job of beachmaster was thought to not require the stamina and strength of combat, and was thus available to any older man who wanted to get in on the action. Beachmasters might not have to move much, but they did require nerves of steel. Their mission was to arrive behind the first assault wave of an amphibious invasion, then turn their back to enemy gunfire and direct troops and vehicles that arrived on the beach. Haffenden volunteered and put in for a transfer.

In October of 1944—less than a month away from his fifty-third birthday—Haffenden reported for duty at Camp Pendleton near San Diego. He was too late for any amphibious operations in Europe, as the rest of the European war would be increasingly fought in the air and on the ground. Instead, he would fight against the Japanese somewhere in the Pacific Ocean. At this stage in the war, the American advance was moving at a feverish pace. The Philippine Islands had just been invaded, and there wasn't much left after that. It was looking as though Haffenden might be a part of the invasion of the Japanese home islands themselves.

News from the front in Europe had been bad for a while, but things were starting to look better. Lucky Luciano had a map of Europe on the wall in his cell, and every day he updated the front lines of the Allied advance based on what he read in the newspapers. His obsession with the progress of the war had him up and down emotionally. When advances slowed, as they did in September 1944, with the Allies' disastrous attempt to take the Port of Antwerp, Luciano railed against Allied leadership for not giving more resources to General Patton.[10] When things were going well, and the Allies were advancing, his mood was better.

On Thursday, November 23, 1944—Thanksgiving Day— Luciano was in a good mood and had much to be thankful for. It was looking like the Allies would take the Port of Antwerp after all, albeit two months behind schedule.

He was also thankful that the District Attorney's Office was finally bringing charges against Vito Genovese in the murder of Ferdinand Boccia seven years earlier, which is what Genovese had been fearing all along. One of the six gunmen had flipped, and was ratting out Genovese, Michael Miranda, Tony Bender, and the other two gunmen. Miranda was now a fugitive, as he skipped town when the charges were filed.[11]

Luciano knew that Genovese would have to stay away from New York City as long as that indictment hung over his head. That meant Luciano would have no interference from Genovese when he got out of prison, as long as he remained in New York.

Another reason Luciano was thankful was because it was the day before his birthday, and as much as he hated to think about the fact that he was turning forty-seven years old, and spending another year in the can, he was happy that he was going to be visited by a friend he hadn't seen in a very long time. That, in and of itself, was something to be thankful for, as Luciano's contribution to the war effort was clearly over, and yet no one had called off his special privileges of receiving off-the-record visits from whomever he wanted. Somewhere down the line, and even though they never met, he'd have to thank Commander Haffenden for that.

On Thanksgiving morning, at 9:30 a.m., Warden Morhous didn't bother splitting up the large delegation that was led by Moses Polakoff. Among Luciano's guests that day were John Martini, who had visited from Saratoga back in August 1942, and Luciano family underboss Willie Moretti. There was also his good friend Michael Lascari, and another friend from his childhood who was an original member of Luciano's board of directors—Benjamin "Bugsy" Siegel.

Siegel was a good-looking man—even better-looking than Joe Adonis. He had blond hair and blue eyes, and an extremely confident stare that the ladies absolutely loved. Siegel had spent the last few years in California, and his looks were one of the reasons he had been sent out to Los Angeles and the West Coast in the first place, as he fit right in with actors and celebrities. He certainly wasn't sent out there for his brains—he spelled his name incorrectly in Morhous's unofficial registry.

It had been a while since Luciano had been in a good mood when he received his guests, but on that day he had much to be thankful for, and the guards had to remind the men to keep it down. Laughter and hugs went all around, as Polakoff, as usual, sequestered himself in the corner.

On that Thursday morning the conversation was almost entirely about gambling. Martini was part of Luciano's holdings in Saratoga, including the Piping Rock Club. Willie Moretti owned several sports books and casinos in Upstate New York and New Jersey. These men were working with Frank Costello and Frank Erickson ("the two Franks") to connect all of the sports books on the East Coast to the same wire service, so that bets could be taken from any of their establishments on horse races, ball games, boxing matches, and other sporting events that were held around the country.

And because Moretti liked to brag, he had to tell Luciano about an entertainer he just recently signed. This young man had the voice of an angel, but his manager had him in a terrible contract. Good thing for the singer his godfather was Moretti, who paid the singer's manager a visit. When the manager got mouthy, Moretti put a gun in the manager's mouth and made him an offer: Either the manager would transfer managerial rights of the singer to Moretti for one dollar, or Moretti would pull the trigger. The manager signed the deal with black ink instead of his red blood. Moretti told Luciano that the singer—a man named Frank Sinatra— was going to be a star and sing at every casino, hotel, and dance hall where the Luciano family had an investment.

The news from Moretti was fantastic, which put Luciano in an even better mood. Luciano really had to hand it to Lansky and Costello, as their vision of creating gambling havens that were all connected was a stroke of genius. Not only that, but Luciano could see that it was coming together perfectly. But then Luciano's mood began to change for the worse, when Siegel started talking.

Siegel tried to sugarcoat his situation and told Luciano that he was tapped into Costello and Erickson's wire service for his sports book in California too, but Luciano saw right through him.

Did Siegel have his own place to run his operations?

No, Siegel didn't. He didn't have a casino, or even a restaurant for that matter, to run a proper sports book.

How was Siegel supposed to expand his sports book if he didn't have an actual establishment?

Siegel didn't really have an answer, so he changed the subject and started talking about a new place that he thought had a lot of potential as a gambling haven. It was in Nevada, which was the only state in the union where gambling was legal.

Siegel was talking about a small railroad depot town with a lot of potential called Las Vegas. Lansky had previously told Luciano about Siegel's efforts in Vegas, and this was the main reason why he was visiting Luciano. Luciano had never been to Vegas, so he let Siegel tell him all about it. Siegel told Luciano that Las Vegas was the future of gambling. There were places opening up all the time. And these places were huge. They weren't just casinos, but giant hotels with swimming pools, tennis courts, vast entertainment venues, and air-conditioning.

Luciano liked the sound of Las Vegas. Was Siegel building one of these casinos and hotels on his own?

Siegel was not building a casino and hotel of his own.

Was Siegel going to buy one of his own?

Siegel had tried. He made an offer to the owner of a place called El Rancho, which was a beautiful establishment, but the owner refused.

This enraged Luciano, who reminded Siegel that he needed to be tougher. It was all or nothing with Siegel; either he was too skittish or he was an unflinching murderer.

Siegel told Luciano that the owners in Las Vegas were all locals, and they had a thing about preventing out-of-towners from becoming a part of it. It was going to be hard to get a gambling license there, let alone operate a casino.

Luciano told Siegel to stop giving him excuses. Siegel needed to quit wasting his time with his low-level bookmaking and start thinking bigger. If he wasn't going to run his own casino in the one state where gambling was legal, then what was he doing out there? After all, it used to take a week to get to California, and now, with all the new technological innovations from the war, it would only take hours from New York via airplane. Luciano had bought into Lansky's assessment that when this war was over, people were going to want to have fun in places like Las Vegas.

Luciano's plans for post-prison life, and the plans of the Commission, included westward expansion.[12] Luciano told Siegel that the Commission would be happy to back him out there if he found something worthy of investing in. Luciano then told Siegel to open his own place in Las Vegas, or the Commission would replace him.

On February 19, 1945, at 8:59 a.m., beachmaster Charles Radcliffe Haffenden arrived on the sands of Iwo Jima right behind the first wave of Marines. As his landing craft lowered its ramp on the southeastern beach, a fifty-three-year-old Haffenden hopped out and ran ahead with his troops.

For all the resistance that Haffenden and the Marines were expecting on Iwo Jima, when they landed there was no contact with the enemy at all. Haffenden and his men landed to the right of the invasion forces on the five-mile-long atoll. On the southeastern side of the island, the invasion force was just in the shadow of the dominating geological feature on the island—a volcano called Mount Suribachi. Though it was only just over five hundred feet high, it looked over an island that was otherwise entirely flat. It was a hot and sunny day, and in the beginning phase of the battle it might have even been pleasant if it didn't smell like sulfur from the volcano.

Equipment and men were landing on the beach in waves, and Haffenden directed Marines to start pushing inland. The only problem was that planners had failed to understand that the fifteen-foot sandy slopes would make it difficult for Marines to climb, and impossible for equipment to drive over. Equipment started piling up on the beach, and as Haffenden and his fellow beachmasters looked for solutions, they had no idea that letting the Americans land all of their men and equipment without incident was exactly what the defenders wanted.

At 10 a.m., one hour after landing, the enemy rose from their positions on Mount Suribachi and opened fire like the volcano itself was erupting. The preinvasion bombardment had failed to make a dent in Japanese defenses, as their soldiers had burrowed themselves deep within the mountain and built pillboxes on the ground that were so well camouflaged and protected that only a direct hit from a high-explosive bomb could knock them out.

Machine gun fire seemed to jump out of the ground, as Japanese soldiers emerged from their camouflaged positions to cut down Marines as they advanced. At the same time, big and small guns, and everything in between, fired down on the Marines from positions on Mount Suribachi like "all the pent-up fury of a hundred hurricanes."[13] Within seconds of the start of the barrage, just about every Marine on the island was on the ground trying to escape enemy fire—and praying.

The beachmasters did all they could to try and punch a hole in the sand wall, and eventually they had some success. But artillery from Mount Suribachi and machine gun fire didn't stop for the entire day. All the while, Haffenden was still on the beach, busy trying to help organize the thirty thousand troops that had landed on the tiny island. Then, night came, and Haffenden took stock after surviving his first day in combat. He didn't sleep a wink, as American ships constantly illuminated the island with starburst shells, and Haffenden and the Marines waited for a banzai attack from the Japanese that never materialized.

Just about all of the first-day objectives for the invasion of Iwo Jima had not been met. The Americans hadn't taken the airfields, but a regiment of Marines had successfully crossed the island at its narrowest point—all the while in front of Mount Suribachi and enduring its wrath—and was dug in on the other side of the island.

On February 20, 1945—D-Day + 1—Vice Admiral H. W. Hill gathered his beachmasters and told them that he needed someone to make contact with the Marines on the other side of the island. They were cut off, and Hill had to find a way to get to them, so he needed one of them to conduct a beachmaster's survey of the beach, and then come back. Commander Haffenden, eager to get directly involved in the action, volunteered for the extremely dangerous mission.

On February 21, 1945—D-Day + 2—Haffenden and a contingent of seven Marines began their dangerous quest, as the weather had gone from sunshine to rain with a strong crosswind. Out in the open, the eight men scurried across the island while gunners from Mount Suribachi attempted to zero in on them. It was a short walk of about a thousand yards, but the thinnest portion of the island was also right in front of Mount Suribachi. There were no trees to hide behind, or hills to provide cover. Iwo Jima was mostly flat sand from shore to shore, open territory that was perfect for Japanese gunners. Machine guns from pillboxes on the ground opened up on Haffenden and his men. The men pushed along, trying to avoid contact with the Japanese and evade fixed positions in order to achieve their objective.

They made it across to the southwest side of the island, and Haffenden took his time assessing the terrain, and American troop strength. If the Marines were going to reinforce the contingent on the southwest beach, commanders were hoping they could land troops instead of making all of them run the gauntlet in front of Mount Suribachi. Haffenden then started collecting data on the black sand beach. The situation was desperate, as the Marines were suffering heavy casualties. The beach was a problem, and it wasn't so much the sand, but the fact that the weather was making the surf so violent that a landing was impossible. He and his men then started their dangerous trek back across the island, running through the Japanese field of fire one more time.

When they arrived back on the southeast beach, Admiral Hill was elated with Haffenden's report. The information the beachmaster provided was exactly what Hill needed, and commanders started moving heavy equipment across the island instead of landing on the beach. Landing craft were having a tough time getting men and equipment on the island because of rough seas, and Haffenden's report reinforced this problem. Haffenden had also proved his mettle, and the feeling of satisfaction was palpable. At fifty-three years old he had conducted himself admirably during combat, while commanding a group of men who were half his age. But the Battle of Iwo Jima was far from over, and in just three days of combat, the Americans had suffered thousands of casualties.

On February 22, 1943—D-Day + 3—Haffenden was gathered with his unit, hunkered down in the rain, in an area that they thought was safe from enemy fire. All of a sudden, shells came pouring in and exploded dangerously close to Haffenden. As he tried to take cover, the unthinkable happened—a Japanese shell exploded right on top of him. The concussion knocked Haffenden senseless as shrapnel rained down upon him. Molten metal shards somehow missed his body, but all of the damage had been done by the blast itself.

The concussion caused severe internal bleeding, and his stomach began to hemorrhage. Amid the shelling, corpsmen attended to him immediately, and he was transferred off the island to a nearby hospital ship, where doctors infused him with several pints of blood.

Haffenden needed surgery to repair his hemorrhaging stomach. Surgeons took his stomach out[14] and discovered that he had a fairly sizable tumor there. It had been growing inside him for years and causing pain that he tried to ignore. The surgeons cut it out, placed his stomach back in his body, and stopped the bleeding.

CHAPTER 15

Banished from Heaven

In early May 1945, Mary Haffenden received a phone call at her home in Flushing from Lucky Luciano's attorney, Moses Polakoff. Polakoff introduced himself and asked if he could speak with Commander Haffenden.

"Haven't you heard?" Mary asked.

"No, what?" Polakoff replied.

"Well," Mary started, "he was wounded in the Battle of Iwo Jima. He's now in the Brooklyn Navy Yard." That was a godsend to her, as it was less than ten miles from the Haffenden residence. Then she added, "I'm sure he would like to see you when he's able to receive visitors."

A couple of days later, Polakoff arrived at the Brooklyn Naval Hospital. Once there, he came upon Commander Haffenden in a bathrobe, gingerly walking around. The two hadn't seen each other in almost two years, and greeted each other like old friends. As the two began chatting, Haffenden told Polakoff all about his harrowing ordeal on Iwo Jima. He also told Polakoff that this was only the second day he had been able to "move about." Polakoff asked about some of the sailors whom he had worked with under Haffenden's command, and Haffenden asked about some of Polakoff's prestigious Mafia clientele.

Then Polakoff revealed the real reason for his visit—he was preparing an application for executive clemency for Luciano, and he wanted to know if Haffenden would write a letter attesting to Luciano's efforts to help the war effort.

The timing was perfect, claimed Polakoff, as it was clear that the Germans were whipped and the war was coming to an end soon. Hitler had committed suicide days earlier, and the Red Army had taken Berlin. It was only a matter of days. Surely victory in Europe, and not a complete conclusion of World War II, would suffice to get the ball rolling on Luciano's clemency.

As for the letter he was requesting, Polakoff explained that their application for executive clemency would first be reviewed by the New York State Parole Board. Polakoff also explained that Governor Dewey and the Governor's Counsel would ultimately base their decision on the Parole Board's recommendation.

Would Commander Haffenden write a letter stating the facts of Luciano's involvement with the navy to the Parole Board or the Governor's Counsel?

Haffenden told Polakoff that a stenographer would be in to see him in a couple of days, and that he would be happy to dictate a letter for Luciano. Polakoff thanked him and then left.

Haffenden had never really had a problem before with carrying on without clearance, and at the moment, he didn't really have a commanding officer. MacFall and Howe were on a different coast and in San Diego. His beachmaster superiors wouldn't know what he was talking about if he checked with them, so Haffenden was fine dictating a letter to the Governor's Counsel without any clearance from ONI, or the entire navy for that matter. When his stenographer arrived, Haffenden dictated his letter that included the following:

"For the purpose of reaching Sicilian-born Italians who could give pertinent information regarding the conditions in Sicily . . . large numbers of informants were constantly sent to my office. . . . It is difficult to say how many such informants came to my attention through the cooperation of Charlies [*sic*] Luciano. . . . Additional assistance on various subjects came from this same informant, which can be explained to you at a later date."[1]

Haffenden felt good about his gesture of goodwill toward Lu-

ciano. He hoped that it would help Luciano get out of prison. The
Luciano connection had done wonders for Haffenden, after all,
and if Luciano did get out, he might even do Haffenden a favor
down the line. Haffenden may have been right about that, but he
had no idea about the storm that began gathering the moment he
sent that letter to the Governor's Counsel.

On May 8, 1945, the United States celebrated as Germany for-
mally surrendered to the Allies, marking V-E Day (Victory in
Europe Day). As so many servicemen and -women, and people
the world over—including in Times Square, where crowds par-
tied well into the first illuminated night in over three years—
rejoiced over peace on the continent of Europe, Lucky Luciano
also celebrated because it was finally time for Polakoff to submit
his application for executive clemency. After Polakoff submitted
Luciano's application, the Parole Board began an exhaustive investigation of the merits of Polakoff's reasons for clemency. One
of those reasons was Luciano's aid to the United States' war effort.

Polakoff had requested that the Parole Board contact Commander Haffenden with questions. He also requested that Murray
Gurfein be summoned to provide his testimony to corroborate the
application. Gurfein, who was busy helping with the prosecution
of German war criminals at the Nuremburg Trials, wrote a letter
to his former boss Frank Hogan, and provided all the facts, as he
knew them, of Luciano's participation in Operation Underworld.
But he also did something that Haffenden neglected to do—
Gurfein told Hogan to get clearance from ONI *before* submitting
his letter to the Parole Board.

Hogan then provided the new commanders at the Third Naval
District Intelligence Office at 90 Church Street a copy of Gurfein's affidavit, and requested that it be provided to the Parole
Board. After reading the facts presented by Gurfein, this request
was unequivocally denied by ONI.

Hogan, who had been rebuked, was sensing trouble from the
navy. Never afraid to take matters into his own hands, Hogan

phoned Polakoff, and on his own authority offered to give him copies of the affidavit provided by Gurfein. "You may need something like this in the future," Hogan told him.

Meanwhile, the Parole Board came calling to ONI because of Haffenden's letter. The board was then effectively stonewalled and were told they were seeking classified information. Naval Intelligence was sure that information about the Luciano connection would embarrass the navy, and they were not going to surrender anything.

Then on May 23, 1945, the stakes grew larger—there had been a leak to the press.

"Luciano Seeks Clemency Says He Helped Navy," read the headline in the *New York Herald-Tribune*. The article went on to say, "Tells of Getting Friends to Aid Sicily Invasion Asks Cut in His 30-Year Term." Some in Naval Intelligence were finding out about the Haffenden-Luciano connection for the first time and were appalled. Some of these men didn't like Haffenden in the first place, and they began making preparations to defend the navy's reputation, lest they let a renegade officer drag the navy's reputation through the mud.

But Haffenden was unaware of the gathering storm, and over the course of the next month he carried on by cooperating with the Parole Board's investigation. He spoke with a man named Joseph F. Healy, who was the Parole Board's investigator for the matter. Investigating Luciano's clemency application was his first case, and he was eager to do an extremely thorough job. He even spoke to Haffenden on three separate occasions, and Haffenden was happy to talk about Operation Underworld for the first time out in the open.

On June 26, 1945, Healy—armed with Commander Haffenden's details of Operation Underworld and Luciano's involvement in it—showed up unannounced at the Third Naval District Intelligence Office at 90 Church Street. Healy demanded an audience with Haffenden's successor—Lieutenant Commander Harold MacDowell.

MacDowell had previously been a member of the Executives

Association, and had known Haffenden since 1933. Haffenden respected MacDowell so much that he had him open an Executives Association branch in New Jersey. Haffenden also recruited MacDowell to become one of the civilian agents working for B-3 section, and in May 1942 MacDowell was commissioned as an officer in the navy. His job was mostly administrative, as he worked with the commander to screen the men and women coming in and out of Haffenden's command. When MacDowell received Healy, he was alarmed by Healy's intimate knowledge of the filing system at 90 Church Street. Haffenden had told Healy about flimsies and giant maps, and he even told Healy about his little black book.

Healy told MacDowell that he wanted to see any and all records about Luciano. MacDowell told Healy that none existed. Healy then asked MacDowell if Haffenden's little black book was in his care, as Haffenden had stated that it was in his office when he left for combat training. Since MacDowell now occupied that office, perhaps he was in possession of it.

MacDowell assured Healy that he didn't know what he was talking about. But Healy, in his need to prove himself on his first case, persisted, and demanded to see their files. MacDowell then briefed another officer on what was happening and had this officer show Healy "the filing system." The officer took Healy into a room wall-to-wall with filing cabinets, and directed him to the letter "L." There was nothing there with the name "Luciano." Healy left Church Street unsatisfied, and sure that the navy was hiding something.

The whole encounter spooked MacDowell, and since Healy didn't get what he wanted, the Parole Board now wanted a search of all of Naval Intelligence—including Washington, DC—for any records about Luciano. MacDowell and his superiors didn't immediately deny the request, as they were extraordinarily curious about what the Parole Board knew and didn't know.

Following Healy's ambush at Church Street, men from ONI finally contacted Haffenden and told him to keep his mouth shut. It was classified information, and if he kept informing the Parole

Board about Operation Underworld, he could be court-martialed. The threat had its desired effect, and the next time Haffenden was contacted by Healy, he said that he could only speak on matters if he received official clearance from the navy, which he did not have.

But merely silencing Haffenden wasn't enough, as the navy set their sights on attacking his reputation. On July 5, 1945, the navy assigned a man to the Third Naval District's Office of Naval Intelligence who already had it in for Haffenden. Captain Wallace Phillips had been one of Haffenden's commanders before the war, and Phillips despised him.[2] Haffenden was a free-wheeling free thinker, and Phillips was a by-the-book sailor to his core. He would've been Haffenden's commander had he not been transferred out of the Third Naval District prior to the beginning of the war.

Through the channels of Naval Intelligence, Philips arrived at Church Street with a copy of the letter that Haffenden had sent to the Governor's Counsel. On July 20, 1945, Phillips then penned a letter to Haffenden wherein he referenced an anonymous letter that had been received by the commandant of the Third Naval District. In part, it read: "A recent disloyal and disgraceful performance perpetrated by a Naval officer reported to be attached to the Intelligence Dept. 3rd naval [sic]/AA District is hereby brought to your attention. . . . The writer and a few other newspapermen and members of the District Attorney's office have been aware of a recent abortion on the Altar of Justice unequaled in history. . . . Commander Haffenden supported Luciano in his false and repulsive claim."

Who the hell wrote that letter? Haffenden's style had clearly created enemies, and it appeared they were aligning against him. Phillips had a meeting with Healy and denied any involvement between Luciano and the navy. He also ordered Haffenden to answer a series of questions regarding his disclosure of information to the Parole Board.

On July 25, 1945, Haffenden wrote a letter back to Phillips answering all of his questions, including the one where Phillips asked if Luciano had indeed provided any assistance to the war effort. Haffenden wrote about Joe "Socks" Lanza and Fulton Fish Market, Meyer Lansky and the ILA, Joe Adonis and Brooklyn, and Luciano and the entire city.

Having now confirmed what his superiors feared—that Luciano helped the navy in the war effort—Phillips carried out the next phase of his orders. He directed that all files created by F section (formerly B-3) be destroyed immediately.

Ninety Church Street, the site of the Third Naval District's Office of Intelligence and the *official* headquarters of Operation Underworld, became the site of a massive purge of classified information. Thousands of names of informants and the information they had provided were incinerated. Reports detailing information obtained from painstaking intelligence work were burned. Even Tarbox's masterpieces of illustrations and maps at 50 Church Street were fed into the fires of Naval Intelligence boilers. At ONI in Washington, DC, all of the flimsies sent from the Third Naval District Intelligence Office were turned to ash. Phillips's purge amounted to the entirety of Haffenden's work for Operation Underworld being completely destroyed and lost to history.[3]

Even though he had destroyed his legacy, Phillips wasn't done with Haffenden. When Phillips threatened Haffenden with a court-martial if he spoke out of turn again, he effectively silenced him. Then he went on damage control regarding Haffenden's letter to the Governor's Counsel back in May. Phillips wrote a letter first to the Parole Board: "Commander Haffenden's letter to the Governor's Counsel was not forwarded through official channels nor were its contents approved. . . . Further, it is believed that the appearance of Commander Haffenden before Justice McCook in 1943, in connection with this case, was without official approval."

That last part was an out-and-out lie. Captain MacFall had given Haffenden clearance to speak with Judge McCook. Haffenden reached out to MacFall for help, and though MacFall spoke up for his subordinate, he could not loosen the noose tightening around Haffenden's neck. Phillips's letter to the Governor's Counsel ended by saying, "You are informed that the statements made by Commander Haffenden in his letter of May 17 cannot be substantiated by the files of this office." That last part was true; all evidence had been torched. Phillips, however, wasn't done telling lies.

In an interview between Healy and Phillips, Healy asked about Haffenden, and Phillips denied him access to the commander. Then Phillips said that Haffenden was recovering from wounds that he had received after spending only four hours on Iwo Jima. Phillips said that Haffenden hadn't actually been wounded by a shell, but was actually suffering from a rectal hemorrhage. Phillips' hatred for Haffenden was one reason for insulting him. The other part was that, as Haffenden's technical superior, Phillips had recently been forced to pin a Purple Heart on Haffenden's chest, an act that seemed to stir Phillips's jealousy to no end.

Haffenden was still recovering from his wounds when he was silenced, reprimanded, and embarrassed, and to him it felt a lot like being disavowed, and like he had been banished from heaven. He loved the navy with all his heart, and even though it seemed that they were expelling him from the outfit he loved, he resolved to protect the navy and keep his legacy a secret. But that was only if they stopped coming after him.

By the end of World War II on V-J Day (Victory in Japan Day), September 2, 1945—a day when a *Life* magazine photographer captured a jubilant sailor kiss an unsuspecting dental assistant in Times Square, and at a time when the free world breathed a collective sigh of relief—Charles "Lucky" Luciano was wondering why the hell it was taking so long for a decision to be reached about his application for clemency. Polakoff told Luciano that he had done his part. He told the Parole Board that the navy—with the exception of Commander Haffenden—was denying the whole thing. The navy had also successfully frustrated Parole Board investigator Healy. But just as Healy was about to throw in the towel,

Polakoff had produced the affidavit written by Murray Gurfein and provided by Frank Hogan. Not only that, but Polakoff got Meyer Lansky himself in his office when he met with Healy, and he corroborated everything.

So what the hell was taking so long?

The eager Parole Board investigator had his information. But the Parole Board itself was thorough. They even visited Joe "Socks" Lanza in Auburn prison. He had been there for two-and-a-half years and corroborated everything that Lansky had told the Parole Board.

Summer turned into fall, and fall turned into winter. Then on December 3, 1945, the Parole Board finally made its recommendation to Governor Dewey and his counsel. The Parole Board recommended dropping a few outstanding warrants against Luciano, which was good news. They also recommended that Luciano's sentence be commuted immediately, but it came with the exception he had dreaded for so long: "The Parole Board, therefore, recommends that commutation be granted for deportation only."[4]

For Luciano it was a devastating blow. But quite incredibly, he falsely believed that he had one last hope—Governor Thomas Dewey. Dewey, who Luciano claimed had paid prostitutes to testify against him and cooked up an entire conspiracy claiming that Luciano was at the head of the combination that ran all prostitution in Manhattan, was going to be his savior, he thought. Dewey owed Luciano, after all.

Back in 1936, when Dewey had come at Luciano with ninety counts of compulsory prostitution, Luciano felt there was no way that he would get convicted. Absolutely no way in hell.

As always when confronted with a serious situation, though, Luciano had summoned the Commission to discuss his situation. Luciano's friend Albert Anastasia was adamant that they kill Dewey before they all ended up in jail. It was the second time the issue of whether Dewey should live or die had come up before the Commission. Luciano held firm that killing Dewey wasn't the way—any notion of their syndicate being legitimate would go out the window if they killed a district attorney, and every cop in the land would be against them. Luciano also believed there was no way Dewey was going to get him on prostitution charges. Even if Dewey did get Luciano, it couldn't be for that.

What was Dewey's angle? Luciano thought for sure that the prostitution charges were a Trojan horse for something else. Maybe Dewey was using it to force him into a deal. And even though Luciano hadn't figured out Dewey's angle, the Commission voted and sided with Luciano—Dewey was not to be touched. So Luciano had saved Dewey for a second time, and Anastasia, who didn't get a vote because he wasn't a member of the Commission, mumbled that Luciano would regret his decision.

But the idea that Dewey had owed him—because he had saved his life twice—was all a construct that Luciano had created in his mind. He had saved Dewey's life twice, to be sure, but Dewey didn't live in a world where the good guys cut deals with the bad guys. People did the right thing because it was the right thing to do, and a person shouldn't be rewarded for not doing something terrible. Dewey didn't care to dignify Sicilian traditions or get on square terms with Luciano. By the book until the end, Dewey simply granted Luciano clemency for deportation because that's what the Parole Board recommended. Luciano couldn't get Dewey out of his head as the only foe he never bested.

He then began trying to wrap his head around the fact that he would only live in the United States for two more months of his life.

In early January 1946, Luciano was transferred to Sing Sing prison to await deportation. On January 9, 1946, he received two guests from Frank Hogan's office. Luciano was brought out of his cell and placed in the office right next to the warden's. He smiled, remembering all the meetings that he'd had in the office next to Warden Morhous's at Great Meadow prison.

But this meeting was more like the one he'd had in the office next to the warden's back at Dannemora. Two men from the District Attorney's Office sat down in front of Luciano at a table and began asking him about a crime—the murder of Carlo Tresca.

The two investigators were curious if Luciano knew the identities of the killer or killers. The police had previously picked up
Carmine Galante, but had to let him go because of a lack of evidence. They found the car—registered in Brooklyn—with all
four doors open, and a loaded pistol inside. Beyond that, the case
had mostly gone cold.

Did Luciano know who killed Carlo Tresca?

Luciano reminded the men that he had been in prison at the
time of the murder. What could he possibly know?

Maybe Luciano had received information in prison about the
murder. Or perhaps Luciano would be interested in obtaining "information from sources that were close to [Luciano]," as one of
the investigators put it.

In adherence to the *omertà* code, Luciano was bound to not say
anything to the authorities about a case like this. But then Luciano added, "but, as far as finding out from some friends [of
mine], [I can] do it on one condition, and that [is] to be free and
remain in this country." Getting that condition satisfied might be
worth violating *omertà*. After all, Luciano recognized that he had
a golden opportunity to take out Miranda, Bender, and Genovese
in one deft move. They were (with Galante) responsible for
Tresca's murder, and the way he saw it, they were also the biggest
threat to his empire.

The two investigators brought this information back to Hogan.
When the investigators came back to see Luciano, they said that
Hogan would make sure that the proper channels were made
aware of his assistance, if he cooperated.

Luciano was unconvinced. "No soap," he said, staying true to
his code, but also putting to bed his last chance at remaining in
the country.[5]

On February 2, 1946, the Parole Board and Governor Dewey
made it official that Luciano was to be deported. In the end, to
save face for the navy, Luciano's contribution to the war effort
was left out of the Parole Board's findings. That way, nobody
could trace the story in what were public documents. However,
Dewey, in affirming the Parole Board's recommendation, wrote

this: "Upon the entry of the United States into the war, Luciano's aid was sought by the Armed Services in inducing others to provide information concerning possible enemy attack. It appears that he cooperated in such effort, although the actual value of the information procured is not clear."[6]

The Parole Board knew Luciano had aided the navy, and so did Dewey and the governor's office, but Luciano's service wasn't included in any reports, so nobody outside of the Operation Underworld participants knew what Luciano actually did during World War II. Not even Dewey.

Luciano was then turned over to the Immigration and Naturalization Service. They were not wasting any time—if Luciano's sentence was commuted, then he had to be deported immediately. Luciano said goodbye to Sing Sing prison forever[7] when he was ushered into the backseat of a four-door sedan with two officers in the car. They made the journey south to Ellis Island, and to get to the ferry terminal, they drove through Manhattan—Luciano's kingdom.

As Luciano rode in the backseat—shackled—he couldn't believe that he was going to see Manhattan for the first time in ten long years. He had lived there for nearly thirty years, and had so many fond memories that he struggled to control his emotions. He just couldn't wrap his mind around the fact that this would be the last time he was ever there.

Along the east bank of the Hudson River, Luciano looked out the window at the tall buildings on the West Side of Manhattan. They drove past Central Park, and he looked to his right to see a waterfront alive with enormous passenger ships tied up to the piers, and getting ready to take free people on adventures to distant lands. Though an adventure aboard a ship and freedom awaited him, he didn't feel the notion at the time, and just thought about how he was riding through Manhattan and couldn't get out of the car.

Then, emotion got the better of Luciano. He couldn't stand going through the city without touching it, without feeling it underneath him, and without smelling it. He had to know that he had actually walked in New York City one last time when he had the chance. He spoke up, and asked the officers in the car if they could stop for just a couple of minutes. The officers denied his request.[8]

Luciano was taken aboard a ferry and arrived at Ellis Island for the second time in his life. He hadn't been there in forty years, and through all the twists and turns in his life he couldn't believe that he had arrived there as a boy with freedom and was now leaving as a man in shackles. Luciano was then placed in a cell, just waiting for the fast-approaching day when he would be placed on a ship and say goodbye to America forever. Dewey had made it clear—if he ever came back, he would be arrested on sight, and be forced to serve out the rest of his prison sentence. As if things couldn't get any worse for Luciano, his prison cell at Ellis Island had a window, and it gave him a view of Manhattan.

On December 3, 1945—the same day that Luciano found out he was to be deported—Commander Charles Radcliffe Haffenden was placed on inactive status by the navy. Due to the wounds that he had sustained at the Battle of Iwo Jima, the subsequent surgery, and the fact that he had exceedingly high blood pressure, he was considered to be unfit for active duty. His time as a sailor—the pride of his life—was over.

Captain Phillips had done his damage spearheading the navy cover-up at Church Street and ONI in Washington, DC, and after just a two-and-a-half-month appointment, Phillips was reassigned. And yet pressure from ONI persisted. The reputation of the navy—an institution of the highest order and prestige—was at stake, and it could never let it get out that there had been a navy-Mafia alliance.

Haffenden believed it was unrealistic that this entire episode—with its hundreds of officers and their countless informants—could stay under wraps forever. Yet he complied with every request and assured the navy that even if he were subpoenaed to testify in Luciano's parole hearing, or any future case for that matter, "I will protect the Navy interest to the best of my ability."[9]

Haffenden, as it turned out, was just buying time, as he had made other plans. On January 1, 1946, Haffenden, Frank Costello, and Tammany Hall rejoiced as Democrat William O'Dwyer—the former district attorney who had let Anastasia and so many murderers in Brooklyn off the hook—became mayor of New York City.

On the same day O'Dwyer took office, Charles R. Haffenden was appointed as New York City's commissioner of Marine and Aviation. It was a position of prestige that he had waited his whole life for, and a fitting reward for all his years of service for the navy. With his war record and a position in government, perhaps the fifty-four-year-old could make a run at politics. He was active in veterans' affairs in his community, and he even had a neighbor who was the head of the Queens County Democratic Committee and a US congressman, named James A. Roe. Roe had even previously sponsored Haffenden for his current position.[10] Plus, Haffenden had made all the right friends in the underworld to make a run at office happen.

But something nagged at him: He had no idea what was happening at the Third Naval District. Instead of guessing, on January 22, 1946, Commissioner Haffenden walked into 90 Church Street and politely asked for Admiral Kelly, who was the commandant of the Third Naval District. Permission was granted, and Haffenden met with Kelly in his office.

Haffenden still had his infectious energy, and Kelly was put at ease by his charm. Kelly was even impressed with Haffenden's new position as a commissioner. Haffenden then told Kelly that he was there because he wanted to know if he was going to be court-martialed. He had nothing to hide and he would cooperate with anything the navy wanted, but Haffenden needed Kelly to make inquiries to see if he was going to be charged. Haffenden then left, and Kelly searched for answers.

The day after their meeting, Kelly wrote a letter to Haffenden that stated: "There is nothing I have found in our files to indicate that you are under such consideration [for court-martial]. I do not know who, if anyone, here at Headquarters, furnished information to the effect that you are in that status, and as far as I am aware, such information is without foundation in fact."

Now that Phillips was gone and the Luciano Parole Board investigation was over, the inquiries had subsided. The navy was now satisfied with Haffenden's word, and the pressure was off him. Admiral Kelly's letter was good news to Haffenden, who could now put Operation Underworld, and it appeared Lucky Luciano also behind him.

Haffenden looked toward the future, which for the commissioner of Marine and Aviation, meant overseeing all aerial and maritime freight and transportation. It also meant that contracts on every pier on the waterfront of New York City had to go through him. If Haffenden decided to help his friends in the Mafia, he was in a dream position to do it. There was also a major project that he was overseeing—the construction of Idlewild Airport. Costello and the Luciano family had grand plans for exploiting the airport, and felt that Haffenden was the right man to oversee its construction and operation.

Haffenden—the brains behind Operation Underworld, who put together a team of New York's finest investigators and paired them with the city's worst criminals to protect the home front— could now smile, knowing that he had proved all the naysayers wrong and was the accomplished war veteran and leader he had always known he could be. He felt like he could do anything—he was on top of the world—and nothing could make him fall. He could finally forget about following rules that he'd never had an interest in, in the first place.[11]

On February 3, 1946, Luciano sat in his prison cell on Ellis Island, gazing at the Manhattan skyline, and waiting for his personal effects to be delivered to him by a familiar delegation— Meyer Lansky, Michael Lascari, and Moses Polakoff. The three of them took a cab to the Ellis Island ferry, with three heavy bags of personal items and clothes—that Luciano hadn't worn in ten years—in the trunk. When the three men arrived at the ferry ter-

minal lobby they received guest passes that were normally designated for lawyers or family members of the detained.

"These men are with me," said Polakoff, and the three of them
were waved through.[12]

Then as they turned around, they saw a dapper man with a familiar face—Frank Costello. He had heard about the meeting the
day before, and somehow acquired a "family" pass of his own.

Costello joined the party, and the four men took the ferry to
Ellis Island. Upon arrival, the bags full of Luciano's personal
items were searched, and then guards escorted them to a private
room where Luciano was waiting.

The mood was somber, and they only had twenty minutes to
speak. Luciano told them that he needed cash, and he had been
told that he'd be shipped out in about a week. Polakoff told him
that he was only allowed to take $60 in cash with him. Luciano
had $388—cash from his prison commissary account—so he
gave most of it to Polakoff.

First, Luciano gave instructions to Costello. He was very clear
that no matter what, he wanted Costello to remain acting boss of
the Luciano family. He was also in charge of just about all of Luciano's gambling interests in the United States. The only exceptions were the investments Luciano had made in casinos where
Lansky was the principal owner.

He also wanted Costello and Lansky to send word to the other
bosses that the two of them would be overseeing any business
ventures that were already in motion. His leaving the continent
did not mean that they could go to town with his money.

Then Vito Genovese, who had fallen onto Luciano's shit list
once again, came up. Shortly after Genovese became an inter-
preter in Naples, he was arrested for his black-market activity.
The man who arrested him did some research and found out that
Genovese was wanted for murder back in Brooklyn, New York.
Genovese was then repatriated to the United States and impris-
oned. He was now awaiting trial for the murder of Ferdinand
Boccia.

Here Luciano was incarcerated in the United States and being
deported to Italy, and now Genovese, incarcerated in Italy, had
been sent back to the United States. If Genovese set foot in New
York before he did, that would really set Luciano off. Luciano
had hedged that Genovese going to Italy was a good thing, because if Luciano did get paroled and deported, Genovese would
be there to help him. And now Luciano was headed to Italy, and
Genovese wasn't there. Luciano said to Lansky and Costello, "I
have a feelin' in my bones that someday Vito [is] gonna be bad
news for everybody. I have something special in mind for the little bastard, and I'll hold you responsible to see that Genovese
keeps his nose clean."

Part of Luciano was very content with Genovese's current situation, but if Genovese managed to beat the rap, get out, and return to the Luciano family, Luciano wanted him watched like a
hawk. He reminded Lansky and Costello about the Carlo Tresca
murder, and how Genovese had ordered that killing against his
wishes. Luciano was sure that it was a sign of things to come.
Hopefully though, Genovese would get convicted of murder, and
executed.

The last thing that Luciano told Lansky and Costello was to tell
all the bosses that they would see him again soon. Luciano said
that he had every intention of coming back to New York, and he
wanted them to know it.

Then, their twenty minutes were up. Luciano said goodbye to
Polakoff, who told him that he wouldn't be back. Costello said
that he'd try to see Luciano one last time before he left. If they
could find out which ship Luciano was departing on, maybe they
could meet again there. Lansky and Lascari said they'd return,
and they'd bring Luciano traveler's checks.

Over the next couple of days, Lansky and Lascari visited Luciano and gave him $2,500 worth of traveler's checks. Since
Luciano had never used the checks before—he was a cash-only
type—Lansky had to explain how to use them.

Then Luciano received a visit from his two brothers—Bart and
Joseph Lucania. Luciano was terribly sad to say goodbye to his

brothers. He hadn't seen Joe since his days at Dannemora. No matter how much Luciano deviated, and became bad news for his family, the three brothers loved each other. Luciano and his brothers wept together, as Luciano thought about saying not to worry, that he'd be coming back. He just couldn't bring himself to say it, because he didn't believe it. When his brothers were gone, he banged his head against the wall.

On February 7, 1946, Luciano received Lansky and Lascari one more time at Ellis Island. He had been saving one last piece of information that he wanted Lansky to know, so he excused Lascari.

He told Lansky that when he was in Sing Sing a month ago, he had made his own contacts with people in Italy who could help him. Luciano told Lansky that he was having visas made under his original name—Salvatore Lucania—for Cuba, Mexico, and several countries in South America.[13]

Luciano said that he would lie low in Italy for about six months, and get things set up for himself over there. Then, if he could, he'd make his way to Cuba and move in there and, if he had to, become a Cuban citizen. If it came to that, Luciano would need Lansky to help, since Lansky had a personal relationship with Fulgencio Batista, who was a high-powered Cuban government official. Lansky also had an investment in the Hotel Nacional in Havana.

Lansky agreed to help. Then Luciano added one more thing— he wanted a meeting with all of the bosses in Cuba at Christmastime of 1946. Christmas would be great because it would just look like a holiday and wouldn't attract too much attention. Lansky agreed to help arrange Luciano's first meeting with the Commission in over a decade.

On Friday, February 8, 1946, Lucky Luciano was escorted from his prison cell on Ellis Island to a room in the hull of a seven-thousand-ton Liberty ship called *Laura Keene*, which was anchored off of Pier 7 in Brooklyn.[14] Luciano couldn't believe his bad luck that the last view he'd have of New York was going to be of Brooklyn, where he had purposely only set foot a handful of times since truant school thirty-five years earlier.

Everybody had heard that Luciano was about to be deported. When Costello was leaving Ellis Island after previously visiting Luciano, he got bushwhacked by a reporter who recognized him. The journalist made quite a fuss when he wasn't allowed to interview Costello, and he wrote about Luciano's impending deportation in the *New York Times*.[15] Members of the press wanted to be there to interview him one last time, and they were even invited to the pier by the Immigration and Naturalization Service to cover Luciano's debarkation.

At 10 a.m. on Saturday February 9, 1946—four years to the day since *Normandie*[16] was accidentally set on fire and ignited the battle for control of the Port of New York—eighteen reporters gathered at the foot of 41st Street in the cold rain and began walking toward the Bush Dock Terminal in front of Pier 7. They approached a large warehouse with a skeleton of steel columns and beams surrounded by sheet metal. When they reached the entrance, there were men inside moving three thousand tons of flour. Suddenly, the reporters were stopped dead in their tracks.[17]

"Get those guys out of the entrance!" yelled the head stevedore. "Throw them out!"[18]

Seventy hookers—burly stevedores and longshoremen—stopped what they were doing, looked toward the entrance, and started to advance. They didn't have their intimidating heaving hooks, as they would have damaged the flour packaging, but they looked mean as they collected into a line that came at the retreating reporters from three sides. The reporters were looking at dozens of strong men with leather skin, scars on their faces, and dripping sweat. Some even had eye patches, and all were hardy men. As the reporters backed toward 41st Street, a female photographer demanded that they be let through. A frightening longshoreman by the name of Henry "the Bull" stepped up and yelled, "Beat it!"[19]

The press backed off and searched for someone in charge who

would help them get through. The dock bosses emerged and told them that Luciano didn't want to conduct any interviews, and that it was too dangerous for them to be walking around the pier that was loaded with flour, which in the rain was easy to damage. Eventually, the reporters left.

For a while it looked like no one was going to get through, but a few hours later, a black limousine with a large grill and white-wall tires emerged and slowly approached the entrance to the warehouse. As longshoremen re-formed to block the limousine, a window opened and someone inside flashed an ILA union badge. The longshoremen then opened up a gap and made way to let the car go through. Once past the warehouse and the longshoremen, it inched down the uneven pier that was long enough to support the over-five-hundred-foot-long *Laura Keene.*

When the limousine got to the entrance of *Laura Keene*, there were more longshoremen loading flour onto the boat. A ship's mate on the boat watched as a half dozen of the most well-dressed men he had ever seen stepped out of the limousine. The delegation—led by Frank Costello—flashed credentials to the ship's mate, who was very impressed by Costello's diamond ring. They were let on board and then permitted to go see their friend Charlie.

Luciano had been confined to his quarters—a five- by eight-foot room aft of amidships—and the delegation tried to meet in there, but the room was too small. The group was then moved to the gun crew's quarters (now empty since the war was over), where Luciano could properly say hello to the men who comprised the combination that he'd created for Operation Under-world. After Costello, Joe Adonis greeted Luciano, after not having seen him in a decade. Bugsy Siegel was in from the West, and he was happy to report that he was opening up a new hotel and casino called the Flamingo in Las Vegas any month now. There was also Costello's cousin and underboss, Willie Moretti.[20] And finally, there was Meyer Lansky, who'd had someone check into a hotel in Maryland under his name just in case anyone tried to claim he was there.[21]

There was wine and champagne, and everyone was reminiscing about old times. They were laughing and telling lies, but as much fun as Luciano was having, he couldn't drink his wine. As was often the case when he was under extreme stress, his stomach was too upset to consume much of anything. It had been ten long years since a bottle of wine was opened in front of him, and now he couldn't even bring himself to drink it. He also couldn't bring himself to eat the greasy veal cutlets served by the ship's crew. It was a huge step up from what he had been eating in prison, but his stomach wasn't having any of it.

So what did Luciano want to have?

The only thing he could think of was seafood.

Costello and Adonis knew exactly where they could get that. The two walked off the boat and back to the limousine.[22] They drove past the longshoremen, across the Brooklyn Bridge, and all the way to the Lower East Side of Manhattan. There, they stopped at Fulton Fish Market, which was where Operation Underworld more or less began. Socks Lanza wasn't there, but just about all of the Italians there knew who Frank Costello and Joe Adonis were. The bottom of a sawed-off crate was loaded with precooked lobsters and escorted to their limousine.

After 3 p.m., they brought the lobster back to the pier and the ship's steward cooked some spaghetti and sauce to go along with it. Luciano ate, but still couldn't touch his wine, so he drank milk, which always helped his stomach. It was too bad, as there were two cases of wine, and also brandy and whiskey.

Then, after several hours, Luciano said goodbye to his final combination in the United States. He assured all of them that he would be back, and he kept a straight face as he tried extremely hard not to cry. The men left after dark, when there were still over a dozen longshoremen guarding the boat from the press.

In the early morning of Sunday, February 10, 1946, Luciano heard *Laura Keene* start up her boilers. He was breathing heavily and trying not to panic. The room he was in was tiny, and the walls began closing in. Then, at 8:50 a.m., Luciano's stomach dropped. The pilot's horn sounded and shook him so violently that he felt like the vibrations came out of his guts. The thing that he had tried so hard to prevent from happening—that he had dreaded at a constant for ten years—was happening.

How could Luciano have let this happen? How could it have come to this?

Luciano wept, as he banged his head against the wall. He had been kicked out of his home, like he had been by his parents when he was younger, and sent on his way back to a place he couldn't remember. He wished he couldn't remember Dewey, or the whores who got him busted. He wished he couldn't remember when Walter Chrysler used to ask him for a marker at his casinos, and when he could just smile at a broad and that would be enough to get her in bed.

As *Laura Keene* began the first feet of her four-thousand-mile journey, Luciano began to feel defeated. He fought back, and rose to his feet and told himself he'd make it back. He told himself that this was not goodbye. He told himself that he would do whatever it took to show the Commission that he was still as much of a big shot as he always was. "Fuck 'em all," he said. "I'll be back."[23] He had to tell himself that, otherwise he'd have to face the truth—that he was never coming back to his home, nor the underworld kingdom over which he'd reigned.

CHAPTER 16

The Hopeless Sinners

Ever since Commander Charles Haffenden wrote that letter to the Governor's Counsel about Lucky Luciano's contribution to the war effort, there had been a lot of nasty rumors circulating about the commander. Former Mayor Fiorello La Guardia got involved indirectly, when he wrote a letter to J. Edgar Hoover asking him to look into how Frank Costello could be "strutting" around during Luciano's debarkation—clearly New York City was lost to racketeers, so federal assistance was all that was left.

The FBI already had an investigation going prior to La Guardia's letter. They had been looking into the reasons behind Luciano's deportation, apparently unsatisfied by the work of the Parole Board. They even managed to get an agent aboard *Laura Keene*, but he was unable to locate the Luciano party. As part of that investigation, Hoover and the FBI wanted to know if there was any truth behind Luciano's contribution to the war effort. This led them to Haffenden and several very bad rumors about the commissioner. There was a rumor that Luciano had paid $250,000 to Haffenden to get him out of prison. Another rumor was that Murray Gurfein, of all people, had gotten Haffenden his job as commissioner. And there was a more menacing rumor that Haffenden had started a dummy corporation with two congressmen from Brooklyn to create a monopoly on all retail contracts coming to Idlewild Airport.[1]

The most persistent of rumors was that Haffenden's appointment as the commissioner of Marine and Aviation of New York City was in repayment for helping Luciano obtain clemency. So the FBI came calling one day, and Haffenden didn't do himself any favors when he denied that he knew Frank Costello.

Hadn't Haffenden golfed with Costello at Pomonok Country Club in Flushing?

Haffenden suddenly remembered that he had indeed golfed with Costello.

Haffenden was slipping cognitively. Something in that bomb blast on Iwo Jima had rattled him so hard that a part of him was broken. He still tried to approach life with energy and swagger, but he kept coming up short. Mary Haffenden was noticing that his energy would come in waves, and he would tire easily.[2]

Then on Friday, May 24, 1946—less than five months since his appointment as commissioner—he was forced to resign by Mayor O'Dwyer. Haffenden wasn't cutting it and wasn't getting along with the mayor. Allegations were piling up, and O'Dwyer had enough crimes of his own to cover up. If he helped Haffenden, he'd be dragged into whatever scandal came next. O'Dwyer acted so fast that nobody could come to Haffenden's rescue, as the mayor sent a policeman to the Haffenden residence in Queens. He gave Haffenden a telegram stating that he'd be off the city payroll by midnight. In response, Haffenden wrote a letter that stated:

"I am making a statement that I no longer wish to serve in the present City administration, this to become effective immediately as of this hour, as there are certain actions unbecoming sound administrative policy."

Haffenden was determined to go down swinging, and his letter, with its open challenge to the mayor, was published in the *New York Times*. As a parting shot to the administration, Haffenden wrote, "And I hereby order all advertised contracts at Idlewild Airport canceled and they must be re-advertised in proper form under my successors after this resignation becomes effective."

In that statement he showed signs of his old self, as he cleverly saved himself from any contracts that might cause him trouble in the future by cancelling all of them. This incensed Mayor O'Dwyer to no end. O'Dwyer later announced that all contracts would be honored and that Haffenden didn't have the authority to make such a decision. "Case closed," O'Dwyer said.

The loss of his position as commissioner was a heavy blow to Haffenden, and in effect the end of any chance at a run for office. His unorthodox approach had offended yet another group of leaders. Five months later, in November, his application for retirement from the navy was approved after a physical examination revealed that he had "arterial hypertension and a ventral hernia," the latter of which had resulted from his stomach surgery after the Battle of Iwo Jima. The former started a long time ago, and sped up when he became the leader of Operation Underworld.

Over the course of the next year, the FBI, the Treasury Department, and the Bureau of Narcotics all sent investigators to the Third Naval District Office of Intelligence at 90 Church Street. The navy dug in deeper with every encounter, as they denied the existence of Operation Underworld and continued to focus on the fact that Haffenden had acted outside of the chain of command, as well as the lie that he was a subpar officer and buffoon. The very mention of the name "Luciano" at 90 Church Street made the mood change, as the Mafia boss's name became like a plague.

Then in February 1947, a broadcaster and gossip columnist named Walter Winchell reported that Luciano was being considered for the Congressional Medal of Honor.

Had Luciano parachuted into Sicily ahead of Operation Husky?

As ridiculous as the rumor sounded, it actually had some basis in truth; it was an idea that had been presented through the channels of ONI. It only made the navy even more defensive. The article also put Haffenden on the spot, as he was the one who had suggested to the navy that Luciano take this action in the first place. The navy lambasted Haffenden again, and this time they did it publicly as a way to respond to Winchell.

Not one to stand on the sidelines, Haffenden fought back, and later in the month he divulged some of the details of Operation

Underworld to the *New York World-Telegram and Sun*. He broke his promise to remain silent because he felt compelled to attack when put on the defensive. Then another punch to the gut hit Haffenden—Captain MacFall, who was retired in San Diego, California, contradicted Haffenden with an article he contributed to in the *New York Post*. MacFall was even quoted as saying, "Luciano had done nothing for the war effort."

After losing MacFall's confidence, and seeing his old commanding officer and friend side against him, Haffenden was finally silenced.

The United States government thought they were done with Charles "Lucky" Luciano, but he was determined to prove them wrong. When Luciano arrived in Genoa, Italy, on February 28, 1946, after a seventeen-day journey across the Atlantic Ocean, he was promptly arrested by Italian authorities and told he would have to reside in his old home town in Sicily—Lercara Friddi.

Nearly forty years to the month later, Luciano was back where he came from, only this time the sky was blue and not clouded with volcanic ash. When he arrived, he signed his name into the town registry, "Salvatore Lucania."

Over the course of the next few months, Luciano moved north to Naples, and then to Rome, staying at the Excelsior Hotel in both cities. All the while, he was establishing contact with Vito Genovese's connections in the smuggling and narcotics rackets. Luciano was determined to come back to the Commission with something profitable for everyone. He needed to show that he had something to bring to the table, because he had two goals to accomplish if he was going to win back his American empire, and then return to it.

First, Luciano needed to take care of the Genovese problem. Genovese, while in jail and awaiting trial, had managed to orchestrate the murder of his co-conspirators and the witnesses to his killing of Ferdinand Boccia. One was shot six times in the backseat of a car and thrown out while it was still moving. Another was somehow poisoned in prison. And the final witness—

Ernest Rupolo—disappeared.[3] Anthony "Tony Bender" Strollo refused to testify. And as for Michael Miranda, he turned himself in after all the witnesses were dead, and pleaded not guilty.[4]

On June 10, 1946, all charges against Genovese, Bender, and Miranda in the murder of Boccia were dropped. Genovese was a free man in the United States for the first time in almost a decade. It was a fate that made Luciano beyond jealous. As for Genovese, he wanted his authority back as underboss of the Luciano family— for starters. Luciano knew exactly what that meant, and what it would lead to.

Word from Costello and Lansky to Luciano was not good. Genovese was muscling in on Anastasia's territory in Brooklyn. He was also reestablishing drug networks without the Commission's consent and was even talking about how he should be running the Luciano family, since Luciano wasn't even there. This threat had to be dealt with.

Luciano's second goal was to retain his American businesses and connect his drug connections in Europe and Africa to the United States. The way he figured it, he could solve the Genovese problem and expand his business in one fell swoop—declare himself *Capo di Tutti Capi*.

It was not a card that Luciano wanted to play, but since he'd arrived in Sicily, something had changed in him. Having once been reticent about the narcotics trade and becoming a leader on an old-world model, Luciano no longer cared about what he had to do to make it back to the top. He had won his freedom, to be sure, but his home was New York City, and he would do anything to get back there. In the meantime, if he couldn't make himself relevant, he knew that it was only a matter of time before Genovese pushed him out.

Then, in the fall of 1946, Luciano received a telegram from Lansky: "December—Hotel Nacional."

The meeting of the Commission—the first in over ten years with Luciano present—was set for Havana, Cuba, around Christmas.

* * *

During the late 1930s, Lucky Luciano had been effectively cut off from communication with his capos. Communication still occurred, but certainly not in the capacity he was used to prior to being incarcerated. When Luciano became part of Operation Underworld, and was given access to anyone he wanted, he learned how to run an empire from afar. When he arrived in Havana, Cuba, in late October 1946, he was ready to duplicate the process from a place that was closer to the United States than he had been to Manhattan when he was in Great Meadow prison.

Nobody outside of the Commission and the Mafia knew that Luciano was in Cuba—his passport read "Salvatore Lucania." He arrived via a roundabout route—Rome to Caracas, Caracas to Mexico City, then finally Mexico City to Havana.

The first order of business was Lansky's idea. Luciano needed a legitimate front to restart his business in Cuba, and he needed to make friends with Lansky's government contacts. Lansky figured out a solution that solved both problems, as he encouraged Luciano to invest $150,000 to buy a share in the Hotel Nacional. The only problem was that Luciano was strapped for cash at the moment, but Lansky solved that problem too.

On December 22, 1946, the underworld elite began arriving in Havana to form what became known as the Havana Conference. There were bosses from all over the US, including Chicago, New Orleans, Miami, and Buffalo. The leaders of the Five Families of New York were present—Lucky Luciano, Vincent Mangano, Joe "Bananas" Bonanno, Joe Profaci, and Tommy "Three Finger Brown" Lucchese, who was representing Tommy Gagliano. There were also members of Luciano's combination for Operation Underworld—Meyer Lansky, Frank Costello, Joe Adonis, Michael Miranda, and Willie Moretti. Present as well were Albert Anastasia and Vito Genovese, the two of whom were not getting along, and whose conflict was a topic of discussion when the Commission met.[5]

The Havana Conference was held in a banquet hall at the Hotel

Nacional.[6] The entire mezzanine floor was off-limits to visitors so that the Commission could meet in total privacy. The meeting kicked off with a tribute to Luciano. He sat at the head of a long rectangular table in a room of the same shape that had long rows of arches on two sides. One by one, the wealthiest racketeers in America walked up to Luciano as he sat, and gave him envelopes stuffed with cash. When each was done displaying his respect to their leader—his fealty—Luciano had over $200,000, and more than enough to buy into the Hotel Nacional. Lansky and Luciano were back to playing their game.

Once everyone was seated, Luciano stood up and addressed the Commission by thanking them for accepting his invitation to meet. Then Luciano brought up the fact that the Commission had gone too long without a leader. He understood that the men in the room were preconditioned to recognize one leader—one king of the underworld. This was especially true for members of the Commission, who were all Sicilian, and accustomed to *Capo di Tutti Capi*. Luciano could have been this person fifteen years ago if he had wanted it, and by the end of 1946 he believed he had made the wrong decision.

What had it gotten Luciano?

He still ended up in jail and deported, and all his business interests had been shrinking while he was away. His legal defense came to well over a million dollars, and every penny he had was tied up in gambling and casino rackets that had yet to pay out.

Luciano would not lose another chance to declare himself "the Boss of All Bosses."

Anastasia was the first to speak in favor of the idea. As he sat across from Genovese, Anastasia stood up and told everyone that the way he saw it, Luciano had always been the boss of all bosses.

Then, Anastasia looked Genovese in the eye, and asked if anyone disagreed. Genovese read the room and didn't say a word, but underneath, he seethed with anger at Luciano and Costello, whom he was trying to replace, and Anastasia, who was in his way.

But Genovese would get his victory, as the conversation shifted to the future of the narcotics racket. There were two factions on the Commission, one led by Costello, who wanted nothing to do with narcotics, and one led by his rival Genovese, who believed the profits were too lucrative to ignore. Luciano bridged the gap, knowing that if they didn't embrace the sale of narcotics, somebody else would. However, his name had been dragged through the mud because of narcotics in the past, and Costello's concerns were valid, so they structured the drug trade to try and leave Luciano's and Costello's names out of it. In the end, Genovese got what he wanted, as Luciano and the Commission agreed to invest more money into the narcotics racket.[7]

The final topic of discussion was the gambling racket, which was what Luciano and his combination from Great Meadow prison had been working on for years. Everywhere in the country things were looking up, as they were operating casinos in dozens of major cities and beginning to connect all the sports books to the same wire service. Cuba had also certainly won all of them over too. Profits weren't soaring yet, but they all awaited a postwar economic boom. There was only one problem—"the Siegel situation."

Meyer Lansky stood before the Commission and made a damaging case against one of his best friends. Benjamin "Bugsy" Siegel had been purposely left out of the Havana Conference because he was mishandling the Commission's investment in the Flamingo Hotel in Las Vegas. Lansky explained that construction was way behind, and a $1 million investment had turned into $6 million. Siegel was also taking in outside investors, and much to the chagrin of the Commission, he was even extorting funds from their investments.

The Commission wanted Siegel's blood, but Lansky had calculated that he could convince the Sicilians to go another way. The Flamingo was opening the day after Christmas, and if that was a success, then maybe there was a chance that Siegel could still turn a profit. The Commission sided with Lansky and decided that he should get one more chance, and Luciano agreed.

When Luciano called the meeting adjourned after an entire day, the men were met by girlfriends and wives. The women had been flown in for the holiday, and to listen to a popular singer with a magical voice named Frank Sinatra. Willie Moretti, as his manager, was happy to show off Sinatra. It was a grand gala of gangsters toasting to good times ahead, and the *Capo di Tutti Capi*—"Salvatore Lucania," which he was to be called by everyone from then on. Evidently, the name of "Charles Luciano" had worn out its charm—and worn out its luck.

Now that he had his title, Luciano could focus on what he had been obsessing over for the last decade while at Dannemora and Great Meadow prisons—getting back to New York City. He was so close that he could taste it. There was good news on the horizon too—Thomas Dewey was going to run for president in the 1948 election. He was a shoo-in to beat the incumbent, President Harry S. Truman. Dewey running for president was wonderful news for Luciano—the man owed him, after all. Once Dewey became president of the United States, Luciano would be king of the American underworld and Dewey the leader of the overworld. Luciano was sure that it was only a matter of time.

In the late 1940s, Commander Charles Radcliffe Haffenden's health was declining, and so too was his reputation. Apparently, there had been some truth to one of the rumors that the FBI caught on to—Haffenden had awarded what appeared to be an illegal contract. As commissioner of Marine and Aviation, Haffenden had rented Pier 42 on the Manhattan side of the East River to a stevedore company that didn't operate any ships, which was against the rules. The benefactors were indeed two congressmen from Brooklyn. There was also some evidence that someone had been murdered as a result. Mayor O'Dwyer hid evidence that would have uncovered all of it, and fired Haffenden as a precaution. Though Haffenden would never admit it, O'Dwyer had actually saved him from a lot of trouble.[8]

Haffenden hadn't set out to be a criminal, but having spent every day with underworld figures during Operation Underworld, and then becoming part of Tammany Hall's collection of shady leaders, he could not shake the spell and the excitement he felt working with criminals. He would not be the last person with good intentions to be spellbound by the wicked wizardry of the underworld.

Haffenden had never saved anything for retirement. He never lasted long in high positions, had squandered investments, and all that he could rely on was his navy pension. He and Felix Sacco worked together for a few years selling aluminum wheels for hand trucks that operated in the fish market. It was a business they were both trying to develop based on observations made in Fulton Fish Market during Operation Underworld.

Haffenden became good friends with Moses Polakoff and he and Mary attended parties with Polakoff and his wife. On at least one such occasion—when Polakoff's daughter was married—Haffenden again came into contact with some old underworld friends. Haffenden spoke with Frank Costello and Meyer Lansky, the latter of which was now retaining Polakoff as his lawyer.

In mid-June 1948, Haffenden's daughter, Mary, got married in Flushing. She had been attending art school in Macon, Georgia, when she met a sailor named Bernard Webb, who had served as an officer aboard the battleships USS *New York* and USS *Alabama*.[9] Haffenden was very proud that his daughter married a navy man.

After the wedding, the Haffendens began spending most of their time in their second home in Saluda, North Carolina, where they had been married. The mountain town had only around six hundred people, and was a very far departure from life in Flushing and work in Manhattan. Haffenden was slowing down even more, and his heart was in terrible shape. Then, on November 21, 1949, he was hospitalized. He spent a month at the Naval Hospital in Bethesda, Maryland, and was diagnosed with "hypertensive, cardiovascular disease." His systolic blood pressure was holding steady at 250.[10]

In March 1951, Haffenden received a telegram in Saluda. Evidently, a US senator named Estes Kefauver, who was the chairman of the Senate Special Committee to Investigate Organized Crime in Interstate Commerce, was asking Haffenden to appear as a witness. This made Haffenden nervous and put him in an awkward position. He had previously said in writing that if questioned about Luciano as part of any investigation he would protect the navy.

The Haffendens nonetheless made the short journey north to Washington, DC, where Haffenden met with staffers of the committee members. They coached him through the questions he was likely to be asked by a panel of US senators. If the panel of senators wasn't intimidating enough, the hearings were being broadcast across the nation on live television.

Among witnesses that were called were Meyer Lansky and Frank Costello, each of whom was represented by a former lawyer of Luciano's—Moses Polakoff and George Wolf, respectively. The hearings spotlighted the underworld that was organized by Italian and Jewish Americans. For the first time, the word "Mafia" became a household name. And amid all of that exposure, an aged, frail, and haggard-looking Commander Haffenden took the stand with the lights on and the cameras rolling.

What was left of Haffenden's hair was mostly gone, and he had dark and saggy bags under his eyes and looked much older than fifty-eight years old. Then, as he tried to keep his pulse under control, the senators started asking him questions out of left field. Evidently, the men he'd met the day before had set him up for failure and made him anticipate a completely different line of questioning. As the senators asked Haffenden about Charles "Lucky" Luciano's participation in the war effort, the commander fell on his sword, and lied under oath for the navy.

He said he hadn't met Lansky until 1950, at the wedding of Polakoff's daughter, which was a blatant lie. He mixed up the sequence of events of Operation Underworld, and even said that Luciano's contribution to the war effort had made no "celebrated case" or "major job." He was contradicting all sorts of facts from the letter that he wrote to the Governor's Counsel almost five years earlier. Haffenden knew the navy was embarrassed about his work during Operation Underworld, so he tried to bury it, just as the navy had burned all of the evidence that would've corroborated Haffenden's work anyway. Operation Underworld was being effectively erased from history.[11]

In Haffenden's final days, he accepted his fate as a hopeless sinner, and was happy that at the end of the day, he had protected the navy, which he absolutely still loved. Still though, until his dying day, he made it known to his family and friends at the Executives Association that he hoped someday his story would be told, that someday people would learn about Socks Lanza, that Haffenden did develop Luciano as an informant, from whom he extracted information that was vital to the war effort.[12] He hoped that one day people would know he was not a wannabe, but an accomplished commander, who presided over a section that used some of the most unique measures in all of World War II to accomplish its mission. But the fact was that at the time, his doubters and enemies seemed to have won the battle, and tarnished his reputation beyond repair.

On Christmas Eve 1952, when Haffenden was sixty years old, he had a heart attack at a friend's home in Flushing.[13] Clinging to the past, his final job had been as a salesman for a company selling Dictaphones. He died in shame, as the Haffenden family name had been dragged through the mud. Clearly, he had not profited from any connection to the Mafia, as his assets (his Flushing house, insurance policies, and a two-door Hudson sedan) at the time of his death totaled $27,061.66.

Until the end of his days he thought, against all odds, that someday everyone would know about the valuable service he provided for the navy and his nation during the most uncertain and darkest times of World War II.

Somehow, in an extreme upset, Thomas Dewey lost the presidential race of 1948. His political career had reached its zenith, so he returned to his office as governor of New York until December 31, 1954. During this time Dewey was under periodic attack that he had been bribed by Lucky Luciano to take up to forty years off of his prison sentence. Though he had only commuted Luciano's sentence based on the recommendation of the Parole Board, and even deported him after that, there were so many rumors and tidbits of hearsay regarding Luciano's war contributions that suspicion began to grow about a secret deal between the two men.

Luciano, for his part, obsessed over Thomas Dewey for the entire second half of his life. Dewey, however, was getting very tired of the rumors piling up, and being powerless to stop them. But he couldn't—he wouldn't—reveal classified information that the navy very much wanted to keep under wraps.

In 1952 a writer named Michael Stern reported about Haffenden's letter to the Governor's Counsel. Stern claimed that it was this letter—not the Parole Board's investigation—that led Dewey to commute Luciano's sentence.[14] Then Luciano, taking a shot at Dewey, told Stern that he had contributed $75,000 to Dewey's campaign fund back in 1943.[15] Dewey was sick of the rumors, and in his last year in office, he finally took action.

On January 28, 1954, Dewey hired a forty-eight-year-old investigator named William B. Herlands. Herlands and a small team of investigators were tasked with figuring out if Dewey had been telling the truth when Luciano was paroled—that Luciano had aided the war effort. Herlands was tasked with answering two questions, which included quotes from what Dewey wrote in Luciano's commutation statement:

Was Luciano's "aid sought by the Armed Services in inducing others to provide information concerning possible enemy attack"?

Did it appear that "Luciano "cooperated in such an effort"?

Over the course of the next eight months, with permission from the navy, and the promise that all civilian agents would not be publicly identified, Herlands and his team talked to thirty-one naval officers and enlisted men: Paul Alfieri, Tony Marzulo, and Roscoe MacFall; five civilian agents, including Dominick and Felix Sacco, George Tarbox, and Charles Hoyt; former and current members of the District Attorney's Office, including Frank Hogan (with his wiretap transcripts) and Murray Gurfein; the lawyers involved—Moses Polakoff, George Wolf, and Joseph Guerin—and also, because Charles Haffenden had already passed, Mary Haffenden. Herlands was permitted as well to talk to five "prominent racketeers," including Meyer Lansky, Benjamin Espy, and Socks Lanza, who had been freed from prison in 1950 after serving seven-and-a-half years.

The navy, for its part, permitted the investigation to continue because Naval Intelligence was also interested in the outcome, especially if it could prove that the answer to both of Dewey's questions was no. Thus the navy permitted its men and women to talk to Herlands, provided no classified information was revealed in their interviews. The Mafia also stuck to their *omertà* code of silence on specific events (and crimes). The result was 2,883 pages of testimony that talked about very few actual events. It was clear that several crimes had been committed during Operation Underworld, but everyone was very careful not to implicate themselves and others who were involved.

Even still, at the end of the investigation, Herlands wrote a 101-page document with supporting appendices that became known as the Herlands Report. In essence, Herlands wrote that the answer to both questions was unequivocally yes—Luciano had indeed been sought out and cooperated with the navy to provide information regarding possible enemy attack that was beneficial to the United States' war effort.

But if Dewey was hoping that the Herlands Report would be his salvation and silence the rumors, he was dead wrong. The navy did not like what Herlands had found, and proceeded to cover it up once again. The commander of ONI, a man named Rear Admiral Carl Espe, wrote to Herlands: "Study of the report raises apprehension that its publication might bring harm to the Navy. . . . Publication of this report would inspire a rush of 'thriller' stories allegedly based therein. Enterprising authors would waste no time in exploiting the persons it names, including Naval officers."

Thus, the Herlands Report, along with all the evidence and testimony that Herlands had collected, was marked as "classified"

and would only be made available to future generations, long
after Dewey's death. He would never be able to silence rumors of
an illegal connection to Luciano while he was still alive. What he
did succeed in, however, was giving future generations evidence
of events that otherwise would've never been known.

Lucky Luciano's trip to Cuba was ended on February 23, 1947,
when the US government, having found out about his presence
there, threatened to stop shipping medical supplies if the Cuban
government permitted Luciano to stay. Luciano was banished
from North America, and deported to Italy again, on a freighter
bound for Genoa. Word was that Vito Genovese was the one who
had tipped off US authorities.

Having been rebuked at the highest level, Genovese bided his
time, as Luciano held on to the title of *Capo di Tutti Capi* for the
next decade while residing in Italy. The gambling empire that Luciano had set up in the United States slowly crumbled, however.
Las Vegas turned out to be a gold mine, but thanks to Bugsy
Siegel, his investment in the Flamingo was a disaster. The Hotel
Nacional was taken over and raided by Cuban Communists, and
Joe Adonis's and Willie Moretti's casinos in New Jersey were all
raided. Luciano then had little choice, and became increasingly
dependent on the narcotics trade.

In 1957, Genovese finally made the move that Luciano had
seen coming back in the early 1940s at Great Meadow prison.
The first domino to fall was when Adonis managed to get himself
deported to Italy. With one of Luciano's key allies out of the picture, Genovese capitalized on the situation by ordering a hit on
Frank Costello. A gunman named Vincent Gigante shot Costello
in the head, but the bullet only grazed him—Costello survived.
The next domino to fall was when Genovese ordered a hit on Albert Anastasia (who had previously killed his boss, Vincent
Mangano) which succeeded, as Anastasia was gunned down at
the Park Sheraton Hotel during his daily manicure, shave, and
haircut.

Having survived his assassination attempt, Costello relinquished control of the Luciano family to Genovese, and remains one of the only Mafia bosses to successfully retire from *Cosa Nostra*. This was the last domino, as Costello's resignation effectively removed Luciano from power. Genovese then changed the family name forever to the Genovese family, and the Luciano family was no longer. And since the king had been deposed, Genovese also declared himself *Capo di Tutti Capi*.[16]

But his reign at the top was extremely short-lived, as Luciano got the last laugh. In 1959 he and a combination of co-conspirators that included Meyer Lansky and Frank Costello convinced an informer to testify against Genovese and twenty-four other defendants, including Vincent Gigante,[17] who had failed to kill Costello. Unlike the last time he had an opportunity to take Genovese out by cooperating with authorities, Luciano finally violated *omertà*. Genovese was given a fifteen-year sentence for distributing heroin and would spend the rest of his days in prison, dying of a heart attack on February 14, 1969.

As for Charles "Lucky" Luciano, aka Salvatore Lucania, though he would try several more times throughout his life, the hopeless sinner would never make it back to the United States while he was alive. In the early 1960s, shortly before his death, Luciano commissioned a movie producer named Martin Gosch to record his life story. Just like Dewey, Luciano was tired of all the lies and rumors that had been written and said about him. But when the Commission—under new leadership—found out about what Luciano was doing, they threatened to kill Luciano if he had it published, as its revelations would certainly jeopardize their business, and their code. Even Meyer Lansky sent word that he did not approve. Thus, Luciano gave Gosch instructions to have his story told only after he had been dead for ten years.

On January 26, 1962, when he was sixty-four years old, Luciano's heart murmurs finally caught up with him, and he died of a heart attack at the Naples International Airport, after a meeting with Gosch. Two weeks later, and after a funeral in Naples which Joe Adonis attended, his body was flown to Idlewild Airport, where his brothers, Bart and Joe Lucania, picked it up.[18] The casket bore the name "Salvatore Lucania."[19] After twenty-six years of trying—ten years in prison, and sixteen years in Italy—Luciano had finally made it back to New York City. Bart and Joe then took their brother's body to St. John Cemetery in Queens, with reporters and photographers in tow.

There, Luciano was placed in a vault that he had bought back in 1935 for $25,000. It had big bronze doors and Greek columns, and enough room for his whole family. Luciano was interred inside with several relatives, including his mother, who had never stopped loving him, and his father, who was ashamed of his criminal son.

Upon leaving the cemetery after the funeral, one of the reporters wondered about a stained-glass window at the back of the vault. The artwork depicted a bearded saint leaning on a shepherd's staff. The reporter chased down the Lucania brothers.

What did it mean?

"I don't know," said one of them. "I'm not acquainted with saints."[20]

AFTERWORD

The Fate of the Rest of the Participants in Operation Underworld

COMMANDER HAFFENDEN'S COMMANDERS AND FERRETS

Paul Alfieri—Alfieri came home from Europe as a highly decorated hero. He received not one, but two Legion of Merit awards for his work in intelligence, in combat, and in Sicily and mainland Italy, along with seven battle stars and many foreign government distinctions. When he got home, he put the knowledge he had gained during Operation Underworld to good use when he became chief investigator of the Waterfront Commission of New York Harbor. He also maintained his status in the Naval Reserve, and even took Haffenden's former job and became a Naval Intelligence section commander while training younger officers. His marriage to Nellie, unfortunately, did not survive their losing a child while he was in Italy. However, Alfieri would remarry, and had a daughter, and a son, named Paul. He died in his home in the Bronx in November 1960 at the age of sixty-four.

William Howe—Unlike his best friend Roscoe MacFall, Howe settled away from the sea and went inland, where he owned a ranch in the Southern California hills. He remained retired from the navy and passed away on December 31, 1968, at the age of eighty-five.

Maurice Kelly—Kelly served in the Third Naval District Intelligence Office until November 1945, and achieved the rank of lieutenant commander. After the war he went back to the New Rochelle Police Department, and retired in 1953 after achieving the rank of captain. He did security work after that, and at the time of his death on December 15, 1964, at age sixty-one, he had a wife, two sons, and nine grandchildren.

Roscoe MacFall—MacFall lived the rest of his days two blocks from the beach in a lovely San Diego seaside suburb called La Jolla. When contacted by William Herlands to lend his testimony to Herlands's investigation, MacFall politely refused to make the journey to New York. Evidently he lived out the rest of his days in serenity, as he wrote to Herlands, "I have no desire to come East unless I have to. Too old to be gallivanting around. . . . Right now my garden is alive with color and the mountains are green and beautiful. This is the best time of the year for flowers." MacFall lived into his nineties and passed away in 1973.

Anthony Marzulo—Marzulo came home with seven battle stars of his own, a Legion of Merit, and a Bronze Star awarded to him by the Italian government. He remained active in the Naval Reserve, and even served during the Korean War years later, eventually reaching the rank of captain. At some point, he changed his last name to a more American-sounding Italian name—Marsloe. In 1961 he was married to the love of his life, Gloria. He died in late 2006 at the age of ninety-five, and in January 2007 he was laid to rest at Arlington National Cemetery.

Joachim Titolo—Titolo achieved four battle stars and several commendations during the war. When he came home, he remained active in the Naval Reserve, achieving the rank of commander. Having previously worked in the prosecutor's office, he started his own practice in New York City while living in Jamaica, Queens. When he retired, he moved away to sunny Arizona. At the time of his death at the age of seventy-six on January 26, 1987, he was survived by his wife Thelma and five children, including three girls and two boys.

Joseph Treglia—Treglia is a bit of a mystery, as he seems to disappear from the historical record starting in 1943. His service during Operation Underworld was invaluable, but the next time Treglia is referenced is in his obituary, as he passed away in 1950, and was thus never given the opportunity to testify for the Herlands investigation.

COMMANDER HAFFENDEN'S CIVILIAN AGENTS

Willis George (Agent G)—George, who was basically a professional burglar, moved on from Naval Intelligence to join the Office of Strategic Services (OSS). At the conclusion of the war, he was teaching men in the OSS how to open safes and pick locks, and of major importance, he was also tasked with opening Nazi safes throughout their previously occupied territories in order to restore countless valuable objects to their rightful owners. In 1946 he wrote a memoir called *Surreptitious Entry*, which explained, in theoretical terms, the events that transpired in Chapter 7. Upon giving her testimony to the Herlands investigation in 1954, Mary Haffenden came to her interview with a copy of this book. George remained a safecracker for the rest of his life, working for various federal government agencies. He died in New York in April 1979 at the age of eighty-one.

Charles Hoyt (Agent H)—Hoyt, already in his mid-fifties during his contribution to Operation Underworld, lived another thirty years. He was retired before the war and remained so after. He spent the rest of his years in North Bergen, New Jersey, and died in August 1973.

Dominick Sacco (Agent X)—This book represents the first time that Dominick Sacco is publicly mentioned as a participant in Operation Underworld. He continued as a civilian agent for a while longer, and then went back to working full-time at the Schindler Bureau of Investigation (he had never actually left during the war). In 1950, he became a claims clerk at the Division of Employment, and in May of 1954 he became the chief security officer of Griswold Country Club. He passed away on June 28, 1976, leaving behind his wife Edith and daughter Gloria.

Felix Sacco (Agent Y)—This book is also the first time that Felix Sacco is publicly mentioned as a participant in Operation Underworld. He left the navy as a civilian agent in 1944, and became an engineer and salesman with Charles Haffenden for aluminum wheels on hand trucks at the fish market. In 1948 he became inspector of housing for the City of New York. Sacco clearly liked to work with his hands, and he passed that down to his son Felix, who became a mechanical engineer. Sacco died at the age of seventy-three, on June 12, 1965.

George Tarbox (Agent T)—Tarbox remained working as a civilian agent for the navy for several more years. He was described as "an investigator's investigator," and was well liked. He retired from the navy in 1959 and passed away at the age of seventy-one years old on March 5, 1966.

OTHER CIVILIANS

Thomas Dewey—Dewey is an interesting character in the entire Operation Underworld episode, in that he didn't know much, if anything, about it until long after it was over, and yet he is responsible for all the knowledge we have about it today. Dewey did not think about Luciano nearly as much as Luciano thought about him, but nevertheless, because of their connection as prosecutor and prosecuted, and pardoner and pardoned, they will forever be linked in history. Dewey retired from politics in 1954, though he was still very much active behind the scenes in the Republican Party, and was never quite able to shake suspicions that there had been some sort of deal between him and Luciano to get the latter pardoned. Dewey returned to the law and ran a private practice until his death at the age of sixty-eight on March 16, 1971. He died of a massive heart attack between rounds of golf in Florida.

Murray Gurfein—Gurfein was one of the most instrumental people in developing the structure of Operation Underworld. During the war, he eventually made his way to Germany, where he was assistant to future Supreme Court Justice Robert H. Jackson in his prosecution of German war criminals in Nuremberg. After the war he returned to New York City and took up a private practice until 1971, when he was appointed by President Richard Nixon to become a judge for the Southern District of New York. He then became a judge in the court of appeals, a position that he held until his death at the age of seventy-two on December 16, 1979. Among his exploits as judge was his upholding of the *Washington Post*'s right to publish what became known as the Pentagon Papers. In his ruling, he wrote something that is highly relevant to Operation Underworld—"The security of the Nation is not at the ramparts alone. Security also lies in the value of our free institutions. A cantankerous press, an obstinate press, a ubiquitous press must be suffered by those in authority in order to preserve the even greater values of freedom of expression and the right of the people to know."

Frank Hogan—Hogan had the wiretap in Meyer's Hotel removed in early February 1943, just days after Lanza went to jail. If it hadn't been for the Herlands investigation, the transcripts from this wiretap might have been all we ever knew about Operation Underworld. After the war, Hogan remained at his post and continued prosecuting New York City's worst criminals. He remained in his position as the district attorney in Manhattan until 1974, when he was forced to retire after having a tumor removed from his lung and suffering a stroke. Later that year, on April 2, 1974, he died of cancer at the age of seventy-two.

Moses Polakoff—Polakoff had one final meeting with Luciano in Naples. As his testimony states, in the early 1950s he was dining outside in Naples while on a vacation when he noticed a champagne bottle effervesce all over Luciano and the women he was with. Polakoff walked over to say hi, and the two men had dinner together that night. He continued his private practice and died at the age of ninety-seven on June 14, 1993. When he was defending Lansky during the Kefauver Hearings, he said something that sums up his view on defending some of the nation's worst criminals. A senator asked Polakoff how he could represent such a "dirty rat" as Luciano, and added, "Aren't there some ethics in the legal profession?" Polakoff responded by saying, "Under our constitution, every person is entitled to their day in court. . . . When the day comes that a person is beyond the pale of justice, that means our liberty is gone. Minorities and undesirables and persons with bad reputations are more entitled to the protection of the law than the so-called honorable people. I don't have to apologize to you . . . or anyone else for whom I represent."[1]

George Wolf—Wolf's underworld clients went beyond Costello and Luciano, as over the years he basically represented an Operation Underworld all-star team that also included Willie Moretti, Vito Genovese, Albert Anastasia, and Frank Erickson. In 1974 he reached national fame when he released a book titled *Frank Costello: Prime Minister of the Underworld.* He too shared Polakoff's belief that everyone deserved a defense in the face of prosecution, and was very proud of the work he did. He died in March 1980 in a Florida nursing home at the age of ninety.

LUCIANO'S COMBINATION FOR OPERATION UNDERWORLD

Joe Adonis—On January 3, 1956, Adonis left New York City for Naples, Italy, after he had served prison time for a crime and was facing deportation. Adonis was not available to be questioned for the Herlands investigation, as he was in prison at the time. There is no evidence that Adonis linked up with Luciano while in Italy, however, when Luciano died, Adonis attended a funeral for Luciano in Naples, and contributed a wreath that said, "So long, Pal." In late November 1971, Adonis was violently questioned about the assassination of a popular prosecutor, had a heart attack during the intense interrogation, and died on November 26.

Frank Costello—If ever there was an underworld figure that embodied class, sophistication, and smarts, it was Frank Costello, later nicknamed "Prime Minister of the Underworld." He was even on the cover of *TIME* magazine in 1949. After becoming a target of the Kefauver Committee, he spent most of the 1950s in and out of prison, while still retaining his hold on the Luciano family. Unlike Luciano, he was able to keep his citizenship and beat most of the charges against him. Costello and Luciano—friends since boyhood—never saw each other again after the Havana Conference. Costello, having successfully retired from the Mafia, gave advice to Lansky when he came calling, and enjoyed gardening in his final days. On February 18, 1974, he died after suffering a massive heart attack days prior.

Johnny "Cockeye" Dunn—Upon being released from prison in 1945, Dunn immediately resumed his endeavor with the Dunn-McGrath Gang to gain control of the waterfront on the West Side of Manhattan. On June 8, 1947, he ambushed a stevedore hiring boss named Andy Hintz, and shot Hintz six times. Somehow, Hintz survived long enough to make a dying declaration that Dunn had shot him. He died weeks later. As for Dunn, he was convicted of murder, and on July 7, 1949, he was executed in an electric chair known as "Old Sparky" at Sing Sing prison. District Attorney Frank Hogan and Governor Thomas Dewey may or may not have known about Dunn's help during Operation Underworld, but either way, while Hogan and Dewey combined to commute the execution of one of Dunn's co-conspirators, they did not do the same for Dunn.

Benjamin Espy—Not much is known about the fate of Espy, but what is known is that after his time at Fulton Fish Market, he worked for years at Meyer Lansky's legitimate business, the Emby Distribution Company. After that, he worked at a pet food corporation in Brooklyn as an office manager. During his testimony for the Herlands investigation, he said that he was a little lost in the world, and his turn from enforcer to legitimate businessman shows that that was certainly true.

Meyer Lansky—Lansky has since been nicknamed the "Mob's accountant." That is an apt title, given that he was the source of so many investments by members of the Mafia. Because of business, Lansky and Lucky Luciano kept ties when Luciano was in Italy, but it appears that the two lifelong friends last saw each other prior to Luciano being deported from Cuba. Lansky lost millions of dollars in the Cuban revolution of 1959, and never even made back his initial investments. Afterward, he focused much of his attention on an emerging Las Vegas. While Siegel failed with the opening of the Flamingo, shortly before his death it reopened as the Fabulous Flamingo, and Lansky enjoyed heavy profits until it was sold in 1960. Biographers and historians have debated Lansky's true impact on the underworld's control over gambling. His influence in setting up a nationwide, and world-wide, gambling network is certainly major; however, he did not achieve the financial success that many attribute to the smart lit-tle man who was really good with numbers. He died at the age of eighty on January 15, 1983, in Florida, from lung cancer.

Joe "Socks" Lanza—When he was released from prison in 1950, Lanza wept because his wife, Ellen Connor, was there to greet him. The two would finally produce a child, a boy that they named Harry, in the same year Lanza got out of prison. Lanza then promptly returned to Fulton Fish Market, where, as the judge in his case had feared, he returned to his life of racketeer-ing. In 1954, he provided an extraordinary account of Operation Underworld to the Herlands investigation. When asked to come back in for another round of questioning, he feigned a cold and was excused from giving more testimony. He went back to prison from 1957 to 1960, for violating his parole, and died of cancer at the age of sixty-eight on October 11, 1968.[2]

Michael Lascari—Mikey Lascari was such a friend to the Lucania family that he even donated his business—Riverside Music Company—to one of Luciano's brothers when he was out of work. In 1950 he visited Luciano in Italy and is reported to have given him $2,500. In 1951 he went to work for a tobacco company.

Vincent Mangano—Mangano didn't last long after Operation Underworld, as Albert Anastasia, having reached the rank of un-derboss, eventually wanted to run the family himself. Mangano disappeared on April 19, 1951, and was never seen again. He was ruled dead in absentia in 1961. Anastasia took over his family, until he was killed in 1957. Then, a gangster named Carlo

Gambino took over, and renamed the family after his own name. Gambino helped Luciano, Lansky, and Costello set up Genovese in 1959, and he became *Capo di Tutti Capi* after Genovese went to prison.

Willie McCabe—McCabe died of natural causes at City Hospital in New York City on January 28, 1953. Thus, he was unable to testify for the Herlands investigation.

Michael Miranda—Miranda remained active in the Mafia, and rose to the prestigious level of consigliere in the Genovese family. When Genovese went to prison, Miranda and two other men formed a triumvirate that ruled the family. He was a bit miffed that he never achieved the rank of boss, but he was able to retire in 1972, and in a rare case with Mafia members, he died of natural causes outside of prison (it should be noted, however, that Luciano, Lansky, and Costello all died of natural causes). This happened in Boca Raton, Florida, on July 16, 1973, just ten days shy of his seventy-eighth birthday.

Willie Moretti—Moretti had success after the war with his gambling operations in New Jersey. He was instrumental at getting celebrities such as Dean Martin and Jerry Lewis to perform there, and continued to work with Frank Sinatra. He famously helped Sinatra by buying out his contract for $1 after making the man who currently held Sinatra's contract *an offer he couldn't refuse*. By the early 1950s, his fellow gangsters were becoming wary of Moretti's declining mental state, evidently the result of advanced syphilis. Since he liked to talk, his partners in crime grew concerned about what he might say to authorities. The Kefauver Committee hearings were the last straw, as he talked way more than he should have, famously saying, when asked if he was in the mafia: "What do you mean, like do I carry a membership card that says 'Mafia' on it?" Costello protected him for a long time, but eventually Genovese got his way and had Moretti killed in what other Mafia members called a "mercy killing." He was shot in the back of the head at Joe's Elbow Room restaurant in Cliffside, New Jersey, on October 4, 1951, at the age of fifty-seven.

Benjamin "Bugsy" Siegel—Siegel's opening of the Flamingo Hotel on December 26, 1946, was an absolute disaster. He lost money and had to shut down the hotel to resume construction. His good buddy Lansky saved his life again in the face of pressure from the Commission, but couldn't stop them a third time when Siegel continued to lose money. On June 20, 1947, a sniper shot Siegel four times with an M1 Garand as Siegel sat in the living room of his movie star girlfriend's house in Beverly Hills. Knowing that Siegel was practically immortal in gunfights, the shooter didn't let himself be seen.

EPILOGUE

When I first read Rear Admiral Carl Espe's assessment of the Herlands Report, noting that "enterprising authors would waste no time in exploiting the persons it names, including Naval officers," I had a powerful feeling that he was talking directly to me. And while I was uneasy about becoming the "enterprising author" he dreaded, I reminded myself of several points to the contrary.

This section will cover how my recounting of Operation Underworld differs from previous ones; my feelings on the navy, the trustworthiness of sources, and gaps in the historical record; and my approach to research and creative liberties.

As of the writing of this book, Operation Underworld ended successfully nearly eighty years ago, and all participants have long since become deceased. And perhaps even more relevant, the Herlands Report was declassified in 1977 and has been available to the public ever since. For forty-five years, this story has been lying in wait.

In 1977, an English journalist named Rodney Campbell, who had previously edited Thomas Dewey's memoir, was entrusted with revealing the contents of the Herlands Report, and the nearly three thousand pages of testimony that came with it, to the public. Campbell used the information to write and publish the book *The

Luciano Project. It is a factual accounting of the events that purposely avoids the drama and excitement revealed in this book.

The Luciano Project also leaves several holes that Campbell didn't address (perhaps on purpose), as connecting the dots of Mafia activity while also being involved in Operation Underworld would have certainly opened the navy up to embarrassment. As the first to break this story, Campbell treated it with extreme care and, for example, chose not to expose the names of Agent X, Agent Y, or the spymaster. I have identified them in this book as Dominick Sacco, Felix Sacco, and Wallace Wharton.

My book has several key findings that Campbell didn't know, but the names of the secret agents, as identified in Haffenden's little black book, do not qualify as such findings. Having spent the better part of two years researching testimony from the Herlands investigation, I can only conclude that Campbell absolutely knew the names of the three men mentioned above, but chose not to disclose their names out of respect for their memories, for their wishes (the Saccos initially did not want to testify to Herlands), and for the navy.

Furthermore, the navy contended that the publication of the material that makes up this story could jeopardize future operations of a similar type, should they become necessary. That is true, but given that the report and all the material that comes with it has been declassified, and the fact that it happened so long ago, it's unlikely that this book is blowing the lid off of anything going on today. The use of underworld informants against a foreign power was not unique, however; it was repeated during the Cold War. The use of fishing boats as a means to gather reconnaissance was also not unique to Operation Underworld. And finally, it has to be mentioned that while these measures by Naval Intelligence were extraordinary, they were faced with incredible circumstances in the early days of World War II, and one must remember that the ultimate goal of victory was very much in doubt.

I can only hope that the navy, having previously signed off on the publication of the Herlands Report, doesn't bat an eye at the telling of a page in its history, which happened so long ago and under such extreme circumstances that certainly it should not reflect negatively on the fine men and women sailors who serve in the US Navy today. I have always been an avid learner about and extreme fan of the navy's traditions and fantastic collection of sailors. This is the prevailing accepted conclusion about Operation Underworld, but admittedly, this book brings to light things that the navy was probably trying to hide when they burned almost everything related to Operation Underworld.

And given the proud traditions of the navy, and the fact that several high-ranking officers believe that Commander Haffenden dishonored these traditions, it's not surprising that they took this step. This is especially true when you consider that maybe Haffenden did overstep and was party to some significant crimes. His friend and successor Harold MacDowell perhaps put it best when he said that he wanted nothing to do with underworld informants because "when you go to sleep with dogs you get up with fleas." This is certainly true in Haffenden's case.

On a personal note, I'd like to add that in a society that embraces liberal democracy and is funded by the taxpayers (especially for defense), it is the right of the citizens of that society to have any and all of the military's activities revealed at some point, to maintain civilian oversight. These activities should also be revealed because if we as a society actually do want to learn from history, then the only way to get it right is to be provided with sources of truth. I recognize that at times information is difficult to share, but I believe that this is not one of those times. The only bad thing I'll say about the navy is that I'm deeply disappointed that they incinerated so much about these events that is now lost to history forever. To my earlier point, I certainly don't blame anyone in the navy now for what happened eighty years ago.

As for Lucky Luciano and his role in this book, it is absolutely amazing how little there is in the historical record of his activities during Operation Underworld. Campbell spends two pages on the first six visits to Luciano in Great Meadow prison, while this book devotes at least that amount to each visit.

Piecing together what was going through Luciano's mind, and

what he was planning, was a bit of reverse engineering. The first thing that struck me when reading *The Last Testament of Lucky Luciano*, by Martin Gosch and Richard Hammer, was how much Luciano obsessed about Thomas Dewey. Even though the book was written in the late 1950s and early 1960s, Luciano was still obsessing over Dewey, and it seemed that the obsession was left over from constantly thinking about him in prison. It was certainly a case where one man thought about the other way more than the other did about him.

That Luciano believed Dewey owed him was a ridiculous line of thought on his part. Dewey held little if none of the same values that Luciano did. Maybe Dewey let Luciano out and deported him because he felt bad for him, but Dewey never said anything to that effect, and there is no evidence that it was the case. In fact, it must have killed him that he went to such great lengths to put together the Herlands Report to clear his name, and yet he would never get to tell his version of the story while he was alive.

As for conversations that Luciano had in prison, this book reveals for the first time a complete list of all of Luciano's visitors. Never before had it been known that M. Einsberg, John Martini, and Willie Moretti visited Luciano at Great Meadow. This was crucial, because when you look at his visitors, and see what they were into, you begin to see that everyone except Joe "Socks" Lanza and Moses Polakoff had something to do with gambling. When you look at what Lansky was able to accomplish with his gambling empire after the war, and consider that he was present for almost every single meeting with Luciano, how could you not think that a lot of their conversations were about gambling? Especially when you also consider their massive devotion of energy and funds toward the gambling racket before Luciano went to prison. Luciano and Lansky were thick as thieves. Constantly plotting and planning—aside from a little chitchat, that's all Luciano and Lansky could really do together at Great Meadow prison.

As a source for this material, Luciano presented other problems. He had several different versions of events. In *The Last Tes-*

tament of Lucky Luciano, Luciano claims he ordered Albert Anastasia to set fire to a boat in New York Harbor so that the navy would come to Luciano for help with security. It's a ludicrous claim (I'm not the only researcher to arrive at the same conclusion, as many major publications such as the *New York Times* have refuted plenty of its claims), and there are plenty more in his recounting of events.

And that's a difficult thing to keep in mind—what's real and what isn't. In Luciano's case, there were too many inaccuracies in his memoir to count. If this book were a common history book, with a recitation of facts that drive toward a narrative, then I couldn't use *The Last Testament of Lucky Luciano* as a source, because if large facts are tainted, then so too is the rest. But for this format—narrative nonfiction—I was afforded the latitude to assess what might be real and what might be fabricated. I did my best to read between the lines, and not get drawn in by the most extravagant claims, while also permitting myself to believe that some of these crazy events actually happened. It was my belief that if I found source material about Luciano's habits, motivation, and documented actions, I could construct an accurate picture of what his life must have been like while he was helping the navy with Operation Underworld. It's a task that no one has attempted before now, but it was a worthy challenge to take on, as there turned out to be a lot more information available than I initially anticipated.

Commander Charles Radcliffe Haffenden was no easier to construct, as he presented other challenges. It should be noted that while most of the characters in this story provide some sort of testimony in the Herlands investigation, the two main characters were not a part of the interviews, given that Haffenden was already dead and Luciano wasn't allowed in the country. In that regard, I was able to dig up more on Haffenden than has been revealed before, and I hope I did the reader justice in bringing his true self to life. As for the Haffenden family, who felt that Charles's fate was unwarranted, this account must make them no more comfortable. Certainly, my research indicates that Haffenden danced with the devil, but also the devil danced with him. Haffenden was never really successful in doing anything wrong (though we will never know his full activities during Operation Underworld). Like so many FBI agents and informants would be in the coming years, he was a victim of the spell that wiseguys have been casting on the rest of us for a century. I think that his memory should be honored for what it is, as he was a truly creative thinker, and his devotion to his country, the navy, and the job he was tasked with was never in question.

I'm reminded of a couple things that one of my favorite authors said in his books. In *Dead Wake*, Erik Larson wrote in the "Sources and Acknowledgments" section that "no matter how deeply I immerse myself in a subject, I still like having actual, physical proof that the events I'm writing about really did occur." That's the mark of a true historian.

But Larson also wrote something else. In his "Sources and Acknowledgments" for *The Devil in the White City*, he explains that he recreated two of the finest parts of the book based on the best evidence available, and provided endnotes for his rationale when he filled in the holes with his own imagination. As a reader of Larson, I trust that his approach has delivered the most likely scenario, even though he admits, as do I, that it's possible he could be off, given that he has presented only one path of history without presenting other possibilities in the narrative. I've researched these events exhaustively, and where necessary, to move the story along for the reader, I've taken some creative liberties. In doing so I've asked readers for a certain amount of trust in retelling history. For those whose job it is to scrutinize, I've done my best to explain these decisions in my endnotes, and I welcome any discussion.

As for Operation Underworld, there are still many dots that have not been connected, and dozens of characters, now easy to identify, whose stories have yet to be investigated. This book, having been researched and written during the Covid-19 pandemic, is the result of a large amount of digital methodology. In the past I have not been a proponent of using mainly digital sources, because there is no comparison to actually visiting libraries, archives, museums, and historical sites. However, it is absolutely incredible how many resources can now be accessed digitally. That includes the testimony that makes up the Herlands investigation. I had always assumed that I would have to spend a significant portion of my time at the University of Rochester, where the investigation is archived among the Thomas Dewey papers. However, because of pandemic restrictions, archivists from the University of Rochester and everywhere else are now digitizing primary source documents upon request, and they are working hard. As digital archiving becomes commonplace (hopefully one of those positives that comes from the terrible pandemic), everyone with access to the internet will be able to read all of the testimony for themselves and be free to evaluate if my conclusions on these extraordinary events are the most appropriate. The more easily available digitized material is, the better.

Finally, I was not able to locate Herlands's personal notes, the many exhibits that he collected (including private notes from civilian agents), Dominick Sacco's union cards, or the photograph of Robert Jordan. I also wasn't able to locate the eighteen documents that were apparently spared from the navy cover-up back in 1946. And I will never know what happened to Haffenden's little black book; I can only assume that it too was burned, but hope that maybe the wily intelligence officer hid it somewhere. If any of the above are located, then they can enrich this tale even more. As it is, I believe I have treated the narrative with the care it deserves and have given an accurate depiction of events as they happened, in perhaps one of the last great lesser-known stories of World War II.

ACKNOWLEDGMENTS

John F. Kennedy once said that "Victory has a thousand fathers, but defeat is an orphan." Given the success of this project, there indeed are so many people who are responsible. For me it's easy to know where to start, and that is with my agents Eileen Cope and Julie Checkoway of Mark Creative Management. You discovered me, gave me the opportunity that I've been dreaming of my entire life, and guided me through the process in a way I only could have imagined. When I praise you, you constantly put it back on me, but without your contributions in so many ways this would not have been possible.

You two presented me with this opportunity during an extremely difficult time in all of our lives, which was during the Covid-19 pandemic. This was a challenging time to take on such an exhaustive project, as travel restrictions and health requirements in libraries and archives across the country hampered my ability to get my hands on so much primary source material. Instead, I had to rely on digital uploads and the fantastic collections that some people are still making to this very day. One of the good things to come out of the pandemic, in my belief, is the digitization of so much historical material. The more that is available to the public at large, in my opinion, the better.

In that regard, I want to thank archivist Melissa S. Mead at the University of Rochester. Over the course of a year and a half,

Melissa diligently responded to my every request and uploaded nearly the entirety of the Herlands Investigation for my use. Without the University of Rochester allowing this, and Melissa's devotion to her job, this book would not be the complete work that it is, as just about every single new discovery that I made was something I uncovered from what she shared.

Thomas P. Hunt deserves a lot of credit for creating a fantastic collection of Mafia material (especially his timeline of Lucky Luciano in prison) on his website mafiahistory.us. Likewise for Julian Boilen, who created an incredible website (https://1940s.nyc/map) that uses thousands of old black-and-white photos from 1939–1941 to enable users to see what amounts to a Google street view of New York City in that era. It's like looking through a window into the past. Thank you also to Tim Newark, who has written extensively about this subject and provided fantastic accounts of both Lucky Luciano's life and the events of Operation Underworld.

To all of my family and friends mentioned or unmentioned in this section, thank you for your personalities and for constantly keeping me entertained and interested. Jack Kerouac once wrote, "The only people for me are the mad ones," and I mean this in the best way possible—you're all "mad." Thanks to you, never in my life has there ever been a shortage of characters.

I want to say thank you to my uncle Bruce Naito, who has always shown enthusiasm for my interests. In this case, it shined through so much during this project that you provided tremendous help with some very much needed sleuthing. Thank you to my father-in-law, Paul Frichtl, for some very much needed last-minute editing. I also want to thank my nanny, Ellen Donley, who in her late nineties and battling Parkinson's is the most talented painter I'll ever know. Our conversations about the creative process and art have been an inspiration.

Thank you to my mom, Carol Black, for all of your love and encouragement, and for always being my biggest fan. Your enthusiasm for my work helped keep me moving toward my dreams even when they didn't seem possible. And you also taught me the importance of reading books, and reinforced it with your decades-long involvement in the Fifth Business Book Club, which has shown me that books still very much matter. And thank you to my dad, Kevin Black, for your love, and for pushing me to bring my success to a higher level. You've had so much influence over my life, and perhaps none greater than the passion for history that we share. Thank you also to my brother, Jason Black, whose love is never in doubt, who is a fantastic role model as one the most compassionate people I know, and who is always challenging me intellectually.

Lastly and most importantly, thank you to my bride (my "Darlin'"), Kristin Black, who without a doubt is the reason this book was possible. You have been the best partner a guy could ask for in guiding us through the rough and thin times and being a shoulder for me to cry and lean on. When you said to me, "Don't let your dreams be dreams," I knew I had found the love of my life. And of course, we've had another love in our lives since the day you gave us our incredible little girl, Brooklyn, to whom this book is dedicated. Brooklyn, your constant epiphanies sprang a fountain of creativity in my mind that carried me through the writing of this book. Like your mom, you have the joie de vivre, and it has been apparent from the beginning. You're an inspiration, and your life made this possible.

Notes

Following the narrative with supplementing endnotes will lead to a richer experience and understanding of the events, settings, and people in this story. At times, it also reveals perhaps more than you'd like to know at a given point. For example, much of the information that led to this narrative was gathered from a formerly classified investigation in 1954—over a decade after Operation Underworld—called the Herlands Investigation. To preserve the reader's experience, I'm going to leave it at that, and simply note that just about everything the navy gathered in reference to Operation Underworld was destroyed in the closing days of World War II and shortly after. Therefore, the Herlands Investigation and the Herlands Report represent the vast majority of what we know about these events. The investigation and report are so pervasive as sources that after the first introduction of testimony or a file in the Herlands investigation, it is only referred to as "Testimony" or "File."

These endnotes also contain references to events that fell just outside of the narrative. These instances are still rich with interesting information, but just didn't fit into the overall flow.

This is also a problem with endnotes, as they break up the story if you're constantly flipping to the end to go deeper into events. I certainly didn't write the narrative with that intention. But for the readers looking to the endnotes to find a trail of my findings, the information is all there for you to examine.

These endnotes also contain explanations of certain sources, as some were far more prevalent than others. The sources themselves, in certain instances, have a great story of their own. If the source was prevalent in the narrative, then it deserved an explanation of how it relates to the story.

Finally, these endnotes will also help clear up confusion about the historical record. There are passages where I have bridged the gaps in the record (see the Epilogue for a much more detailed explanation of this process). Exhaustive efforts have been made to adhere to the historical record at all times, but the record itself at times produced conflicting accounts, was incomplete, or was suspect because the sources were known to have a loose relationship with the truth. Whereas historians must often discount such sources, they are valuable for narrative nonfiction, and if they are examined with open eyes, empathy, and a clear filter, the complete story can be found somewhere in the fog. In all instances that fit this criteria, the endnotes are meant to clear up the confusion and explain my thinking as to the choices I made to bring this narrative to life.

Prologue

1. "12 Hour Fight in Vain—Waterlogged Vessel Is Turned Over by Tide After Disastrous Fire," *New York Times*, February 10, 1942, https://timesmachine. nytimes.com/timesmachine/1942/02/10/85252086.html?pageNumber=1, https://timesmachine.nytimes.com/timesmachine/1942/02/10/85252086.html? pageNumber=7 (accessed 12/16/2020).

Chapter 1—Cerberus at the Gates

1. Campbell, Rodney, *The Luciano Project: The Secret Wartime Collaboration of the Mafia and the U.S. Navy* (New York, NY: McGraw-Hill, 1977), print, page 26.

In Lieutenant James O'Malley's Herlands testimony he stated that in the beginning phases of Operation Underworld one of the threats B-3 section needed to combat and investigate was "whether any information could be developed as to the means by which the submarine packs operating off the Atlantic coast were able to refuel without returning to their bases."

A note on *The Luciano Project*: When the Herlands investigation was declassified, an English journalist named Rodney Campbell was given the task of writing a book about it by Thomas Dewey's family. Campbell was a trusted writer, as he had previously edited Thomas Dewey's memoir, *Twenty Against the Underworld*. Since *The Luciano Project*'s publication in 1977, it has been decidedly recognized as the authority on the Herlands Report and Herlands investigation. The book was commissioned under certain conditions (e.g., certain names, such as MacFall's and Haffenden's civilian agents', would have to be omitted). This book will reveal much of what he left out of the story, and these instances, or material where there are discrepancies, will typically be highlighted out in the following endnotes.

2. Johnson, Malcolm, *On the Waterfront: The Story Behind the Story* (New York, NY: Chamberlain Brothers, 2005), print. *On the Waterfront* was a Pulitzer Prize–winning series of articles by Malcolm Jenkins (later adapted into an Academy Award–winning movie starring Marlon Brando) in the late 1940s that shed tremendous light on the situation confronting longshoremen and stevedores on the waterfront. Thanks to Jenkins's groundbreaking reporting, the plight and day-to-day toil of longshoremen along many Manhattan and Brooklyn piers became a known quantity, and details from this book have and will figure in this narrative often.

3. Strausbaugh, John, *Victory City* (New York, NY: Hachette Book Group, 2018), print, page 257.

4. Thomas E. Dewey Archive in the University of Rochester Library, New York, Herlands Report of 1954, http://www.lib.rochester.edu/IN/RBSCP/ATTACHMENTS/Series-13-17-2-Herlands-report.pdf, page 21.

5. "USS President Grant (ID # 3014), 1917–1919. Later USS Republic (AP-33), 1941–1945," *DEPARTMENT OF THE NAVY—NAVAL HISTORY AND HERITAGE COMMAND*, https://www.ibiblio.org/hyperwar/OnlineLibrary/photos/sh-usn/usnsh-p/id3014.htm (accessed 3/8/2022).

6. Julian Boilen, "35-35 167th Street. Flushing, New York," *Street View of 1940s New York*, https://1940s.nyc/map/photo/nynyma_rec0040_4_05291_0029#17.64/40.764353/-73.798609 (accessed 3/5/2022).

7. Strausbaugh, *Victory City*.

8. Digital Testimony of George Mack Tarbox (Herlands Investigation, 1954), Thomas E. Dewey papers, D.58, Rare Books, Special Collections, and

Preservation, River Campus Libraries, University of Rochester, page 11. At
various points in the Herlands investigation, interviewees were given the opportunity to provide their opinion of Commander Haffenden. This particular
exchange happened to include an especially pointed question about other officers not respecting Haffenden because he had no investigative experience. The
interview was promptly stopped after Tarbox answered in the affirmative,
which indicates they were heading outside the purview of the investigation.

9. Digital Testimony of Wallace Phillips (Herlands Investigation, 1954),
Thomas E. Dewey papers, D.58, Rare Books, Special Collections, and
Preservation, River Campus Libraries, University of Rochester.

10. Digital Testimony of Moses Polakoff (Herlands Investigation, 1954),
Thomas E. Dewey papers, D.58, Rare Books, Special Collections, and
Preservation, River Campus Libraries, University of Rochester.

11. Herlands Investigation; Campbell, *The Luciano Project*; and Haffenden's
obituary: "Charles R. Haffenden," *New York Times*, December 25, 1952,
https://timesmachine.nytimes.com/timesmachine/1952/12/25/84382360.html?
pageNumber=29 (accessed 11/01/2020).

12. Shrapnel and debris even managed to damage the Statue of Liberty.
Exploding fragments hit the arm and torch of Lady Liberty, and even over
one hundred years later, this damage is part of the reason the public is not
allowed to access the torch of the statue.

13. Thomas E. Dewey Archive in the University of Rochester Library, New
York, Herlands Report Appendices of 1954, http://www.lib.rochester.edu/
IN/RBSCP/ATTACHMENTS/Series-13-17-3-Herlands-appendices.pdf.
Pages 16 and 34 provide information regarding Allied shipping losses. All
future mentions of Allied shipping losses come from this source.

14. Digital Testimony of Dominick Sacco (Herlands Investigation, 1954),
Thomas E. Dewey papers, D.58, Rare Books, Special Collections, and
Preservation, River Campus Libraries, University of Rochester, page 61;
Digital Testimony of Maurice Kelly (Herlands Investigation, 1954), Thomas
E. Dewey papers, D.58, Rare Books, Special Collections, and Preservation,
River Campus Libraries, University of Rochester, page 10.

15. Thomas E. Dewey Archive in the University of Rochester Library, New
York, Herlands Report of 1954, http://www.lib.rochester.edu/IN/RBSCP/
ATTACHMENTS/Series-13-17-2-Herlands-report.pdf, pages 14–15.

16. Digital Testimony of Charles Bonner (Herlands Investigation, 1954),
Thomas E. Dewey papers, D.58, Rare Books, Special Collections, and
Preservation, River Campus Libraries, University of Rochester, page 7.

17. Bettman/Contributor, "Frank Hogan Taking Oath," Getty Images, Editorial #: 517218030, December 28, 1941, https://www.gettyimages.com/ detail/news-photo/scene-in-the-new-york-district-attorneys-office-today-as- news-photo/517218030?adppopup=true; New York Police Department, Bettman/Contributor, "Mugshot of Suspect Joseph Lanza," *Getty Images*, Editorial #: 515162662, December 1,1937, https://www.gettyimages.co.uk/ detail/news-photo/named-as-associate-of-new-york-county-clerk-joseph- lanza-news-photo/515162662. These photos were taken in Frank Hogan's office (previously occupied by Thomas E. Dewey) just a couple of months prior, when Hogan assumed the office of district attorney.

18. Digital Testimony of Roscoe MacFall (Herlands Investigation, 1954), Thomas E. Dewey papers, D.58, Rare Books, Special Collections, and Preservation, River Campus Libraries, University of Rochester; Campbell, *The Luciano Project*, page 30.

19. Campbell, *The Luciano Project*, page 30.

20. Ibid., pages 23–33.

21. Ibid; Herlands Report. After the war, Anthony "Marzulo" changed his last name to "Marsloe," which indicates that he was likely changing his name to sound less Italian, which was common at the time.

22. Digital Testimony of Anthony Marsloe (Herlands Investigation, 1954), Thomas E. Dewey papers, D.58, Rare Books, Special Collections, and Preservation, River Campus Libraries, University of Rochester.

Campbell, *The Luciano Project*, page 27.

23. It's generally believed, though there is nothing in the historical record, that Joe "Socks" Lanza was a caporegime in the Luciano family by the time he died. A capo is a high-ranking figure, as there would only be a couple, or maybe a handful, in any one family. Lanza held his own territory and had a direct line to the underboss of the family, Frank Costello. However, it isn't known when Lanza was made a capo, and it's more likely that at this point he was a rank under that, which would've been soldier, or perhaps lieutenant.

24. Lena Presner, "South Street Perks Up: New Fulton Fish Market Corlear's Hook Park, Gives It Air of Modernity." *New York Times*, June 11, 1939, https://timesmachine.nytimes.com/timesmachine/1939/06/11/113355574. html?pageNumber=172 (accessed June 6, 2020).

25. Herlands Report, pages 35–36.

26. Campbell, *The Luciano Project*, page 37. Given Marzulo's exploits as a Naval Intelligence officer during World War II, it's evident that he was will- ing and able for any mission that came his way.

27. Digital Testimony of Harold MacDowell (Herlands Investigation, 1954), Thomas E. Dewey papers, D.58, Rare Books, Special Collections, and Preservation, River Campus Libraries, University of Rochester, page 71.

28. Less than two hours earlier, at 8:50 a.m., the oil tanker *Dixie Arrow* had been hit by three torpedoes launched from *U 71*, right off the North Carolina coast. Because it was so close to shore, aircraft were dispatched to the scene and captured photos of the ship burning and breaking into two pieces. It was *U 71*'s second kill in a week.

29. Herlands Report Appendices, page 34.

30. Digital Testimonies of Joseph Lanza (Herlands Investigation, 1954), Thomas E. Dewey papers, D.58, Rare Books, Special Collections, and Preservation, River Campus Libraries, University of Rochester; Campbell. *The Luciano Project*, page 35.

31. Ibid., page 36.

32. Ibid.

Chapter 2—An Unholy Alliance

1. Miller, Tom. "The Lost 1907 Hotel Astor—1511 Broadway." *Daytonian in Manhattan*. January 4, 2016. http://daytoninmanhattan.blogspot.com/2016/01/the-lost-1907-hotel-astor-1511-broadway.html (accessed February 14, 2022).

2. Herlands Report, page 32; Campbell, *The Luciano Project*, pages 34–35.

3. Digital Testimony of Murray Gurfein (Herlands Investigation, 1954), Thomas E. Dewey papers, D.58, Rare Books, Special Collections, and Preservation, River Campus Libraries, University of Rochester, page 16.

4. Ibid.; Campbell, *The Luciano Project*, page 32.

5. Gurfein Testimony, page 15.

6. D. Sacco Testimony, page 14. There's some discrepancy in the testimony, as the Herlands Report says Dominick Sacco was introduced to Lanza later, but Sacco says that he met Lanza here, at this meeting. Sacco took meticulous notes about his actions during this time, and that's why his account is accepted over the report's, which doesn't say whose testimony it draws facts from. Also, Sacco still made a mistake, and said that he met DA Murray Gurfein at this meeting. Perhaps he meant Joseph Guerin, but it's interesting because he definitely says the "District Attorney." Other accounts do

not corroborate this part of the meeting, including Gurfein's and Guerin's testimony. Plus, the Herlands Report and Guerin testimony clearly state that he was in the meeting, so Sacco would've had to have met Guerin.

The point of bringing this to light is the fact that the Herlands investigation took place over ten years after these events, and it's completely understandable that some of the witnesses' recollection of events were a little fuzzy.

7. D. Sacco Testimony, page 61.

8. Digital File of Charles R. Haffenden (Herlands Investigation, 1954), Thomas E. Dewey papers, D.58, Rare Books, Special Collections, and Preservation, River Campus Libraries, University of Rochester, page 2. There is only one surviving document that shows Haffenden's roster, and it's dated April 1, 1943. There are more than a few discrepancies from squad member testimony as to what their jobs were, so there's evidence that squad members and leaders were swapped out, changed, transferred out of B-3, or added.

9. This is the first time this information has been revealed—that Dominick Sacco is indeed "Agent X" and Felix Sacco is "Agent Y." The Saccos gave their testimony to the Herlands investigation under the condition that their names would never be revealed to the public. This account of events not only reveals their names, but also concludes that Campbell must have known the names of the Sacco brothers, and chose not to reveal their names, presumably out of respect for their story, anonymity, and the traditions of the navy.

10. Lanza testimony. According to Lanza's testimony, his number was either "63" or "67."

11. Campbell, *The Luciano Project*, page 48.

12. Details of Lanza's crime are derived from the following *New York Times* articles: "Convict Testifies to Lanza's Tactics—Says He Demanded Appointment of Aide as Union Official," New York Times, January 8, 1941, https://timesmachine.nytimes.com/timesmachine/1943/01/08/87407679.html?pageNumber=27 (accessed 3/8/2020); "Dewey Says Lanza Ran Racket in Jail—Accuses Him of Extorting $120 a Week from Union by Murder Threats," *New York Times*, January 9, 1941, https://timesmachine. nytimes.com/timesmachine/1941/01/09/85182531.html?pageNumber=23 (accessed 3/8/2020); "Lanza, Racketeer, Admits Extortion—Four Co-Defendants Also Make Unexpected Move in Fish Market Union Case," *New York Times*, January 13, 1943, https://timesmachine.nytimes.com/times machine/1943/01/13/88510384.html?pageNumber=25 (accessed 3/8/2020); " 'Socks' Lanza gets 7 ½ to 15 Year Sentence—4 'Strong Arm' Men of Fulton Market Labor Racketeer Also go to Prison," *New York Times*,

January 30, 1943, https://timesmachine.nytimes.com/timesmachine/
1943/01/30/87410794.html?pageNumber=17 (accessed 3/8/2020);
Perlmutter, Emanuel. "Lanza: Case History of a Thug—Often In and Out of
Trouble with the Law," *New York Times*, April 21, 1957, https://times
machine.nytimes.com/timesmachine/1957/04/21/90798450.html?page
Number=167 (accessed 3/8/2020).

13. "Lanza Is Indicted with Aides in Plot—Accused of Extortion Against
Union While in Prison," *New York Times*, January 1, 1941, https://times-
machine.nytimes.com/timesmachine/1941/01/18/85276747.html?page
Number=17 (accessed 3/8/2020).

14. Johnson, *On the Waterfront*, pages 40–41. The loading racket was occurring all over the Port of New York. In *On the Waterfront*, Malcolm Johnson
reveals a meeting between heavily armed representatives that took place in
the fall of 1942. The loading racket was getting so out of hand that truckers
were not only scared and powerless to combat it, but they never knew how
much they were going to be charged from pier to pier. It was a shakedown
with no predetermined scale, leaving gangsters like Socks Lanza free to
charge what they wanted. The truckers appealed to International Longshoreman Association (ILA) president Joe Ryan, and his right-hand man
Jerry Sullivan. The two men really weren't willing to help out the truckers, as
the only thing they cared about was that the men doing the loading were ILA
members who were up to date on paying their dues. At the meeting, the truckers invited the ILA strongmen to shoot them because they were through being
harassed. After that they reached a compromise, and a scale for the illegal
loading of supplies that was based on the weight of cargo. It went into effect
early in 1943.

15. Campbell, *The Luciano Project*, page 49.

16. Ibid., page 49.

17. MacDowell Testimony, pages 71–73. MacDowell was known to
Haffenden through the Executives Association, and Haffenden signed him on
early to help screen men and women coming in and out of B-3. The final
page of MacDowell's file in the Herlands investigation has a hand drawing of
Haffenden's office setup. It's unknown who drew it, but it was produced from
descriptions made by MacDowell.

18. Digital Testimony of Benjamin Espy (Herlands Investigation, 1954),
Thomas E. Dewey papers, D.58, Rare Books, Special Collections, and
Preservation, River Campus Libraries, University of Rochester, page 8.

19. Campbell, *The Luciano Project*, page 50.

20. There is no indication in the Herlands investigation as to who named Operation Underworld. But given that MacFall and Haffenden were largely responsible for setting it in motion, it's presumable that at least one of them conceived the name.

Chapter 3—Operation Underworld

1. Holt, Jane, "News of Food—50 Varieties of Fish Available to Break Monotony of Lenten Diet," *New York Times*, April 3, 1941, https://timesmachine.nytimes.com/timesmachine/1941/04/03/110051554.html?pageNumber=20 (accessed 11/3/2019).

2. Digital Testimony of Felix Sacco (Herlands Investigation, 1954), Thomas E. Dewey papers, D.58, Rare Books, Special Collections, and Preservation, River Campus Libraries, University of Rochester, pages 9–10.

3. "American Ships Sunk During WWII," World War II U.S. Navy Armed Guard and World War II U.S. Merchant Marine, https://www.armed-guard.com/sunk.html (accessed 8/25/2020).

4. Herlands Report; Campbell. *The Luciano Project*, page 59.

5. Digital Testimony of William de Waal (Herlands Investigation, 1954), Thomas E. Dewey papers, D.58, Rare Books, Special Collections, and Preservation, River Campus Libraries, University of Rochester, page 3.

6. "2 Police Officials Suspended on Amen's Charges of Graft," *New York Times*, April 10, 1942, https://timesmachine.nytimes.com/timesmachine/1942/04/10/85029037.html?pageNumber=1 (accessed 8/3/2020).

7. Ronald Michne and Ronald Michne, Jr., "Historical Profiles of Eastport, Speonk, Remsenburg, West Hampton." January 2004. https://www.southamptontownny.gov/DocumentCenter/View/865/Historical-Profiles-Eastport—-Speonk-Remsenburg—-Westhampton-PDF (accessed 3/3/2021).

8. De Waal Testimony, page 6.

9. Digital Testimony of Ellis Tuthill (Herlands Investigation, 1954), Thomas E. Dewey papers, D.58, Rare Books, Special Collections, and Preservation, River Campus Libraries, University of Rochester, page 4.

10. Out of pure coincidence, April 18, 1942, was the same day that a daring army colonel named Jimmy Doolittle led a raid of bombers over mainland Japan. The mission almost resulted in disaster when the naval task force that the bombers were to launch from was discovered by a Japanese fishing boat. Admiral Halsey, who was in command of the task force, ordered the fishing

boat sunk. This happened quickly, but Halsey feared that the fishing boat had alerted the Japanese fleet. As a result, Halsey and Doolittle decided to launch from hundreds of miles farther than planned, which severely jeopardized the range of the bombers and the mission as a whole. It's unknown if that fishing boat actually had a radio, but it's worth noting, because the use of fishing boats for naval purposes was a common theme of World War II in several different theaters.

11. Digital Testimony of Clement le Vesconte (Herlands Investigation, 1954), Thomas E. Dewey papers, D.58, Rare Books, Special Collections, and Preservation, River Campus Libraries, University of Rochester.

12. Lanza Testimony; Campbell, *The Luciano Project*, page 52.

13. "Dewey Says Lanza Ran Racket in Jail—Accuses Him of Extorting $120 a Week from Union by Murder Threats," *New York Times*, January 9, 1941, https://timesmachine.nytimes.com/timesmachine/1941/01/09/85182531.html?pageNumber=23 (accessed 3/8/2020). At his bail hearing over a year ago, Guerin had argued that Fulton Fish Market was all Lanza knew and that he would never leave. At the hearing, Lanza's lawyer had even said to the judge, "You couldn't drive this man away from New York with a 13-inch gun. He's here to stay." The irony was that the navy was the only outfit in the country that possessed a bigger gun, as they had fourteen-inch guns affixed to their massive battleships.

14. Lanza Testimony, pages 28–33; Espy Testimony, pages 20–21.

15. Lanza Testimony, page 30.

16. In May 1926, when Lanza was just twenty-five years old, he'd had a run-in with an Irish gangster. Just up the street from Fulton Fish Market, on the second floor of 105 South Street—in a speakeasy named "M Slavin and Sons"—an Irish labor organizer named William Mack was having a drink in the wrong neighborhood. Mack was no saint, with a rap sheet just as long as Lanza's.

Someone from the speakeasy alerted the Patrol Association of Mack's presence, and soon, four men approached him from behind—one of them was Lanza—and they shot him several times.

Tough Irishman that he was, Mack managed to get out, and walk nearly three blocks before he collapsed and died in front of the headquarters of the United Seafood Workers Union, of which Lanza was a founding member. Lanza was arrested shortly thereafter and tried for murder. Whether he was one of the gunmen was of little dispute, but it didn't matter, as Lanza beat the rap. Of course, winning the case was made much easier by the fact that no witnesses turned up to testify against Lanza—no one would dare. Indeed,

Mack was not welcome on Lanza's turf, and in turn, Lanza was not welcome in Irish territory.

17. Lanza Testimony.

18. Campbell, *The Luciano Project*, page 65.

19. In Dominick Sacco's testimony, he makes it sound like Haffenden already knew about the idea. It also seems more than likely that Socks Lanza didn't come up with this idea, though there is almost nothing in the historical record that indicates otherwise. Would Lanza really get Luciano involved without consulting Frank Costello first? Definitely not. So once Costello got wind of Operation Underworld (from Lanza or one of the people he reached out to), it was one of those two who came up with the idea of having Luciano help. But there is no evidence that supports this theory, with the exception of statements made later by other top gangsters whose testimonies have been refuted. Because of this, it is Lanza who is credited with being the one who came up with using Luciano in Operation Underworld.

Chapter 4—"The Devil Himself"

1. Campbell, *The Luciano Project*, pages 83–85; Gurfein Testimony; Polakoff Testimony.

2. Meyer Lansky and "Bugsy" Siegel were too young to be drafted in 1917 and 1918. Costello wasn't eligible because of a throat problem. Luciano, however, contended that he purposely got the "clap" in order to fail his physical. Whether that was true or not is a matter of debate, but what isn't debatable is the fact that Luciano avoided the draft, and did indeed get the "clap"—seven different times.

3. Gosch, Martin, Hammer, Richard, and Lucania, Charles, *The Last Testament of Lucky Luciano* (Boston, MA: Little, Brown & Company, 1974), print, pages 25–30. Much about Luciano is derived from this book, which was a memoir published posthumously. There are many factual inaccuracies in it, leaving writers of history with a source that they, for the most part, have trouble using. It is used as a source in this story, however, as it reveals much about the man himself, and the majority of events did actually happen. And any events described by Luciano in his memoir that are not corroborated elsewhere will be pointed out in these endnotes, and proper explanation will be given as to why the anecdotes were used.

4. Fritz Kuhn was convicted of embezzlement in 1939, and was sent to Dannemora prison, where he did time with Luciano. It's unknown if they met.

5. Digital Testimony of Meyer Lansky (Herlands Investigation, 1954), Thomas E. Dewey papers, D.58, Rare Books, Special Collections, and Preservation, River Campus Libraries, University of Rochester.

6. Campbell, *The Luciano Project*, pages 85–87; Meyer Lansky, Moses Polakoff, and Murray Gurfein Testimony, quoted from *The Luciano Project*.

7. Polakoff Testimony, page 9; Lansky Testimony, page 11.

8. Somehow, in the course of Murray Gurfein's meetings with Moses Polakoff, then Polakoff and Meyer Lansky, and finally with Haffenden as well, Gurfein was under the impression that Polakoff and Lanza were going to visit Luciano, not Lansky. Either Haffenden, Polakoff, and Lansky deliberately deceived him, or Gurfein made a typo in his memo to Hogan, giving permission for Lanza to visit, instead of Lansky. He was in the middle of building a case against Lanza, after all.

9. Digital Testimony of Harold Lamberson (Herlands Investigation, 1954), Thomas E. Dewey papers, D.58, Rare Books, Special Collections, and Preservation, River Campus Libraries, University of Rochester, pages 1–3.

10. Campbell, *The Luciano Project*, page 92; John Lyons and Harry Bonesteel, quoted from *The Luciano Project*. Though Haffenden certainly knew at the time, as it stands now, nobody has any idea who this man was.

Chapter 5—A Deal with the Devil

1. Resko, John, *Reprieve* (Westport, CT: Greenwood Press, 1956), print, page 67. *Reprieve* was a memoir by a man named John Resko. Resko was convicted of murder in 1933 and was given a life sentence and confined at Dannemora prison. Nineteen years later, he was pardoned, and four years after that he wrote *Reprieve*. It depicts his daily life in Dannemora, and many of Luciano's personal activities are derived from this source. Several sections in *Reprieve* are devoted to talking about Luciano, as Resko and Luciano were friendly, and spoke often in prison (Resko mostly spoke, and Luciano mostly listened).

2. Newark, Tim, *Boardwalk Gangster: The Real Lucky Luciano* (New York, NY: Thomas Dunne Books & St. Martin's Griffin, 2010), print, page 137. Newark quoted Leo Katcher, who wrote an article in the *New York Post* in 1938 that caught the last quote from Luciano for almost a decade. Katcher visited Luciano at Dannemora after his last appeal was rejected. Katcher asked Luciano what he'd do if he got out, and Luciano said he'd "follow the horses from Saratoga to Belmont to Florida to California. *I'll sleep with my windows open so I can reach out and hold the air in my hands* [emphasis

added]. I'll never lock a door again. Whenever I hear a noise I'm going to go in and look at people and watch them. I'll watch women laughing and dancing. I'll laugh and dance too. When I get out, I'm going to be free."

3. Gosch, Hammer, and Lucania, *The Last Testament of Lucky Luciano*, page 6.

4. Resko, *Reprieve*, page 76.

5. Gosch, Hammer, and Lucania, *The Last Testament of Lucky Luciano*, page 272.

6. Ibid., page 19.

7. Ibid., page 7–8.

8. Ibid., pages 18–22.

9. Newark, *Boardwalk Gangster*, pages 17–18.

10. Gosch, Hammer, and Lucania, *The Last Testament of Lucky Luciano*, pages 18 and 272.

11. Ibid., pages 19 and 272.

12. Ibid., pages 271–272; Campbell, *The Luciano Project*.

13. Gosch and Hammer, *The Last Testament of Lucky Luciano*, pages 271–272.

14. Resko, *Reprieve*, page 106.

15. Even though Luciano was looking at a sentence of thirty to fifty years, he would be up for parole after twenty years, which would have landed on April 24, 1956.

16. Hunt, Thomas, "Mob Boss 'Luciano' in the Hands of the Law," The American Mafia, mafiahistory.us, December 8, 2021, http://mafiahistory.us/a004/f_prisonlucky.html; "Charlie Luciano Prison Cash Transfers," New York State Archives, Series B0123-77, Box 27, pdf (accessed March 3, 2022).

17. Meyer Lansky's favorite historical figure to read about, not surprisingly, was Napoleon, who was actually three inches taller than Lansky.

18. Campbell, *The Luciano Project*, page 71.

19. Ibid., page 81.

20. Lansky Testimony, page 12; Polakoff Testimony, page 13; Campbell, *The Luciano Project*, pages 96–98.

21. Polakoff Testimony, page 13.

22. Gosch, Hammer, and Lucania, *The Last Testament of Lucky Luciano*, page 273.

23. Ibid., page 187.

24. Ibid., page 75.

25. Polakoff Testimony, page 13.

26. Ibid., page 17.

27. Herlands Report Appendix II, page 37.

28. Gosch, Hammer, and Lucania, *The Last Testament of Lucky Luciano*, page 273.

29. Lanza Testimony, pages 51–52.

30. Ibid., pages 51–52. Though Socks Lanza testified that Johnny "Cockeye" Dunn was brought up in this meeting, it seems very unlikely that he would have been. Meyer Lansky later made inroads with Joe Ryan and Jerry Sullivan, and it's likely that Dunn's involvement stemmed from their recommendation.

31. In the late 1930s there emerged a bright shining light in the gloomy borough of Brooklyn, when a man named Peter Panto openly challenged his employer's treatment of his fellow longshoremen.

Between the Brooklyn Bridge to the north and 20th Street to the south, the lives of four thousand hardworking longshoremen—mostly poor Italian immigrants—were run by the six "pistol locals" that operated along the five-mile stretch. The area was full of pre–Civil War warehouses and businesses that operated like a company town—everyone paid tribute to the Mangano family.

Panto grew tired of it, so he did something that hadn't been done in decades on the waterfront—he gathered his union brothers for a meeting. Members of ILA Local 929 huddled together in the dark of night on the waterfront and listened to Panto speak in Italian about union democratization. By mid-1939, Panto's gatherings were growing. Hundreds of men came to listen to him speak, and drink in the hope that he poured. The Mangano family eventually grew tired of this crusader's open challenge to their system.

On July 8, 1939, just six days after his biggest rally, Panto "went for a ride" with an ILA vice president, Emil Camarda, and a vicious murderer named Anthony "Tony Spring" Romeo. The trio, under orders from Albert Anastasia, invited Panto into that car, and Panto was never seen alive again.

Even in the fall of 1942, many shops and warehouses that made up the buildings of the Brooklyn waterfront were still tagged with the words, *"Dov'e Panto?"* Translation: "Where is Panto?"

Panto's disappearance showed who the real power was on the Brooklyn waterfront. And even though Emil Camarda was shot dead because of an extremely petty dispute two months before the Japanese bombing of Pearl Harbor, the hydra that was the Camarda family still had three leaders in Local 327, two in Local 1199, and a restructured Camarda leadership in Local 929 after Emil was shot in the head. Outside of that, Locals 903, 338, and 346 were governed largely by the Manganos, and men loyal to Anastasia. With Anastasia absent because of his enlistment in the army, Joe Adonis and the Camardas were the best options for helping Operation Underworld.

32. War, Nathan, "The Tragic, Violent History of the Brooklyn Waterfront," *Crime Reads*, July 17, 2019, https://crimereads.com/the-tragic-violent-history-of-the-brooklyn-waterfront/ (accessed 12/5/2019).

33. Lanza Testimony, page 52.

34. Gosch, Hammer, and Lucania, *The Last Testament of Lucky Luciano*, page 37. Frank Scalise was also named as one of Luciano's board members, but he later fell out of favor. The other names mentioned had been working with Luciano for a long time, and at this time, he still very much trusted them.

35. Lanza Testimony; Herlands Report; Campbell, *The Luciano Project*. According to all three sources, which stem from Lanza's testimony, "Tony Spring's" name came up in this discussion. By June 4, 1942, Spring had been on the run for two years, so his involvement on the waterfront had long since ended. Therefore, it's unlikely that his name came up for anything related to Operation Underworld. And given what happened to Tony Spring shortly after this meeting (you'll see), it's possible, even plausible, that this is the context in which his name came up.

36. Espy Testimony, page 30.

Chapter 6—The Enemy Arrives

1. Goldstein, Richard, "John Cullen, Coast Guardsman Who Detected Spies, Dies at 90," *New York Times*, September 2, 2011, https://www.nytimes.com/2011/09/03/nyregion/john-cullen-coast-guardsman-who-detected-spies-dies-at-90.html (accessed 9/20/2021).

2. Digital Testimony of Lindsay Henry (Herlands Investigation, 1954), Thomas E. Dewey papers, D.58, Rare Books, Special Collections, and Preservation, River Campus Libraries, University of Rochester, page 10.

3. The warship in question was *U 202*, which landed the four men as part of her sixth patrol. It's unknown if *U 202* was also the U-boat that was sighted off of Montauk two months earlier. During World War II, *U 202* sank nine Allied ships, and was destroyed by depth charges from a British warship on June 2, 1943.

4. Bonner Testimony, page 63. The fishing fleet had also already been organized, and over the course of the last couple months, reports about things they saw came flooding into Riverhead and to Haffenden in New York. The captains found wings from airplane crashes, body parts—including a human skull—and one even accidentally snagged a US submarine.

Charles Bonner later testified that a fishing trawler was dragging its net and was abruptly stopped. The captain went full throttle, and not only did the boat not go forward, but it also started moving backward. Evidently, the net had caught a US submarine.

5. Digital Testimony of Charles Hoyt (Herlands Investigation, 1954), Thomas E. Dewey papers, D.58, Rare Books, Special Collections, and Preservation, River Campus Libraries, University of Rochester.

6. Henry Testimony. Lieutenant Henry later testified to Haffenden's handling of the case: "He came out there and sort of took charge of the investigation and completely ignored my official connection with it. I don't say that unkindly, but that's the factual part of it. I was not asked anything at all." Campbell, *The Luciano Project*, page 113.

7. Hoyt Testimony. Haffenden also had Hoyt investigate the involvement of a local, who was a former bootlegger and rumrunner. The man's name was Otto Steinfeldt, and Haffenden called him the "biggest crook in the world." Hoyt also said that there were three saboteurs and not four, but this was clearly a mistake.

8. Digital Testimony of Elizabeth Schwerin (Herlands Investigation, 1954), Thomas E. Dewey papers, D.58, Rare Books, Special Collections, and Preservation, River Campus Libraries, University of Rochester, page 21.

9. Digital Testimony of Hiram Chester Sweezey (Herlands Investigation, 1954), Thomas E. Dewey papers, D.58, Rare Books, Special Collections, and Preservation, River Campus Libraries, University of Rochester, page 12.

10. This is truly amazing: Lanza was under indictment for violent measures taken against Teamsters Local 202—of which he was not a member, and not even in the same industry—and still managed to come up with a legitimate union card from that local.

11. Hoyt Testimony, page 44; Sweezey Testimony, page 9; D. Sacco Testimony, pages 31 and 59.

Dominick Sacco was sent back to the waterfront shortly after. His middle-aged body couldn't keep up with the constant loading and unloading of heavy ice. After three days, he told Haffenden he'd had enough.

12. Hunt, Thomas, "Mob Boss 'Luciano' in the Hands of the Law," The American Mafia, mafiahistory.us, December 8, 2021, http://mafiahistory.us/a004/f_prisonlucky.html; Clinton, "Charles 'Lucky' Luciano inmate file," Clinton State Prison, Series 14610-77, Box 26, pdf (accessed March 3, 2022).

13. Gosch, Hammer, and Lucania, *The Last Testament of Lucky Luciano*, page 272.

14. Ibid., page 48.

15. Ibid., page 126.

16. The man in question is Gaetano Reina, whom Luciano respected. Luciano didn't want to have him killed, and for that matter, nobody wanted to do it. In the end, it had to be done if Luciano was going to survive. Genovese had no qualms.

Luciano had Reina's routine figured out and decided Reina would meet his end in the Bronx, where he visited his aunt every Wednesday. On the evening of February 26, 1931, Genovese hid outside of Reina's aunt's house until Reina emerged at around eight o'clock. Genovese called to him, as the two were well known to each other. Reina smiled as he waved his hand to say hello. Genovese then leveled his shotgun and shot Reina in the head. In doing so, Genovese had done right by Reina, by killing him in what was considered by the Mafia to be the most honorable way—face-to-face. Genovese never seemed to have a problem killing someone while looking them in the eye.

17. Gosch, Hammer, and Lucania, *The Last Testament of Lucky Luciano*, page 130.

18. Ibid., pages 130–132.

19. Newark, *Boardwalk Gangster*, pages 58–59. Newark concluded that Luciano did not place this card in Masseria's hand, but a member of the press did. There's no direct evidence to conclude this is definitely true, as it was reported that Masseria was found with the card in his hand.

Chapter 7—Surreptitious Entry

1. Bjorkman, Jacob, "Then and Now: Carmine's at the Seaport, Manhattan," *Then and Now—Let's See Cities Change*, November 4, 2018, http://guns.

filminspector.com/2018/11/then-and-now-carmines-at-seaport.html (accessed 3/10/2022).

2. Espy Testimony, pages 30–31.

3. Herlands Report Appendix III.

4. Melton, Keith H., *The Ultimate Spy Book* (New York, NY: DK Publishing Inc., 1996), print, pages 124–125. Harmless-looking letters could contain secret messages, as invisible ink was typically applied between the lines of visible writing. The letter was inconsequential; the invisible writing was the actual message. Matchsticks dipped in lemon juice were typically used, and the team looked at these letters under candlelight, as heat revealed the writing. They also treated the letters to various chemical baths.

5. Digital Testimony of John R. McNaught (Herlands Investigation, 1954), Thomas E. Dewey papers, D.58, Rare Books, Special Collections, and Preservation, River Campus Libraries, University of Rochester, pages 4–5; Campbell, *The Luciano Project*, pages 43–44.

6. George, Willis, *Surreptitious Entry* (Boulder, CO: Paladin Press, 1946, reprint 1990); Thomas O'Toole, "Spanish Diplomats Spied on U.S. for Japan in WWII," *Washington Post*, September 10, 1978, https://www.washington-post.com/archive/politics/1978/09/10/spanish-diplomats-spied-on-us-for-japan-in-wwii/b16527e5-7781-4603-9f5b-d0cff3f24a75/ (accessed 4/1/2021).

Much of what happens next comes from the book written by Willis George (Agent "G") in 1946 called *Surreptitious Entry*. In it, George toes the line of truth about classified information and between writing about hypothetical situations versus actual events. Willis's superior officer in the book is a "Lieutenant Commander" who is never identified by name, but he is clearly Lieutenant Commander Haffenden. The methods described in the book are directly linked to what happens in this chapter. The information presented in *Surreptitious Entry*, though hypothetical, is highly likely true. Paul Alfieri, Maurice Kelly, and the Sacco brothers all touch on "surreptitious entries" in their testimony, and Felix Sacco even goes so far as to talk about lockpicking.

At the end of the section about surreptitious entries, George explains that they were investigating a plot that involved a neutral nation. If this is true, and given that there were dozens of neutral nations with consulates in New York City, and that there are indications that it was a country where Spanish was the official language (such as the text on the envelope being written in Spanish), then the most likely country was Spain.

In 1978, the National Security Agency (NSA) declassified thirty thousand pages of documents that describe what was known as the "TO" spy ring. Oddly enough, the "TO" spy ring wasn't spying for the Germans, but actually the Japanese, with Spanish diplomats in America passing information to them. There are several clues about information gathered in 1942 that match information shared by George in *Surreptitious Entry*. For example, George claimed that the chain involved spies in six major cities. It's revealed by the NSA in the "TO" reports that there were six to eight operatives, each in a different city. The "TO" reports also indicate that the members of the Spanish diplomatic corps who were being used as spies were especially active in Washington, DC, and New York City, among other cities. There's even a confirmed instance in 1942 when the Spanish consulate in New York City transmitted information about the movement of sixty-six ships coming out of New York Harbor. The Japanese received this information and passed it on to Germany. Because the US was able to break Japanese diplomatic codes early in the war, high-level military planners knew that this spy ring existed. However, planners did not try to break up the spy ring, out of fear that the Japanese would catch on to the fact that their code was broken.

While Spain is the most likely country that George wrote about in *Surreptitious Entry*, it's not possible to say with 100 percent certainty that it was indeed Spain. There's plenty of evidence to support that it was Argentina or even Mexico, both of which had consulates in New York City in 1942. Therefore, Spain is mentioned in these endnotes, but not the narrative itself.

7. George, *Surreptitious Entry*, page 103.

8. *The World Almanac & Book of Facts 1942* (New York, NY: New York World Telegram, 1942), digital, page 422.

Spain's consulate was in the DuMont Building at 515 Madison Avenue, a forty-two-floor art deco and new gothic building that was just over a decade old. Argentina's consulate was a few blocks away at 9 Rockefeller Plaza.

9. Haffenden File, page 2.

10. Felix Sacco was just back from duty at the Norden Bombsight Plant, where there had been incidents of sabotage. He had worked as a bench hand sniffing out enemy spies. There's very little information about this episode, but there is a fascinating account written by Haffenden's spymaster in Washington, DC, about how Germany had sabotaged world industry in the years prior to the war by making the world dependent on their skilled laborers. Most of the skilled laborers in the Norden plant were of German descent. They could have stolen plans, sabotaged work, or what was more common, slowed the work to a crawl. (Wallace Wharton, "Nazi-Industrial-Espionage-and-Sabotage," *NCISA History Project*, December 24, 1942, https://ncisa-history.org/wp-content/uploads/2020/01/Nazi-Industrial-Espionage-and-Sabotage-Dec-24-1942.pdf (accessed February 12, 2022).

William Hoyt testified that Sacco was able to gain access to the Norden Bombsight Plant by obtaining a legitimate union card from a Greenwich Village–based gangster named Tony Bender (Hoyt Testimony, page 29).

There was also a lot going on at the Norden plant; later in the war a fraud case stemming from sabotage activity at the plant was prosecuted. "Navy Aide Charges Bomb-Sight Faults," *New York Times*, August 30, 1944, https://timesmachine.nytimes.com/timesmachine/1944/08/30/87467010.html?pageNumber=19 (accessed February 10, 2020); "Navy Seizes Plant of Remington Raid—Slow, Faulty Production of Bomb-Sights Is Alleged—Company Defends Its Work," *New York Times*, November 30, 1943, https://timesmachine.nytimes.com/timesmachine/1943/11/30/88582469.html?pageNumber=24 (accessed February 10, 2020); "Plot to Restrict Bomb-Sight Output Laid to Norden, Inc—2 Corporation Officials, Navy Commander and Associate Named in Indictments," *New York Times*, December 20, 1944, https://timesmachine.nytimes.com/timesmachine/1944/12/20/86890430.html?pageNumber=1 (accessed February 10, 2020); "Pleas of Not Guilty Made in Norden Case," *New York Times*, December 29, 1944, https://timesmachine.nytimes.com/timesmachine/ 1944/12/29/87479597.html?pageNumber=11 (accessed February 10, 2020).

11. George, *Surreptitious Entry*, page 105.

12. Ibid., page 103.

13. The crimes of Johnny "Cockeye" Dunn and Joe "Socks" Lanza are virtually the same, and give us a very clear picture of what business was like on the waterfront before and during World War II. After the war, Malcolm Johnson's *On the Waterfront* series of articles showed the plight of longshoremen and stevedores all over the Port of New York, and the men who took advantage of them. Cockeye and Socks were much like these men, who kept the dockworkers under control. Each man was definitely the muscle in his territory.

14. Lansky Testimony.

15. Arnaldo Cortesi, "Spies in Argentina Still Big Problem," *New York Times*, May 26, 1943, https://timesmachine.nytimes.com timesmachine/ 1943/05/26/87419035.html (accessed 5/14/2021). In Buenos Aires, for example, U-boat captains were receiving information about shipping from many places, including New York City.

16. Lansky Testimony, page 21. There is no specific reference to Dunn ever roughing anybody up; however, when Meyer Lansky was asked how Dunn confronted problems on the waterfront, Lansky said "I know he took care of it." There is evidence of only a couple instances during Operation

Underworld that accomplices engaged in violence, but it is highly plausible, given that most of the historical record was destroyed to hide something, that there were instances when Dunn, Lanza, the Camarda brothers, or others beat up someone for saying something they shouldn't have.

17. D. Sacco Testimony, page 47.

18. MacDowell Testimony, page 69.

19. George, *Surreptitious Entry*, page 106.

20. Campbell, *The Luciano Project*, page 58.

21. D. Sacco Testimony, page 59.

22. Haffenden File, page 2.

23. Kokomolock, "File Cabinet Lock Picked and Bypassed," YouTube, April 17, 2011, https://www.youtube.com/watch?v=7R5VIz2U_MI. This video shows how to bypass a simple lock that can be found in file cabinets in modern times that were also in use in the 1940s.

24. F. Sacco Testimony. Page 28

25. George, *Surreptitious Entry*, page 107.

Silversmyth, Julie. "How to Secretly Open a Sealed Envelope." YouTube. April 9, 2020. https://www.youtube.com/watch?v=4VZyXjWfHXI

George does not describe the process in *Surreptitious Entry*, but the above YouTube video gives us an idea of how this delicate process was accomplished.

26. D. Sacco Testimony, page 44.

27. Digital Testimony of Ben Jacobs (Herlands Investigation, 1954), Thomas E. Dewey papers, D.58, Rare Books, Special Collections, and Preservation, River Campus Libraries, University of Rochester. All quotes and descriptions from this conversation are taken from Jacobs's testimony.

Chapter 8—Thick as Thieves

1. Campbell, *The Luciano Project*, page 106.

2. "Slaying Is Linked to Brooklyn Gang—Rome, Ex-Longshoreman Delegate Found Murdered Near Wilmington, DE," *New York Times*, July 2, 1942, https://timesmachine.nytimes.com/timesmachine/1942/07/02/85559265.html?pageNumber=23 (accessed July 24, 2020).

3. Gosch, Hammer, and Lucania, *The Last Testament of Lucky Luciano*.

4. Ibid., page 29.

5. Lacey, Robert, *Little Man* (Boston, MA: Little, Brown and Company, 1991), print, page 92.

6. Gosch, Hammer, and Lucania, *The Last Testament of Lucky Luciano.*

7. Field, Brian, "Can't Wait First by a Head at Spa in $14,200 Stake," *New York Times*, August 23, 1942, https://timesmachine.nytimes.com/timesmachine/1942/08/23/85580483.html?pageNumber=138, (accessed September 4, 2020).

8. Most months, Costello would be at another of his clubs, like the Copacabana, which he had opened less than two years earlier. Business there was beginning to boom with the massive influx of servicemen and -women. Consumer goods were hard to come by with the war on, so many people began spending more of their money on entertainment. Since it was August, Costello had his Manhattan maître d's and chefs come out to Lake Lonely to entertain Piping Rock's ritzy patrons, who were all impressed with the engraved silverware from the Copa.

9. Digital Testimony of Vernon Morhous (Herlands Investigation, 1954), Thomas E. Dewey papers, D.58, Rare Books, Special Collections, and Preservation, River Campus Libraries, University of Rochester. This is the first time that this list of visitors has ever been revealed. Vernon Morhous had listed Moses Polakoff in his letter to Commissioner Lyons after the meeting, and the FBI was able to find out that Costello joined for this meeting. But unseen by those viewing the testimony in the Herlands investigation was a roster list that Morhous provided to Frank Hogan a month later. It included the names of every visitor during this meeting. Until now, it was not known that Socks Lanza was a part of the meeting. M. Einsberg and John Martini were names that didn't yield any search results, and although they certainly could be real names, it's likely that they were aliases. They weren't required to provide identification or fingerprints either.

10. Campbell, *The Luciano Project*, page 108.

11. Lacey, *Little Man*, pages 108–109.

12. United States Senate, *Special Committee to Investigate Organized Crime in Interstate Commerce: Part. 1-1A* (Florida, 1951), digital. This commission—often referred to as the Kefauver Committee, named after Tennessee Senator Estes Kefauver—took testimony from the country's top gangsters, and because it was televised to a national audience, the word "Mafia" became a household name for the first time. Among the people who testified were Frank Costello, Frank Erickson, and George Levy. Their testimony is the basis for the information presented in this section.

13. Erickson Testimony, *Special Committee to Investigate Organized Crime in Interstate Commerce*. Frank Erickson had so much money that he was often approached to place "lay off" bets, which sports books used to hedge against bets that were considered to be a sure thing (like having to pay out bets against Seabiscuit). Frank Costello even got a cut of 5 percent if he brokered the deal for Erickson.

14. In this instance, Costello demonstrated a notable difference between his and Luciano's approach. Costello didn't use violence, but instead asked the right people to do him a favor, noting that it would make him happy if they did (and unhappy if they didn't, which carried an implied threat without having to say it). The Brooklyn outfits couldn't understand that—especially Anastasia—but Costello had learned the old maxim that you can shear a sheep many times, but you can only skin it once. He garnered his reputation by showing restraint, and keeping violent murders out of his repertoire, thus giving him a whiff, however tiny, of legitimacy. This was important, because he needed to maintain a reputation that made it easy for more legitimate businessmen and politicians to do business with him.

15. Hunt, Thomas, "Mob Boss 'Luciano' in the Hands of the Law," The American Mafia, mafiahistory.us, December 8, 2021, http://mafiahistory.us/a004/f_prisonlucky.html; "Charlie Lucky Luciano's visitor lists," New York State Archives, Series B0123-77, Box 27. pdf (accessed March 3, 2022).

16. A singular meeting at the Madison Hotel between Frank Costello and Haffenden, however, is not spoken about in Socks Lanza's testimony. He says that he had dinner and drinks with Haffenden at the Madison Hotel, which was later revealed via wiretap transcripts to be a frequent meeting place for Frank Costello. This will be touched on later, but Costello and Haffenden developed a relationship at some point during Operation Underworld.

17. Gosch, Hammer, and Lucania, *The Last Testament of Lucky Luciano*, page 269.

18. "Filipino Agitator Seized Here by the FBI—Spent Years in Stirring Up 'Dark Skinned Races' Against U.S. J. E. Hoover Says," *New York Times*, August 1, 1942, https://timesmachine.nytimes.com/timesmachine/1942/08/01/85571329.html?pageNumber=3 (accessed 2/3/2020).

19. It's even plausible that members of the audience alerted authorities. African Americans were still dealing with segregation and Jim Crow laws, but overall, there were very few instances where their loyalty to the United States during World War II was in question. Instances such as the Harlem Draft Riots in 1943 were the exception, but the motivations behind that did not reflect the views of the entire African American community, and it

certainly wasn't about overthrowing the US government, as Guzman was suggesting.

20. "Disloyalty Denied by Black Hitler," *New York Times*, December 24, 1942, https://timesmachine.nytimes.com/timesmachine/1942/12/24/292389392.html?pageNumber=10 (accessed 2/3/2020).

21. Lanza Testimony. Socks Lanza actually recalled the name as "Gordan," but "Jordan" is likely who it was. The only other Gordan in the movement was a woman, and when Lanza identified the photograph of "Jordan" twelve years later, it was revealed that the person was definitely a man.

22. Lanza Testimony, page 106.

23. "Disloyalty Denied by Black Hitler," *New York Times*, December 24, 1942, https://timesmachine.nytimes.com/timesmachine/1942/12/24/292389392.html?pageNumber=10 (accessed 2/3/2020).

24. Campbell, *The Luciano Project*, page 116. Rodney Campbell claims that he didn't know what Haffenden was looking for in Harlem. Campbell also never mentions "Jordan," or anything about this episode. Therefore, this is the first time that this information regarding Naval Intelligence's work in Harlem has been revealed to the public.

25. Gosch, Hammer, and Lucania, *The Last Testament of Lucky Luciano*, page 231.

26. Resko, *Reprieve*, page 202.

27. Hunt, Thomas, "Mob Boss 'Luciano' in the Hands of the Law," The American Mafia, mafiahistory.us, December 8, 2021, http://mafiahistory.us/a004/f_prisonlucky.html; Clinton, "Charlie Luciano Medical/Psychiatric Reports," Charles 'Lucky' Luciano inmate file, Clinton State Prison, Series 14610-77, Box 26, pdf (accessed March 3, 2022).

28. Gosch, Hammer, and Lucania, *The Last Testament of Lucky Luciano*, pages 117–118.

29. Newark, *Boardwalk Gangster*, pages 43–52. I accept Tim Newark's conclusion in his chapter in *Boardwalk Gangster* titled "Surviving the Ride," because Newark cites *New York Times* articles from the time period that refer to Luciano as "Lucky." Presently, this is the accepted story of Luciano's facial scars.

30. Gosch, Hammer, and Lucania, *The Last Testament of Lucky Luciano*, page 51.

31. Jeff Burke, author interview, March 9, 2022. The probability of this case of iritis being caused by previous trauma is actually so low that it's highly unlikely. What's more likely is that it arose from some sort of infection.

Luciano's Wassermann test (syphilis test) had previously come back negative, so his iritis in this case was possibly due to herpes, toxoplasmosis, TB, or an undiagnosed autoimmune disease (none of which have been confirmed).

32. Gosch, Hammer, and Lucania, *The Last Testament of Lucky Luciano*, page 109.

33. Newark, *Boardwalk Gangster*, page 46.

34. This is true, but they were drug addicts, and they may have been threatened, and therefore, their testimony was deemed inadmissible. However, there is some truth to this speculation, as it was widely known that Cokey Flo took a vacation in Paris after the Luciano trial, which was considered highly suspicious in criminal circles.

35. Gosch, Hammer, and Lucania, *The Last Testament of Lucky Luciano*, page 269. Luciano contends that he offered Thomas Dewey a $90,000 bribe for his "campaign fund," and that Dewey accepted it. Dewey, for his part, not only vehemently denied that he ever took a bribe from Luciano, but his commissioning of the Herlands Investigation eleven years later was largely to disprove this claim and, instead, prove that Luciano's contributions to the war effort had indeed contributed to his parole. Prior to the Herlands Investigation, Luciano's contribution had been hearsay, but nonetheless written about extensively, as rumors of Dewey and Luciano's pact ran rampant. This book is not contending that Dewey accepted a bribe from Luciano—in fact, quite the opposite—but this book is written with the belief that Luciano, one way or another, did offer a bribe to Dewey.

Chapter 9—Spying on Spies

1. Contrary to popular belief, Major League Baseball did not shut down during the war years. The MLB just lost a significant number of players, including their biggest stars. One star who did not immediately serve, however, was Yankees legend Joe DiMaggio. He had recently become a father, so he was 3A and exempt from service. However, he was very unpopular in 1942 for not volunteering to fight and was just as likely to hear boos as cheers. In fact, despite the Yankees making it to the World Series (they lost in five games), DiMaggio had one of the worst statistical seasons of his career. Given that he was facing less than stellar opponents, this was a surprising result, and his declining public image may have contributed to him having an off year. The public's stance and his poor performance that season contributed to him enlisting in the army early in the following year.

2. D. Sacco Testimony, page 54.

3. Lanza Testimony, page 89.

4. Ibid., pages 83–84; Campbell, *The Luciano Project*, page 104.

5. Haffenden File, page 2. This conclusion is based on analysis of Haffenden's roster from February 1, 1943. It's noteworthy that every last name in Squad #1 seems to have Irish origins, while the other squads are nearly devoid of any Irish names.

6. D. Sacco Testimony. When questioned about his role in thwarting certain plots, Dominick Sacco revealed that for the men in B-3 section in 1942, "sabotage" events could have been fraud cases involving American war materials, theft, slowing of work, or labor unrest.

7. Polakoff Testimony; Campbell, *The Luciano Project*.

8. "Lanza Is Jailed on New Charges—Labor Racketeer, Facing Trial in Union Extortion, Accused Also of Election Fraud," *New York Times*, November 12, 1942, https://timesmachine.nytimes.com/timesmachine/1942/11/12/96560959.html (accessed 2/6/2022).

9. The two detectives were demoted as a result of this incident.

10. Polakoff Testimony, page 26; Campbell, *The Luciano Project*, page 122.

11. Digital Files of Frank Hogan (Herlands Investigation, 1954), Thomas E. Dewey papers, D.58, Rare Books, Special Collections, and Preservation, River Campus Libraries, University of Rochester; Campbell, *The Luciano Project*, page 110. The fugitive Frank Hogan was looking for was Patsy Murray. Upon being contacted by Investigator William Herlands in 1954, Hogan provided a transcript that showed conversations from two of Socks Lanza's phones in Meyer's Hotel. There are large gaps in the dates of the conversations, indicating that Hogan did not provide all of the transcripts produced between November 23, 1942, and February 24, 1943 (when the tap was removed). It's likely that Hogan only included portions that had to do with Operation Underworld, as that is what Herlands would have been after. These transcripts give us a unique look into Operation Underworld, and the majority of these conversations are revealed to the public for the first time in the following pages.

12. Espy Testimony, page 46.

13. Hogan Files. Socks Lanza has one of the best nicknames of anyone in Operation Underworld, and it's revealing that Haffenden calls him Socks there. Evidently, it was common that people (probably mostly friends) called him that, which also indicates how close Lanza and Haffenden had become.

14. Hogan Files.

15. Espy Testimony. Espy and Lanza were actually shown Hogan's wiretap transcripts by Herlands investigators. Espy identified the name "Brown" in

his testimony, and said it had to do with Communists and Harlem. "Brown" also came up in the Hogan transcripts as having to do with a cabaret in Harlem. It is unknown which cabaret this was, but if this information were discovered, it would help identify the informant known as "Brown."

16. D. Sacco Testimony, page 63.

17. Morhous Testimony. On December 4, 1942, presumably after reading the phone tap transcripts, DA Frank Hogan contacted Warden Morhous and demanded a list of visitors to Luciano. Morhous had been getting lazy with lists that he was providing to Lyons, referring to visitors merely as "parties."

18. Hogan Files.

19. Ibid.

20. Lanza Testimony, page 65; Campbell, *The Luciano Project*, page 123. Did Socks Lanza actually hit Bridges? Why not? His name was "Socks," after all, and Bridges was very well known as an agitator to the US government and the Mafia. However, Lanza's recollection of this event is the only account in the historical record, and it should be noted that it cannot be and has not been corroborated by anyone else.

21. Polakoff Testimony, page 26; Campbell, *The Luciano Project*, page 123.

Chapter 10—When You Dance with the Devil . . .

1. United States Senate, *Special Committee to Investigate Organized Crime in Interstate Commerce*. Frank Costello also received a special visitor during the Christmas holidays. His name was William O'Dwyer, and he was in the army at the time. Previously, O'Dwyer had been the district attorney of Brooklyn, and it was later proven that he committed several instances of extreme dereliction of duty in not following up to prosecute certain underworld individuals—Albert Anastasia among them. The fact that O'Dwyer visited Costello's house came up in the Kefauver Committee hearings in 1951.

2. Resko, *Reprieve*, page 203.

3. Ibid., pages 205–206.

4. Ibid., page 206.

5. While Lansky clearly served Luciano (and his own interests) in the role of advisor, it appears that the common term "consigliere" wasn't used at this time. So even though Lansky fits the description and role that future "consiglieris" would occupy, he is not given that title by Luciano, and therefore is an "advisor."

6. Block, Alan A., *East Side-West Side: Organized Crime in New York, 1930–1950* (New Brunswick, NJ: Transaction Books, 1983), print. Exactly how many murders actually took place during "the Night of the Sicilian Vespers" is unknown. Rumors and lore claim there were dozens across the country, and maybe even hundreds of murders. However, the authority on the issue is Alan Block, who contends that there were only a handful of murders, as a search of national newspaper publications in and around the time revealed only three or four gangland-type slayings. But it's also possible that some bodies weren't found or weren't reported. So the truth is probably somewhere between Block's research and the exaggerated rumors, which puts the death toll somewhere between a handful and a hundred.

7. Morhous File; Hogan Files. None of the logs or records indicate that Lascari was with them. But his name is penciled in on Morhous's letter, along with "Lansky" and "Mirandi" (Mike Miranda was also known as Mike "Mirandi" and Mike "Mirando"). Also, Hogan's wiretaps record Lanza talking with a guy named "Mick" about his visit at the prison. It's been determined by the detectives who transcribed the tapes that "Mick" was Michael Lascari.

8. "Moses Polakoff Is Dead at the Age of 97—Was Lawyer for Lucky Luciano," *New York Times*, June 14 ,1993, https://timesmachine.nytimes.com/timesmachine/1993/06/14/784393.html?pageNumber=25 (accessed 3/8/2021). In his obituary, it is stated that Moses Polakoff represented the former Heavyweight Champion of the World Jack Dempsey in a divorce proceeding in the early 1940s. The case had started just days after he met Luciano in prison for the first time, so perhaps he was more intent on that case than Luciano's appeal, and needed to outsource the work.

9. Gosch, Hammer, and Lucania, *The Last Testament of Lucky Luciano*, page 285.

10. Morhous Testimony. The detective who read this transcript concluded that "Guy" was either Frank Costello or Joe Adonis. Since the topic involved Brooklyn, and the navy yard there, which was close to the Camarda Locals, then it's far more likely that this person was Adonis.

Chapter 11—Black January

1. Berger, Meyer, "400,000 Revelers Fill Times Square in Dim New Year's—Chill of War Felt as Vast Crowd Toots Sluggishly on Old and Second-Hand Horns, *New York Times*, January 1, 1943, https://timesmachine.nytimes.com/timesmachine/1943/01/01/83892198.html?pageNumber=1 (accessed February 15, 2022).

2. Lanza Testimony, pages 92–95.

3. Ibid. According to Lanza, he brought up no fewer than a dozen Italian men in connection with Haffenden's requests for native Italians and Sicilians. But this is the only specific instance that he speaks about in his testimony.

4. "Convict Testifies to Lanza's Tactics—Says He Demanded Appointment of Aide as Union Official," *New York Times*, January 8, 1941, https://times machine.nytimes.com/timesmachine/1943/01/08/87407679.html?page Number=27 (accessed 3/8/2020).

5 "Lanza, Racketeer, Admits Extortion—Four Co-Defendants Also Make Unexpected Move in Fish Market Union Case," *New York Times*, January 13, 1943, https://timesmachine.nytimes.com/timesmachine/1943/01/13/88510384.html?pageNumber=25 (accessed 3/8/2020).

6. Newark, Tim, *The Mafia at War: The Shocking True Story of America's Wartime Pact with Organized Crime* (New York, NY: Skyhorse Publishing, 2012), print, pages 115–118.

7. Block, *East Side-West Side: Organized Crime in New York, 1930–1950*, pages 108–111.

8. The murder of Carlo Tresca was never solved; however, the handling of his case was later cited as a major dereliction of duty by the District Attorney's Office. There are several theories as to who was behind Tresca's murder and who actually killed him, but the prevailing one presented by Alan Block is that Genovese paid Galante to murder Tresca. Luciano later claimed that Tony Bender was involved too. No claim has been made about Michael Miranda being involved in this murder, but as Block points out, Miranda was good friends with both Bender and Genovese. Not only that, but Bender and Miranda were both involved in Operation Underworld (Bender had previously supplied a legitimate union card to Felix Sacco so he could infiltrate the Norden Bombsight Plant). Miranda was also a contract killer just like Bender and Galante. It's even possible that Miranda was in the car next to Galante or even in the front passenger seat (the car was found with all four doors open). It's also plausible that Genovese sent word through Miranda, or that he found out about the contract. Perhaps Genovese even offered the contract to him or asked him to relay his plan to Luciano in prison. Any way you slice it, it's highly likely that Miranda knew about the order that led to Tresca's murder before it happened, even if he wasn't directly involved.

9. Upon winning the Revolutionary War for the United States in 1783, George Washington stood at the command of the most powerful army in North America. If he had wanted to, he could have marched on the Capitol

and taken the country for himself. Instead, he stood down, and ceded power to the Congress of the United States. When he received news of Washington's unprecedented notion, King George III reportedly said, "If he does that, [Washington] will be the greatest man in the world." Ever since then, the peaceful transfer of power in government has been the hallmark of United States democracy. Luciano was no George Washington, but he was certainly influenced by this American tradition.

10. Hogan Files. Wiretaps reveal that Costello's man, Jim O'Connell, called Lanza's office at Meyer's Hotel. The detectives who read the transcripts say that Costello's code name was both "Frank Casino" and "Murray." There is some evidence to suggest that "Frank Casino" is another man in the Luciano family, but there is no way to be sure.

11. "'Socks' Lanza Gets 7 ½ to 15 Year Term," *New York Times*, January 30, 1943, Lanza gets 7 ½ to 15 Year Sentence—4 'Strong Arm' Men of Fulton Market Labor Racketeer Also go to Prison," *New York Times,* https://times machine.nytimes.com/timesmachine/1943/01/30/87410794.html?page Number=17 (accessed 3/8/2020).

12. Hogan Testimony.

Chapter 12—The Devil's in the Details

1. Schwerin Testimony.

2. Lansky Testimony, page 31.

3. Ibid.

4. Polakoff Testimony, page 55.

5. Lansky Testimony, pages 24–27; Tarbox Testimony, pages 20–25.

6. Marsloe Testimony; Campbell, *The Luciano Project*, page 137.

7. Tarbox Testimony, page 8.

8. Ibid.; Campbell, *The Luciano Project*.

9. Tarbox Testimony; MacDowell Testimony, pages 27–28. In an illustration of just how unprepared the navy was to launch an attack on mainland Europe, George Tarbox testified that the original maps used by ONI were purchased from Rand McNally, or a company like them. The navy had no maps of its own.

10. Digital Testimony of George Wolf (Herlands Investigation, 1954), Thomas E. Dewey papers, D.58, Rare Books, Special Collections, and

Preservation, River Campus Libraries, University of Rochester; Campbell, *The Luciano Project*, page 153.

11. "Lucania's Aid in War Effort Cited in Legal Plea—Suspension of Two Sentences Asked for Ex-Vice Overlord," *New York Times*, February 9, 1943, https://timesmachine.nytimes.com/timesmachine/1943/02/09/88514676.html? pageNumber=17(accessed February 22, 2022).

12. Campbell, *The Luciano Project*, pages 155–56.

13. Wolf Testimony; Campbell, *The Luciano Project*, pages 158–59.

14. "Lucania's Aid in War Effort Cited in Legal Plea."

15. Digital Testimony of Angelo Cincotta (Herlands Investigation, 1954), Thomas E. Dewey papers, D.58, Rare Books, Special Collections, and Preservation, River Campus Libraries, University of Rochester; Campbell, *The Luciano Project*.

16. Cincotta Testimony; Campbell, *The Luciano Project*, pages 161–67. According to Cincotta's file, investigators who were a part of the Herlands investigation cited his report as "false," and further chided Cincotta because his report had been the prevailing theory on Luciano's involvement for the next twelve years. The Herlands investigators commented that this had de-railed future investigations.

17. Campbell, *The Luciano Project*, page 159.

18. Polakoff Testimony, page 30.

19. Kelly Testimony, pages 23–24; Espy Testimony, pages 34–36.

20. Digital Testimony of Paul A. Alfieri (Herlands Investigation, 1954), Thomas E. Dewey papers, D.58, Rare Books, Special Collections, and Preservation, River Campus Libraries, University of Rochester, page 13.

21. Polakoff Testimony, page 29.

22. Digital Testimony of Joachim Titolo (Herlands Investigation, 1954), Thomas E. Dewey papers, D.58, Rare Books, Special Collections, and Preservation, River Campus Libraries, University of Rochester, pages 8–9; Tarbox Testimony.

23. Kelly Testimony, page 31.

Chapter 13—Desperate Measures

1. Lansky Testimony.

2. Once the four officers from New York City arrived in Washington, DC,

they met up with two other officers who had been recruited for the same mission. These two officers served in a reserve capacity.

3. This is the first time that Wallace Wharton's name has been revealed to the public as the spymaster.

4. Digital Testimony of Wallace S. Wharton (Herlands Investigation, 1954), Thomas E. Dewey papers, D.58, Rare Books, Special Collections, and Preservation, River Campus Libraries, University of Rochester.

5. Campbell, *The Luciano Project*.

6. Digital Testimony of Mary Haffenden (Herlands Investigation, 1954), Thomas E. Dewey papers, D.58, Rare Books, Special Collections, and Preservation, River Campus Libraries, University of Rochester.

7. Eisenberg, Dennis, *Meyer Lansky: Mogul of the Mob* (New York, NY: Paddington Press 1979), print, pages 211–12; Tim Newark, *Mafia Allies: The True Story of America's Secret Alliance with the Mob in World War II* (St. Paul, MN: MBI Publishing Company, 2007), print, pages 152–53. Meyer Lansky is the sole source for this story about Paul Alfieri meeting one of Luciano's cousin's sons in Sicily. Lansky claims that Alfieri told him this story after the war. Alfieri didn't corroborate the story during the Herlands investigation, but that is not surprising, as he was not forthcoming with details of his exploits, in consideration of not disclosing classified information. However, Alfieri did say that he was able to contact numerous people in Sicily who were deported to Italy because of crimes in the United States.

8. Campbell, *The Luciano Project*, pages 174–80; Newark, *Mafia Allies*, pages 150–56; Marsloe, Alfieri, Titolo, and Lanza Testimonies.

9. Gosch, Hammer, and Lucania, *The Last Testament of Lucky Luciano*.

10. Newark, *Boardwalk Gangster*, pages 70–72.

11. Luciano didn't really have any long-term relationships with women prior to his incarceration, and the only relationship that came close to long term was his affair with a showgirl named Gay Orlova.

12. Newark, *Boardwalk Gangster*, page 110. Luciano liked to winter in Miami.

13. Ibid., pages 69–70.

14. Gosch and Hammer, *The Last Testament of Lucky Luciano*, page 151.

15. Ibid., pages 150–155.

16. Ibid., page 187.

17. Newark, *Boardwalk Gangster*, pages 80–82

Chapter 14—Unfinished Business

1. Titolo Testimony; Campbell, *The Luciano Project*, pages 179–180.

2. Campbell, *The Luciano Project*, page 182.

3. Titolo Testimony. Meanwhile, on the island of Sardinia, Lieutenant Titolo used the methods taught to him by Alfieri to organize the fishing fleet to work for Naval Intelligence. With his mafiosi and fishing fleet contacts, he foiled a plot organized by nineteen Italian officers. The officers were going to use the fishing fleet to ferry German forces back to Sardinia to retake the island. Thanks to his organization of the Sardinian fleet, Titolo was tipped off, and the officers were captured as they tried to flee.

4. "Costello Boasts of Aiding Kennedy to Win Leadership—Testified Four District Chiefs Voted as He Suggested in Tammany Election," *New York Times*, October 26, 1943, https://timesmachine.nytimes.com/timesmachine/1943/10/26/88575236.html?pageNumber=1 (accessed 10/20/2021).

5. Wolf Testimony, page 2.

6. Lacey, *Little Man*, page 112.

7. The British government did think about assassinating Hitler, with a plot called Operation Foxley. There were various plans made that were to see Hitler dispatched in mid-summer 1944. However, the British government balked at that plan, and among other reasons, it was concluded that Hitler was such a poor strategist anyone who replaced him would ultimately be better than him. It was a lesson the English had learned from their onetime enemy Napoleon Bonaparte, who said, "Never interrupt your enemy when he is making a mistake."

8. Gosch, Hammer, and Lucania, *The Last Testament of Lucky Luciano*, pages 270–271. Luciano claimed that he had this conversation with Tommy Lucchese—a loyal and longtime friend—and Joe Adonis. There are three names that I have been unable to identify on Morhous's witness list, and the names provided are likely aliases. It cannot be proven that Lucchese or Adonis didn't visit Luciano at Great Meadow, but there is no definitive record of them doing so. If this conversation did take place, then it was likely to his normal audience of Meyer Lansky and Moses Polakoff. If the conversation never took place at all, it's still highly plausible that Luciano had these thoughts. The story of "Bugsy" Siegel from 1932 comes to us courtesy of Luciano and Lansky.

9. FBI report, file no. 39-2141-4. In a letter to J. Edgar Hoover that's signed by E. E. Conroy, Conroy states that Haffenden played golf with Costello. Conroy was tasked by Hoover to discover the truth behind Luciano's release

from prison. The fact that Haffenden golfed with Costello was also corroborated during testimony gathered from the Kefauver Committee.

10. Gosch, Hammer, and Lucania, *The Last Testament of Lucky Luciano*, page 270.

11. "Fugitive Miranda Gives Himself Up—Gang Figure Held Without Bail in Boccia Slaying Case, *New York Times*, September 17, 1946, https://times machine.nytimes.com/timesmachine/1946/09/17/102267077.pdf (accessed February 22, 2022).

12. Lacey, *Little Man*, pages 150–51.

13. Leckie, Robert, *The Battle for Iwo Jima* (New York, NY: Random House, 1967), digital, page 28.

14. United States Senate. Special Committee to Investigate Organized Crime in Interstate Commerce: Page 1193.

Chapter 15—Banished from Heaven

1. Campbell, *The Luciano Project*, page 199.

2. Phillips Testimony, pages 1–4.

3. Because of this destruction of the historical record, many details about Operation Underworld will never be known. We'll never know how big the network formed by Luciano's contacts became. We'll never fully understand the scope of Naval Intelligence activity in New York City. So many details about the actions of the men involved will never be known. In fact, if it weren't for the Herlands investigation years later, all the public would have is hearsay and conjecture, and FBI files with more of the same.

4. Campbell, *The Luciano Project*, page 247.

5. Ibid., pages 247–248.

6. Ibid., page 247.

7. Morhous Testimony. During Luciano's time at Great Meadow prison the access he gained to his criminal associates was nothing short of unprecedented. Most of his visitors have previously been identified, with the exceptions of M. Einsberg and John Martini. Also revealed for the first time are R. Filkins, who visited Luciano on May 16, 1944; a person referred to as "Franks" on July 15, 1944; and R. Roseman, who visited on September 19, 1944. Morhous wrote their names down, and then included them in a report that he submitted to John Lyons on July 27, 1945. The last three names could be aliases ("Franks" could be Frank Erickson, Frank Costello, or perhaps

even both, as they were often referred to as the "two Franks"), or they could be real people. Perhaps a motivated sleuth will one day be able to answer the question of who these people were.

8. Campbell, *The Luciano Project*, page 277.

9. Ibid., page 240.

10. Ibid., page 260.

11. Rodney Campbell came to a different conclusion, which was that Haffenden simply had a personality dispute with Mayor O'Dwyer and engaged in no wrongdoing (which is what Haffenden said). His conclusion is based on a couple of fallacies that he was privy to. He claimed that Frank Costello and Haffenden never met (*The Luciano Project*, page 243). Not only was Costello and Haffenden's meeting talked about in the Kefauver Committee proceedings, but the FBI also had testimony from informants who spoke to this fact. Campbell may have overlooked the Kefauver Committee testimony, but there's no way he could have known about the FBI file that made the link, as that wasn't declassified until 1982, which was five years after Campbell came to these conclusions. This means he was also not privy to some of the claims made about Haffenden, and perhaps if he was, he would have reached a different conclusion about him. However, Campbell's conclusions about Haffenden are also consistent with his desire to not "stir the pot" with the navy, and it's possible they come from that notion.

12. FBI report, file no. 39-2141-9–39-2141-10. pdfs; Campbell, *The Luciano Project*.

13. Gosch, Hammer, and Lucania, *The Last Testament of Lucky Luciano*, pages 283–284. Luciano said that when he had his last visit with Lansky on Ellis Island, he had already had visas made. If this is true, then it likely came from a visit on January 14, 1946, at Sing Sing by three men: I. Spieler, James Leesto, and Joseph Leone (Polakoff Testimony, page 59.)

14. "Laura Keene," *Marad Vessel History Database*, https://vesselhistory. marad.dot.gov/ShipHistory/Detail/2964 (accessed 2/15/2022).

15. "Deportation Set for Luciano Today—Vice Overlord to Depart for Italy, Freed for His Aid to the Army in War, *New York Times*, https://timesmachine. nytimes.com/timesmachine/1946/02/09/91609037.html?pageNumber=15 (accessed February 15, 2022). To make matters worse, the attorney general of the United States—Tom Clark—just happened to be touring the facilities at Ellis Island that day. Clark's name was mentioned in an article in the *New York Times* about Frank Costello. Clark then complained to the director of the FBI—J. Edgar Hoover. This complaint, combined with another by former

Mayor La Guardia, caused Hoover to send an undercover agent to Pier 7 to eavesdrop on Luciano's departure and look for criminal activity.

16. In the summer of 1943, *Normandie* had finally been renamed *Lafayette* and towed to the Brooklyn Navy Yard. The salvage operation that got her out of the mud was the most expensive of its kind, coming in at $5,000,000. Eventually, she was sold for scrap, and the job was completed on December 31, 1948.

17. FBI report, file no. 39-2141–(number indiscernible), pdf; Digital File of Daniel Frawley File (Herlands Investigation, 1954), Thomas E. Dewey papers, D.58, Rare Books, Special Collections, and Preservation, River Campus Libraries, University of Rochester; United States Senate, *Special Committee to Investigate Organized Crime in Interstate Commerce*. There are conflicting reports about what follows. The FBI's investigation told a different story (that no one visited Luciano on *Laura Keene*). The guards were even questioned by FBI agents after the event, and they denied that the following incidents happened. However, on the ship was Second Mate Daniel Frawley, who later testified during a Kefauver Committee hearing that he saw men with diamond rings and longshoremen union identification enter the boat. What follows is mostly from Fawley's testimony, as his statements were taken under oath. The guards, for their part, may have lied to the FBI in fear that they would get in trouble.

Also, the agent that was dispatched to Pier 7 by FBI Director Hoover was able to gain access to the pier and the ship. His account of events is described in "the Rosen memo," which was addressed from Agent Alex Rosen to Assistant Director of the FBI E. A. Tamm (FBI report, file no. 39-2141-39), who forwarded the memo to Hoover. In it, Rosen corroborates some events, is the sole source for other events, and also produces parts that conflict with other people's testimony.

Given all of the different sources, this is the most accurate depiction of what happened that day.

18. "Luciano Gets Heave Ho; Bars Press from Pier," Brooklyn Newspapers, February 10, 1946, https://bklyn.newspapers.com/image/52896191/ ?terms=bush%20terminal%20Brooklyn%20piers&match=1 (accessed 3/10/2022).

19. FBI report, file no. 39-2141-39, pdf.

20. Gosch, Hammer, and Lucania, *The Last Testament of Lucky Luciano*, page 286. The FBI agent sent by Director Hoover never saw the room where Daniel Frawley said the meeting happened, so he is not the best witness for what happens next. Luciano is also not the best witness, because it is believed

that he exaggerated events substantially. For example, Luciano claimed that there was a much larger procession that visited him. Frank Costello, Meyer Lansky, Bugsy Siegel, Joe Adonis, and Willie Moretti were all on his list, but so too were Longie Zwillman, Tommy Lucchese, Joe Bonanno, Albert Anastasia, Steve Magaddino, Carlo Gambino, Phil Kastel, Owney Madden, Moe Dalitz, plus top political figures or their representatives, Siegel's mistress Virginia Hill, and "three girls selected by Joe Adonis" to accompany Luciano for the journey across the Atlantic. That certainly would have required at least a few more limousines. It's unlikely that there was more than one car full of visitors, given eyewitness testimony (see Daniel Frawley Testimony). Admittedly, it's also impossible to know who exactly joined Luciano on that boat even if the group was smaller. When they were later questioned, guards failed to identify anyone from pictures provided by the FBI or government investigators. Therefore, the people chosen for this event here were the ones that were closest to Luciano, had active shared business interests (rackets), and had been in Luciano's life more recently (and longer) than others.

21. Polakoff Testimony, page 59. Moses Polakoff made this claim, about Meyer Lansky checking into a hotel, during the Herlands Investigation. It's believable in itself, but Polakoff was either misinformed, or he lied when he said that Lansky's last visit to Ellis Island was during Polakoff's last visit to Luciano. That means that Polakoff was either unaware that his client made two subsequent visits, or he was covering for him. Either way, the fact that he didn't know about those visits leaves room to believe that his testimony about this subject wasn't accurate. Lansky was his client, after all, and that gave Polakoff reason to cover for him.

22. It's impossible to know for sure that it was Costello and Adonis who ran this errand. But Costello was the obvious choice given that Fulton Fish Market was in his territory, and Adonis could have gone too, as he was the only other one who was known at Fulton (Ben Espy knew him for sure).

23. Gosch, Hammer, and Lucania, *The Last Testament of Lucky Luciano*, page 278.

Chapter 16—The Hopeless Sinners

1. FBI report, file no. 39-2141-10, pdf.

2. MacDowell Testimony; Campbell, *The Luciano Project*, page 268.

3. Ernest Rupolo's body was found almost twenty years later in Jamaica Bay, Queens. Concrete blocks had been tied to his legs, and his hands were bound

behind his back. He was identified by dental records. No one was ever charged with his murder, but it's evident that Genovese ordered his killing.

4. "Gang-Ride Victim Thrown in Brush—Link to Genovese Trial Seen in Brooklyn Parolees Killing—Body Found in Jersey," *New York Times*, June 10, 1946, https://timesmachine.nytimes.com/timesmachine/1946/06/10/93128831.html?pageNumber=3 (accessed 2/18/2022).

5. Jewish gangsters like Meyer Lansky were allowed to sit in on the meetings of the Commission and act as consiglieri for various family leaders, but they were not given a vote when the Commission ruled on an issue.

6. Gosch, Hammer, and Lucania, *The Last Testament of Lucky Luciano*, pages 311–19; Hunt, Thomas, "Lucky Called Mob Meet in Havana? Probably Not," *The American Mafia*, January 2, 2022, https://mafiahistory.us/a045/f_havana-convention.html (accessed March 3, 2022). Information about the Havana Conference comes from Luciano and Meyer Lansky. However, the website mafiahistory.us put together a very impressive collection of evidence that suggests that the Havana Conference never really happened (see link above). Instead, they claim various bosses (and also Frank Sinatra) visited Luciano while he was in Havana over the course of months. The authors make a very compelling case, but also admit that they cannot disprove that this event took place as described by Luciano. I've chosen to keep references to the Havana Conference in this narrative, as it was a concise representation of the issues that the Mafia was facing at that time.

7. Gosch, Hammer, and Lucania, *The Last Testament of Lucky Luciano*, pages 311–319. Luciano claimed that he was against the narcotics trade and had learned his lesson from his younger years. What we know now is that for years after the Havana Conference, Luciano busied himself with the narcotics trade and racket quite a bit. It's understandable that he would deny involvement, given his need to separate himself from rackets that were frowned upon by the public, but evidence suggests that he was very much involved in the drug trade.

8. "Morris Declares O'Dwyer Witheld Facts in Pier Deal," *New York Times*, October 24, 1949, https://timesmachine.nytimes.com/timesmachine/1949/10/24/86787758.html?pageNumber=1 (accessed February 18, 2022).

9. "Mary Haffenden a Bride in Queens," *New York Times*, June 15, 1948, https://timesmachine.nytimes.com/timesmachine/1948/06/15/85274088.html?pageNumber=31 (accessed March 4, 2022).

10. M. Haffenden Testimony; Campbell, *The Luciano Project*, page 264.

11. M. Haffenden Testimony; Campbell, *The Luciano Project*, page 269. Murray Gurfein testified to the Kefauver Commission that Haffenden's testi-

mony about events surrounding Operation Underworld was mostly incorrect. But Gurfein also said that he would not speak to the actual facts, given the navy's desire to keep them a secret. The Kefauver Commission, which made some effort toward revealing the facts of Operation Underworld, therefore came up short, and the true story remained a mystery.

12. MacDowell Testimony; Campbell, *The Luciano Project*, page 268.

13. "Charles R. Haffenden," *New York Times*, December 25, 1952, https://timesmachine.nytimes.com/timesmachine/1952/12/25/84382360.html?pageNumber=29 (accessed 11/01/2019).

14. Digital File of Carlo Tresca (Herlands Investigation, 1954), Thomas E. Dewey papers, D.58, Rare Books, Special Collections, and Preservation, River Campus Libraries, University of Rochester.

15. Gosch, Hammer, and Lucania, *The Last Testament of Lucky Luciano*, page 269. In his memoir, Luciano said that the amount was $90,000.

16. Gosch, Hammer, and Lucania, *The Last Testament of Lucky Luciano*, page 405.

17. Vincent Gigante of the Genovese family later became *Capo di Tutti Capi*.

18. "Luciano's Brother Returns," *New York Times*, February 6, 1962, https://timesmachine.nytimes.com/timesmachine/1962/02/06/89498136.html?pageNumber=50 (accessed March 8, 2022).

19. "Luciano Is Buried in Queens Vault—2 Brothers Meet the Plane Bearing Casket from Italy," *New York Times*, February 8, 1962, https://timesmachine. nytimes.com/timesmachine/1962/02/08/87301589.html?pageNumber=52 (accessed March 8, 2022).

20. Ibid.

Afterword

1. United States Senate, *Special Committee to Investigate Organized Crime in Interstate Commerce.*

2. "Socks Lanza Dies—Ran Rackets Here," *New York Times*, February 8, 1962, https://timesmachine.nytimes.com/timesmachine/1968/10/11/76888989.html (accessed October 20, 2021).

Selected Bibliography
(sources not cited in notes)

Archives, Special Collections, and Declassified Official Documents

Digital File of Frank Costello (Herlands Investigation, 1954), Thomas E. Dewey papers, D.58, Rare Books, Special Collections, and Preservation, River Campus Libraries, University of Rochester.

Digital File of Joe Adonis (Herlands Investigation, 1954), Thomas E. Dewey papers, D.58, Rare Books, Special Collections, and Preservation, River Campus Libraries, University of Rochester.

Digital File of John Dunn (Herlands Investigation, 1954), Thomas E. Dewey papers, D.58, Rare Books, Special Collections, and Preservation, River Campus Libraries, University of Rochester.

Digital File of Harry Anslinger (Herlands Investigation, 1954), Thomas E. Dewey papers, D.58, Rare Books, Special Collections, and Preservation, River Campus Libraries, University of Rochester.

Digital File of Michael Lascari (Herlands Investigation, 1954), Thomas E. Dewey papers, D.58, Rare Books, Special Collections, and Preservation, River Campus Libraries, University of Rochester.

Digital File of Luciano–Kefauver Hearings (Herlands Investigation, 1954), Thomas E. Dewey papers, D.58, Rare Books, Special Collections, and Preservation, River Campus Libraries, University of Rochester.

Digital File of Luciano (Herlands Investigation, 1954), Thomas E. Dewey papers, D.58, Rare Books, Special Collections, and Preservation, River Campus Libraries, University of Rochester.

Digital File of Willis George (Herlands Investigation, 1954), Thomas E. Dewey papers, D.58, Rare Books, Special Collections, and Preservation, River Campus Libraries, University of Rochester.

Digital Testimony of Anthony Marsloe (Herlands Investigation, 1954), Thomas E. Dewey papers, D.58, Rare Books, Special Collections, and Preservation, River Campus Libraries, University of Rochester.

Digital Testimony of Charles Siragusa (Herlands Investigation, 1954), Thomas E. Dewey papers, D.58, Rare Books, Special Collections, and Preservation, River Campus Libraries, University of Rochester.

Digital Testimony of Frederick Moran (Herlands Investigation, 1954), Thomas E. Dewey papers, D.58, Rare Books, Special Collections, and Preservation, River Campus Libraries, University of Rochester.

Digital Testimony of George White (Herlands Investigation, 1954), Thomas E. Dewey papers, D.58, Rare Books, Special Collections, and Preservation, River Campus Libraries, University of Rochester.

Digital Testimony of George Wolf (Herlands Investigation, 1954), Thomas E. Dewey papers, D.58, Rare Books, Special Collections, and Preservation, River Campus Libraries, University of Rochester.

Digital Testimony of Harry Bonesteel (Herlands Investigation, 1954), Thomas E. Dewey papers, D.58, Rare Books, Special Collections, and Preservation, River Campus Libraries, University of Rochester.

Digital Testimony of Herbert Kemp (Herlands Investigation, 1954), Thomas E. Dewey papers, D.58, Rare Books, Special Collections, and Preservation, River Campus Libraries, University of Rochester.

Digital Testimony of Howard Nugent (Herlands Investigation, 1954), Thomas E. Dewey papers, D.58, Rare Books, Special Collections, and Preservation, River Campus Libraries, University of Rochester.

Digital Testimony of James O'Malley (Herlands Investigation, 1954), Thomas E. Dewey papers, D.58, Rare Books, Special Collections, and Preservation, River Campus Libraries, University of Rochester.

Digital Testimony of Joachim Titolo (Herlands Investigation, 1954), Thomas E. Dewey papers, D.58, Rare Books, Special Collections, and Preservation, River Campus Libraries, University of Rochester.

Digital Testimony of John A. Murphy (Herlands Investigation, 1954), Thomas E. Dewey papers, D.58, Rare Books, Special Collections, and Preservation, River Campus Libraries, University of Rochester.

Digital Testimony of Joseph Guerin (Herlands Investigation, 1954), Thomas E. Dewey papers, D.58, Rare Books, Special Collections, and Preservation, River Campus Libraries, University of Rochester.

Digital Testimony of Joseph P. Healy (Herlands Investigation, 1954), Thomas E. Dewey papers, D.58, Rare Books, Special Collections, and Preservation, River Campus Libraries, University of Rochester.

Digital Testimony of Joseph Kaitz (Herlands Investigation, 1954), Thomas E. Dewey papers, D.58, Rare Books, Special Collections, and Preservation, River Campus Libraries, University of Rochester.

Digital Testimony of Kathleen Cowen (Herlands Investigation, 1954), Thomas E. Dewey papers, D.58, Rare Books, Special Collections, and Preservation, River Campus Libraries, University of Rochester.

Digital Testimony of Lawrence Cowen (Herlands Investigation, 1954), Thomas E. Dewey papers, D.58, Rare Books, Special Collections, and Preservation, River Campus Libraries, University of Rochester.

Digital Testimony of Louise Pagnucco (Herlands Investigation, 1954), Thomas E. Dewey papers, D.58, Rare Books, Special Collections, and Preservation, River Campus Libraries, University of Rochester.

Digital Testimony of Margaret Grogan (Herlands Investigation, 1954), Thomas E. Dewey papers, D.58, Rare Books, Special Collections, and Preservation, River Campus Libraries, University of Rochester.

Digital Testimony of Paul A. Alfieri (Herlands Investigation, 1954), Thomas E. Dewey papers, D.58, Rare Books, Special Collections, and Preservation, River Campus Libraries, University of Rochester.

Digital Testimony of Samuel Levine (Herlands Investigation, 1954), Thomas E. Dewey papers, D.58, Rare Books, Special Collections, and Preservation, River Campus Libraries, University of Rochester.

Digital Testimony of William B. Howe (Herlands Investigation, 1954), Thomas E. Dewey papers, D.58, Rare Books, Special Collections, and Preservation, River Campus Libraries, University of Rochester.

FBI report, file no. 39-2141-5–39-2141-7. pdfs.

FBI report, file no. 39-2141-17–39-2141-21. pdfs.

FBI report, file no. 39-2141-24. pdf.

FBI report, file no. 39-2141-31. pdf.

FBI report, file no. 39-2141-35. pdf.

FBI report, file no. 39-2141-44. pdf.

Books

Afrasiabi, Peter. *Burning Bridges: America's 20-Year Crusade to Deport Labor Leader Harry Bridges*. Brooklyn, NY: Thirlmere Books, 2016. Print.

Asbury, Herbert. *The Gangs of New York*. New York, NY: Thunder's Mouth Press, 1927. Reprint 1990.

Atkinson, Rick. *An Army at Dawn*. New York, NY: Picador, 2002. Print.

Bayard, Piper, and Jay Holmes. *Spycraft: Essentials*. Lafayette, CO: Shoe Phone Press, 2018. Print.

Bell, Daniel. *The Racket-Ridden Longshoremen: The End of Ideology*. Glencoe, IL: The Free Press, 1960. Print.

Black, Matthew. *Dave Beck: A Teamster's Life*. Washington, DC: The International Brotherhood of Teamsters, 2016. Print.

Block, Alan A. *A Modern Marriage of Convenience: A Collaboration Between Organized Crime and U.S. Intelligence in Organized Crime: A Global Perspective*. Totowa, NJ: Rowman & Littlefield, 1986. Print.

Carroll, Brian. *Combating Racketeering in the Fulton Fish Market: In Organized Crime and Its Containment, eds*. Amsterdam, Netherlands: Kluwer, 1991. Digital.

Clark, Neil G. *Dock Boss: Eddie McGrath and the West Side Waterfront*. Fort Lee, NJ: Barricade Books, 2017. Print.

Devaney, John. *America Fights the Tide. WWII Series: 1942*. New York, NY. Walker and Company, 1991.

Dewey, Thomas E., *Twenty Against the Underworld*, Garden City, NY: Doubleday & Company, 1974. Print.

Diehl, Lorraine B. *Over Here: New York City during WWII*. New York, NY: Harper Collins-ebook, 2010. Digital.

Humbert, Nelli S. *The Business of Crime: Italians and Syndicate Crime in the United States Oxford*: Oxford, United Kingdom: University Press, 1976. Print.

Kelly, Robert J. *The Upperworld and the Underworld: Case Studies of Racketeering and Business Infiltration in the United States*. New York, NY: Klewer Academic, 1999. Digital.

Lacey, Robert. *Little Man*. Boston, MA: Little, Brown and Company, 1991. Print.

Mitchell, Joseph. *Old Mr. Flood*. San Francisco, CA: MacAdam/Cage, 1948. Reprint 2005.

Newark, Tim. *Mafia Allies: The True Story of America's Secret Alliance with the Mob in World War II*. St. Paul, MN: MBI Publishing Company, 2007. Print.

Offney, Ed. *Turning the Tide*. New York, NY: Perseus Books Group, 2011. Print.

Reynolds, Robert G. *Joe "Socks" Lanza: Genovese Family Caporegime*. Kindle Edition, 2010. Digital.

Sondern, Frederic. *Brotherhood of Evil: The Mafia*. New York, NY: Farrar, Straus & Cudahy, 1957. Reprint 1973.

Turkus, Burton B. *Murder Inc*. New York, NY: Tenacity Media Books, 1951. Digital.

Wolf, George. *Frank Costello: Prime Minister of the Underworld*. New York, NY: Morrow, 1974. Digital.

Newspaper Articles

"20-Pound Stray Salmon Netted Off Long Island." *New York Times*. April 20, 1941. https://timesmachine.nytimes.com/timesmachine/1941/04/20/ 85306470.html. (Accessed June 6, 2021)

"Admits Conspiracy in Spy-Ring Case—Last of Three Men Confesses—All Await Sentence." *New York Times*. August 15, 1942. https://timesmachine. nytimes.com/timesmachine/1942/08/15/88111403.html?pageNumber=5. (Accessed June 15, 2021)

"An Older and Wiser New York—The Expatriate Returning After Twenty Years Finds a City Changed in Many Ways." *New York Times*. January 19, 1941. https://timesmachine.nytimes.com/timesmachine/1941/ 01/19/85284182.html?pageNumber=136. (Accessed March 2, 2022)

Barry, Dan. "A Last Whiff of Fulton's Fish, Bringing a Tear." *New York Times*. July 10, 2005. https://www.nytimes.com/2005/07/10/nyregion/a-last- whiff-of-fultons-fish-bringing-a-tear.html. (Accessed January 20, 2021)

"Beef Famine Here Due to End Soon—FDA Predicts Better Supply in 7 to 10 Days as Mayor Appeals to Capital." *New York Times*. July 16, 1943. https://timesmachine.nytimes.com/timesmachine/1943/07/16/85109937.ht ml. (Accessed January 22, 2021)

"Daily Almanac." *New York Daily News*. April 1, 1942. https://www.news papers.com/image/432811596. (Accessed January 25, 2022)

"Daily Almanac." *New York Daily News*. April 3, 1942. https://www.news papers.com/image/432837621. (Accessed January 25, 2022)

"Daily Almanac." *New York Daily News*. March 26, 1942. https://www.news papers.com/image/432830580. (Accessed January 25, 2022)

"Daily Almanac." *New York Daily News*. November 24, 1942. https://www.newspapers.com/image/434671073. (Accessed January 25, 2022)

"Death Notices." *New York Daily News*. June 30, 1976. https://www.news papers.com/image/488427628. (Accessed January 26, 2022)

"Ex Bund Trooper Arrested as Spy—Arrest of Naturalized Citizen Recently Back from Reich Brings Total to 33." *New York Times*. July 3, 1941. https://timesmachine.nytimes.com/timesmachine/1941/07/03/104295551. html?pageNumber=21. (Accessed June 7, 2021)

"Ex-Soldier Guilty of Plot to Aid Nazis—Admits Charges of Supplying Information to Spy Ring." *New York Times*. August 14, 1942. https://times machine.nytimes.com/timesmachine/1942/08/14/85577035.html?page Number=7. (Accessed June 15, 2021)

"FBI Traps Engineer Who Gave Nazi Spy Data on U.S. Arms—Former German Officer Born in Uruguay Admits He Aided Staten Island Air Warden." *New York Times*. June 30, 1943. https://timesmachine. nytimes.com/timesmachine/1943/06/30/87420406.html?pageNumber=5. (Accessed June 22, 2021)

"George Morton Levy, a Pioneer of Night Harness Racing, Is Dead at 89." *New York Times*. July 20, 1977. https://timesmachine.nytimes.com/times-machine/1977/07/20/105374379.html?pageNumber=37. (Accessed September 22, 2021)

Holt, Jane. "News of Food—Fishing Boats Arrive with Huge Catch of Yellowtail Flounders for Fillets." *New York Times*. September 17, 1942. https://timesmachine.nytimes.com/timesmachine/1942/09/17/85051807. html. (Accessed January 22, 2021)

Holt, Jane. "News of Food—Fish Shortage Arrives with Lent—But the Simple Dab Is Plentiful." *New York Times*. February 18, 1942. https:// timesmachine.nytimes.com/timesmachine/1942/02/18/85268138.html? pageNumber=16. (Accessed January 22, 2021)

Holt, Jane. "News of Food—Pedigreed Pears of Northwest Plentiful—Bake Them for a Distinctive Dessert. *New York Times*. April 16, 1942. https://timesmachine.nytimes.com/timesmachine/1942/04/16/88502099. html?pageNumber=25. (Accessed January 22, 2021)

Holt, Jane. "News of Food—Time Now Held Propitious for Fish Dinners Halibut from West Make Final Appearance." *New York Times*. October 15,

1942. https://timesmachine.nytimes.com/timesmachine/1942/10/15/ 85055705.html?pageNumber=20. (Accessed January 22, 2021)

Holt, Jane. "News of Food—'Tuesday Is Bargain Fish Day,' Asserts Commissioner Morgan, and Here It Is." *New York Times.* April 22, 1941. https://timesmachine.nytimes.com/timesmachine/1941/04/22/85482807. html?pageNumber=18. (Accessed January 22, 2021)

"How Spies Were Recruited—German-American Bund Made Them Nazi Sympathizers." *New York Times.* June 28, 1942. https://timesmachine.ny times.com/timesmachine/1942/06/28/99332186.html?pageNumber=30. (Accessed June 15, 2021)

"Jack Dempsey Wins Divorce Suit. Children's Custody to Be Decided." *New York Times.* July 8, 1943. https://timesmachine.nytimes.com/ timesmachine/1943/07/08/88552811.html?pageNumber=21. (Accessed May 25, 2021)

"Joseph Kaitz, Known as Docks Investigator for New York, Was 69." *New York Times.* November 24, 1979. https://www.nytimes.com/1979/ 11/24/archives/joseph-kaitz-known-as-docks-investigator-for-new-york-was-69.html. (Accessed April 20, 2021)

Malcolm, Hilary. "Safe Cracking Secrets of OSS." *Philadelphia Enquirer.* January 26, 1947. https://www.newspapers.com/newspage/172636600/. (Accessed January 28, 2022)

"Maurice P. Kelly, Security Officer—Ex-Policeman, Honored for Captures, Dies at 61." *New York Times.* December 15, 1964. https://timesmachine. nytimes.com/timesmachine/1964/12/15/118544400.html?pageNumber=44 (Accessed September 21, 2021)

"Navy Takes Over Normandie Pier—Deposits $2,610,000 for City in Gamble That Capsized Ship Can Be Righted." *New York Times.* March 17, 1942. https://timesmachine.nytimes.com/timesmachine/1942/03/17/85290955. html?pageNumber=23. (Accessed March 9, 2021)

"Nazi Spy Tells Way Saboteurs Studied—At Trial of Six in Chicago for Aid to Haupt, Burger Reveals Aims to Cripple the U.S." *New York Times.* October 28, 1942. https://timesmachine.nytimes.com/timesmachine/ 1942/10/28/85602037.html?pageNumber=17. (Accessed June 15, 2021)

"News of Night Clubs—El Chico, Down the Village Way, Plans a New Show for This Week." *New York Times.* November 1, 1942. https://times machine.nytimes.com/timesmachine/1942/11/01/96558486.html?page Number=203. (June 20, 2021)

"Obituaries." *Arizona Republic.* January 29, 1987. https://www.newspapers. com/image/120920119. (Accessed January 15, 2022)

"Pardoned Luciano on His Way to Italy." *New York Times.* February 11, 1946. https://timesmachine.nytimes.com/timesmachine/1946/02/11/93047003. html?pageNumber=26. (Accessed March 3, 2022)

"Paul Alfieri, Waterfront Investigator." *Newsday* (Nassau Edition). https:// www.newspapers.com/image/712388247. (Accessed January 25, 2022)

"Prisoner Kayoes Judge, Slugs 3 Cops in Court." *New York Daily News.* March 20, 1933. https://www.newspapers.com/image/414680879. (Accessed January 17, 2022)

"Seafood Arrivals at 25 Year Record—2,000,000 Pounds Received at Fulton Market in Day—All Varieties Represented." *New York Times.* December 24, 1941. https://timesmachine.nytimes.com/timesmachine/1941/12/24/ 105169432.html?pageNumber=20. (Accessed October 20, 2021)

"Sinking of Ships Linked to Spy Ring—Data on Vessels Here Sent by Ludwig to Himmler, Girl Accomplice Testifies." *New York Times.* February 5, 1942. https://timesmachine.nytimes.com/timesmachine/1942/ 02/05/85230132.html?pageNumber=23. (Accessed September 25, 2021)

"Spy Here Admits He Sent Nazis Data on Arms and Ships—Naturalized Citizen Watched Harbor from Staten Island Home—Listened in Bars." *New York Times.* June 29, 1943. https://timesmachine.nytimes.com/times machine/1943/06/29/88548325.html?pageNumber=5. (Accessed June 22, 2021)

"Trigger Men Bare (per link) 'Contract' Murders for Big Racketeers—Dozen Killings by Brooklyn Gang Solved by Confessions of Pair, O'Dwyer Says." *New York Times.* March 18, 1940. https://timesmachine.nytimes. com/timesmachine/1940/03/18/91580280.html?pageNumber=1. (Accessed Mary 22, 2021)

"Union Man Slain—Pier Executive Sought as Killer." *New York Times.* October 3, 1941. https://timesmachine.nytimes.com/timesmachine/ 1941/10/03/99248560.html?pageNumber=1. (Accessed October 20, 2021)

Online Resources and Websites

Allen, Ernest. "When Japan Was 'Champion of the Darker Races': Satokata Takahashi and the Flowering of Black Messianic Nationalism." *JSTOR.* The Black Scholar. Vol. 24. No. 1. Black Cultural History—1994 (Winter

1994). Pages 23–46. https://www.jstor.org/stable/41068457. (Accessed June 17, 2021)

"Art Bartsch—The Ferret Squad." *Heritage Auctions.* Comics, Comic Art & Animation Art / 2017 November 16–18 Comics & Comic Art Signature Auction—Beverly Hills #7169. Lot #93025. February 6, 1942. https://comics.ha.com/itm/original-comic-art/illustrations/art-bartsch-the-ferret-squad-illustration-original-art-with-us-navy-officers-and-officer-s-hat-group-of-2-1942-total-2/a/7169-93025.s. (Accessed March 20, 2021)

Berick, Julia. "Tails and Scales: The Fate of the Fulton Fish Market Hangs in the Balance." *Tenement Museum.* Blog Archive. https://www.tenement.org/blog/tails-and-scales-the-fate-of-the-fulton-fish-market-hangs-in-the-balance/. (Accessed December 15, 2020)

Black, Matthew. "Declassified Information Reveals US Navy's Alliance with the Italian Mob Decades Later." *History 101.* April 2019. https://www.history101.com/lucky-luciano-us-government-wwii/. (Accessed April 2019)

Brooks, Tom. "Naval Intelligence and the Mafia in WWII." *NCISA History Project.* https://ncisahistory.org/wp-content/uploads/2017/08/Naval-Intelligence-and-the-Mafia-in-World-War-II.pdf. (Accessed October 25, 2020)

Bryant, Mary L. "Fine Arts Behind Bars—Painting and Friendship." *New York Correction History Society.* http://www.correctionhistory.org/html/chronicl/state/singsing/finearts/fineartsbehindbars.html. (Accessed February 17, 2021)

"Charles Hoyt—(1886–1973)." *Ancient Faces.* October 6, 2011. http://www.ancientfaces.com/person/charles-hoyt-birth-1886-death-1973/20477018. (Accessed March 15, 2022)

"Counterintelligence: Operation Underworld." US Naval War College Newport, Rhode Island. https://usnwc.libguides.com/c.php?g=661096&p=6277109. (Accessed October 24, 2020)

Deihl, Lorraine. "Smoke Over Manhattan—The Fate of the SS Normandie." *HistoryNet.* January 29, 2010. https://www.historynet.com/the-fate-of-the-ss-normandie/. (Accessed October 5, 2020)

Dezenhall, Eric. "Operation Underworld." *The American Spectator.* September 14, 2011. https://spectator.org/operation-underworld/. (Accessed October 24, 2020)

Erickson, "King of Bookmakers, Admits His Guilt 60 Years in Jail and $30,000 Fine Could Be Imposed." *UCR. Center for Bibliographical Study and Research.* California Digital Newspaper Collection. Madera Tribune, Volume 59, Number 68. June 19, 1950. https://cdnc.ucr.edu/?a=d&d= MT19500619.2.9&e=-------en--20--1--txt-txIN--------1. (Accessed on July 1, 2021)

Hertel, Ed. "Saratoga Springs—A Brief Gambling History." *Casino Chip and Token News* (per link). Volume 22. Number 3. http://www.ccgtcc-ccn.com/ SaratogaSprings.pdf. (Accessed July 7, 2021)

Higham, Nick. "Drawings Reveal Germans' World War Two Boobytrap Bombs." *BBC News.* September 30, 2015. https://www.bbc.com/news/ uk-34396939. (Accessed June 26, 2021)

"Hotel Astor—Photographs, Written Historical and Descriptive Data." *Library of Congress.* http://lcweb2.loc.gov/master/pnp/habshaer/ ny/ny0300/ny0385/data/ny0385data.pdf. (Accessed February 10, 2022)

Klein, Christopher. "What Was Operation Underworld?" *History.* History Stories. https://www.history.com/news/what-was-operation-underworld. (Accessed October 5, 2020)

"Long Island Historical Journal: Long Island as America." Stony Brook, NY: State University of New York, 1992.pdf.

"Ludwig Spy Ring." *FBI.* History. Famous Cases & Criminals. https://www. fbi.gov/history/famous-cases/ludwig-spy-ring. (Accessed May 17, 2021)

"Office of Naval Intelligence Naval Investigative Services Newsletter." *NCISA History Project.* March 31, 1966. https://ncisahistory.org/wp- content/uploads/2017/07/ONI-NIS-Newsletter-31-March-1966.pdf. (Accessed October 24, 2021)

"Principles of Strategic Intelligence First Tentative Edition." *NCISA History Project.* October 1945. https://ncisahistory.org/wp-content/uploads/ 2019/11/War-Department-Manual-Principles-of-Strategic-Intelligence- First-Tentative-Edition-October-1945.pdf. (Accessed October 24, 2021)

"Report of the Attorney General to the Congress of the United States on the Administration of the Foreign Agents Registration Act of 1938, as Amended for the Period from June 28, 1942, to December 31, 1944." June 1945. https://s3.amazonaws.com/s3.documentcloud.org/documents/ 325918/1942-1944-fara-report.pdf. (Accessed June 15, 2021)

"Salty Old World." *Ole Davy Jones* on Tumblr. https://oledavyjones. tumblr.com/post/641484733303390208/longshore-man-at-the-fulton-fish- market-new-york. (Accessed December 17, 2020)

"The Lost 1907 Hotel Astor—1511 Broadway." *Daytonian in Manhattan.* January 4, 2016. http://daytoninmanhattan.blogspot.com/2016/01/the-lost-1907-hotel-astor-1511-broadway.html. (Accessed February 8, 2022)

Wharton, Wallace. "Intelligence-and-CI-Implications-of-the-Reinsurance-Industry." *NCISA History Project.* October 22, 1942. https://ncisahistory.org/wp-content/uploads/2017/07/Intelligence-and-CI-Implications-of-the-Reinsurance-Industry-Oct-22-1942.pdf. (Accessed February 12, 2022)

Wharton, Wallace. "Naval Interest and Responsibility in Movement of Persons of Japanese Ancestry." *NCISA History Project.* August 14, 1944. https://ncisahistory.org/wp-content/uploads/2017/07/Naval-Interest-and-Responsibility-in-Movement-of-Persons-of-Japanese-Ancestry-14-Aug-1944.pdf. (Accessed February 12, 2022)

Wharton, Wallace. "The Navy—A National Investment." *U.S. Naval Institute.* November 1924. https://www.usni.org/magazines/proceedings/1924/november/navy-national-investment. (Accessed February 12, 2022)

Wharton, Wallace. "ONI Tracking the Relocation of Japanese." *NCISA History Project.* July 2, 1943 https://ncisahistory.org/wp-content/uploads/2017/07/ONI-Tracking-the-Relocation-of-Japanese-2-Jul-1943.pdf. (Accessed February 12, 2022)

Wharton, Wallace. "Ward Man and Ship." *U.S. Naval Institute.* November 1946. https://www.usni.org/magazines/proceedings/1946/november/ward-man-and-ship. (Accessed February 12, 2022)

Wilcox, Leroy. "1775–1975 and Eastport Gospel Church 1822–1975." *Long Island Genealogy.* http://longislandgenealogy.com/EastportGospel.pdf. (Accessed February 11, 2022)

Online Photographs

Canadian2006. "1904 Hotel Astor NY floor plans-d." *Wikimedia Commons.* Uploaded June 27, 2019. https://commons.wikimedia.org/wiki/File:1904_Hotel_Astor_NY_floor_plans-d.png. (Accessed February 14, 2022)

Museum of the City of New York/Byron Collection/Contributor. "Hotel Astor, B'way & 44th Street, Interior with Models, the Lobby." *Getty Images.* December 31, 1928. https://www.gettyimages.com/detail/news-photo/hotel-astor-broadway-44th-street-interior-with-models-the-news-photo/111748465?adppopup=true. (Accessed February 14, 2022)

Museum of the City of New York/Byron Collection/Contributor "Hotel Astor, B'way 44th & 45th Streets, Interior, North Mezzanine & Staircase from

Mezzanine." *Getty Images*. December 31, 1934. https://www.gettyimages. com/detail/news-photo/hotel-astor-broadway-44th-45th-streets-interior-north-news-photo/111749550?adppopup=true. (Accessed February 14, 2022)

"Presten's Dock Greenport, Long Island." *Pinterest*. Old Montauk. Uploaded by Wallat, Bill. https://www.pinterest.com/pin/445926800595075673// (Accessed February 3, 222)

Online Videos

AP Archive. "USA: Fulton Fish Market Faces Closure." *YouTube*. July 23, 2015. https://www.youtube.com/watch?v=cbfs2uSeWDw. (Accessed October 29, 2020)

Franzese, Michael. "Frank Costello: The Most Successful Gangster in Cosa Nostra History." *YouTube*. December 10, 2021. https://www.youtube.com/ watch?v=D_sUPXp3LLs. (Accessed January 5, 2022)

Marine Salvage and Offshore. "US Navy—Salvage of the USS Lafayette (SS Normandie)." *YouTube*. July 27, 2017. https://www.youtube.com/ watch?v=4AdWZkdc8BI. (Accessed October 25, 2020)

Pureimaginationvideo. "Fulton Fish Market's Final Days South Street Seaport Morry A." *YouTube*. June 3, 2008. https://www.youtube.com/ watch?v=R2n-0dEuCuY (Accessed October 29, 2020)

INDEX